ON LAND AND WATER

ON LAND AND WATER

IRISH WILDLIFE THROUGH IMAGE AND POETRY

SHEENA JOLLEY and D. J. O'SULLIVAN

First published in 2024.
Second edition 2026.
ISBN 978-1-7395705-5-2

MENMA BOOKS

www.menmabooks.eu

Contact:
Sheena Jolley,
Mill House Gallery, Coosheen, Schull, Co. Cork P81XF64
www.sheenajolleyphotography.com
sheenajolley@gmail.com
+ 353 (0)86 0577456

Edited and designed by Maurice Sweeney

Printed by Inspire, Skibbereen

FSC
www.fsc.org
MIX
Paper | Supporting responsible forestry
FSC® C115691

CONTENTS

INTRODUCTION — Éanna Ní Lamhna

Writers, poets and radio broadcasters have one thing in common. They create pictures with words. Radio listeners to the spoken word can form excellent pictures in their heads if the broadcaster is good at describing things. The pictures are transient, however, unless the listener has a recording and listens again and again. The written word can be taken at the reader's own pace, and re-read if necessary, to help the reader to form the pictures of what is being described. The better the writing, the easier it is for the reader to do this.

D. J. O'Sullivan was a master at writing about nature. In his forty-five years of writing columns about the wildlife that he observed at first hand as a lighthouse keeper, he created images for the reader in an age before colour printing—never mind moving pictures. But prose could never do justice to what he observed, and his finest expressions were in poetry. These poems were love paeans to his beloved wildlife and were received with great acclaim. The images in the poetry were finely drawn.

There is a saying that a picture is worth a thousand words. But Sheena Jolley doesn't need a thousand words per picture. Just seven beautifully chosen words of his are the inspiration for a picture of rounded beach stones whose texture you can almost feel just by looking at it. The amount of time needed to be able to describe the courtship behaviour of the Arctic tern must have been mirrored by the amount of time spent waiting for the exact shot to highlight the words.

A lighthouse keeper in a time when such work meant solitary days on an isolated island, O'Sullivan's work is naturally full of wildlife from these remote places. Many of the wonderful photographs on these pages are of sea birds in their resplendent breeding plumage. And also too of other island wildlife. 'Every window's wind-whistle/Is a blackbird's nesting song' is illustrated with pictures both of the window and of the blackbird. And mammals—'And fed, the otter comes to play/Out on this rock'. Otters on the seashore 'seeking rest on rock remote' are captured by Sheena off Inishtrahull. How much more remote can you get?

O'Sullivan's love of puffins inspired a prize-winning short story and many poetic words. When he was a lighthouse keeper way back in the mid-twentieth century, puffins and indeed all the other sea birds were present in much greater numbers than they are now. We have half the amount of wildlife nowadays compared to what was here before 1970. So, it is greatly to Sheena's credit that she has been able to get such intimate pictures of puffins to accompany the text.

But it is not all island wildlife. O'Sullivan was writing poetry right up till his death at the age of 87 in 1993—long after he had retired and indeed long after the lighthouses became automatic and lighthouse keepers redundant. He had the same lively interest, the same keen eye, the same wonderful ability to describe wildlife wherever he observed it as his forty-five years of 'Land and Water' columns testify. Foxes, hares, blue tits 'in creviced garden wall', little black beetles and clucking waterhens are all worthy of inclusion and of being photographed.

But he didn't live in a fool's paradise. He understood the threats posed to wildlife, even in the remote locations he knew so well. '"Pray that in this generation/Wildlife be saved through conservation/Defilement and pollution no more found'. Almost thirty years later Sheena can find distressing images of defilement and pollution of wildlife to illustrate these words.

But they are as a footnote, as it were, to the book. The joy evoked in the readers who look at the images throughout the book, and who are uplifted by O'Sullivan's words, must inevitably ensure that they are motivated to call stop to the ceaseless, careless destruction. This book is a wonderful panegyric to D. J. O Sullivan and his lifetime of wildlife observations and writings. It is up to us all now to make sure that it does not become a historical record of how wildlife once was, but rather, that it is a clarion call to protect our biodiversity.

ABOUT SHEENA JOLLEY

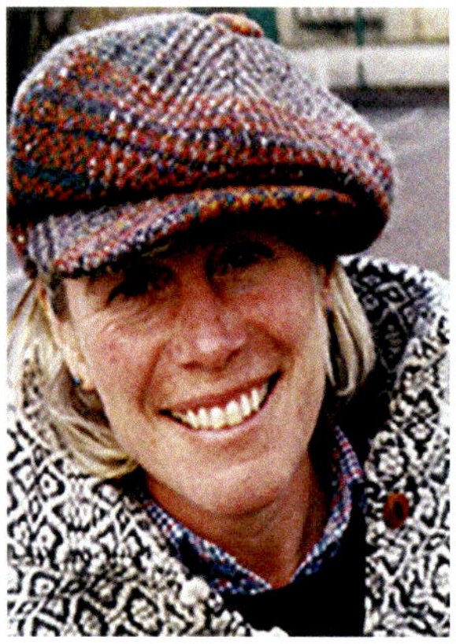

Born in Wicklow, Ireland, Sheena Jolley studied photography full time at the North Oxfordshire College of Art, combining her creative talents with her knowledge and love of nature. She is dedicated to capturing images of the indigenous wildlife of Ireland and in particular that of its islands so that others will be encouraged to preserve our natural heritage.

She believes that the best way to preserve a thing of beauty is to hold the attention of the viewer and encourage a feeling of wonder and nurture. Her work therefore involves tight close-ups as well as a study of animals in their environment.

Her work has been purchased by collectors in Europe and America and has featured many times in a number of national publications. In 2009 one of her photographs made it to the finals of the Veolia Environment Wildlife Photographer of the Year Competition. In 2013 she was awarded The Irish Professional Photographers' Association's Best Wildlife Portfolio. In 2019 she was a finalist in the wildlife category in the FEP European Professional Photographer of the Year Awards.

As well as photographing wildlife, Sheena has been involved in photographing a suppressed community in the West Indies. These are the forgotten descendants of Irish and Scottish people shipped to Barbados as indentured servants more than 300 years ago. With compassion and sensitivity she has managed to give an identity and dignity to a poverty-stricken community living on the edge of society. Her work and provocative images also feature in a documentary shown on both Irish and Scottish television. She has become well know to Irish television viewers as a judge on the RTE 'Eye on Nature' photographic competition.

ABOUT D.J. O'SULLIVAN

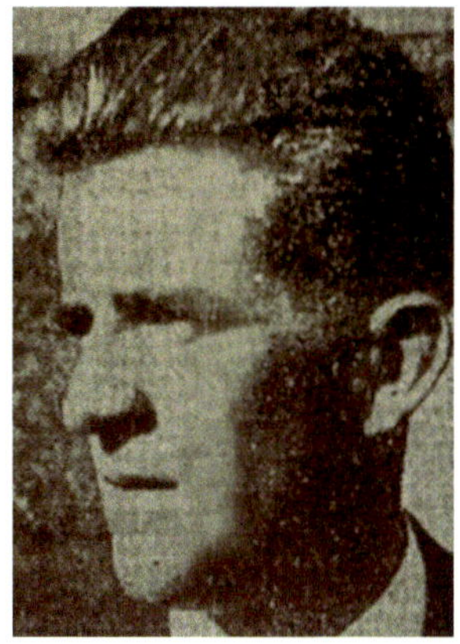

D. J. O'Sullivan was born in Whitegate, Co.Cork, in1906 but spent most of his life in the north-west, where he followed in his father's footsteps to become a lighthouse keeper, as did his three brothers.

While stationed on the remote lighthouse on Blackrock Island off the Mayo coast, he began to express his deep love of nature by recording his observations in poetry and then in a daily column, 'Land and Water', which he wrote for more than forty-five years for *The Irish Press*. His acute eye led him to observe a bird that was new to Ireland, the Madeiran Fork-tailed Petrel, and a moth that he discovered was named after him—*Luperina Testacea, ab sullivani.*

In 1947, his book of poems *Light-keeper's Lyrics* was published by the Dundalgan Press. His short story 'Puffin' was runner-up in the *New York Herald* International Writing Competition and was translated into fifteen languages and published in twenty-two counties. Two of his poems were also included in the Faber 1948 anthology, *Contemporary Irish Poetry*.

In 1993, Lapwing Publications in Belfast published a second collection of his poems, *From Fastnet to Inishtrahull*, with an introduction by John Montague, who noted that a hallmark of O'Sullivan's poetry was authenticity—'the first thing one should demand of a poem.'

'The best of O'Sullivan rivals Ledwidge,' Montague wrote, 'but place it together with the best of prose and, allowing for the lack of literary context, you have an observer as keen as Edward Thomas, a lover of the hedge and the foreshore.'

D. J. O'Sullivan died in 1993, shortly after the publication of his second collection.

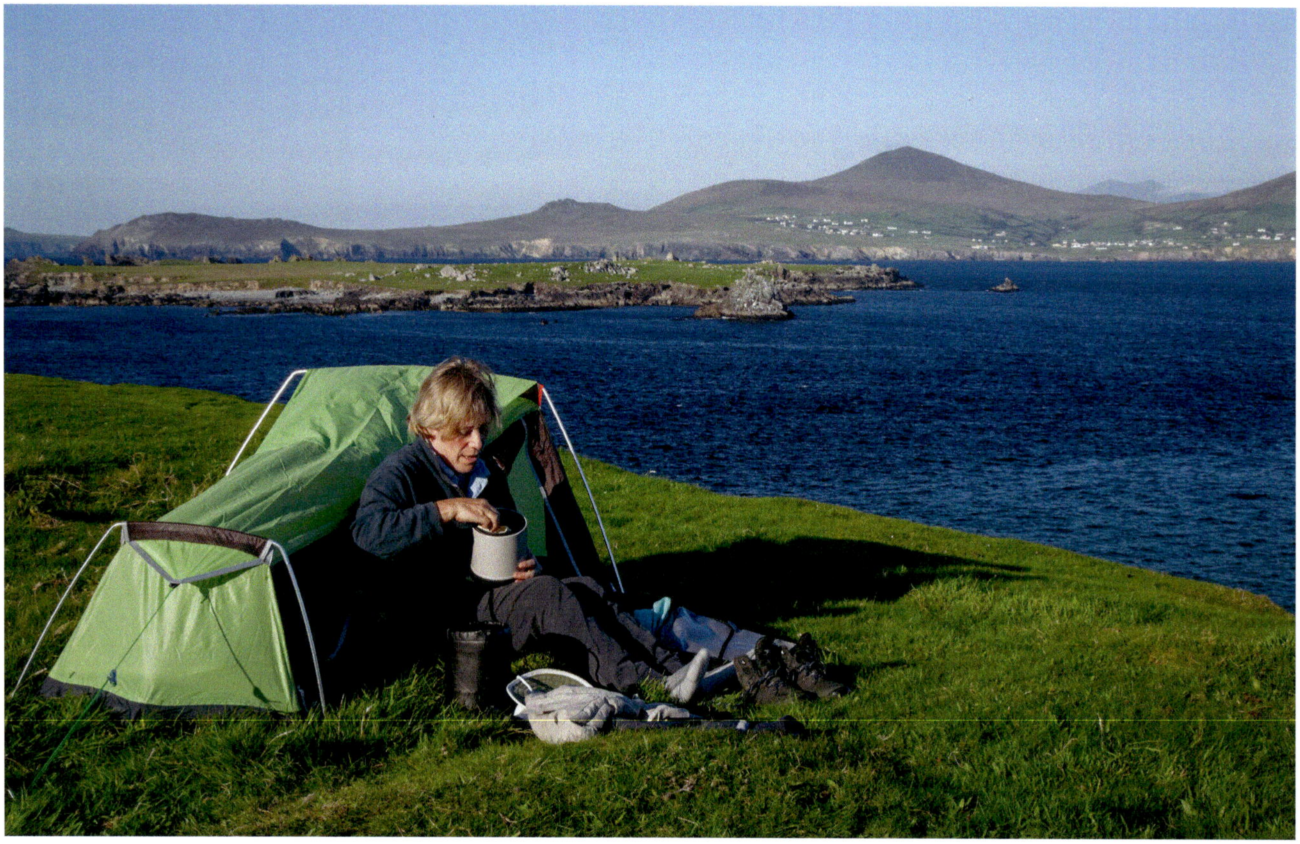

Camping out on the Great Blasket Island off the coast of Kerry.

TAKING THE PHOTOGRAPHS — Sheena Jolley

In 2006 when I was on a visit to Inishtrahull, D. J. O'Sullivan's son, the lighthouse keeper Donal O'Sullivan, asked me if I would be interested in republishing his father's poems with my wildlife images.

As I am passionate about wildlife photography and conservation, this proved to be the start of a wonderful project and a challenge to do justice to D. J.'s poems. Having familiarised myself with the words of the poems, I would preconceive and carefully plan the shots I wanted to capture. It meant being in the right place at the right time with the necessary camera and lenses.

It quickly became apparent that daily visits to the different locations would never work. To achieve the best results, I would have to photograph during the early morning and evening light. This often meant camping in remote places and on islands, which was no easy task. It involved taking cameras, a heavy prime lens, a telephoto zoom lens, a tent, food, and water, making sure that all was kept dry in waterproof bags and finally persuading a boatman that I would be fine left alone on an island. Once I found a spot to camp, I was free to roam, carefully observe the wildlife, concentrate on my technical and creative ability, and wait for the opportune moments to take my images.

Sometimes camping was not possible, and I am grateful to the Commissioners of Irish Lights for their assistance in getting me to certain islands and allowing me to stay in their lighthouses. I was also privileged to be allowed to stay in an O.P.W. hut on Skellig Michael. This support certainly made my job easier and provided me with wonderful opportunities to complete this project. Creating this book has allowed me to share my passion with others, capturing brief moments that I hope will evoke an emotion in the viewer, hold their attention, and enhance the poems of D. J. O'Sullivan. I also hope this book encourages the reader to wonder about nature and do everything we can to take care of it.

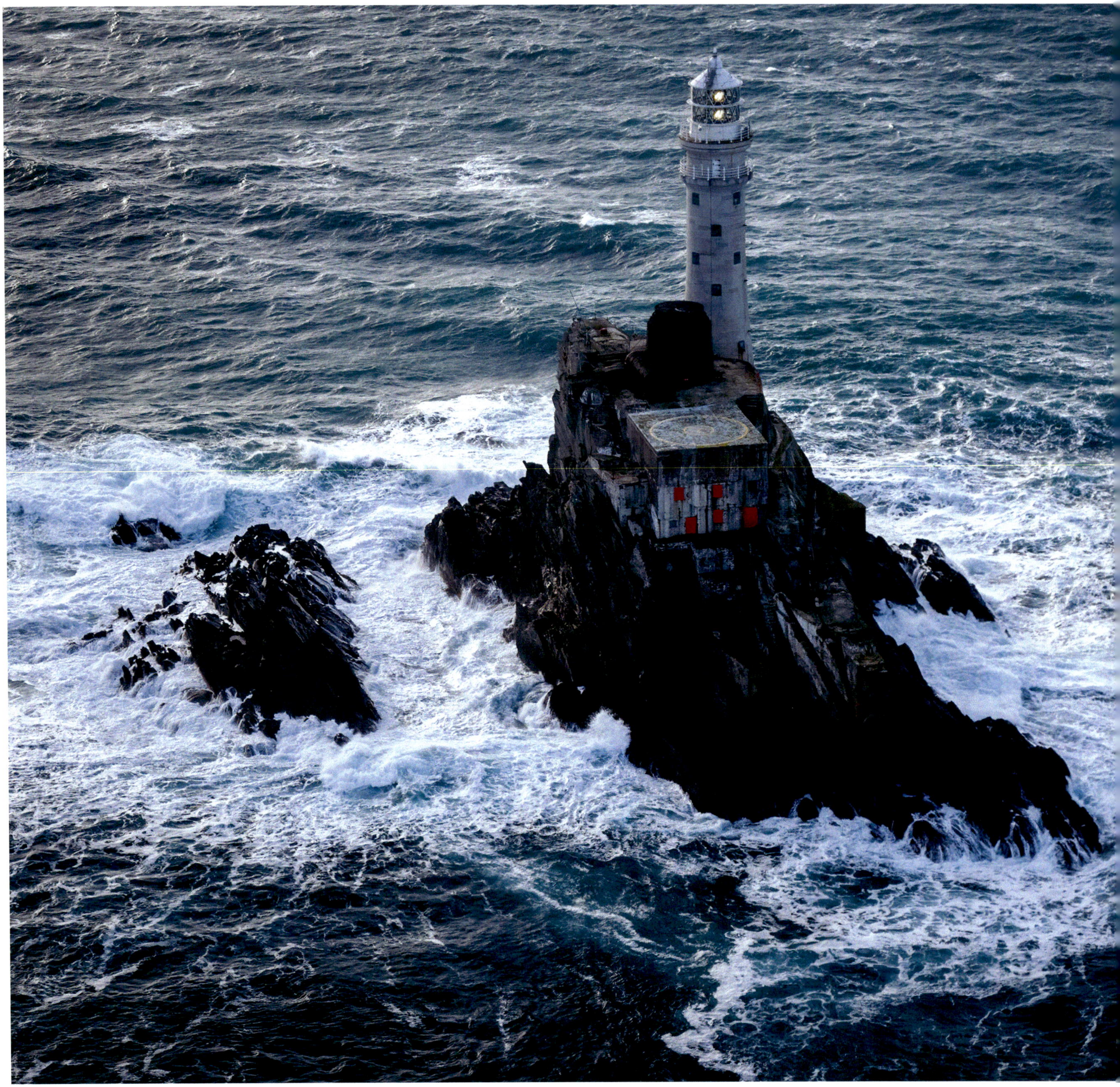

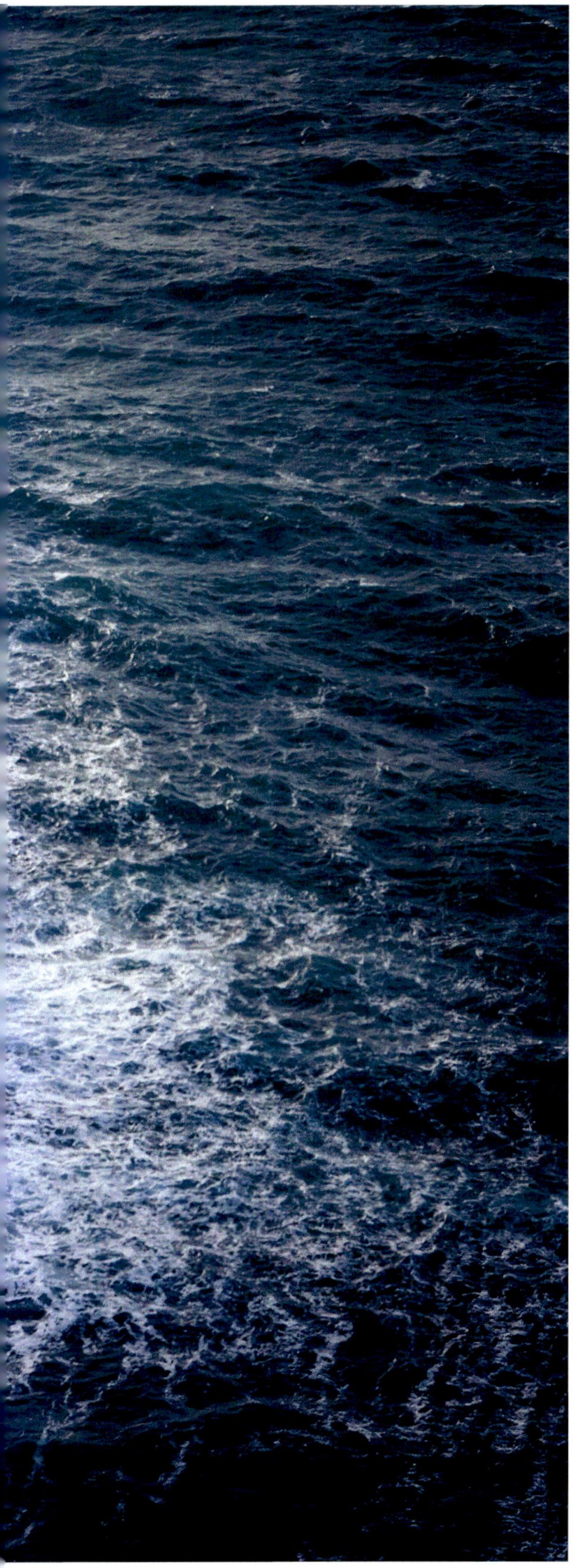

FASTNET

I write a log
In this lighthouse,
Autumn waning,
Winter coming.
Wind from the north
Gelid blowing;
Sun cloud-shadowed,
Shortening days.
Ships wave-battered,
Ploughing ocean;
And every night
Migrant birds calling.
Spindrift sprayed
The tower windows;
A time of change—
That's my log.

Fastnet Rock off the south-west coast of Ireland was one of the lighthouses where D. J. O'Sullivan worked. It is also known as 'Ireland's Teardrop' as it was the last part of the country seen by Irish emigrants to America in the nineteenth century as they sailed past it. It was in solitary places as far south as the Fastnet and as far north as Inishtrahull that D. J. O'Sullivan was able to train his eye to observe nature acutely and express what he saw in his daily nature column in *The Irish Press*, in his contributions to the *Irish Naturalists' Journal*, and in his poetry.

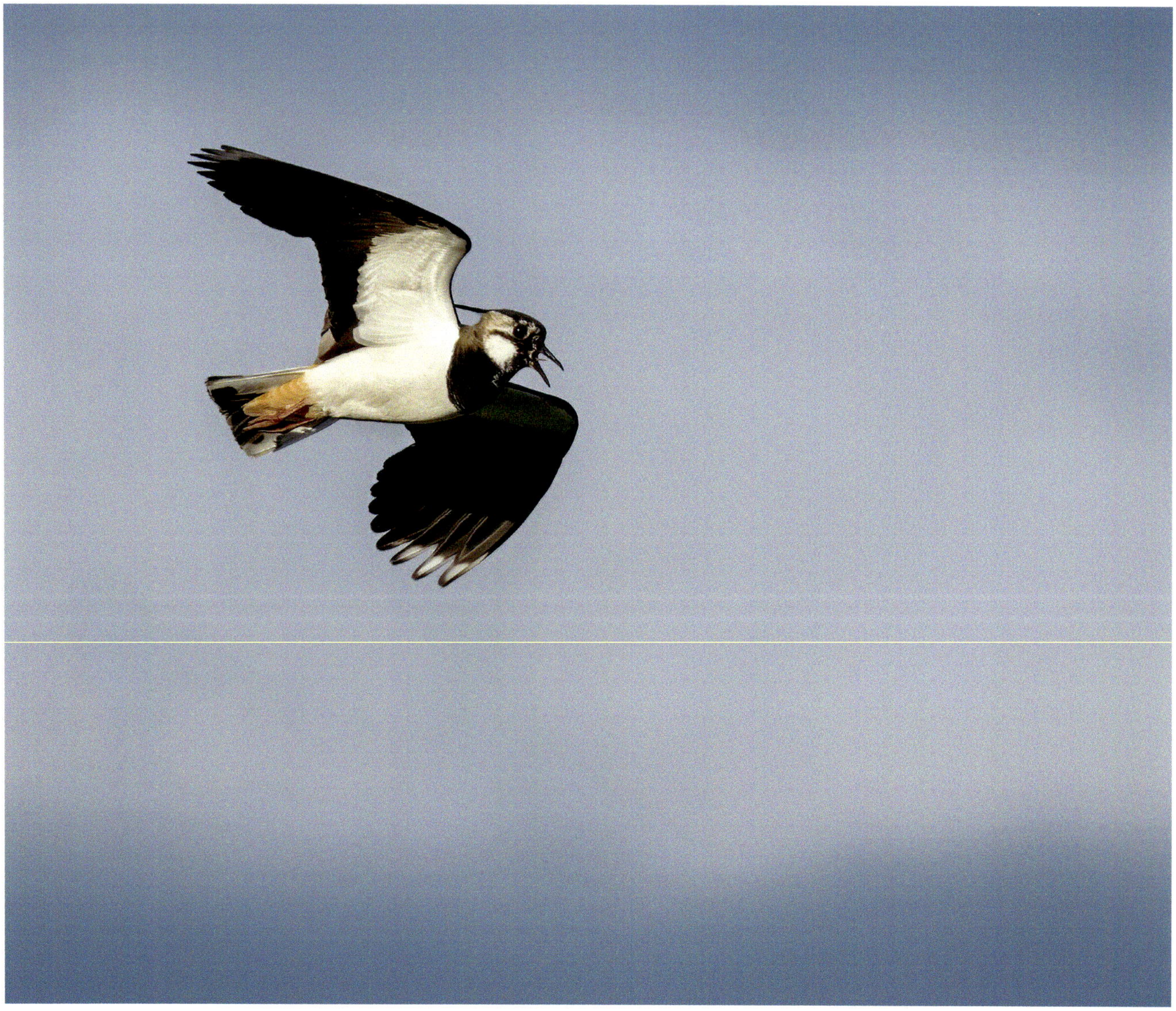

'...when hungry lapwing calls...'

The Lapwing is one of the many migrants that visit Inishtrahull. It feeds on a variety of soil and surface-living invertebrates, particularly small arthropods and earthworms. The Lapwing, like many other ground nesting species in Ireland has undergone severe declines in breeding numbers. Alarmingly, populations of this handsome wading bird have declined by more than 50% in 25 years.

DAWN IN INISHTRAHULL

The moon shines on the Isle of Inishtrahull,
Bejewelling nuptial tinted herring-gull,
May-fly dancing in the balmy air,
And moth returning to its daylight lair.
A shoal of herring breaking out at sea
Sparkle like hoar frost on an aspen tree,
Spindrift in the shaded rocky cleft,
And raised-beach quartz that the ice-ages left.
The droning beetles seek the crevassed walls
To dive into when hungry lapwing calls;
Earwigs, likewise, into earthed homes,
And red-ants under scarred lichened stones.
An otter seeking rest on rock remote
Glistens with phosphorescence on his coat,
The snail *Arborum*, with his watery glue,
And bunch of pearlwort in a crystal dew.
The flaming sun ascends o'er Cantyre's Mull,
Flings out his arms, day breaks on Inishtrahull!

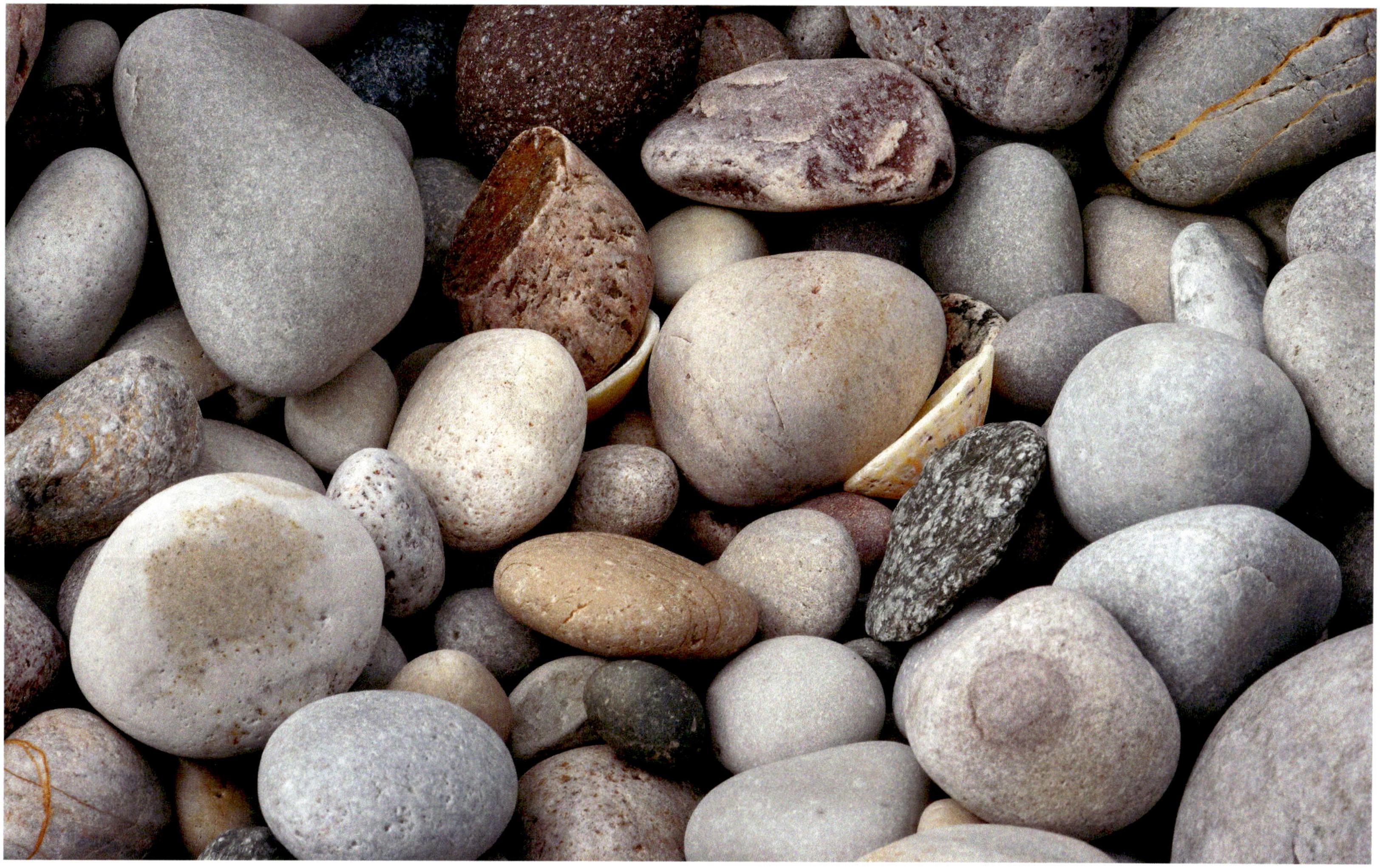

'And raised-beach quartz that the ice-ages left.'

Inishtrahull is a mile across from east to west and lies 5 miles northeast of Malin Head. It is the most northerly part of Ireland and is where Ireland's oldest rocks go back as far as 1,800 million years. It shares geological characteristics more akin to southern Greenland and the Inner Hebrides of Scotland than to Ireland. Repeated episodes of deformation and metamorphism formed the rocks into coarse crystalline banded metamorphic rocks called gneiss.

The Brown-lipped Snail has a large variety of colourations and band patterns but usually has a brown band around the opening of its shell. It is one of the commonest large species of land snail in Europe.

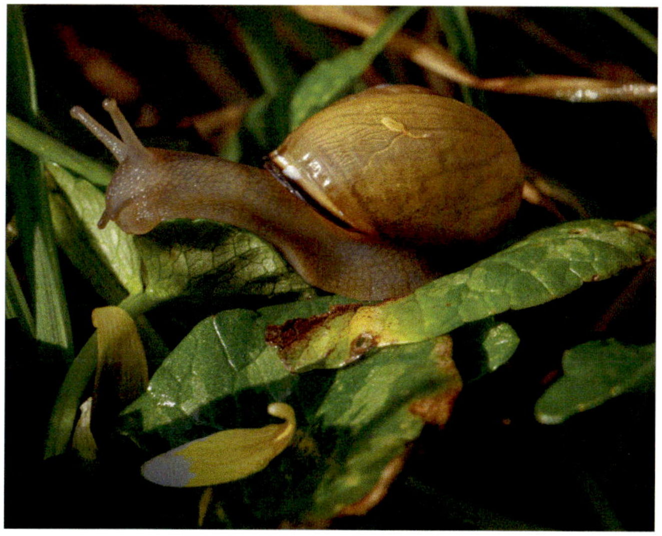

'The snail Arborum, with his watery glue...'

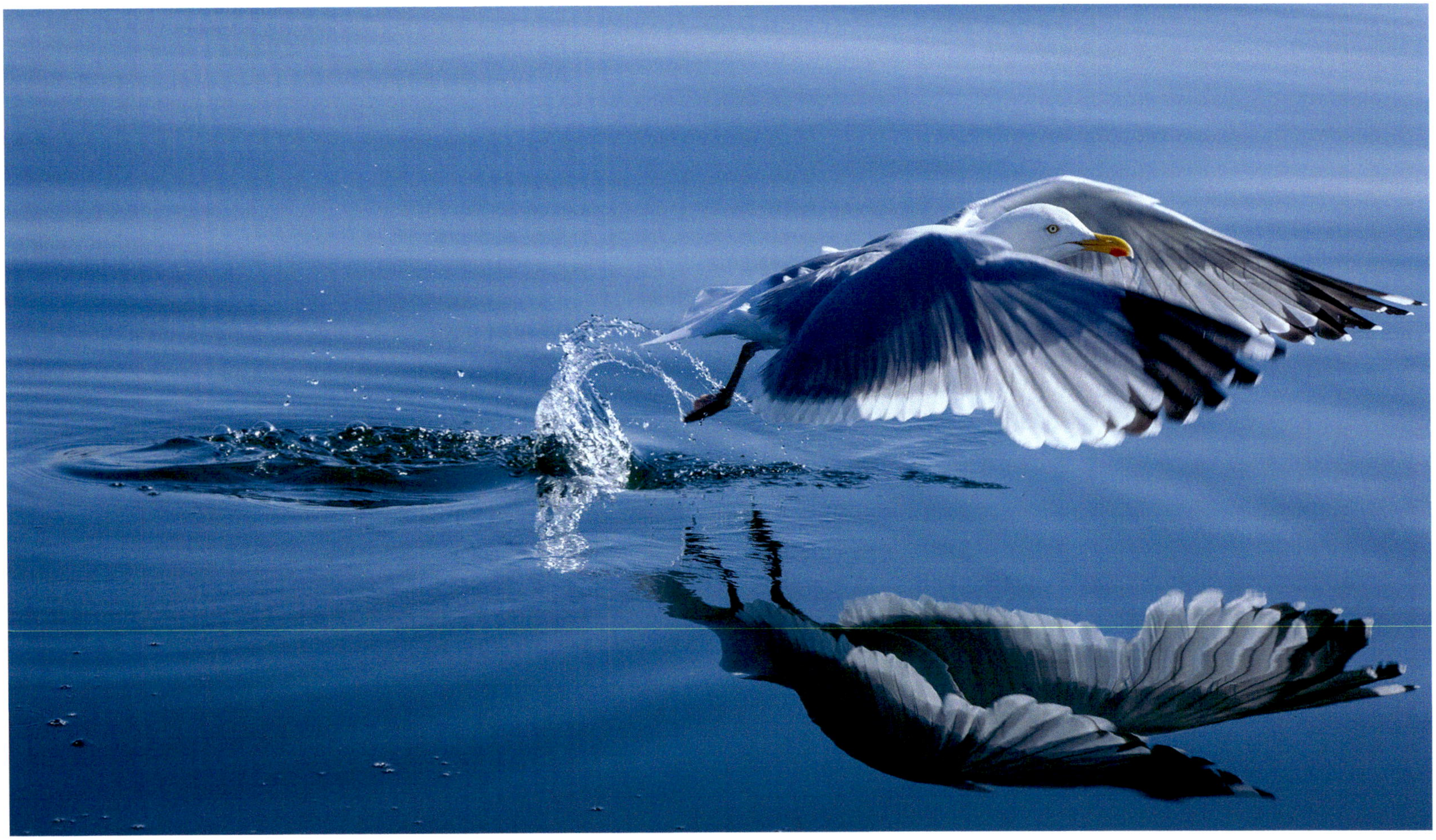

'...Bejewelling nuptial tinted herring-gull...'

The Herring Gull is both predator and scavenger. It often feeds on the coast and follows fishing boats and uses landfill sites. On sea cliffs these dramatic birds add immeasurably to the coastal atmosphere with their strident calls and mastery of flight. The flesh-coloured pink legs distinguish this large gull from other gulls. The heavy yellow bills have an orange spot on the lower bill.

I managed to shoot this photograph by going out to sea on a small boat which put me close to the water level. I hope it shows something special and beautiful in a much seen species.

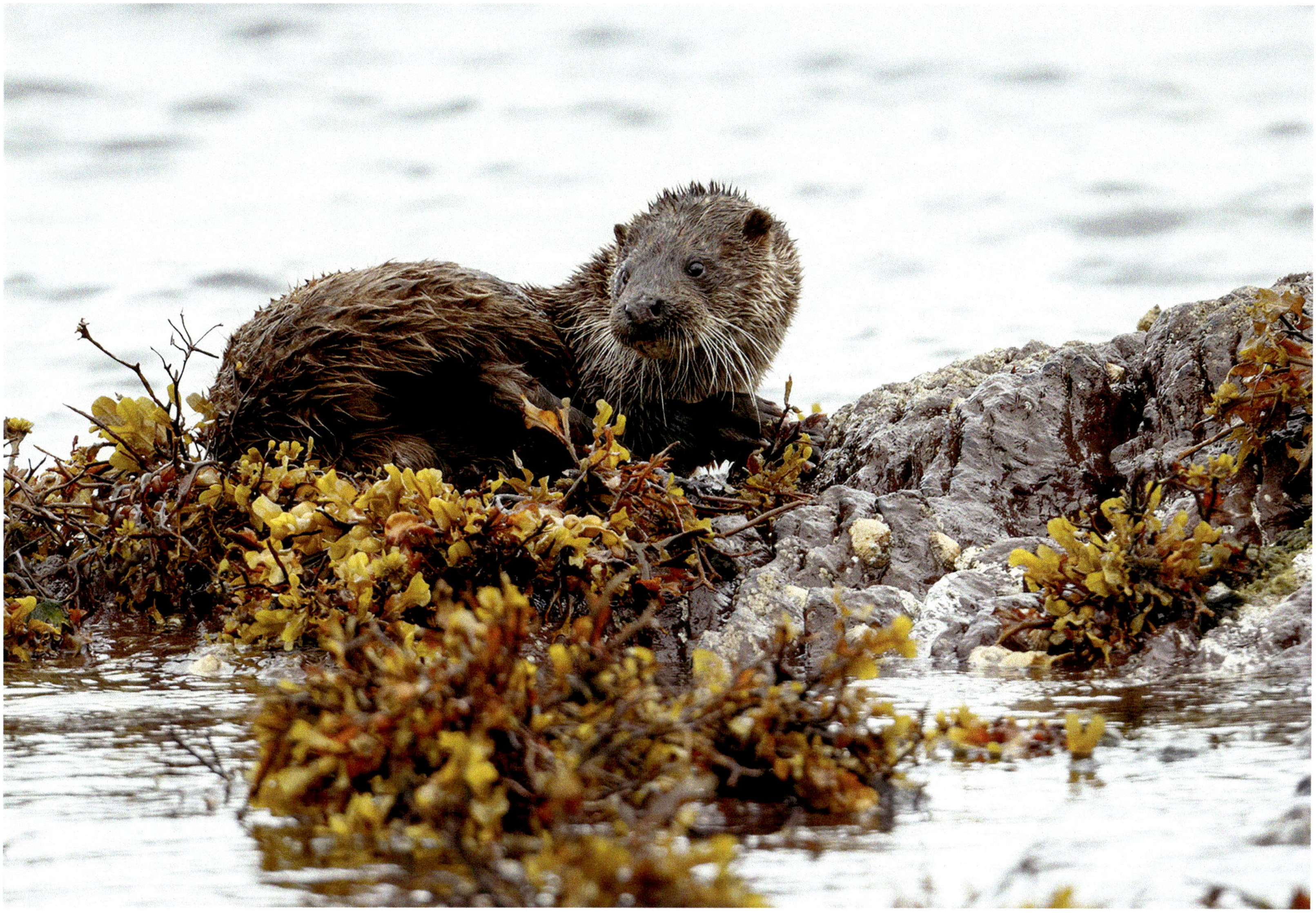

'An otter seeking rest on rock remote…'

Otters are sensitive to disturbance. Wild and beautiful Inishtrahull has been uninhabited by humans since the late 1920s and is a safe place for an otter to seek shelter.

TURNSTONE

A pebble tumbler
At water's edge,
Beak industriously
Probing, flicking.

Receiving reward
In ample repast,
Pellucid sandhoppers
And whiskered shrimps.

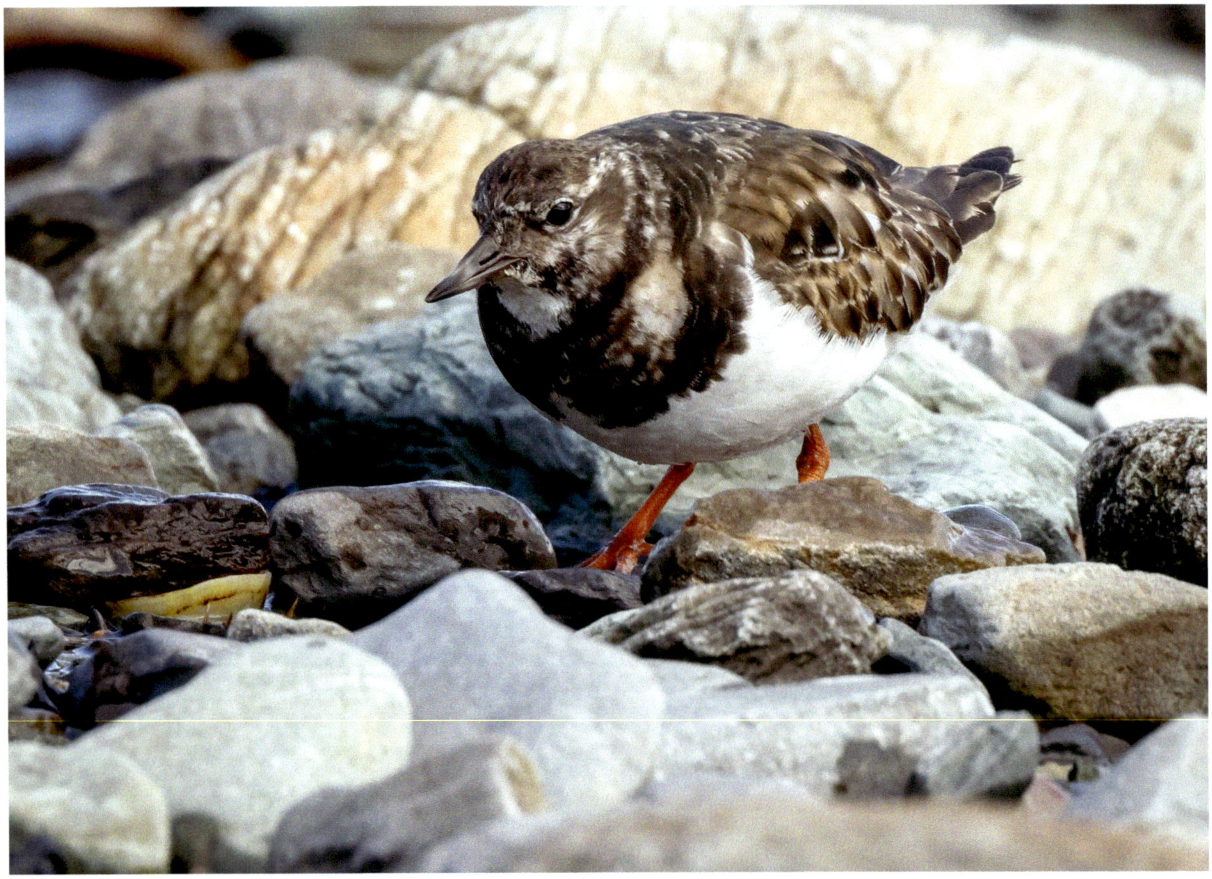

'A pebble tumbler at water's edge…'

The Ruddy Turnstone can be seen throughout the year around the Irish coast but breeds in the Arctic. They forage on the tide-line using their short, strong bill to turn over small stones and seaweed in the search for sandhoppers and other insects underneath. This image shows its unique tortoiseshell breeding plumage, a beautiful patchwork of white, black, brown and bright orange. This is perfect camouflage for the Arctic nesting sites of brown pebbles covered in coloured lichens.

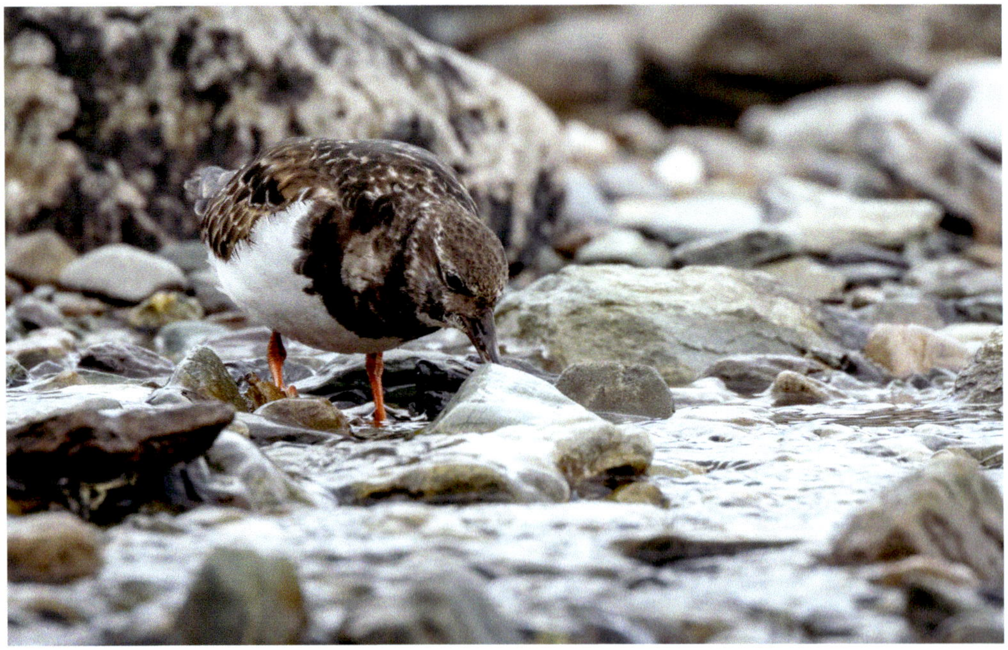

'Receiving reward, in ample repast…'

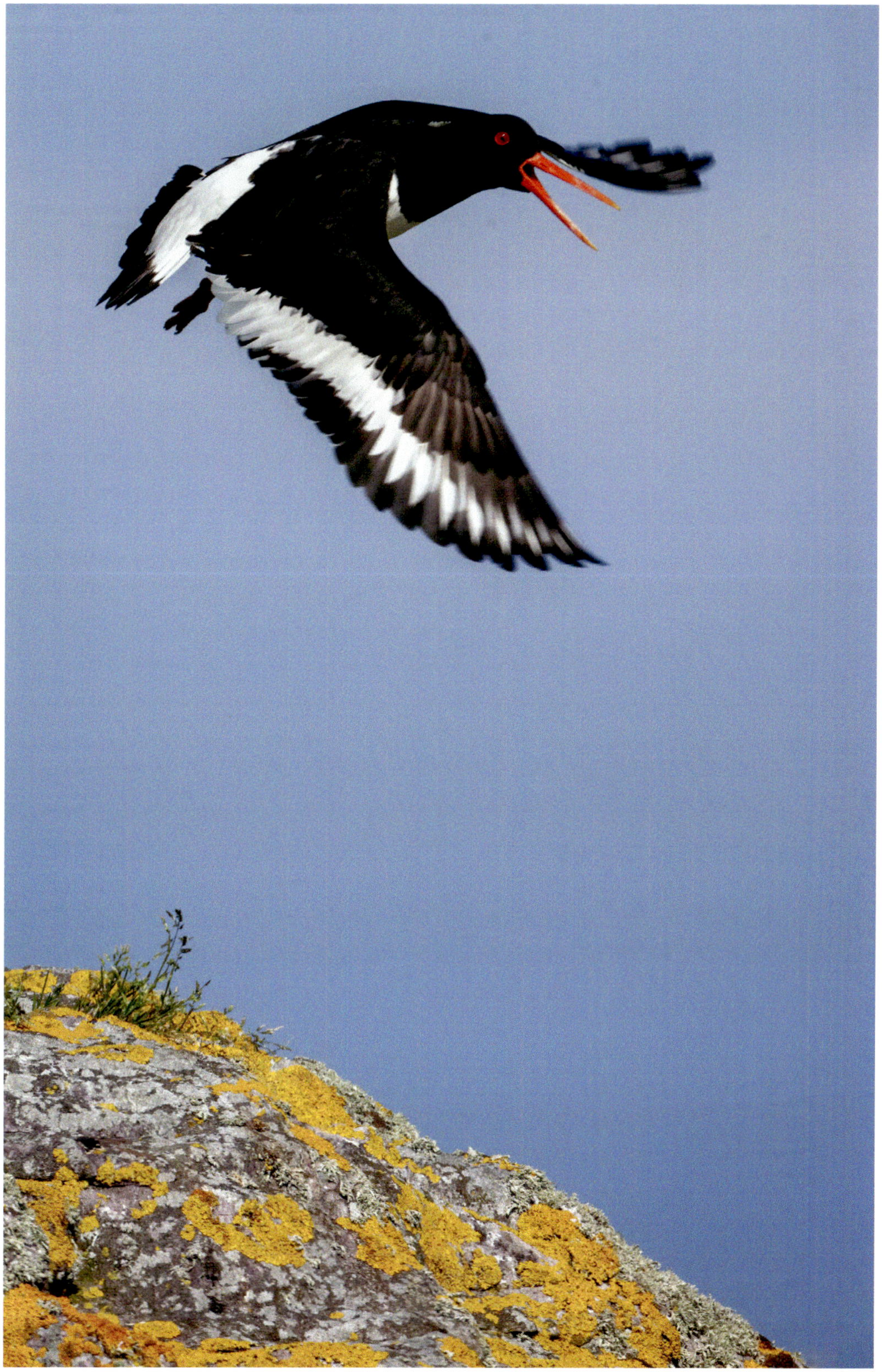

'Flight-cross on back...'

OYSTERCATCHER

Wedge-shaped mandibles,
Flight-cross on back;
St Brigid's servant
Scorning concealement.
Chipping your trade
On rocky coast,
Limpets dislodging,
Piping "kleep-kleep".

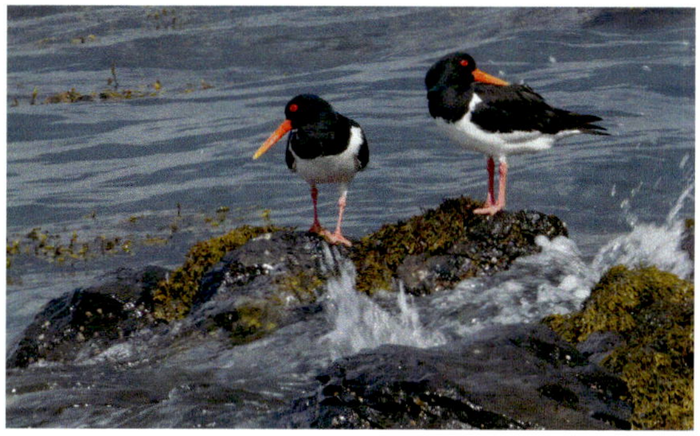

'Chipping your trade on rocky coast...'

The loud 'peeping' call of an oystercatcher is a recognisable and familiar sound of the seashore. They are large, obvious, and noisy bird with massive, long orange bills used for prying open limpets. In flight it shows a wide, white wing-stripe, a black tail and a white rump that extends as a 'V' between the wings. In winter, overseas immigrants mingle with our indigenous species.

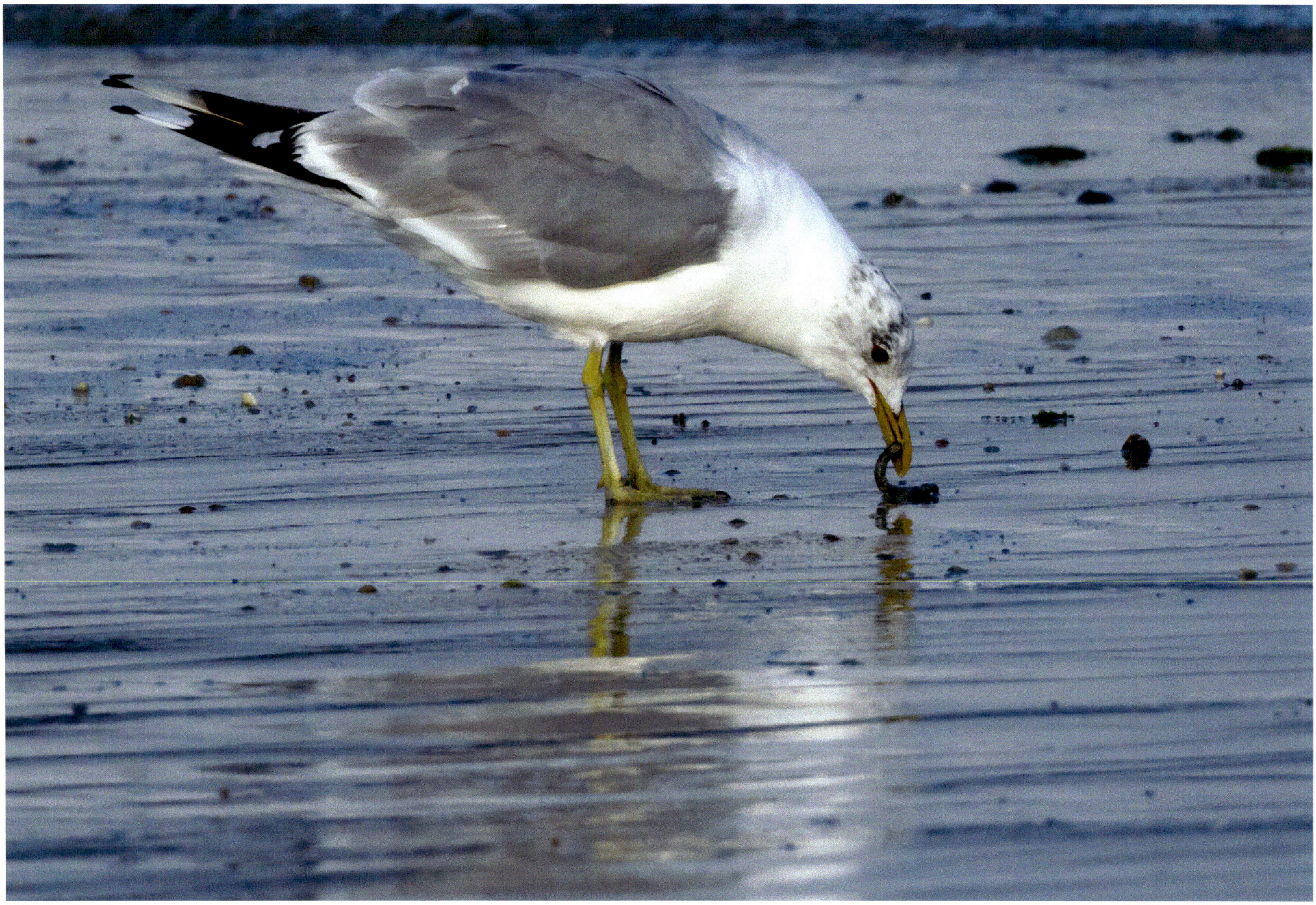

'Imprinting the mudflat with webbed toes.'

SEAGULL

Cockle dropper,
And scavenger,
Imprinting the mudflat
With webbed toes.
Takes off,
Alights on the sea;
Calls; paddles;
Goes fishing.

The Common Gull feeds from water or on the ground, living on a diet of molluscs, fish, worms and insects.

DRAGONFLY

The needle-shaped Aeshna
Hawks along the seaside,
Cerulean blue and brown
Catches the kittiwake's eye.

From aerial manoeuvring
Alights for relief in repose,
Front legs akimbo, basket-fashion,
Trap for the unwary shore moth.

Killer in varnished disguise,
Jaws masticating gnat-victim,
Flight members stiffly outspread
And hinged head swivelling.

Airborne, sunstreak of sapphire,
Golden costa glittering;
Then rainbow of transfixed wings
As kittiwake floats cliffwards away.

Four-spotted Chasers are easily recognised by the two dark spots on the leading edge of each wing. On the wing from May to September, they are active dragonflies, spending a lot of time hawking over water for insects or to mark out their territories. They mate on the wing; the female then hovers over the water, dipping the tip of her abdomen to drop her eggs on vegetation below the surface.

It is believed in Irish folklore that fairies use dragonflies to travel from place to place. In some cases it is believed that dragonflies are fairies in disguise!

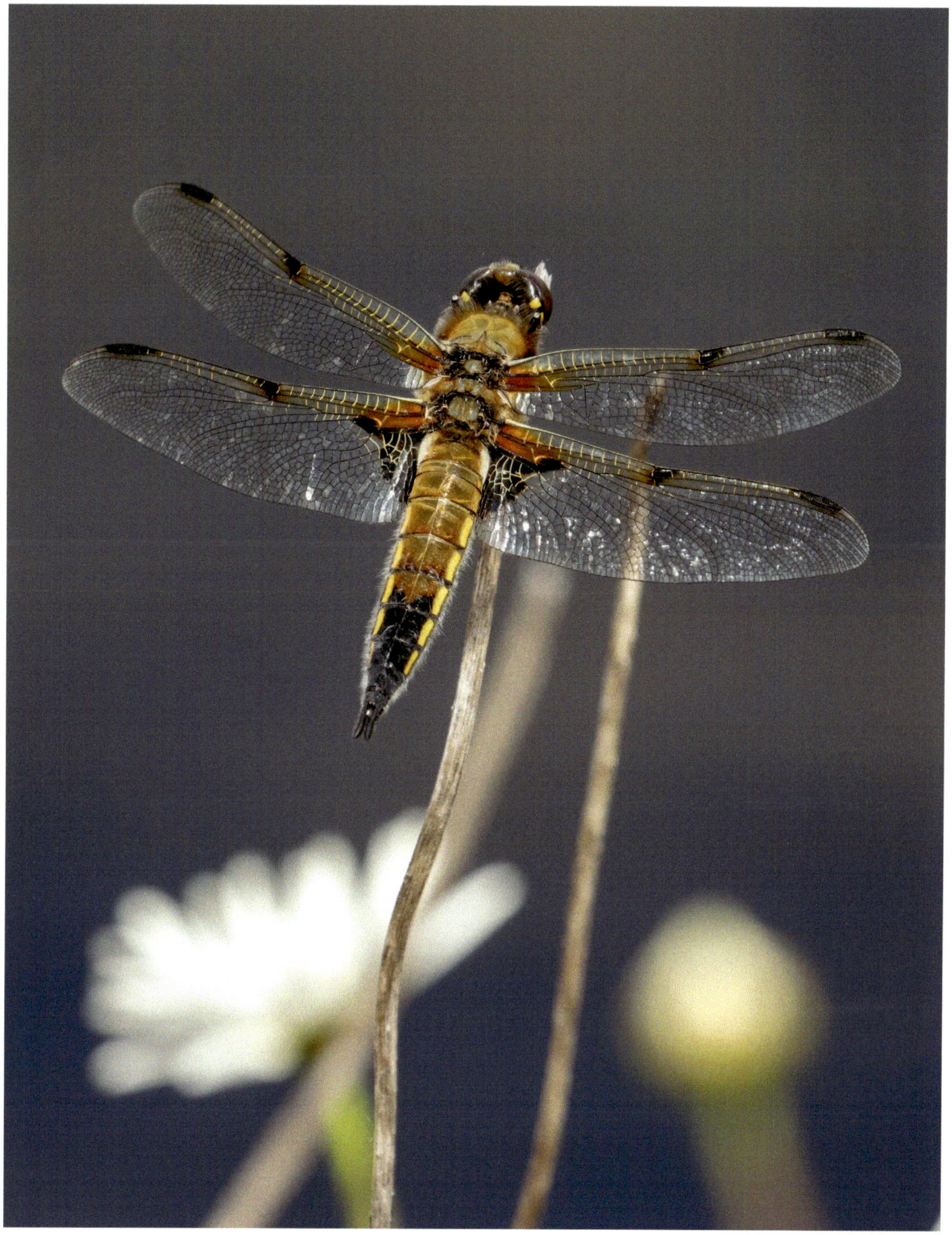

'From aerial manoeuvring alights for relief in repose…'

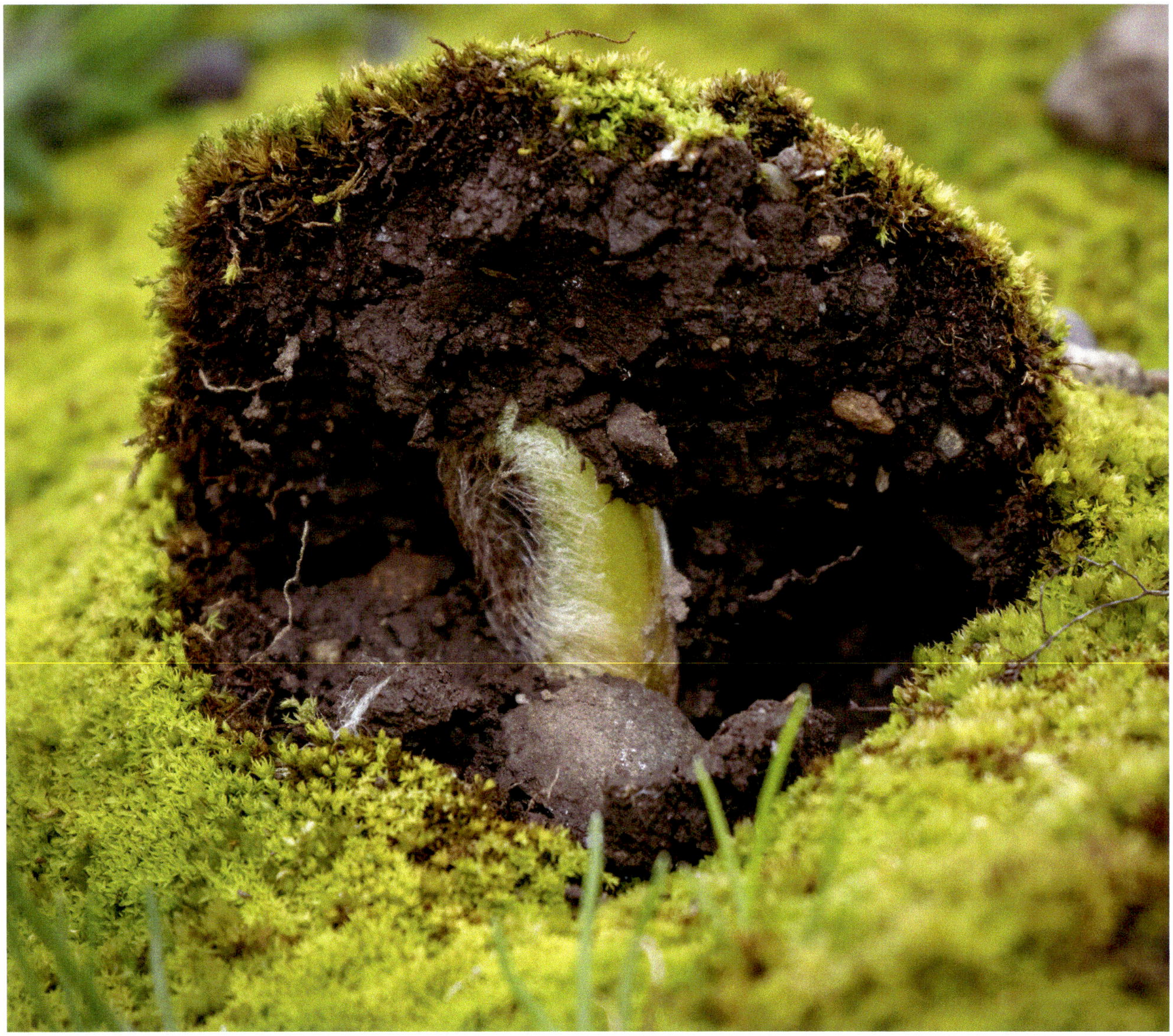

Cocoons are specific to moths, while chrysalides are formed by butterflies. Insects that mature through a process known as complete metamorphosis enter what is called the pupa stage before entering the adult stage. During this time, a cocoon of spun silk protects the moth caterpillar, and this pupa stage is frequently found hiding underground or beneath layers of foliage.

'Chrysalids wrapped on ostracism threads.'

METAMORPHOSIS

Taking a clod of turf, squeezing it,
And having it crumble into debris
Of desiccated fern and fibrous rootlets,
You may find you have liberated
From a hide in the middle
The chrysalis of a moth.

Later, trespassing spade-worked bog,
Bent eyes scanning the windrows,
Clumps, rickles and footings,
Built higgledy-piggledy to air-dry;
The mind registers, entomologically:
"Safe home for insect hibernators."

So, likewise, encamped itinerants,
Withdrawn into themselves, cocooned,
Chrysalids wrapped in ostracism-threads;
An understanding hand of friendship could brittle
The black clay of their apathy,
To set them free—sun-kiss'd imagos.

DRIFTWOOD

When I walked across the strand
Along the edge of the sea,
Mackerel were shoaling close in,
Making a miniature tide-wash.

Climbing the rocks, bubble-wrack popping,
Cast ashore tangles of mermaid's-hair
Added grip to the soles of the wellingtons,
Prevented slipping on the eel-grass zone.

Diving gannets split the water,
Swallowed their catches and surfaced
To flap into airborne circles again,
Repeating the cycle monotonously.

The ozone-scented wall of organic debris,
Flinging the tidal foreshore flats,
Was peopled by scavenging sandhoppers,
with worm-like henichordata burrowing
beneath.

Here in the solitude and quite
Stood a notice, "Beware of rising tide".
So, not wishing to be cut off,
I beachcombed the higher reaches.

My mind registering the oar-weeds
roundness,
The mating call of an Arctic tern;
With a bundle of driftwood safely gathered,
I roped and knotted and carried it home.

The Common Tern is very similar to the Arctic Tern, and both are summer visitors to Ireland, arriving in April and leaving in August. I managed to watch and shoot the courting antics of this buoyant, graceful pair of common terns on Horse Island off the southwest coast of Ireland where the colony is undisturbed by human habitation or predatory mammals. Pairs are established through delightful aerial courtship displays. The bill is deep red at this time and usually with a black tip.

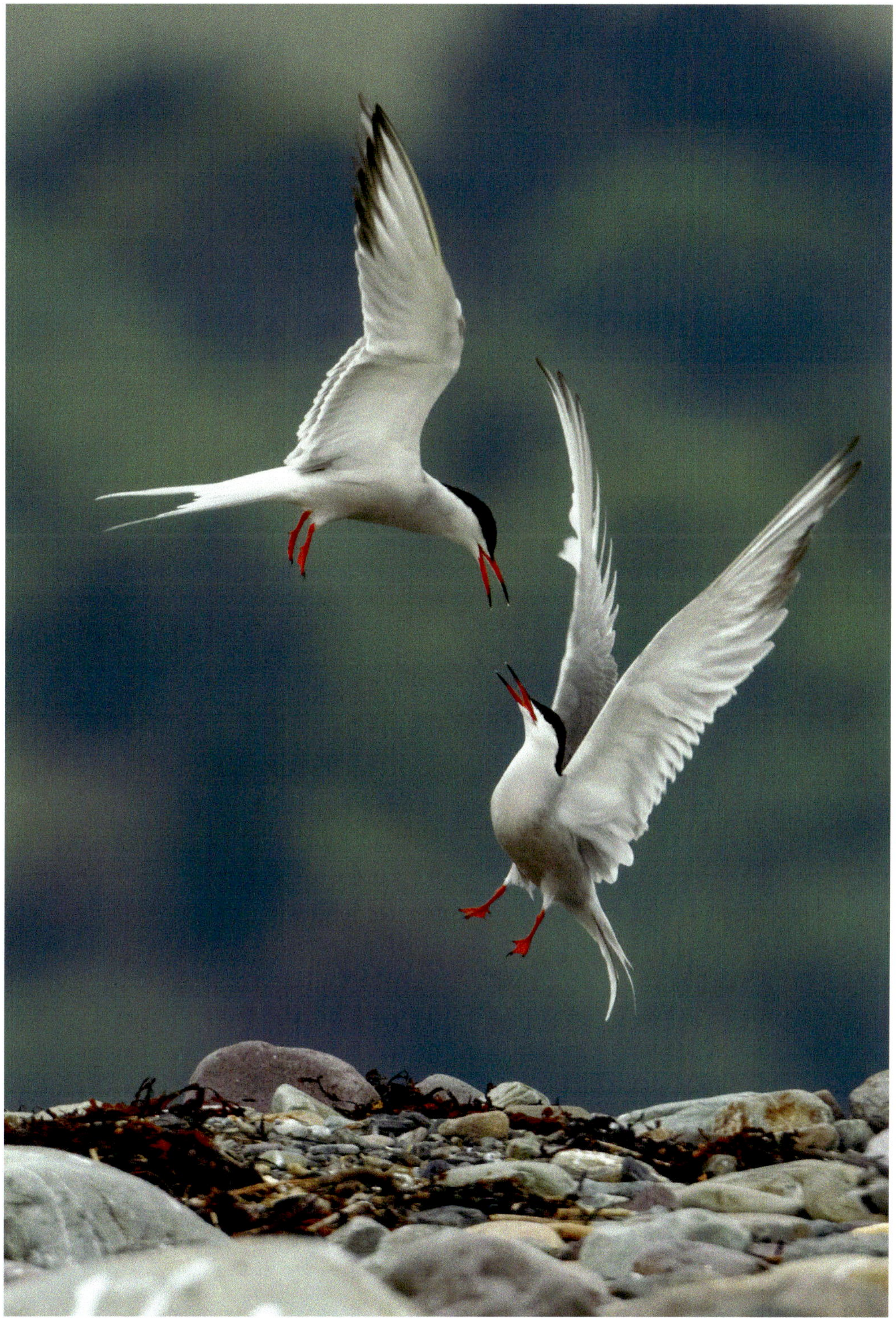

'...the mating call of an Arctic tern.'

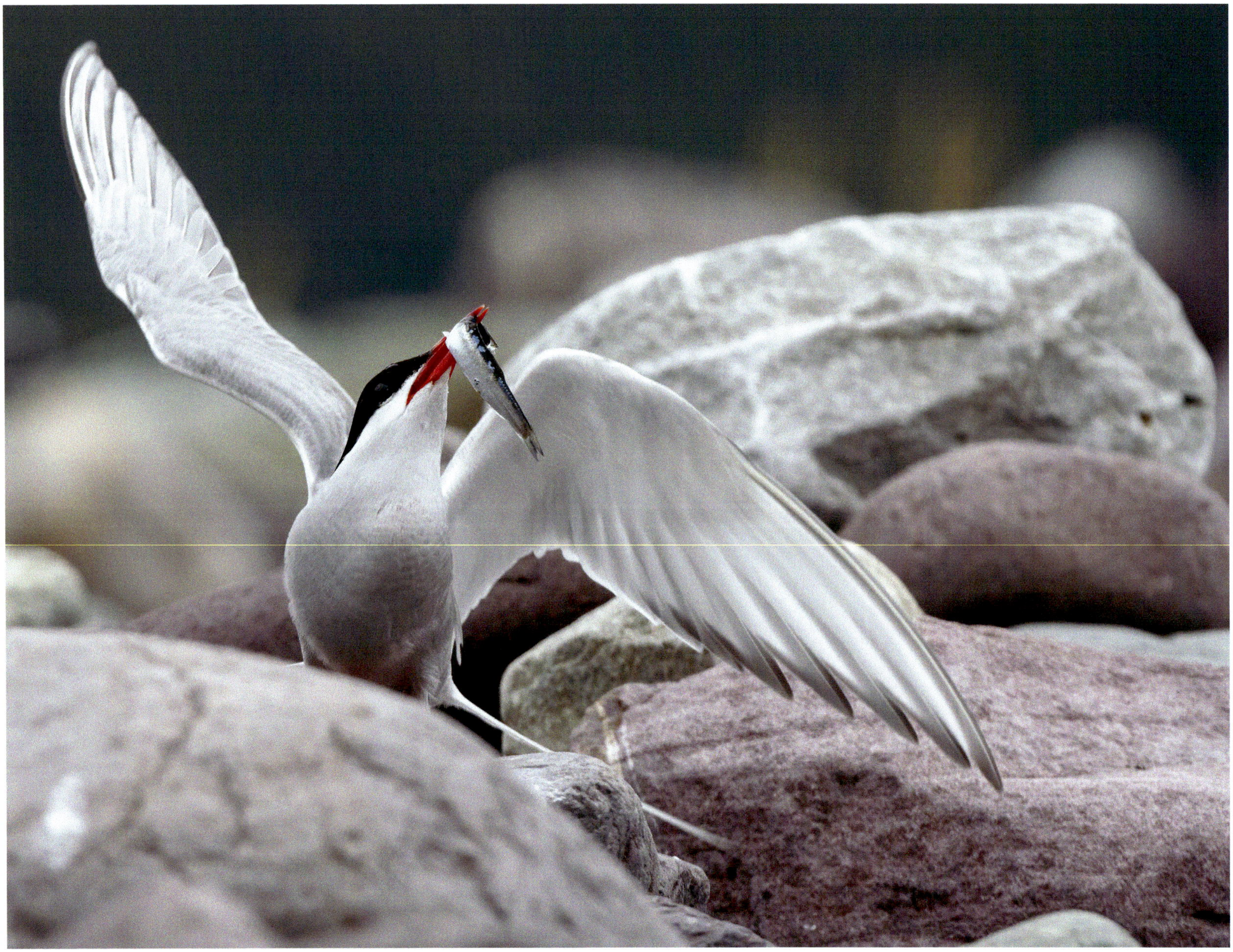

The courtship ritual of terns begins with the female chasing a male up into the air (known as the 'high flight'), after which the pair slowly descends back to the land. Next, the male brings gifts of fish, a ritual called the 'fish flight'. Courtship feeding is a common aspect of tern behaviour. It seems that males that provide the best supplies of fish during courtship also rear, on average, larger numbers of young, so the female is apparently testing his potential as a father before agreeing to partner with him.

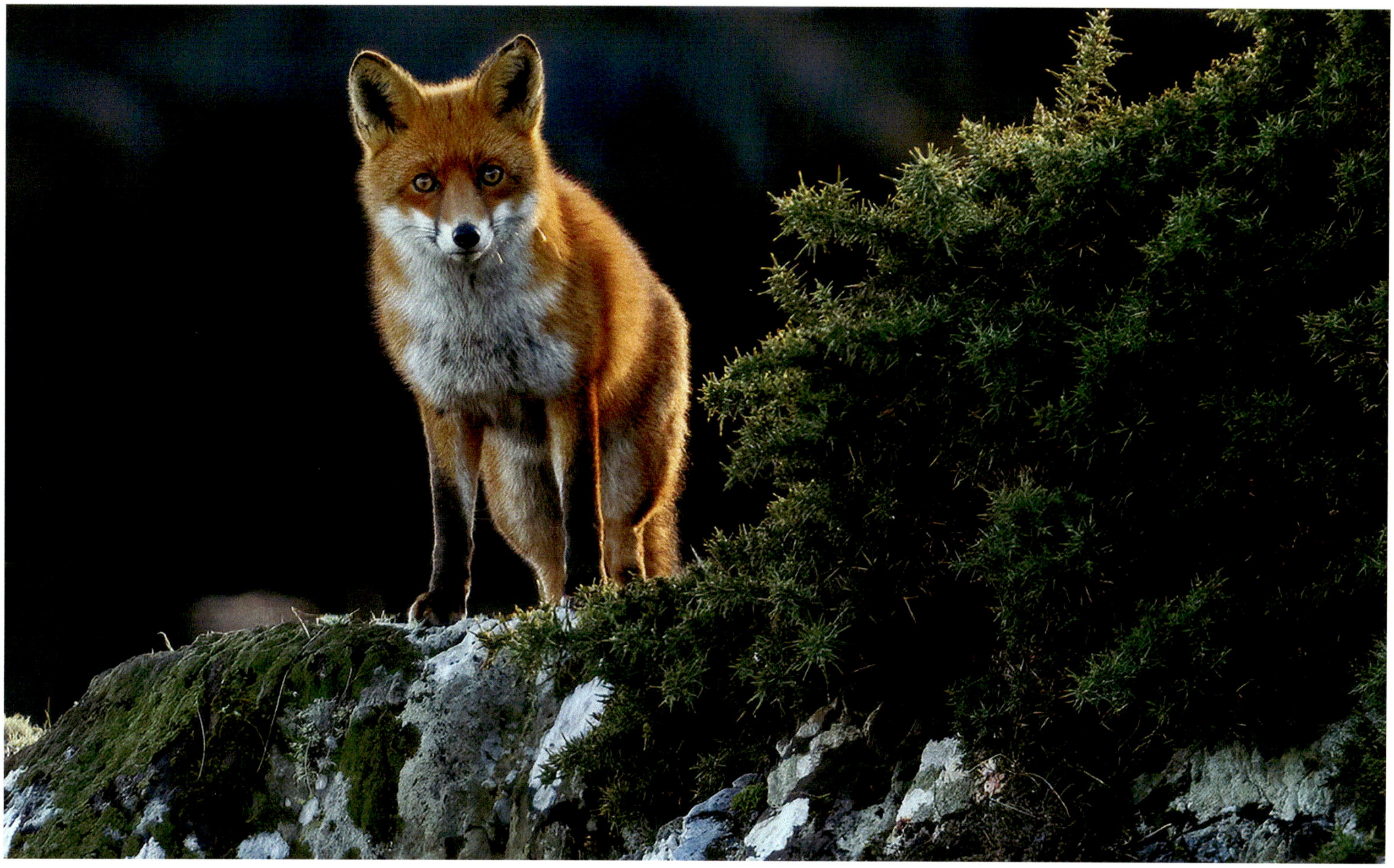

'So also the hill fox wanders, padding the rain-soaked heather, fur ruffed by the barren up-winds…'

DECEMBER NIGHT

Jupiter strides the eastern sky,
Travelling south-west, shouldering stars,
Bombarded by streaming meteorites
From a fixed point in Gemini.

So also the hill fox wanders,
Padding the rain-soaked heather,
Fur ruffled by the barren up-winds,
And black muzzle moon-pointing.

No bird speaks in the dark,
Nor mothy shadow hedge-flits,
But a meandering stream bubbles,
Escalating winter into spring.

Foxes can inhabit any type of land area along the coast or in farmland and from lowlands up to mountainous areas. They mostly remain hidden during the day, emerging at dusk to hunt for prey. Unusually, I spotted this fox before she was aware of my presence. She continued to walk in my direction, and then for a brief moment, her gaze met mine. The evening light added a dramatic flair to my magic moment.

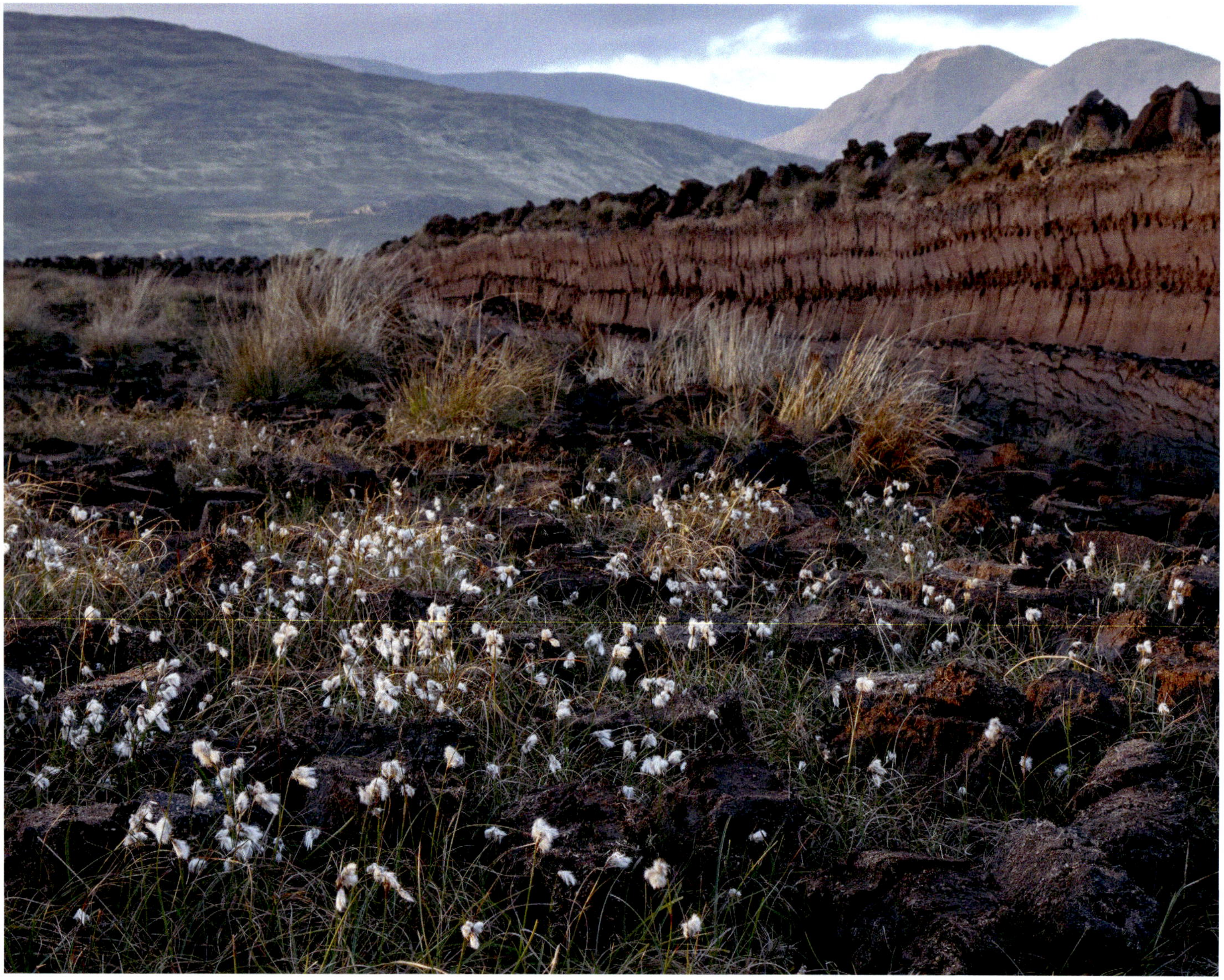

'Bog-cotton waves where pennon-silk, doe-hares to leverets give milk…'

A COUNTRY CALENDAR

Plough-moulded, Arran Banner flower;
Hedge-sparrows nest in bramble-bower,
And shield-bugs glint on musk mallow.

Dissolving mist half-shrouds each hill,
The tumbling of the rock-strewn rill
Stops short where water-beetles row.

Bog-cotton waves where pennon-silk,
Doe-hares to leverets give milk,
Frog-hoppers hide in bubble-sap.

Each day is shot with sunbeams bright,
Star-spangles jewel the sky at night
As June falls into July's lap.

Soon prosaic clouds turn on their tap:
Floods speed the rivers; wild winds blow;
The water-glass moves 'High' to 'Low'.

Bog Cotton is a plant of very damp peaty ground. Its leaves mostly arise from the base of the plant, often being tinged with red or brown. It has tiny insignificant brown flowers in April and May, but it is really when it is in fruit that this becomes a most eye-catching and attractive plant.

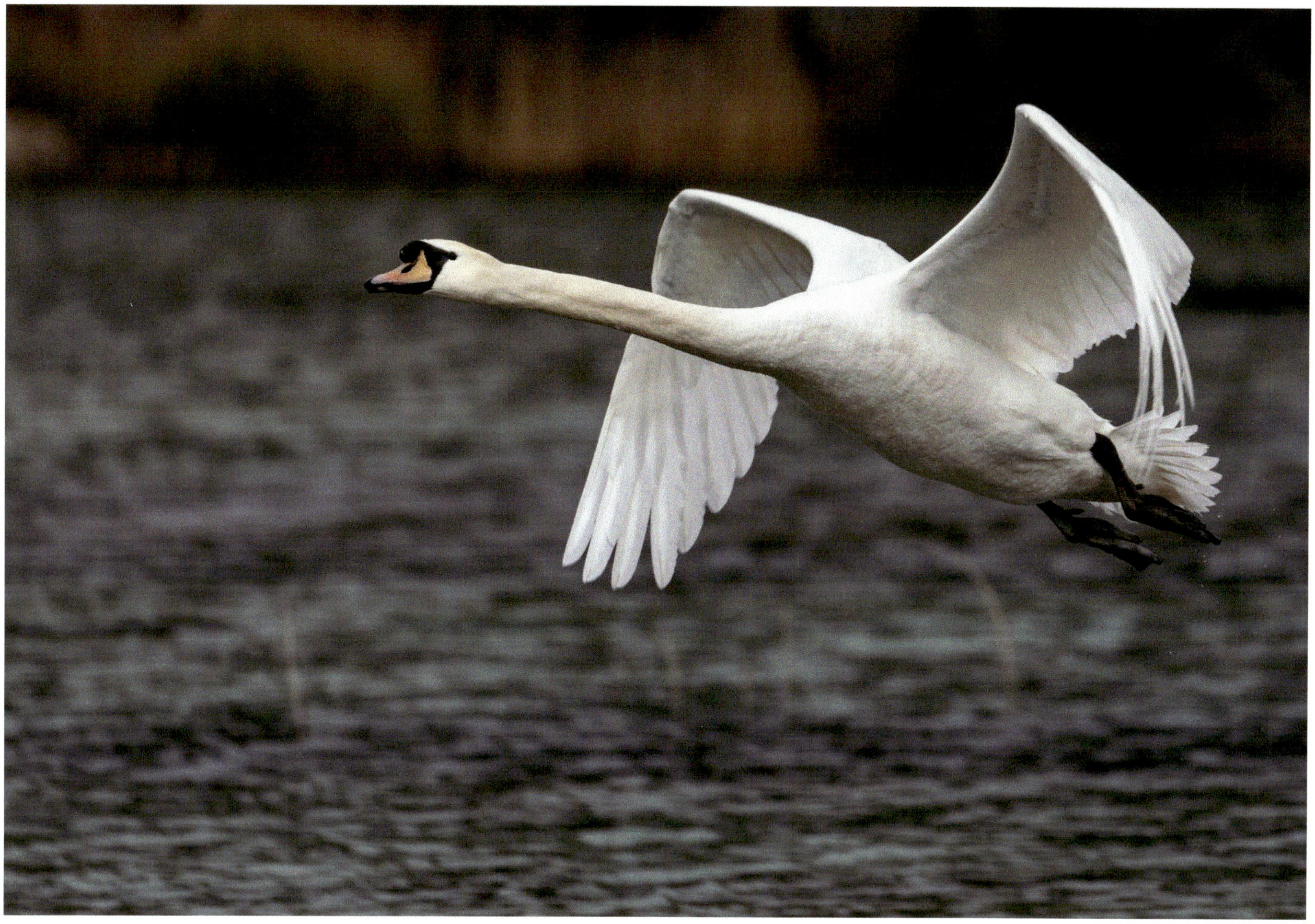

'...the class pedant replied: "Mute swan!" but she corrected 'mute' was a misnomer...'

PHILOLOGY

At grammar teacher asked: "As silent as what...?"
To which the class pedant replied: "Mute swan!"
But she corrected 'mute' was a misnomer,
To think of something else: an owl, a bat...?
When "Silent as a graveyard mouse," I interposed
And took delight in her assenting "Yes!"

Remembering the mound-heaped cemetery
Betwixt the parish church and blacksmith's forge,
The crypt wherein Penrose-Fitzgerald lies
In Whitegate, where in youth I went to school:
I wonder if in truth the rodents small
Are squeakless, sporting nightly round tombstones?

This beautiful bird can be found all around Ireland. The Mute Swan isn't mute. It makes a variety of sounds, often described as grunting, hoarse whistling, and snorting noises. The throaty rumble its chest is a welcome greeting to another swan. During a courtship display, Mute Swans utter a rhythmic song. Cygnets are especially vocal, and communicate through a variety of whistling and chirping sounds when content, as well as a harsh squawking noise when distressed or lost.

MARCH HARE

I unwind from my hidden form
When the west wind is blowing
Down the hill, through the woodland,
Quilting the dunes and shingle;
Exciting the creative instincts
And stimulating my urge for love:
The edict of organised Nature.

Now looping the tattered threshold
Bordering a handkerchief of fields,
I hop in a frenzy of pantings,
Swallowed in a shimmering shadowland
The vernal sun illuminates;
Blood boil into
A heart-transplant of Spring.

The silence of a graveyard
Engulfs the hungry backlands
As I skirmish into the valley.
Eagerly, from my ambuscades,
Seeking another craving release.
We meet at last: Constriction of space—
Swinging heath-bells proclaim our marriage

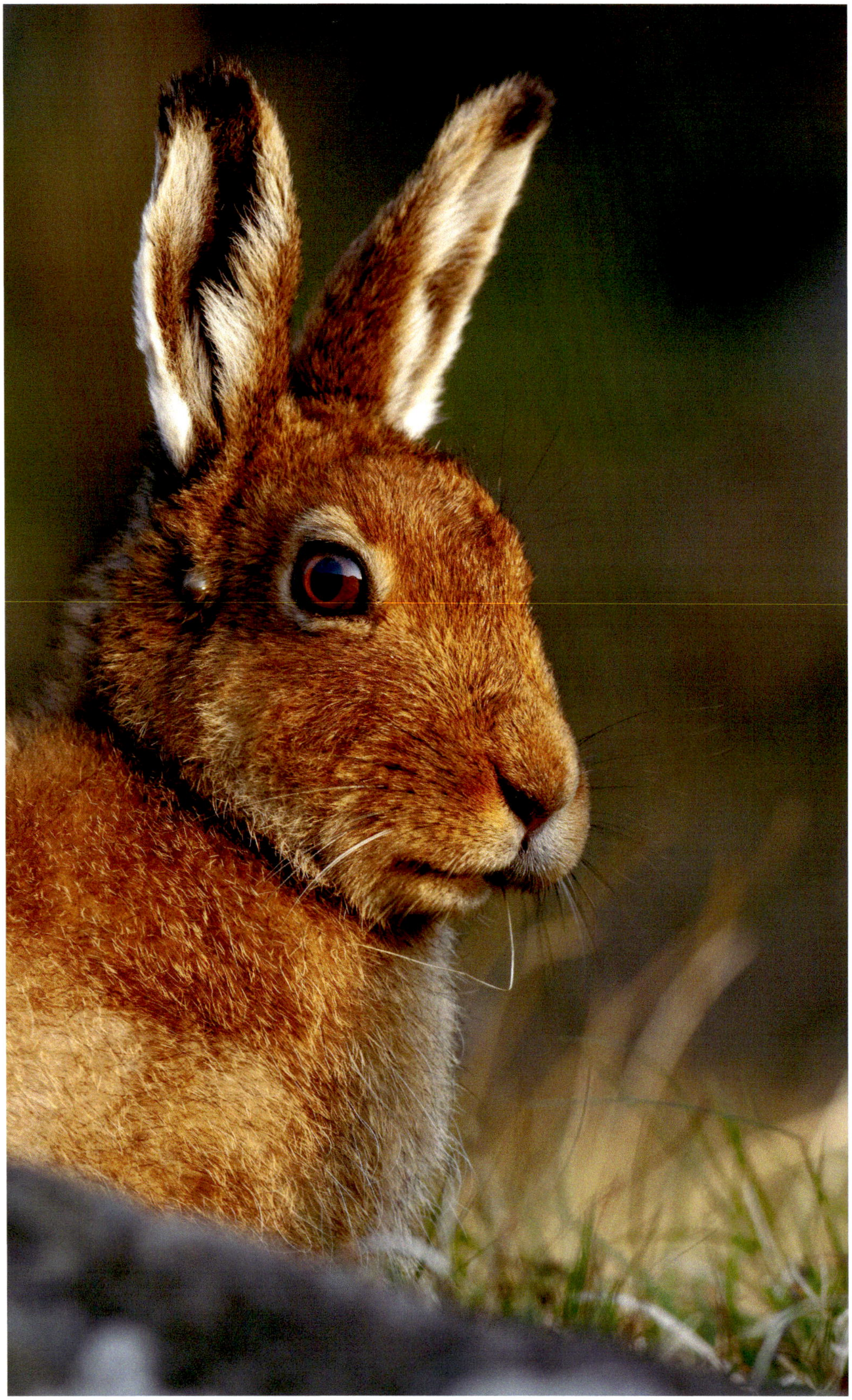

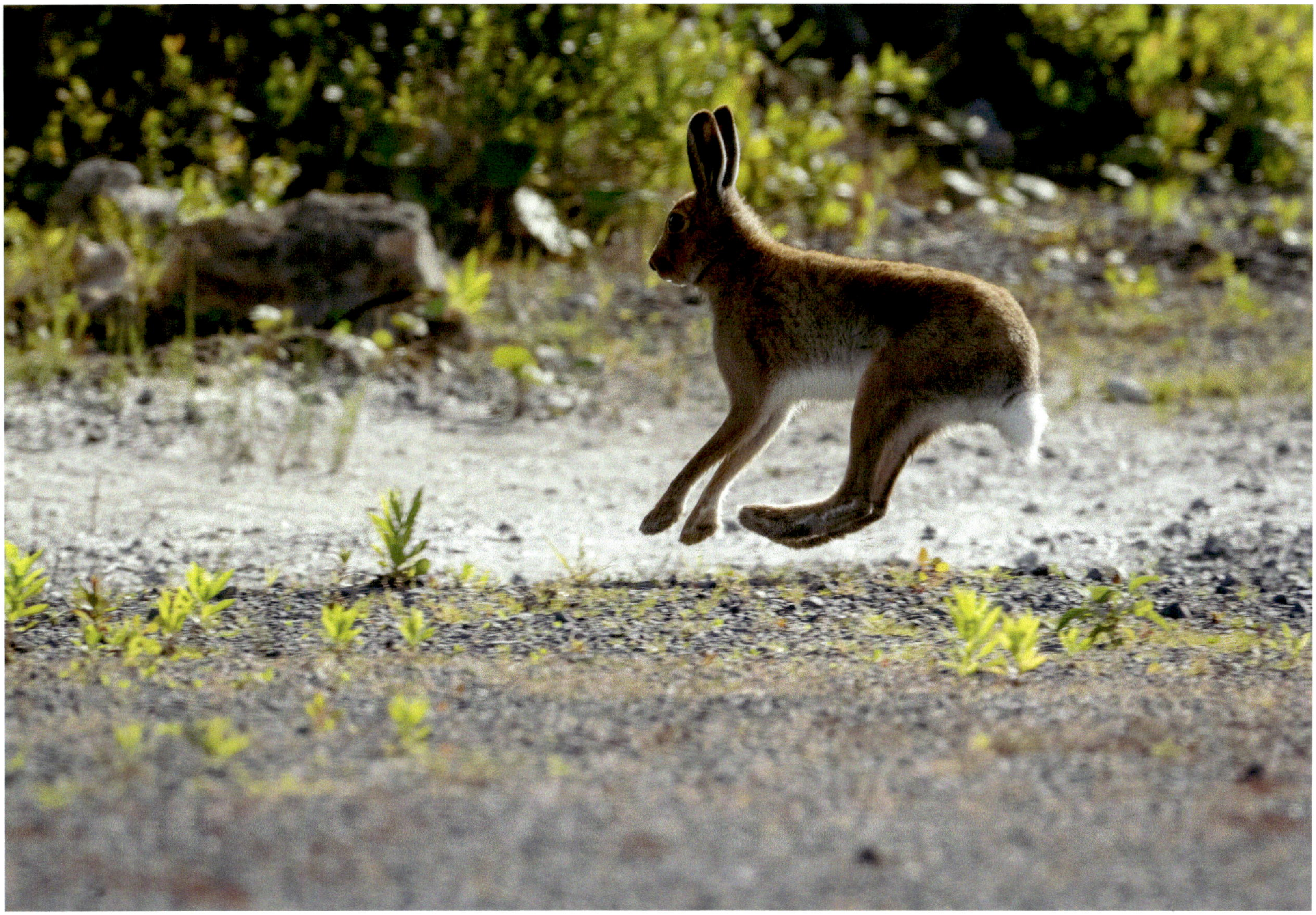

'I hop in a frenzy of pantings, swallowed in a shimmering shadowland…'

The Irish Mountain Hare, *lepus timidus hibernicus*, is an endemic sub-species of the Arctic Hare and is found from sea level right up to the tops of the highest mountains. It is one of Ireland's longest established indigenous species of mammal and has been present on the island since before the last ice age and is thus through evolutionary development and adaptation very much our own. Revered and celebrated in Celtic lore for centuries, the numbers of these noble animals have declined dramatically in the past three decades, but they are now a legally protected species under the Irish Wildlife Act. They can reproduce two or three times a year. The two to five young hares, or leverets, are furred and have open eyes at birth. Unlike rabbits, hares do not burrow and live life entirely above ground, resting in a 'form' in the open.

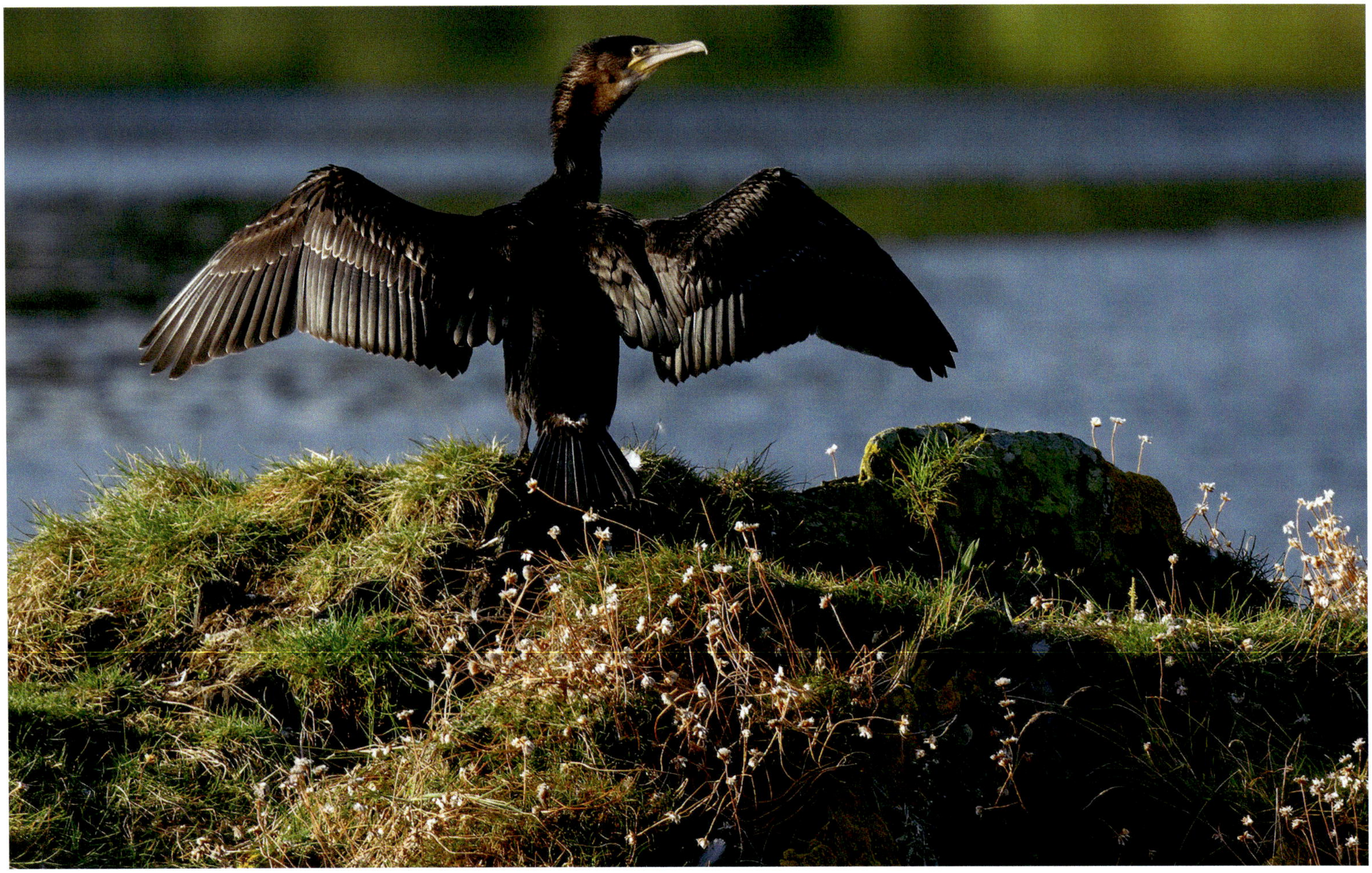

'...shag wing-drying.'

INVOCATION

No more the hissing swish of nacreous wavelets
Flung from the breasting bow of the bouncing boat,
The rattle of chains festooning the pier walls,
Gannets in gyration, or shags wing-drying.

The laws of redundancy bind my late years
With the tangled tapes of enforced retirement,
Self-esteem smothered beneath pension-papers,
Public oblivion, a living death.

"At 18 Join the Navy and See the World"—
Hoary 65 a pilgrim denied destiny.
Looking back...I remember the *Titanic*,
Ark Royal, *Isolda*: and now I look at myself.

Both the Shag and the Cormorant are resident along all Irish coasts. They don't have oil glands like other water birds, so they cannot oil their wings and are not waterproof. This helps with diving as they are less buoyant, but does mean that if they get too wet they could drown, so after a fishing session they must find somewhere to stand with their wings outstretched to dry off their feathers.

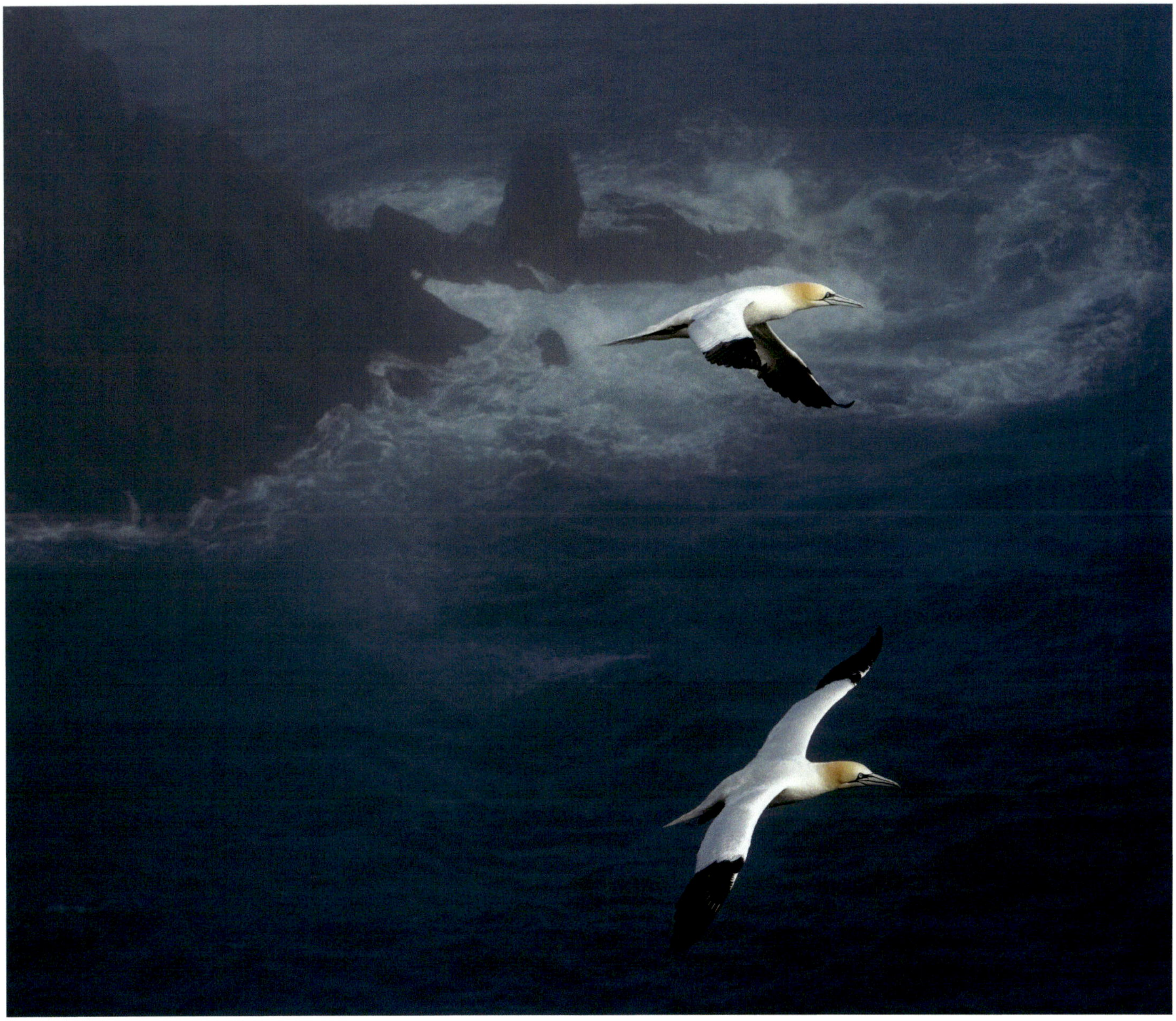

'Gannets in gyration....'

The Gannet is the largest European sea bird and swims and flies almost its entire life in and above the sea, only coming on land to nest. The wings of the Northern Gannet are long and narrow, allowing the bird to cruise along in strong wind. In normal flight, it performs powerful wing-beats interspersed with glides. Even in calm weather they can attain velocities of between 55 and 65 km an hour although their flying muscles are relatively small.

At sea they flap and then glide low over the water. They feed by flying high and circling before plunging into the sea from up to 40 metres, descending with half-closed wings to hit the water in a streamlined arrowhead shape. By visiting the colony on the Great Saltee Island in County Wexford, I had a wonderful opportunity to photograph their flight as they glided past.

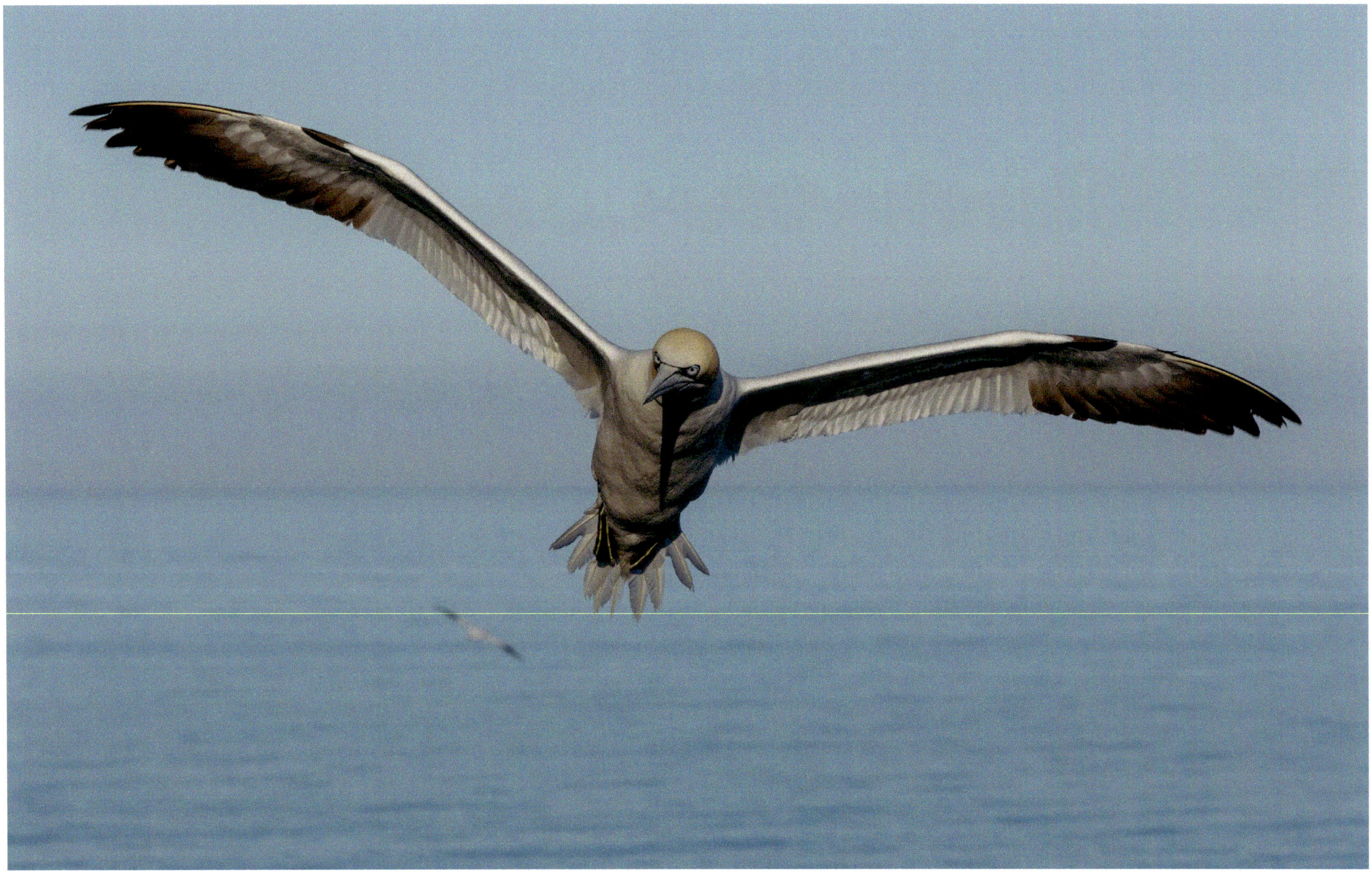

'From cliff-edge in flight, predicament over…'

FIRST FLIGHT

From cliff-edge in flight,
Predicament over:
Grey-brown in the light
World and life-rover.

Earth changed for the air,
No blemish showing;
Desire binding fear
With brain-threads of knowing.

The zephyr low singing
Through pinion and feather
Wing prowess bringing
To battle all weather.

Each member true tested,
Swing back to parent;
Young gull-years invested
With sky-love inherent.

The Northern Gannet is an elegant bird in the air but is clumsy on land. Take-off requires a running start, with wings flapping powerfully, and for this reason the breeding colonies are usually established high up on steep coasts, often on sea cliffs where the wind is forced upwards against the rocky wall. In upward winds, the bird only needs to spread its wings spanning over 6 feet to rise into the air. Like all seabirds, they drink seawater and discharge the salt via nasal glands

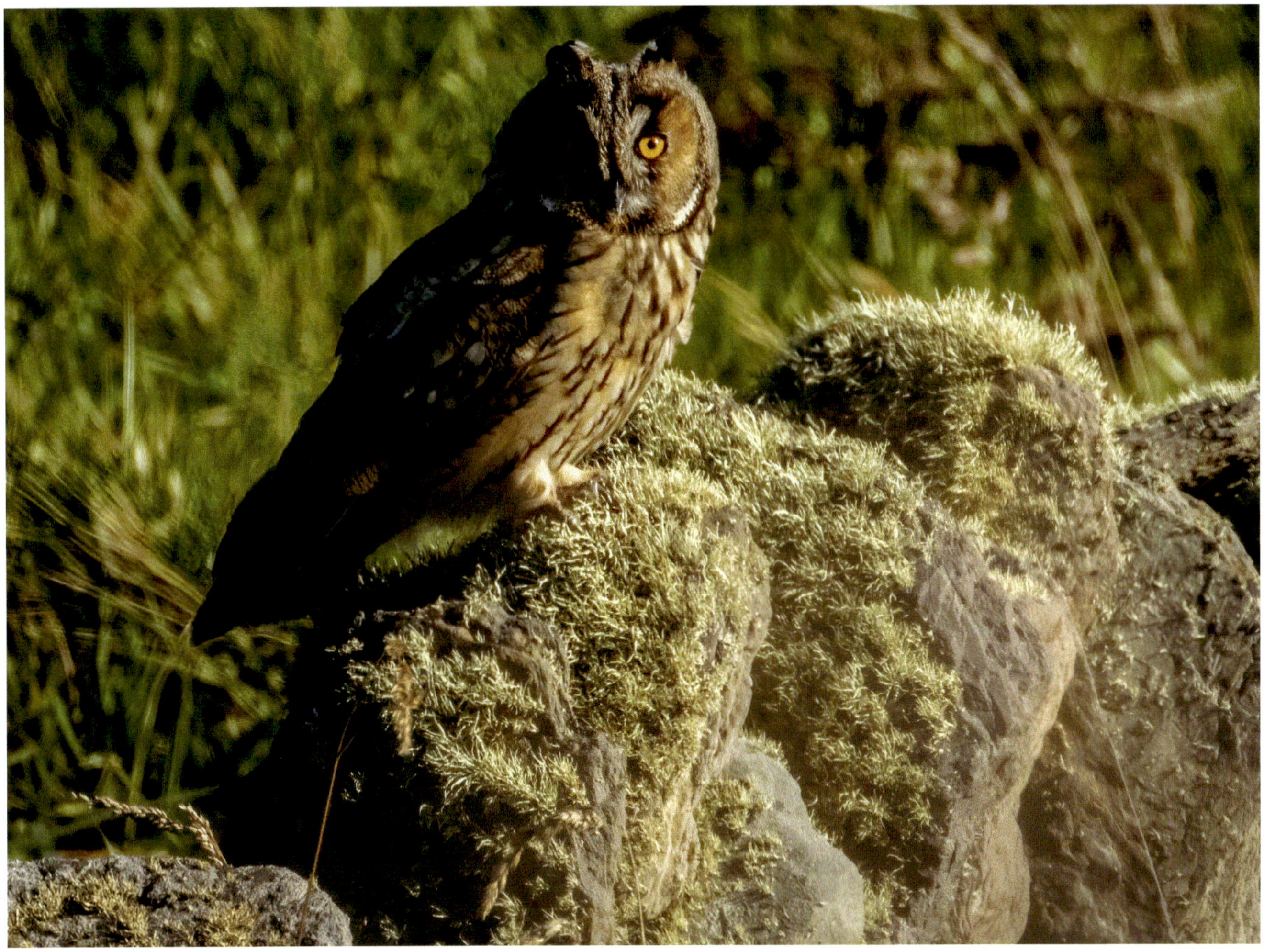

'Great saucer eyes and cat-like head…'

THROWBACK

Loose-feathered,
Soft as silk,
Great saucer eyes
And cat-like head;
The brown owl came
Floating
Out of the dark
With awesome call:
"Hoo-hoo! Hoo-hoo!"
Depicting in prowling ghost-flight
Instinctive knowledge
Of the night.

The Long-eared Owl is distributed all across Ireland and is often found in coniferous woodlands with open grasslands nearby where they hunt their prey. The two tufts of feathers on the top of its head are erect when it is alarmed or focussed and are flat when it is relaxed or flying. The face has two vertical white lines between the eyes. Like all owls the Long-eared Owl has a huge facial disc and can turn its head through 270 degrees in either direction from a forward-facing position. It is strictly nocturnal and is rarely seen foraging at dusk or dawn. This shot, taken during the day on Middle Calf Island in Roaring Water Bay in West Cork, shows perfectly how light effects the pupil of the owl's eye. The pupil has shrunk to block out some of the light from the sun shining on the right side. On the left side of the image, the pupil of the eye in shadow has expanded to let in lots of light. An owl's large pupils help it hunt in the dark.

SOLITUDE

I live out of the world,
Far from the land.
"A lightkeeper?" they ask,
And shake my hand;
"It must be lonely out there?"
They do not understand.

For, rock-bound by the tide,
And free from the throng,
Sweet peace fills my breast
The whole day long,
Every window's wind-whistle
Is a blackbird's nesting song.

The view of the rocks from one of the bedrooms of Skellig Lighthouse, a place of awe and peace.

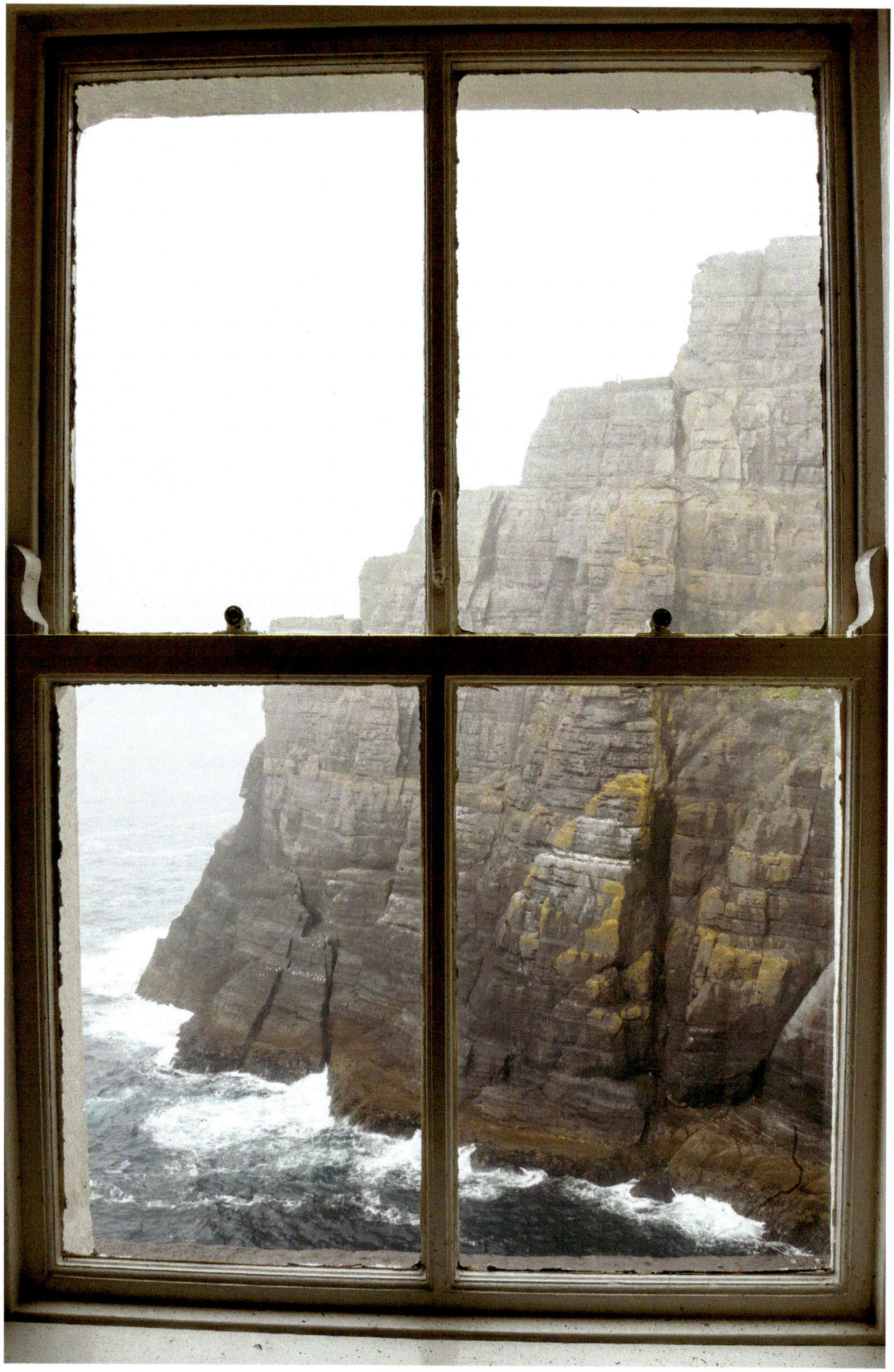

'..rock-bound by the tide, and free from the throng..'

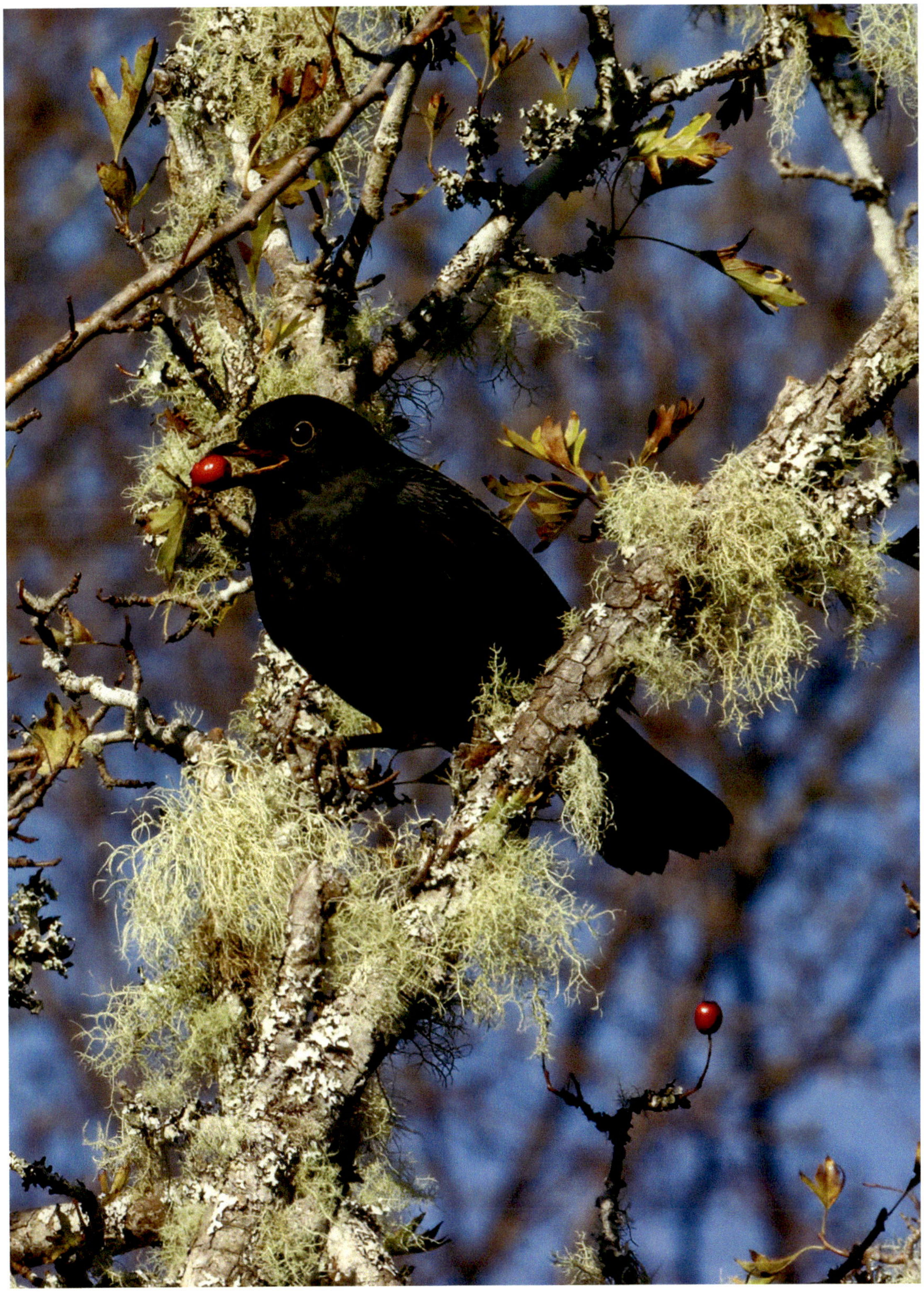

'Every window's wind-whistle is a blackbird's nesting song.'

The Blackbird is the most common and widespread member of the thrush family in Ireland and is one of our favourite songsters. As well as insects and earthworms, they eat berries.

SILHOUETTES

1. Jackdaw:

Chimney-perched
The jackdaw
Calling "Cae!"
Smoke-enshrouded,
Black Beelzebub.

The Jackdaw is a widespread bird and often nests in chimneys. Intelligent and noisy, it is usually seen in pairs.

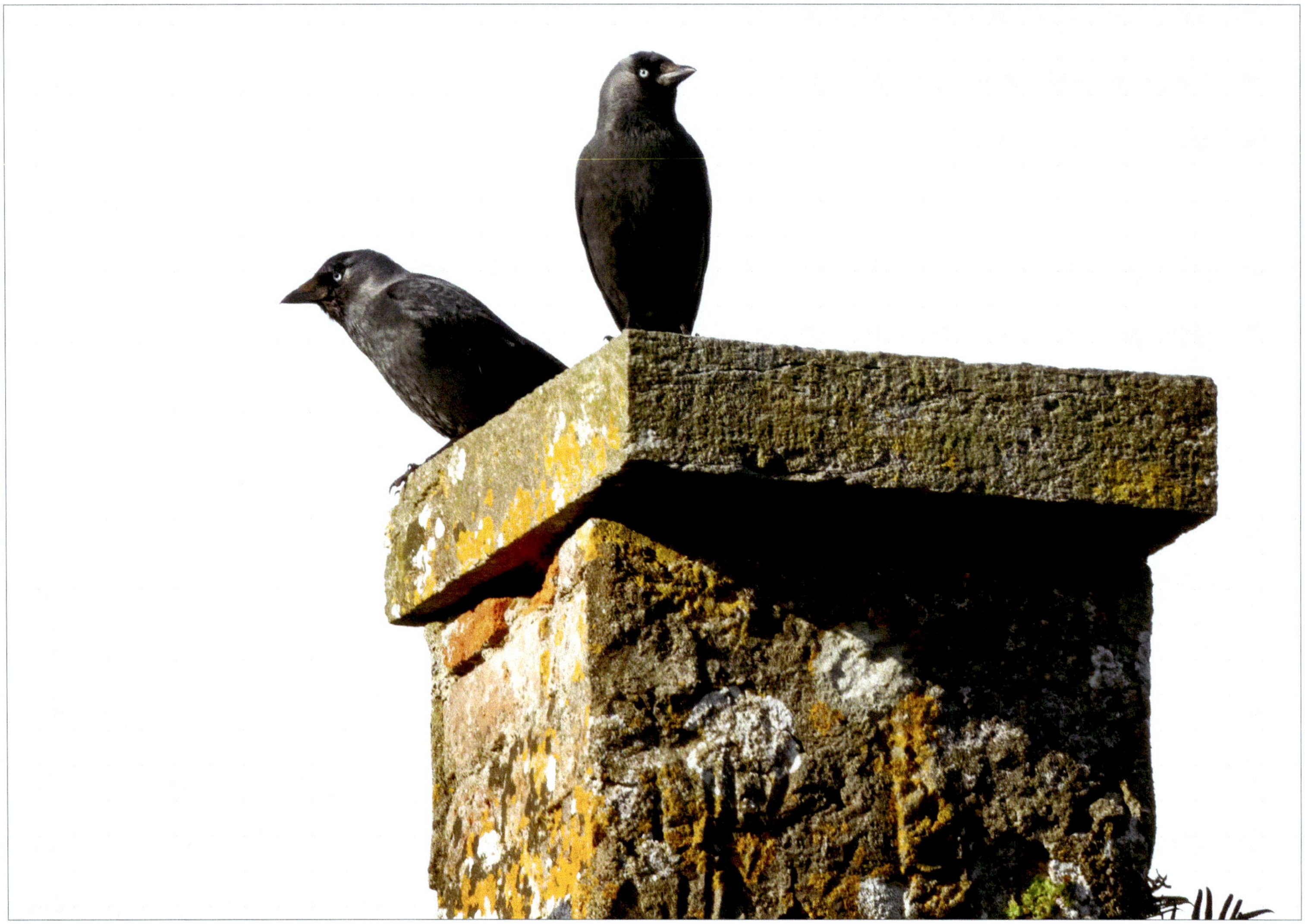

'Chimney-perched...'

2. Seagull

On a storm-tossed sea,
Rising and falling,
The seagull
Better than any boat
Can take to the air,
Fly high.

Gulls fly beautifully on their long, elegant wings using thermals to give them lift. The higher the gull rides up, the faster and further it can glide. They are also acrobats of the air, as they can swoop down quickly and seemingly hover in place to snatch their bit of food and ascend in seconds.

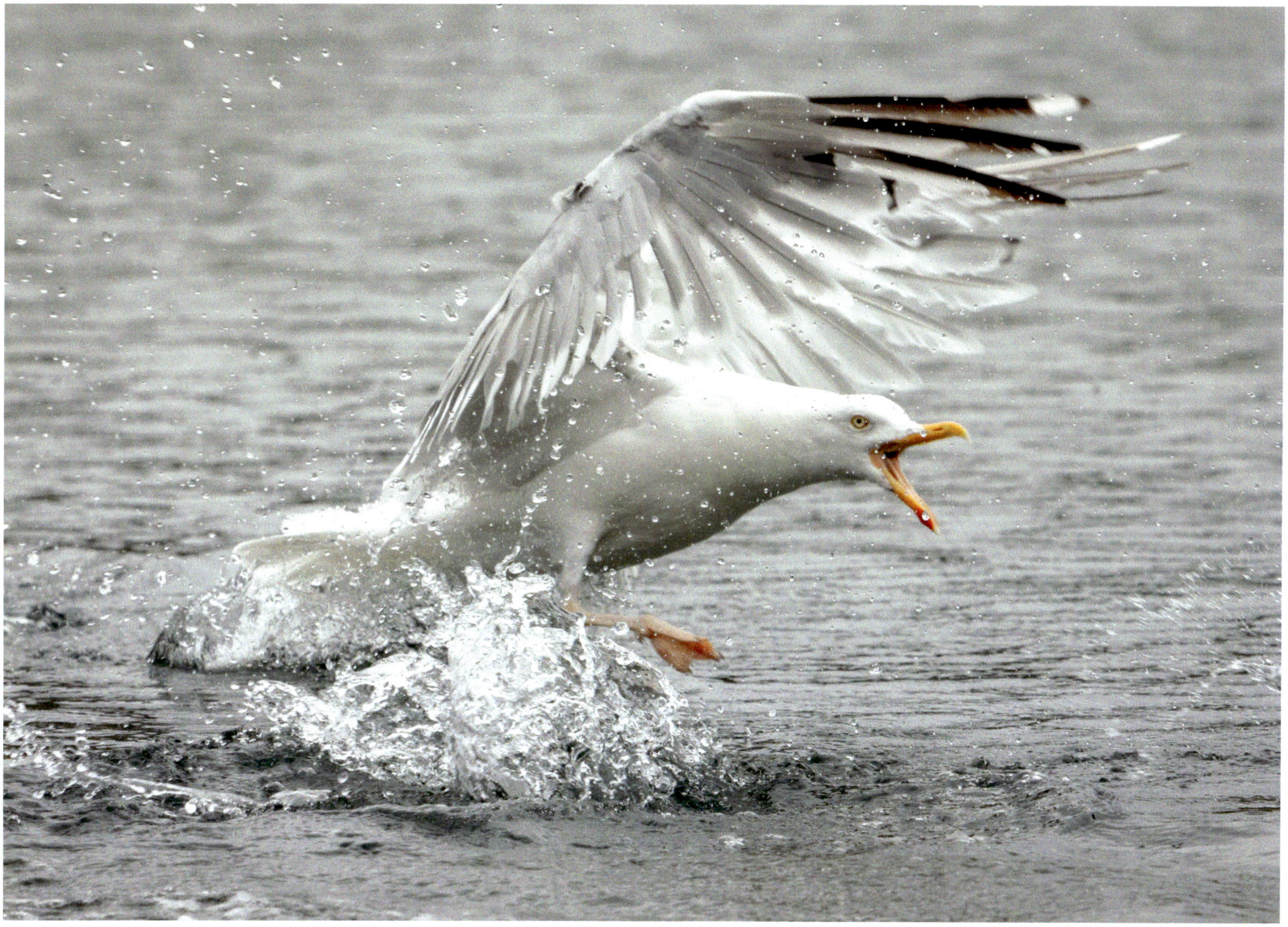

'On a storm-tossed sea...'

3. Kestrel

Sky-hooked
Clothes-hanger,
The windhover
Unslings,
Drops,
Death's arrow.

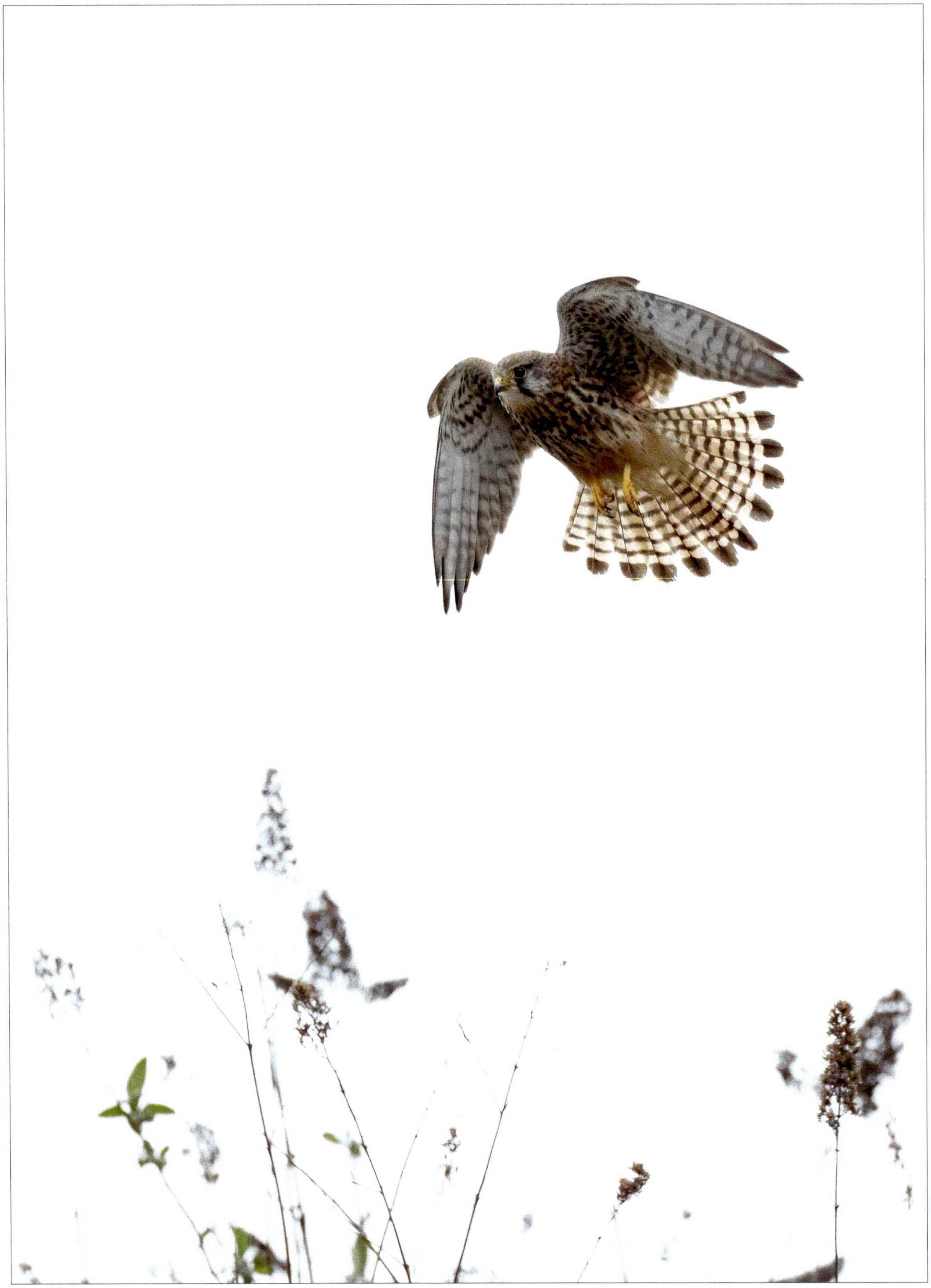

'Sky-hooked clothes-hanger…'

Several hunting techniques are used by kestrels, but the most well-known is the hover. A Kestrel will fly into the wind and use its fanned tail and wings to hold its position in the air. Keeping its eyes fixed on the ground, it will swiftly drop to pounce on any prey sighted. It manages to keep its head stationary despite its rapid wing beats. With extremely sharp eyesight, kestrels can spot a beetle from 50 metres. Characteristic of all falcons and most hawks are the powerful talons that are out of all proportion to the size and weight of the bird.

4. Sparrow

Barn-busker,
Up at dawnlight
Jangling his tune,
No care for tomorrow,
Tattered his brown coat.

The House Sparrow is one of Ireland's most recognisable birds but has suffered a huge population decline across Europe. It is active and noisy around farms and urban areas. Feeding our garden birds is an important contribution to preventing further decline. Seeds are the most appropriate feed for sparrows, as they feed on grain.

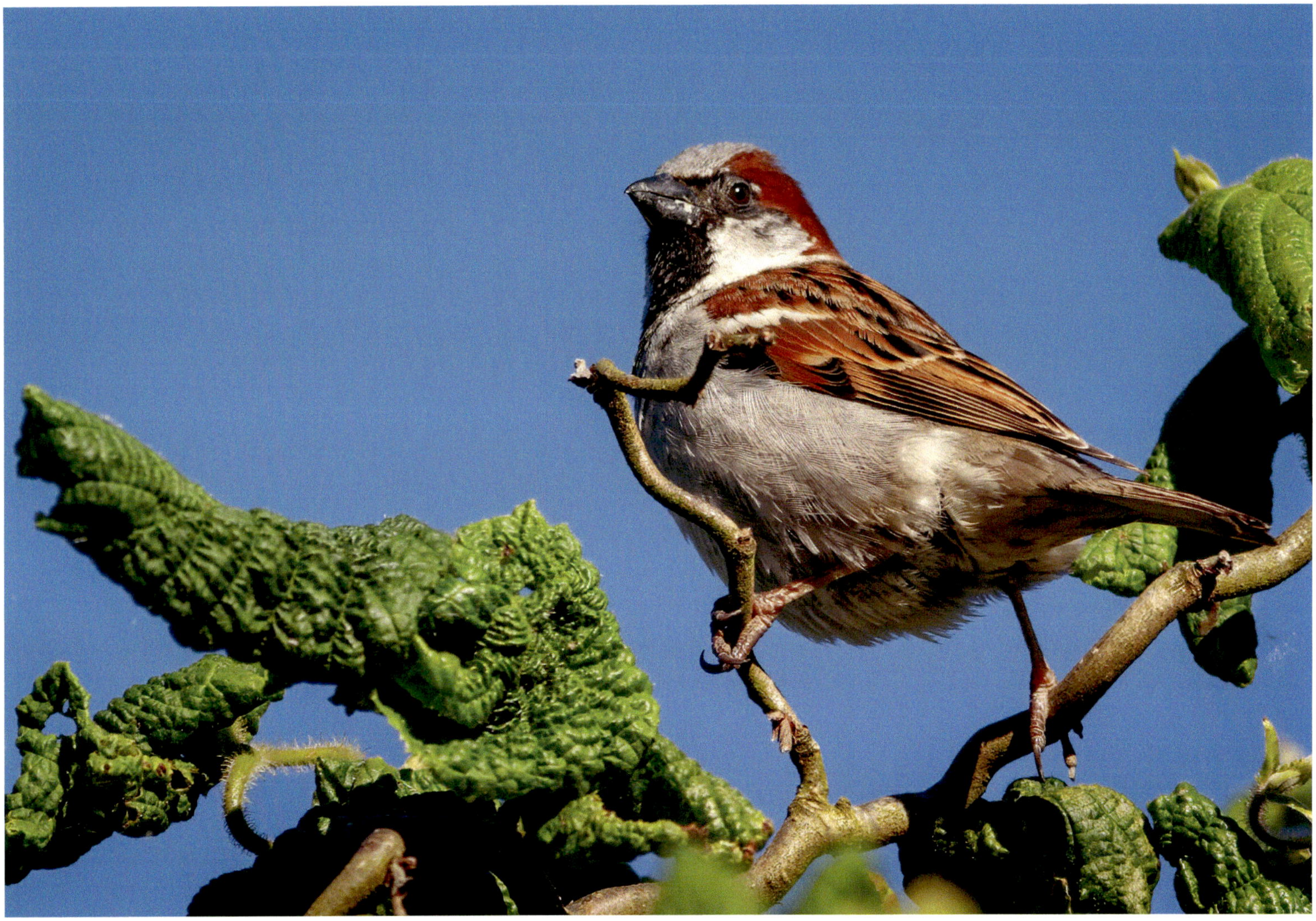

'Up at dawnlight jangling his tune…'

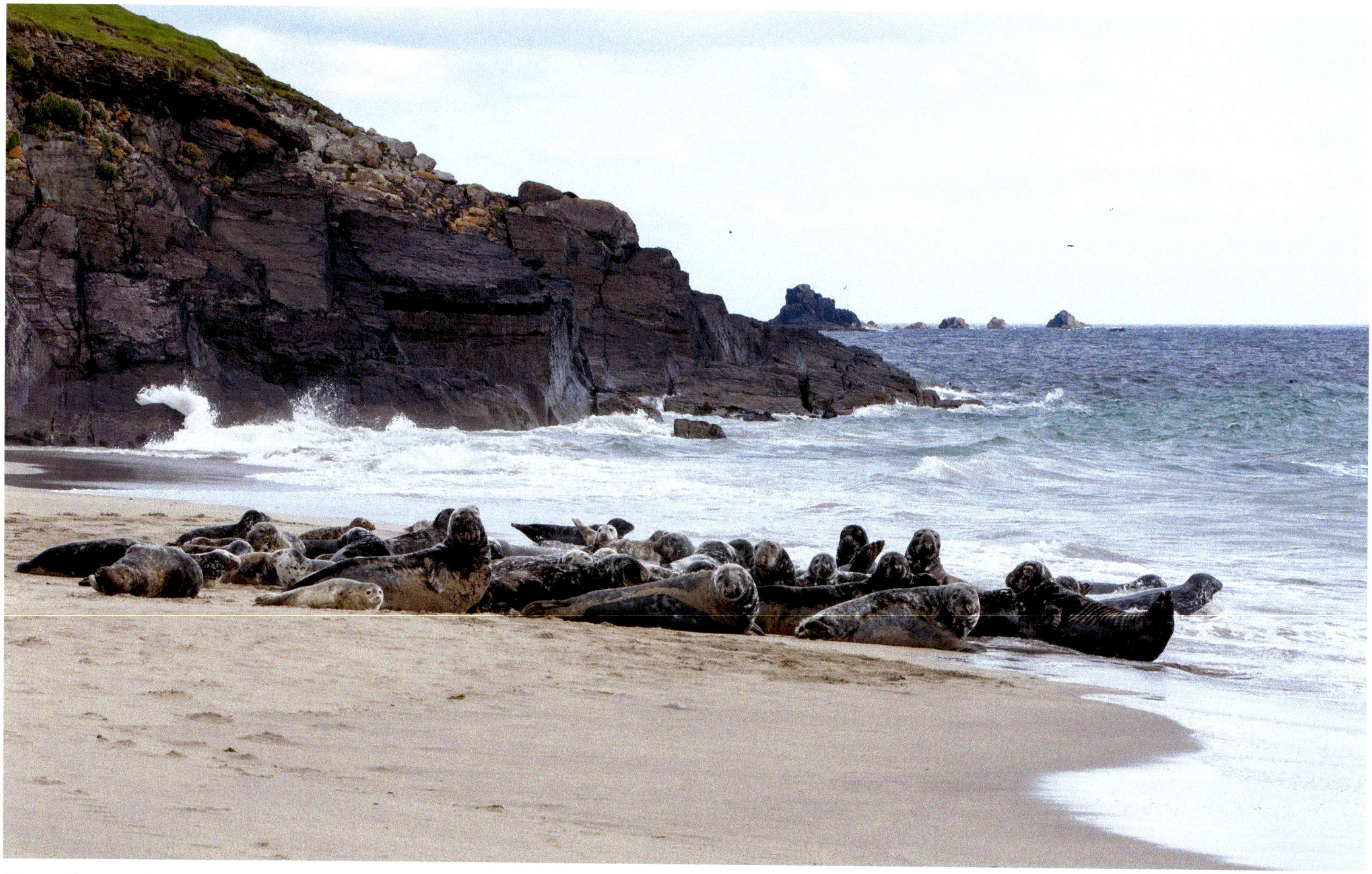

'Otter-dogs and grey north-seal, rest awhile on shingled strand...'

MIGRANTS

Migrants flying round the tower
Of the lighthouse, in the night;
Blinded by its rays they cower
Or keep darting left and right;
Wheatears strike the lantern-glass
Breaking beaks, disjointing wings;
Crumpled up fall to the grass,
Pained, bewildered bleeding things.

Migrants on the lantern-pane
Swarm and glide, and dance,
Diamond-moths from sunny Spain
With butterflies from France;
Bees strayed off the honeyed route,
Dazed by man-made beacon's glare,
And beetles buzzing round about
In hundreds fill the air.

Migrants living in the tide
Sparkling sheets of phosphor showing,
Fishes breaking far and wide,
Salmon to the rivers going;
Sand-eels burrowing in the sand,
Elvers, wriggling threads of flame,
Nature's urge their guiding hand,
From Bermudian seas they came.

Migrants making for the land,
Otter-dogs and grey north-seal,
Rest awhile on shingled strand,
Straying starlight beams reveal:
But when night-time turns to day
Migrants scatter far and wide,
Disappear like wind-blown spray,
All but those that die.

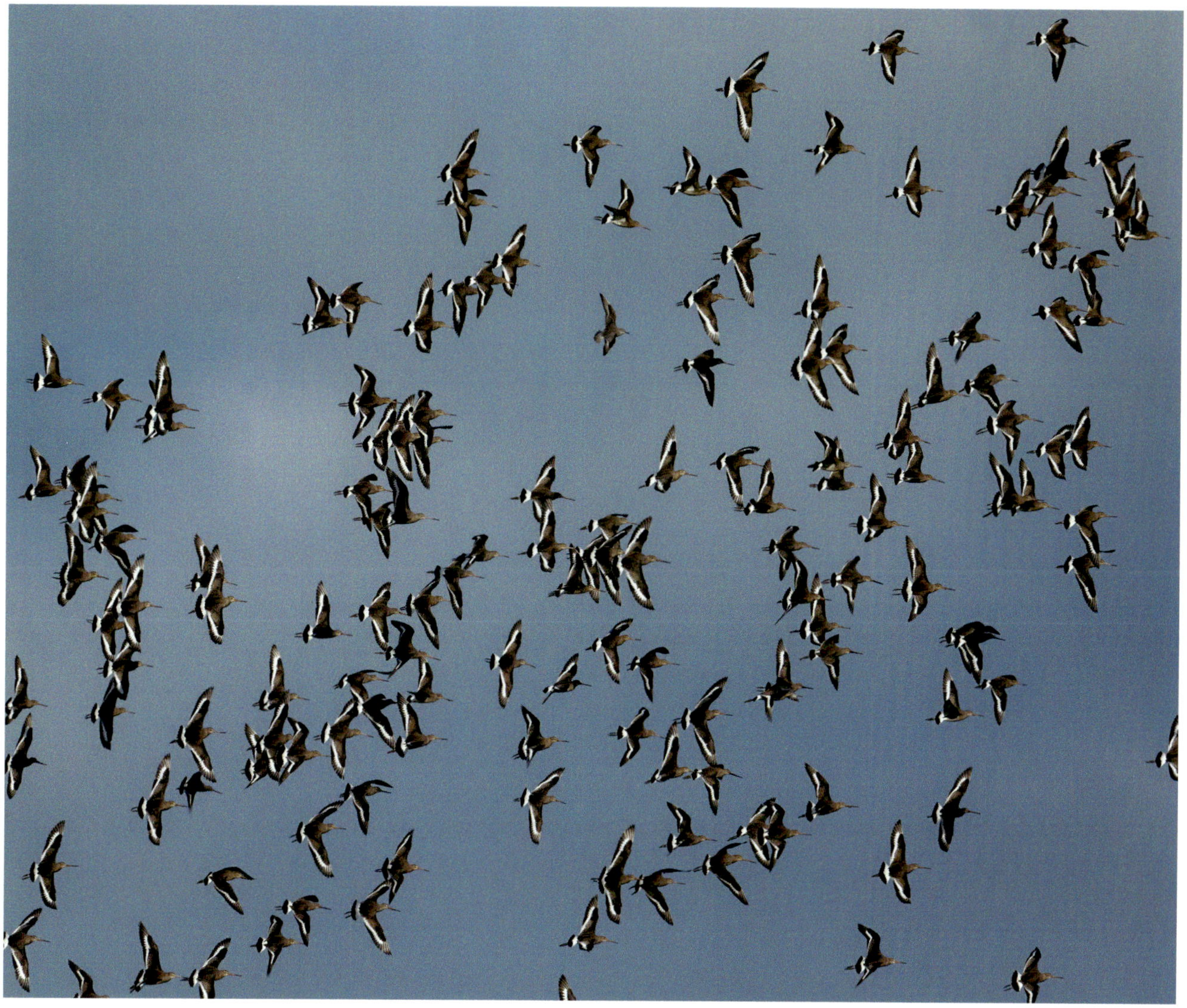

'Migrants making for the land…'

Ireland is important as a winter refuge for many of Europe's wildfowl and waders, most notably because of our mild and typically damp winters and wetland habitats.
The Black-tailed Godwit (left and below) is a large, long-legged, handsome wading bird. Every year these migrants travel from Iceland to wintering areas in Ireland. They are unmistakeable in flight and can occur in large flocks of several hundred birds. Their winter plumage is a greyish brown, but summer plumaged or moulting birds often occur, showing varying amounts of rich orange.

If undisturbed, Grey Seals (facing page) come ashore on Great Blasket Island to rest and nurse their young. The young are born in the autumn on the land, where they stay until they have trebled their body weight and lost their white coats. My quiet, slow approach did not disturb the seals, and they seemed to accept my presence, giving me time to observe them.

The Grey Seal pup is not nearly as independent as a newborn Common Seal, which sheds its furry coat immediately after birth in July and can swim just a few hours later. The Grey Seal pup, after clinging to land for a few perilous weeks, is forced by hunger to enter the water and learn to swim and fish.

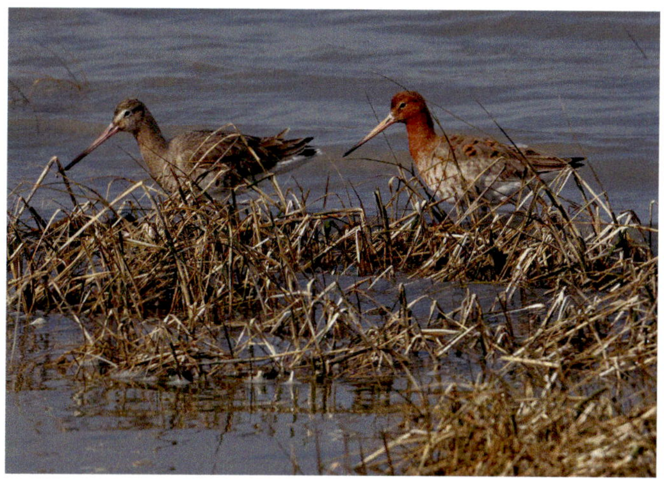

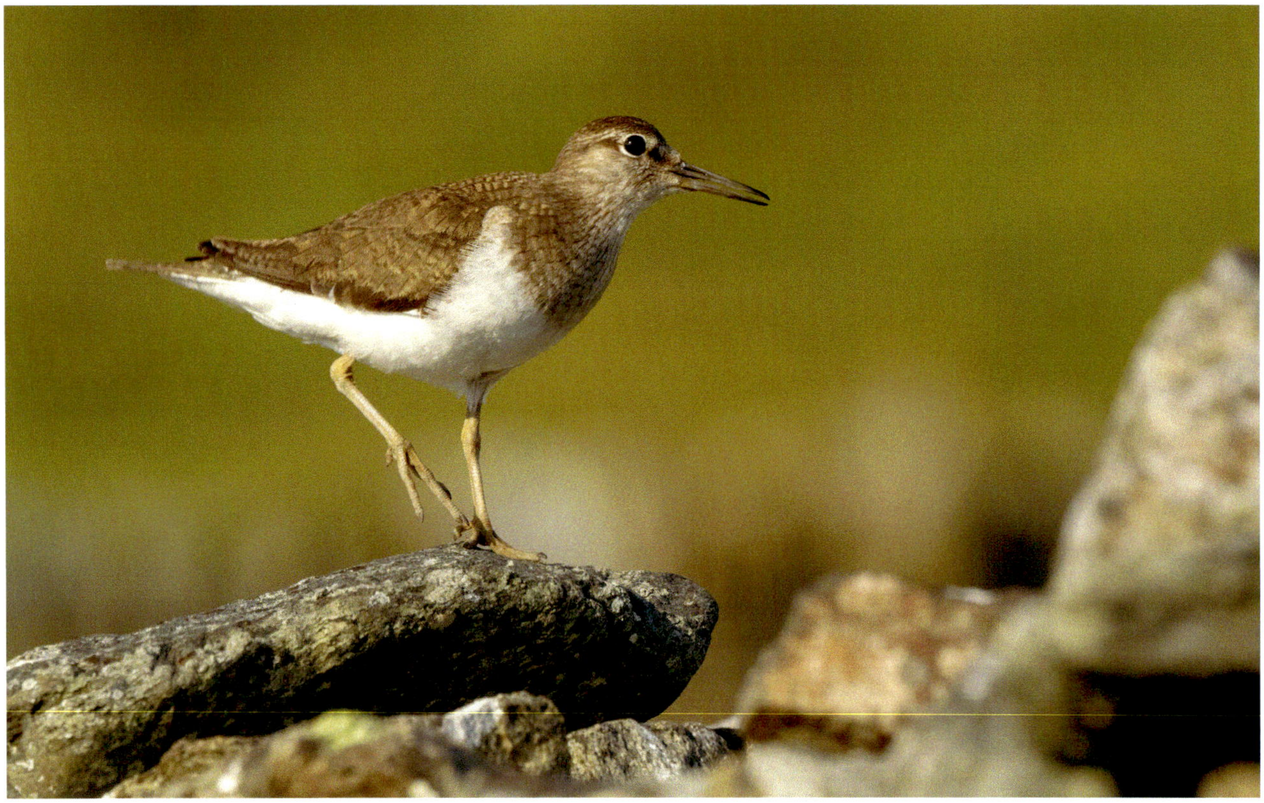

'Migrants scatter far and wide...'

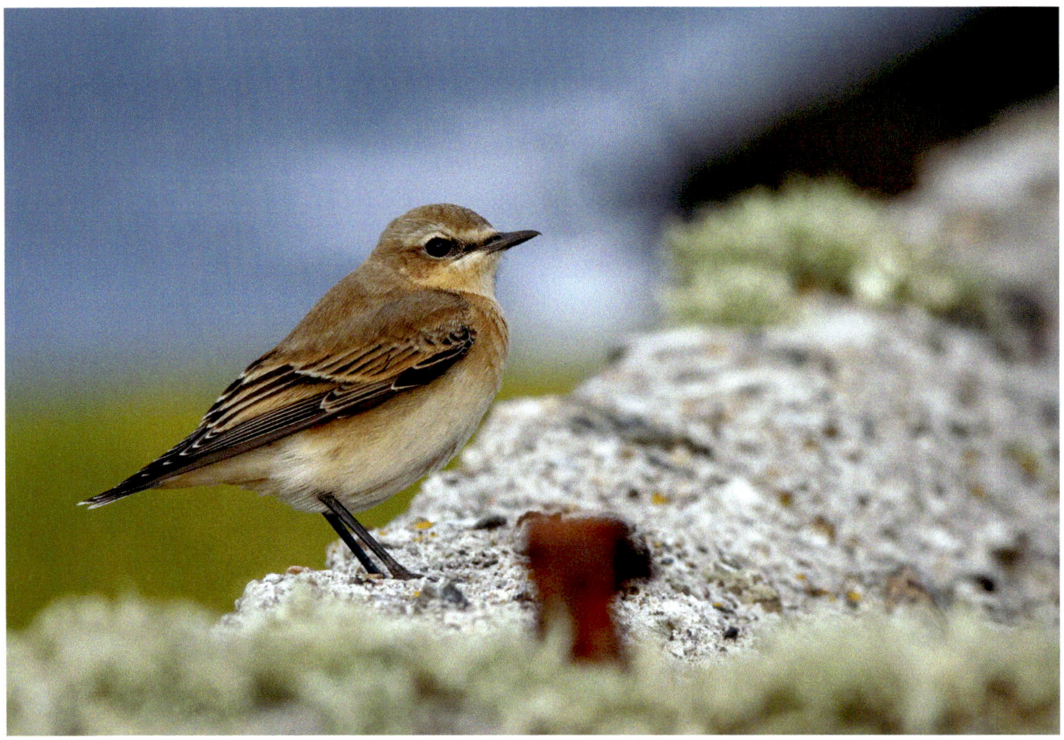

'Wheatears strike the lantern-glass...'

The Common Sandpiper is our only wader that is purely a summer migrant. It nests close to water by inland lakes, streams and sea coast. It flies low over water with rapid beats of down-curved wings alternating with short glides and uttering its high pitched trisyllabic call.

The Wheatear is a widespread summer visitor to the islands, uplands and scrubland throughout Ireland. It winters in southern Africa and has one of the longest migration routes of any songbird. The cock birds are normally the first to arrive to stake out a breeding territory, followed by the females about a fortnight later.

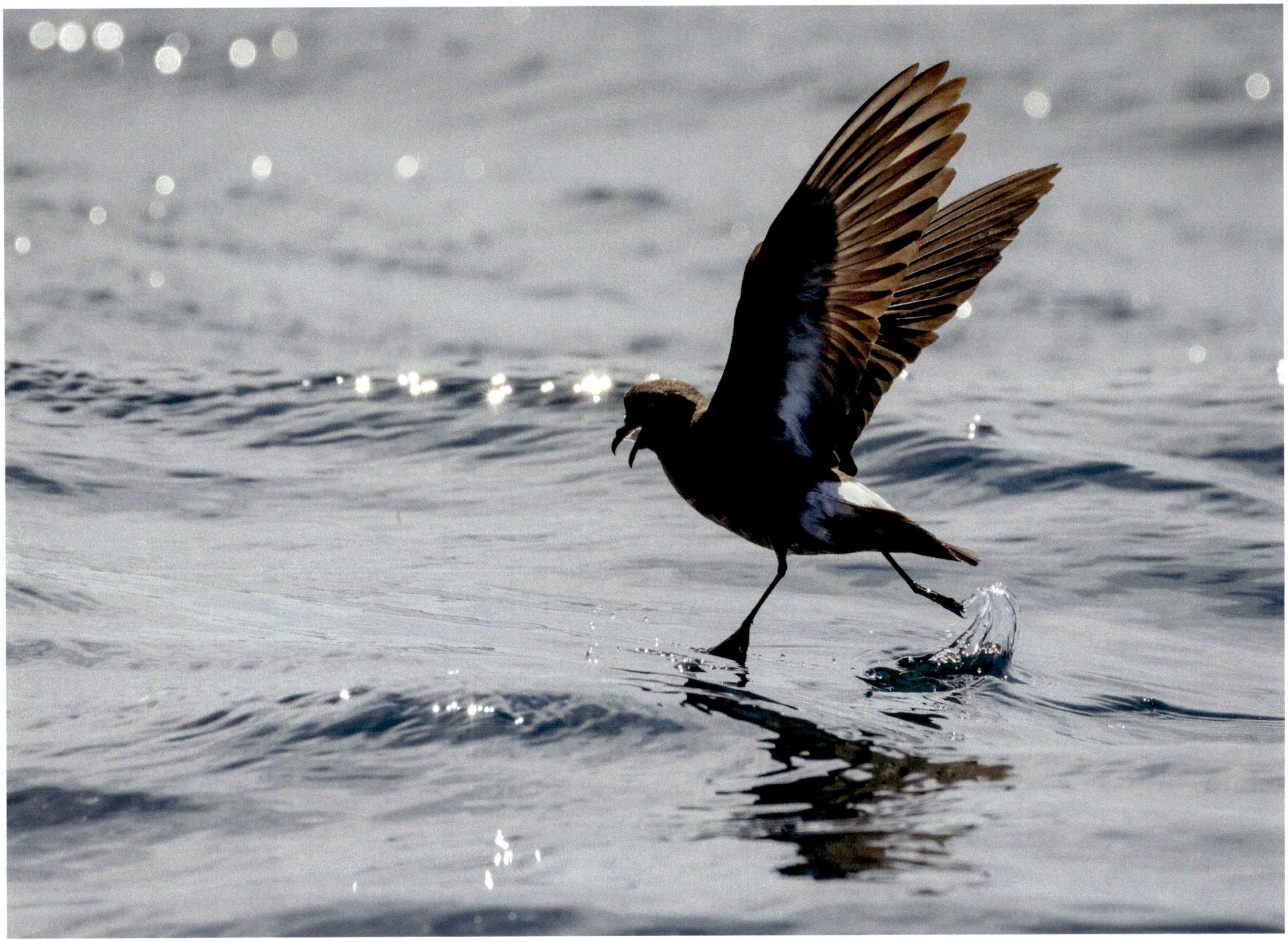

'Migrants living in the tide…'

The European Storm Petrel winters off the coasts of South Africa and its return passage starts in April. Migration is particularly difficult for the storm petrel, as it is one of the smallest sea bird species in the world, weighing an ounce. It flutters over the water, feeding with its wings held up in a 'V' with feet pattering across the waves. They mainly fly at night and rest on the water surface during daylight hours, only setting foot on land to breed.

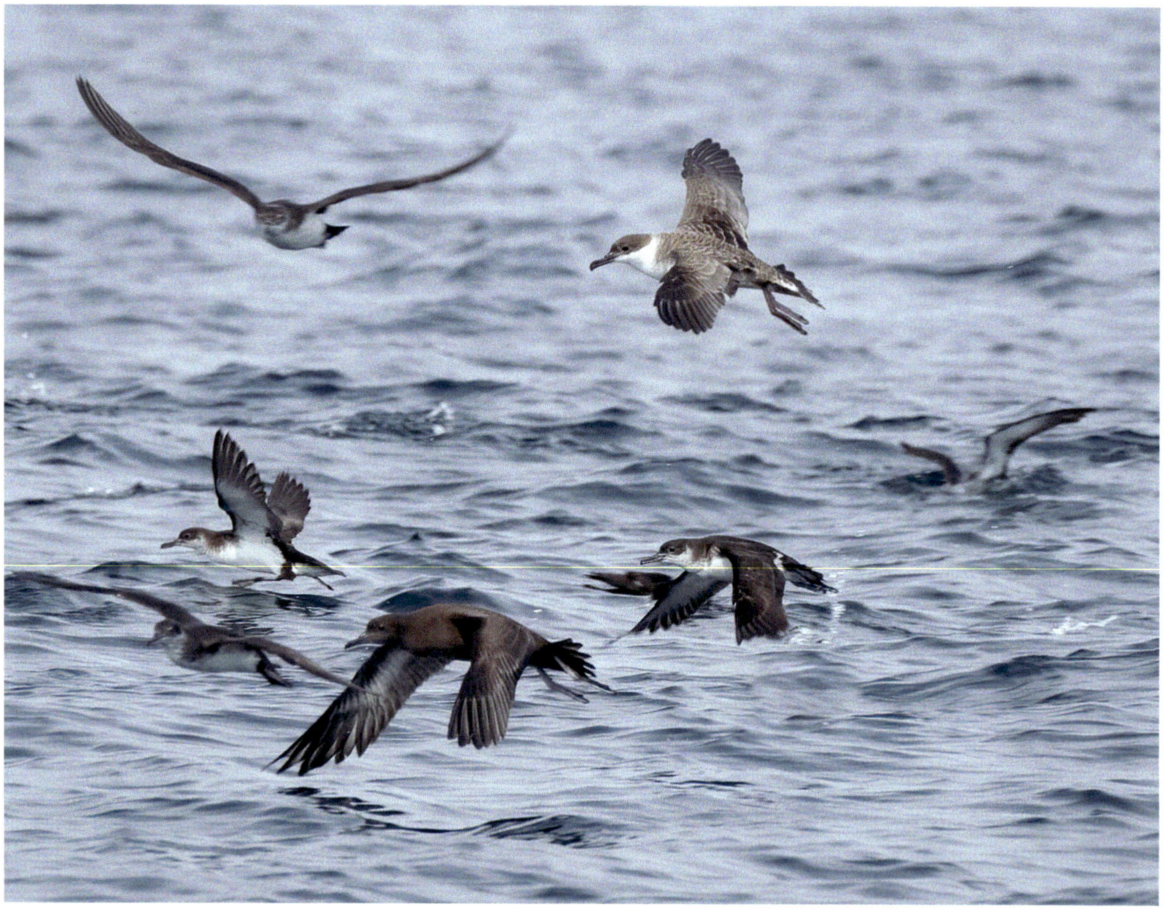

'Migrants making for the land...'

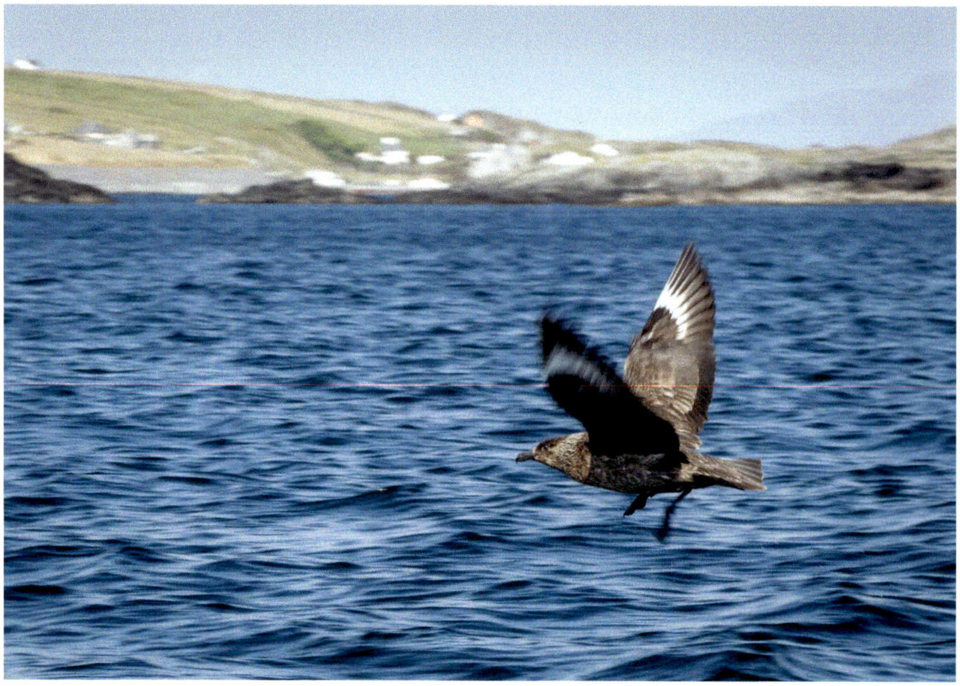

The image above has captured three species of shearwater—namely, the Sooty Shearwater, the Manx Shearwater and the Great Shearwater. Many shearwaters are long-distance migrants travelling between northern breeding grounds and the southern ocean, coming to islands and coastal cliffs only to breed. Sooty Shearwaters in particular undertake a remarkable annual migration of a 40,000-mile round trip, claiming the longest migration of any animal ever recorded

The Great Skua (left) is a passage migrant off all Irish coasts from April to October, arriving from South Africa. This large, powerful bird breeds on isolated islands off the west coast. They are renowned for their piratical behaviour, harrying other birds with their skilful flying until they finally disgorge their catch.

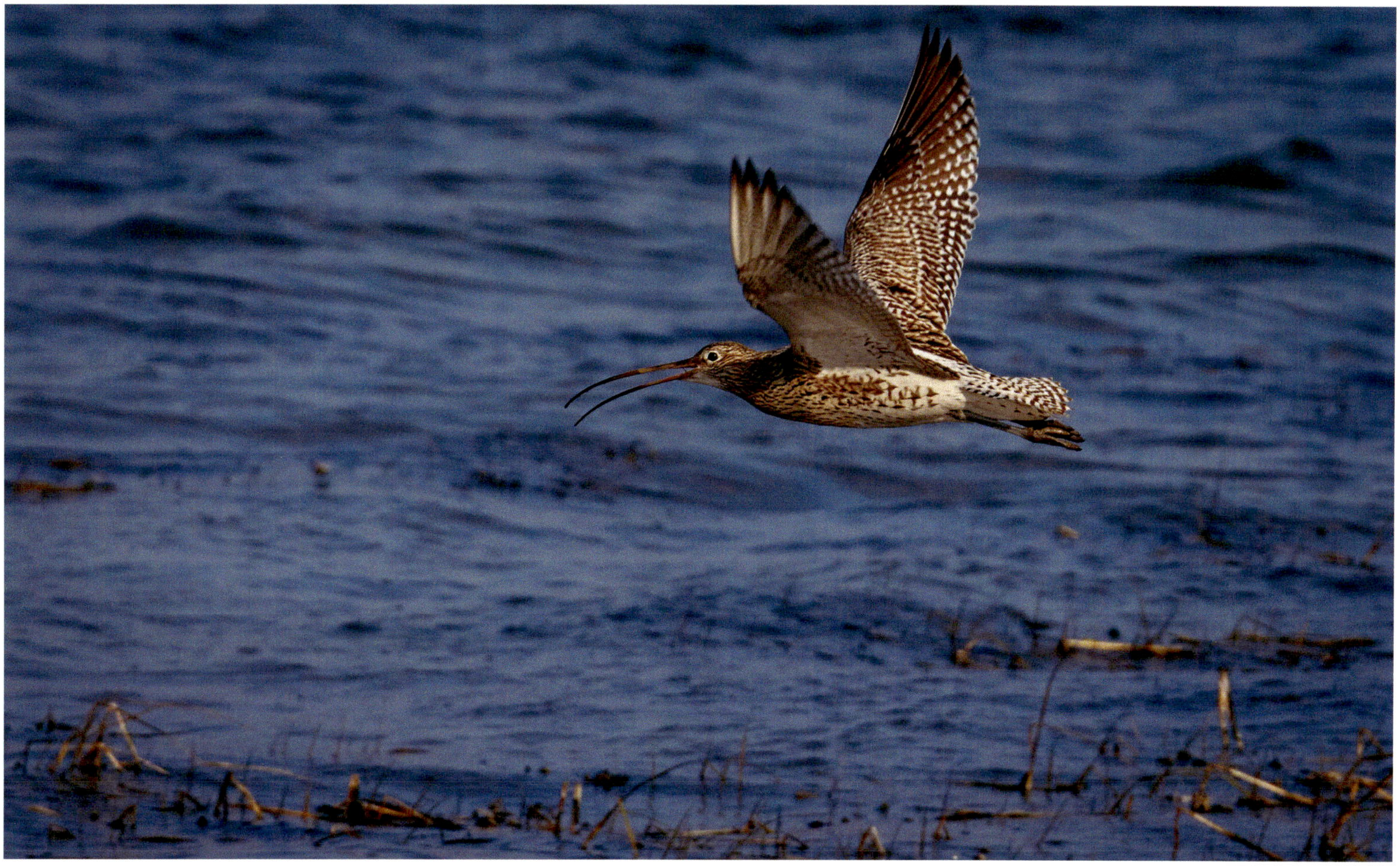

'And by the shore, lone curlew's cry onomatopoeically cleaves the sky.'

VESPERS

The sun sinks west, and twilights falls,
As jumping-spiders climb high walls;
Leap into space, and land below
On insects passing to and fro;
End pulsing life with poison-bite—
Blood-meal potations throughout the night
While harbour-buoy sends beams afar
Flash-warning ships of dangerous bar;
And by the shore, lone curlew's cry
Onomatopoeically cleaves the sky.
The city motorist is gone,
His visit to the country done;
Perhaps he may return again
When honeysuckle scents the lane
With incense from its nectar store
Which hawk-moths search, probe throated
core,
Each slipping though proboscis long,
Enthralled by cricket's chirping-song.
June moon begins to show afar,
Swim cloudlets, race the Evening Star;
Near woodland grey-brown nightjar calls,
The sun sinks west, and twilight falls.

The Eurasian Curlew was once a widespread breeding bird of the Irish landscape. They have suffered a staggering 96% decline in recent decades. The curlew's evocative and haunting cry is one of the most beautiful sounds of the countryside.
It is likely that increased afforestation and agricultural improvement are responsible for the decline of this bird. Without action, it is in danger of becoming extinct.

ROCK PIPITS

Daybreak!
Then comes a beam of filtered light
From out of the Heavens above—
Effulgent,
Golden,
The rock pipit's delight
As he soars in the balmy air…
And there:
His slumbering spouse awakens;
With loving chorus takes to flight
In marital understanding.
Two warbling specks
High in the blue,
Adoring,
Outpouring,
As if their tiny hearts would break.
Sunrise,
Each ray a burnished stalactite;
Singing,
Winging,
The rock pipits alight.

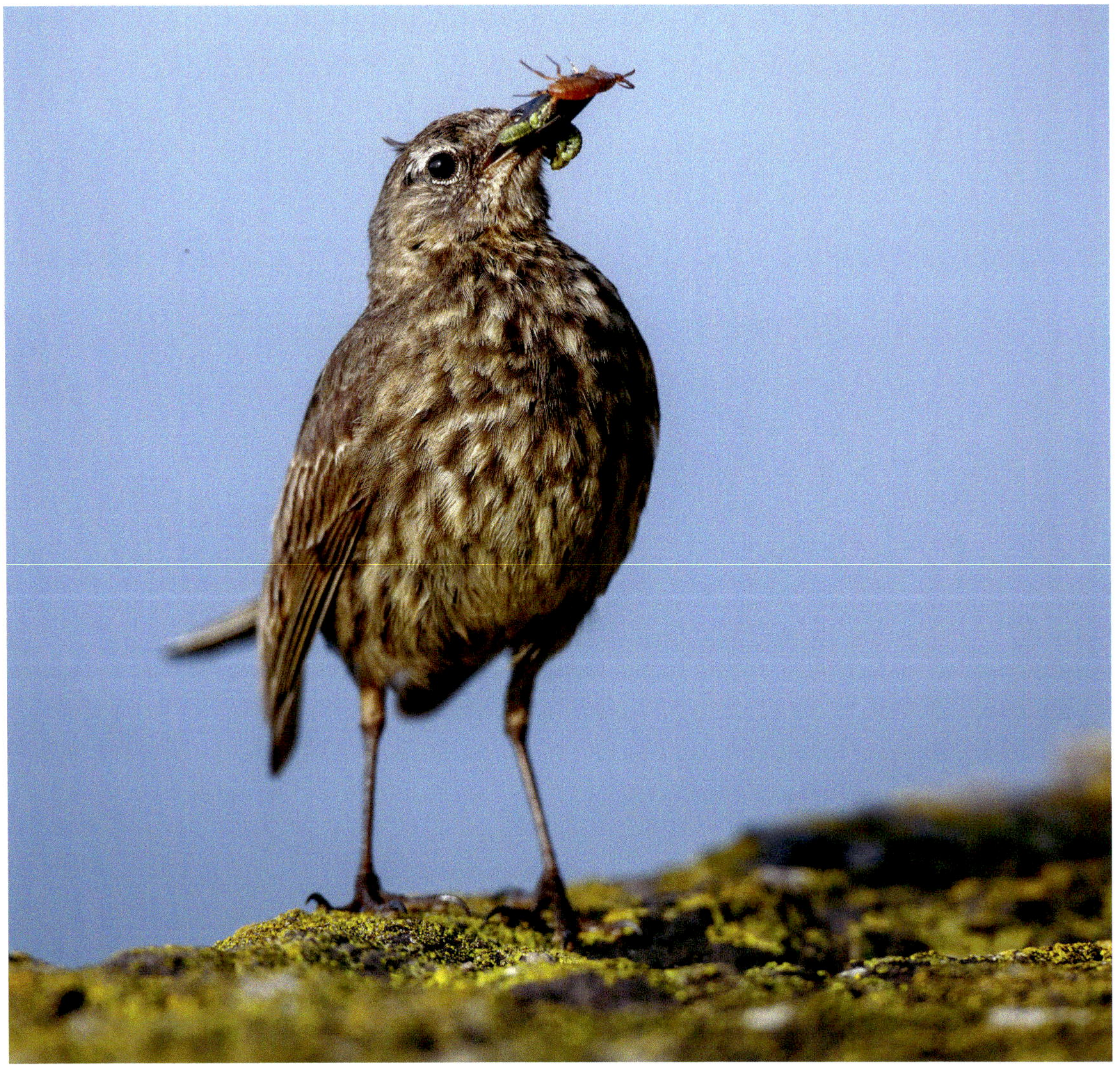

'Each ray a burnished stalactite; singing, winging, the rock pipits alight.'

The Rock Pipit is rarely seen away from the coast. It appears really stock-bodied in flight but breeding males have a song flight which is powerful and agile. The male rises into the air (15-30 metres) while singing, and then descends in fluttering parachute-flight action with semi-open wings and dangling legs for soft landing. This flight is accompanied by loud, harsh notes ending in twittering trills.

FREEHOLD

Rose-scented June:
In creviced garden wall
Two busy blue tits work
Constructing mossy nest
To brood eggs, cradle offspring.
No application there
For tenure rights.
The job completed...
All ground-rent paid
In blossoms purged of insect pests.

These colourful, noisy, active little Blue Tits are nesting in a crevice in the walls of a very old bridge. Both birds are busy feeding the chicks. It is not unusual for a single bird to feed the chicks in the nest at a rate of one feed every 90 seconds during the height of the breeding season. As the young birds grow, the number of feeds per day also increases .

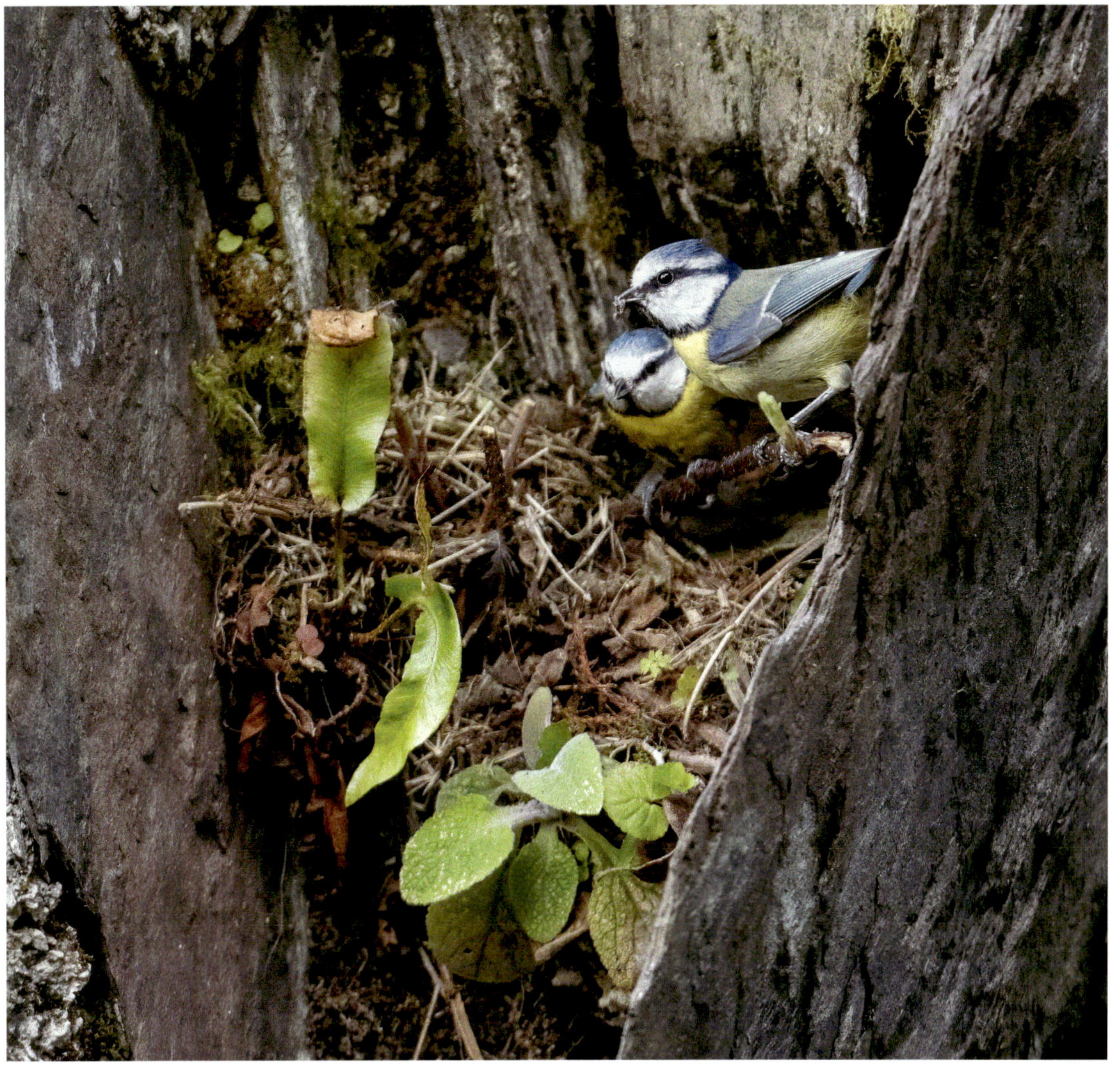

'Two busy blue tits work constructing mossy nest to brood eggs, cradle offspring.'

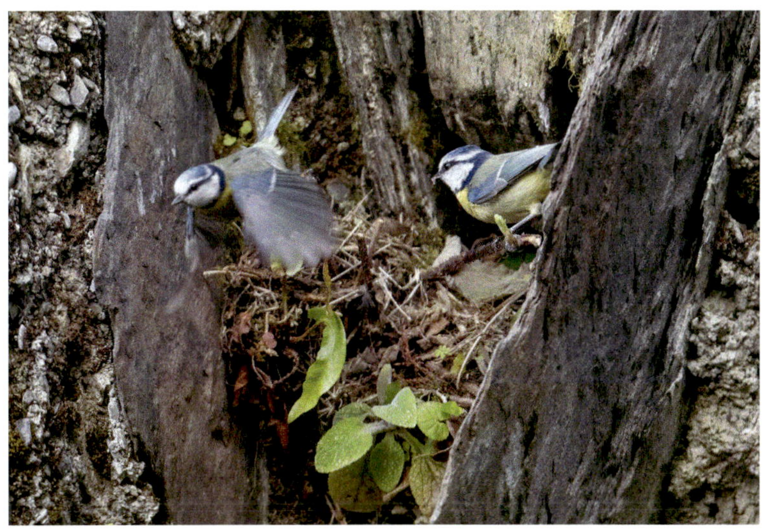

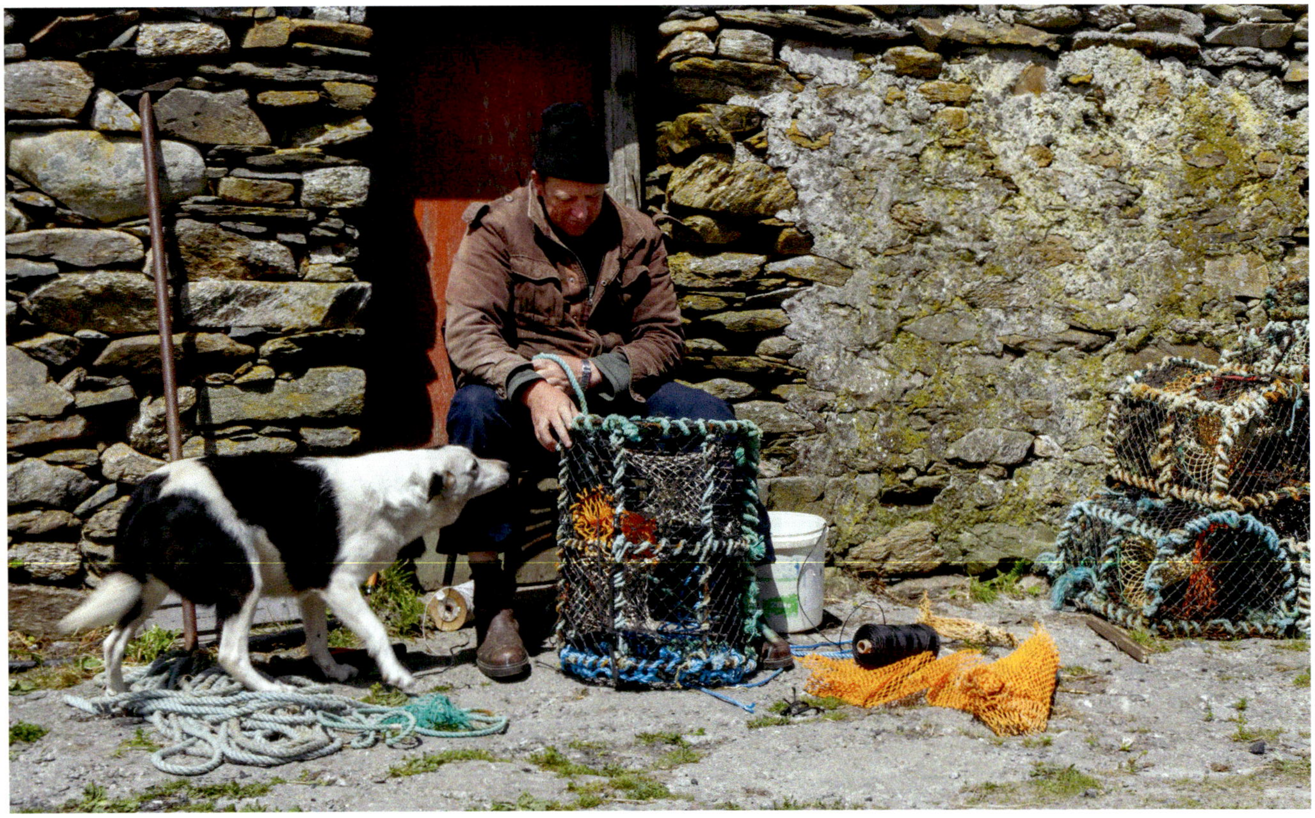

'The fisherman of yesterday…' taken on Inishbofin, Co. Galway.

TIDEWAY

This fisherman of yesterday
Sailed windswept-ruffled waters;
In calm conditions rowed, the task
Hardening his saline-soaked fingers
That gripped tight as grey seal's claws
And moved supple as squirming eel.

Everyone welcomed the fisherman
Gathered around him on the pier-head
To view the catch he brought ashore.
Fresh fish sold "by the foot",
Laid out placed head to tail;
Measured by stepping the line,
Toe to heel and heel to toe;
Coins clinked as bargains made.

The old folk remember the fisherman…
His clay pipe reeking smudge-rings;
Chewing duilseag; rope splicing;
Patched knees of homespun trousers
Bulging over high seaboots;
Fish-scale besprinkled jersey.

An errant hamlet daughter conceived child;
Mothers and sons become disturbed
And fathers felt uneasy—
Wild rumours named the fisherman,
A false premise, as innocent
He fashioned buoys from cured goat-skins;
Re-meshed holes in barked purse-nets;
And baited long-line fishing hooks.

In time passed on. Our world changed
But the tide still comes in and goes out.

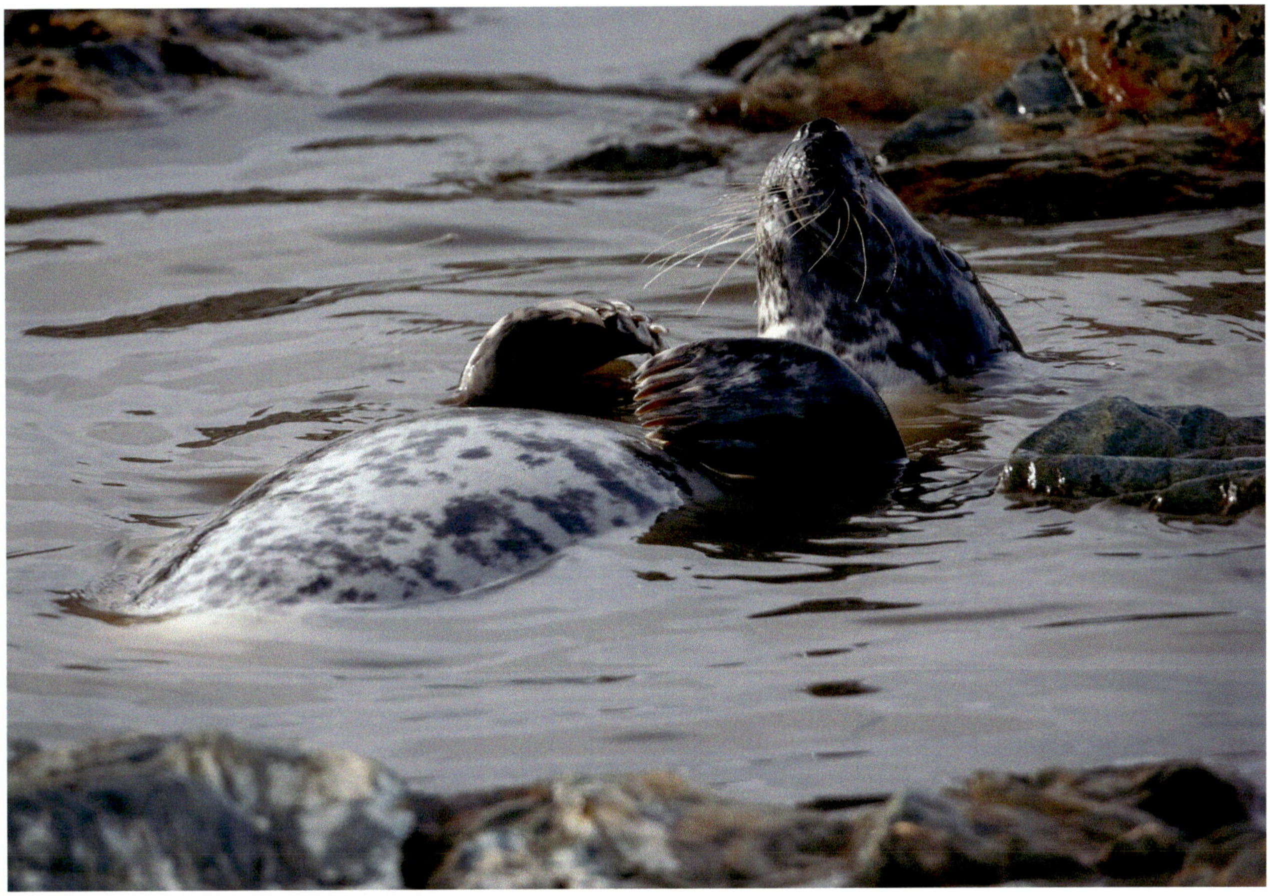

'Hardening his saline-soaked fingers That gripped tight as grey seal's claws...'

Fishing (previous page) in the past was done by line as well as net. In deep water, fishermen would use a spillet line, a weighted line with many hooks strung across the sea bottom and left overnight. A netting technique for herring and mackerel was seine netting, where two boats formed a purse of the net around the fish. Fishermen used pots to trap lobster and crab much as they do today.

Grey Seals (above) have relatively short front flippers with five large protruding claws used for gripping. After securing a large fish in their jaws, they swim up to the surface, tightly gripping the fish with curled flippers and sinking their claws into its flesh. Finally, they pull down their arms to stretch their prey, gradually tearing it between the teeth and claws.

In the past much fishing was done from tarred and canvas curraghs which were a distinctive feature of parts of the west coast. Rowing a curragh strengthens the muscles in the arms, shoulders, and hands, including the grip.

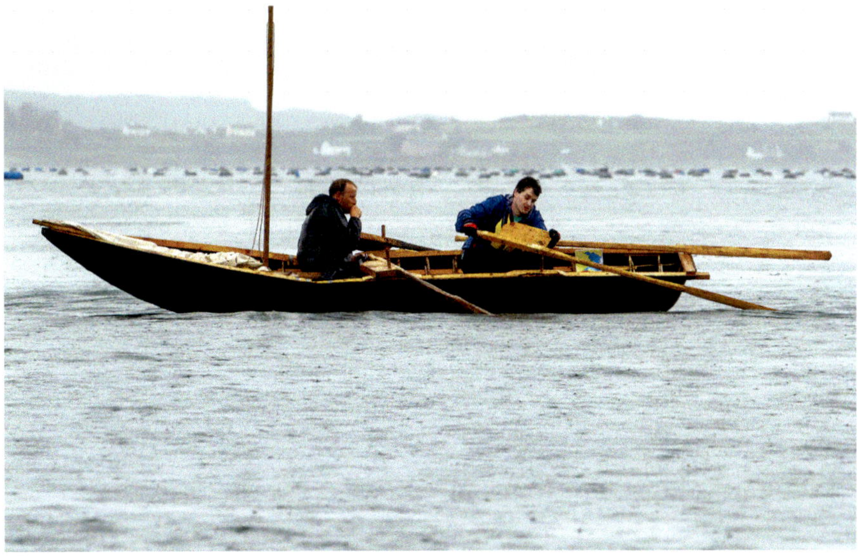

'In calm conditions rowed...'

HELLO SAILOR

Carder-bee voyager, in earth's vast solar sea
You tack port and starboard 'twixt catkin and flower;
Each willow, whin, woundwort, a new port of call,
Collecting mixed cargo of nectar and pollen.

Steering past sand-dunes, coasting 'round rocks,
Lost in hill-haze, your radar instinctive;
Navigating the hazards of wind-tickled waters
Of bog-pool, canal and light-dappled river.

Plotting safe passages despite deviations;
Sextant's arc-image found in the sun's rays;
Orientation of bearings, a true compass-course
Set homeward to dock in the lark-hunted meadow.

Slow glide to full stop: Leg-anchors away
To kedge tin cup-lichens concealing domed nest;
Claw into snug cabin—craft-woven of mosses—
Ground drone of wing-engines subdued...and then
gone!

There are 100 bee species in Ireland. The Common Carder Bee , here visiting the Bird's Foot Trefoil and the Lupin flowers, is a fluffy, gingery bumble bee. It is one of a number of long-tongued bees that feed on flowers with long tubular florets. It is found in gardens, farmland, woodland, hedgerows and heaths: anywhere there are flowers to feed on. It is a social bee, nesting in cavities, old birds' nests and mossy lawns.

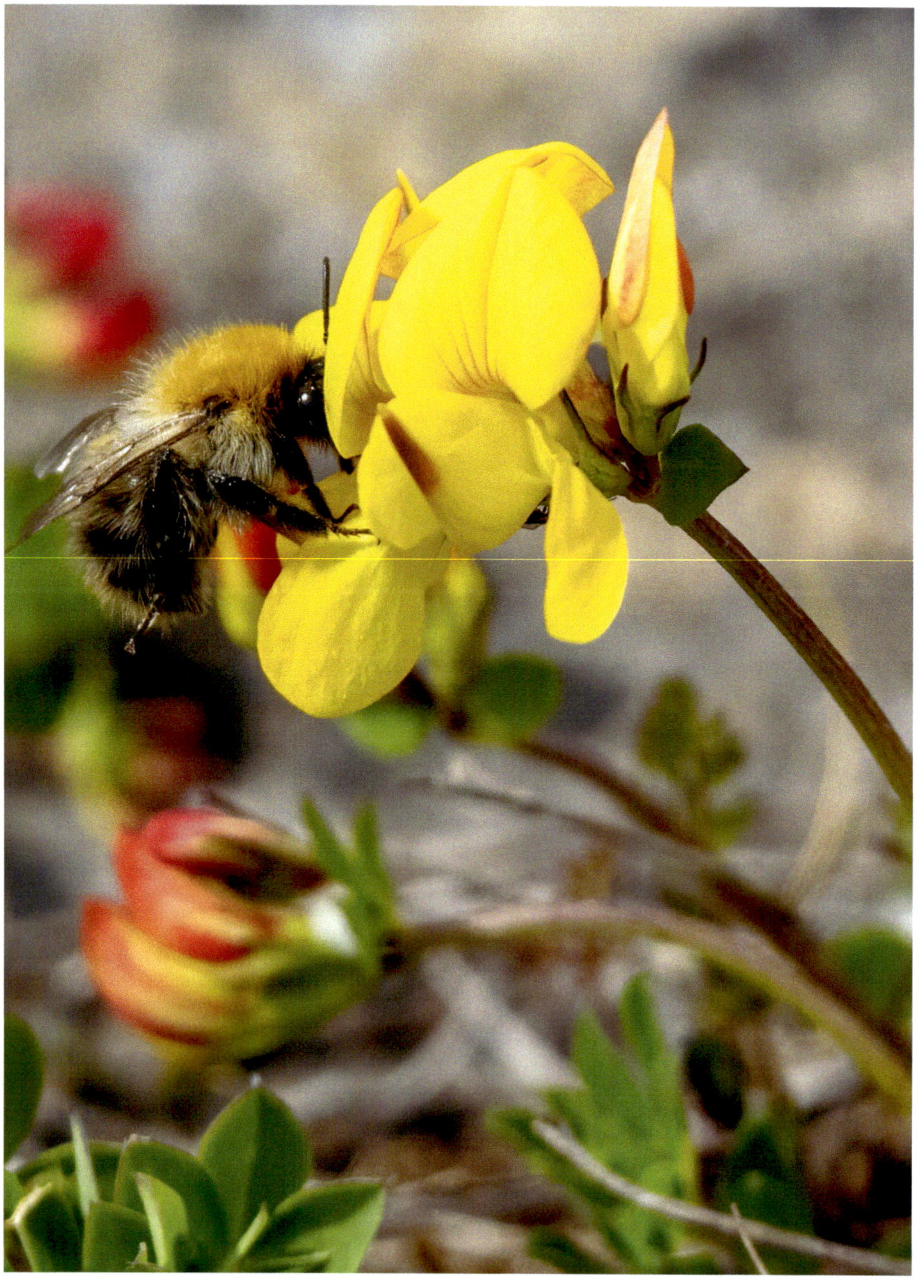

'Carder-bee voyager, in earth's vast solar sea...'

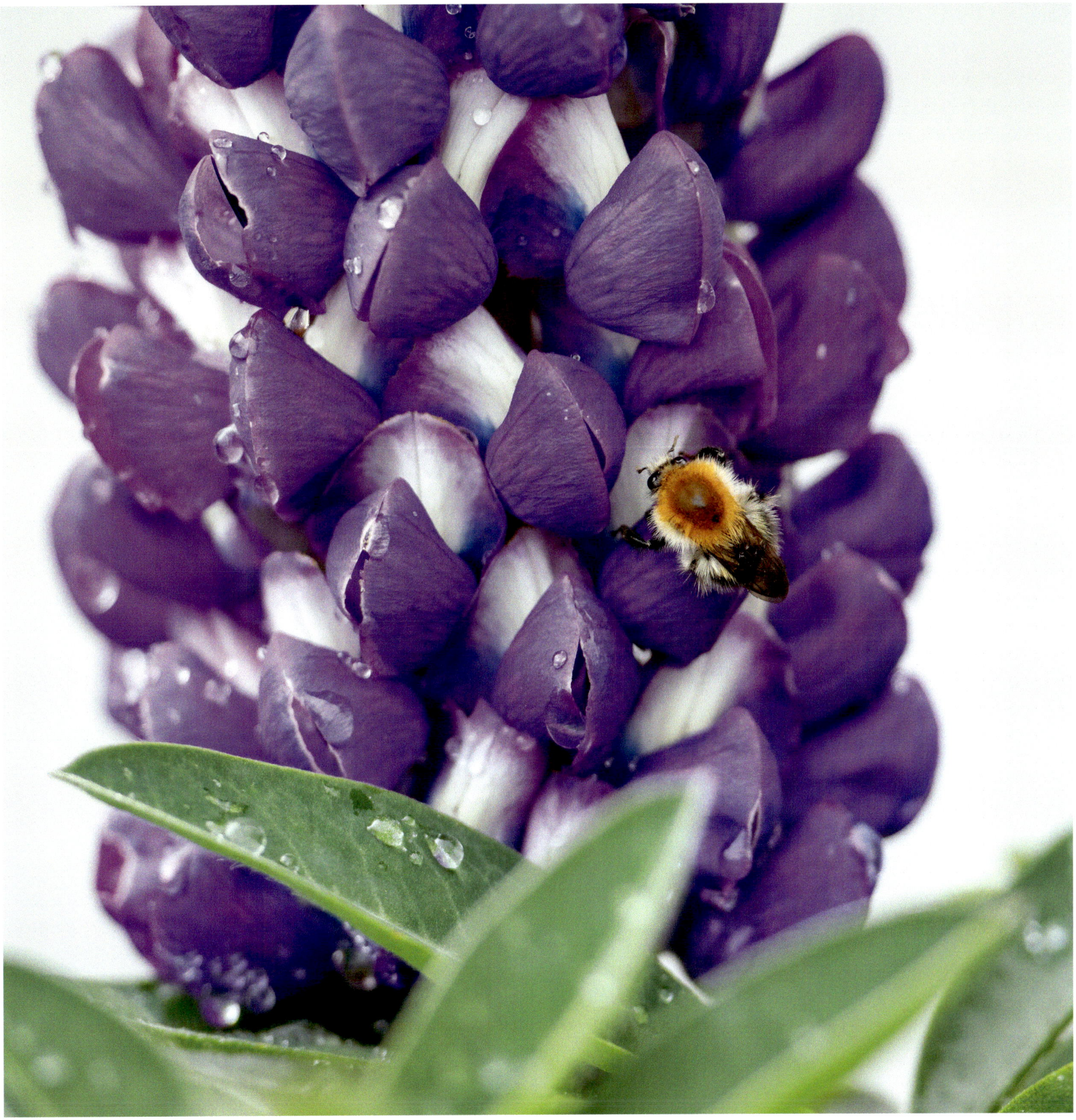

THE MONASTIC LIFE

White collar, front to back;
Cassock faded rust-black;
He walks the chapel nave
Bead-counting, Ave on Ave.

Tomorrow he'll say Mass,
The blessed Eucharist pass
To those free of grave sin,
Souls polished as new pin.

And from raised pulpit mouth
What Christian's life's about,
Hoping that some may hear
Christ's message, loud and clear.

In solitude at night
He dreams of saints in white
At prayer around his bed,
Haloed each tonsured head.

A simple man of God,
Only the graveyard sod
'Twixt him and heavenly bliss;
He asks no more than this.

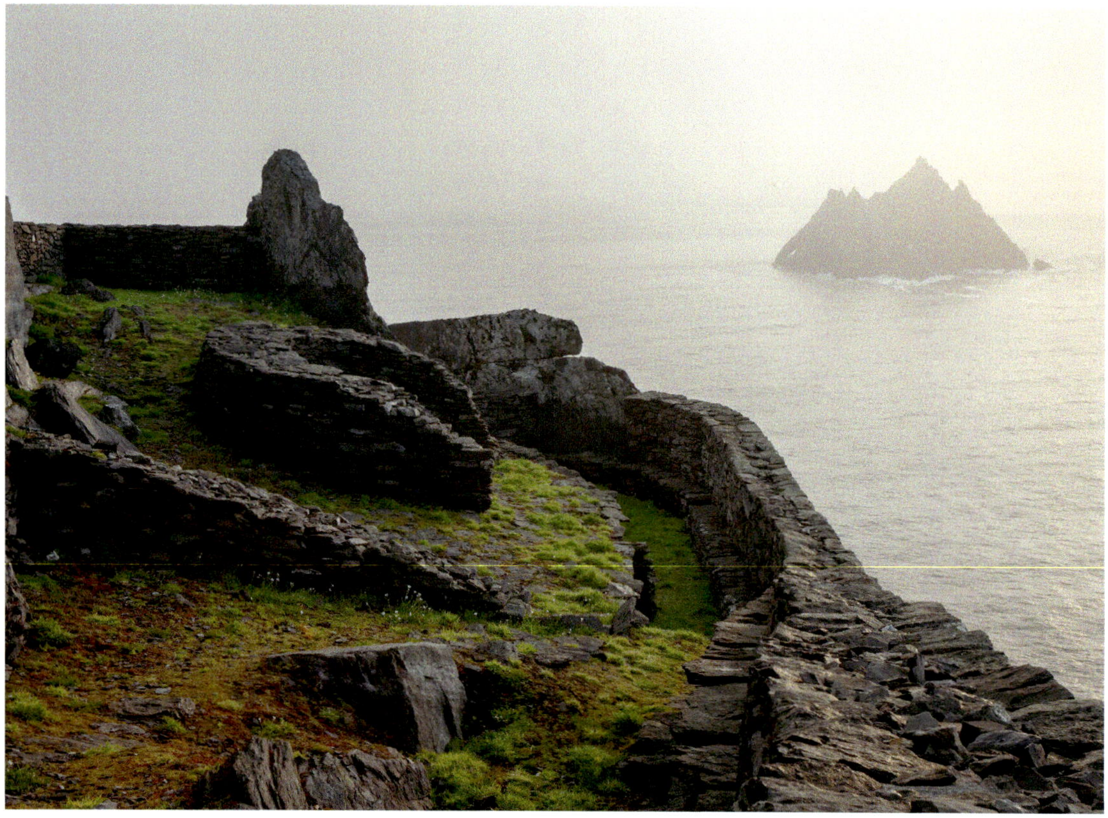

'In solitude at night he dreams of saints in white...'

Skellig Michael was a place of refuge for numerous Catholics during penal times when their rights and beliefs were being suppressed. It is an island shrouded in mystery and , having had the privilege of staying there overnight, I could only wonder and admire the past souls who survived on those remote and ancient rocks. Lighthouse keepers too must surely have had time to reflect when so close to this ancient site. This place is completely exposed to the elements and will always retain a sense of untouched wilderness. An eerie light and still mist added to the changing moods the weather casts on the Skelligs and one could be forgiven for imagining it to be an island between heaven and earth.

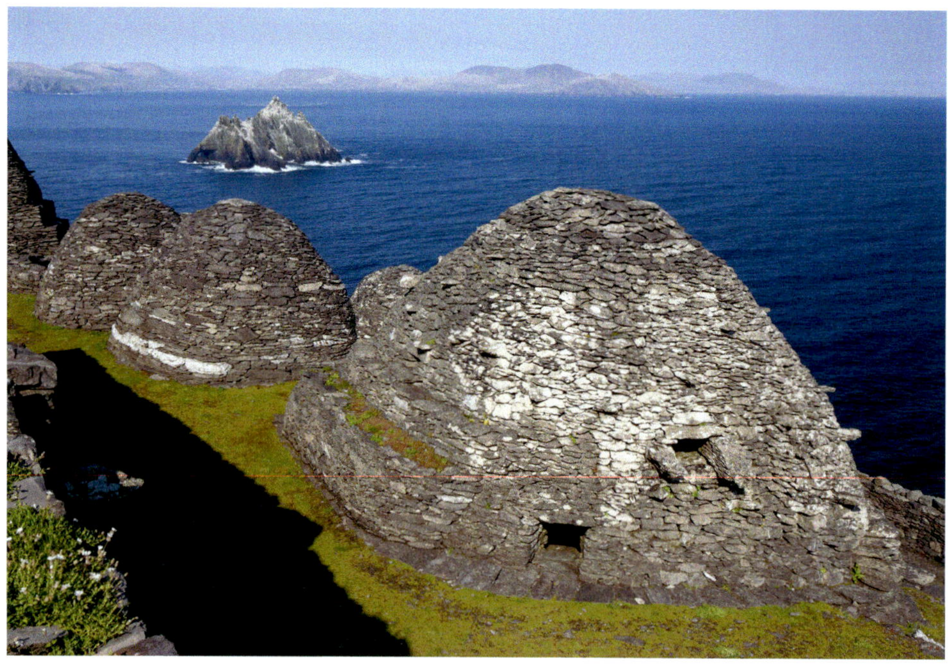

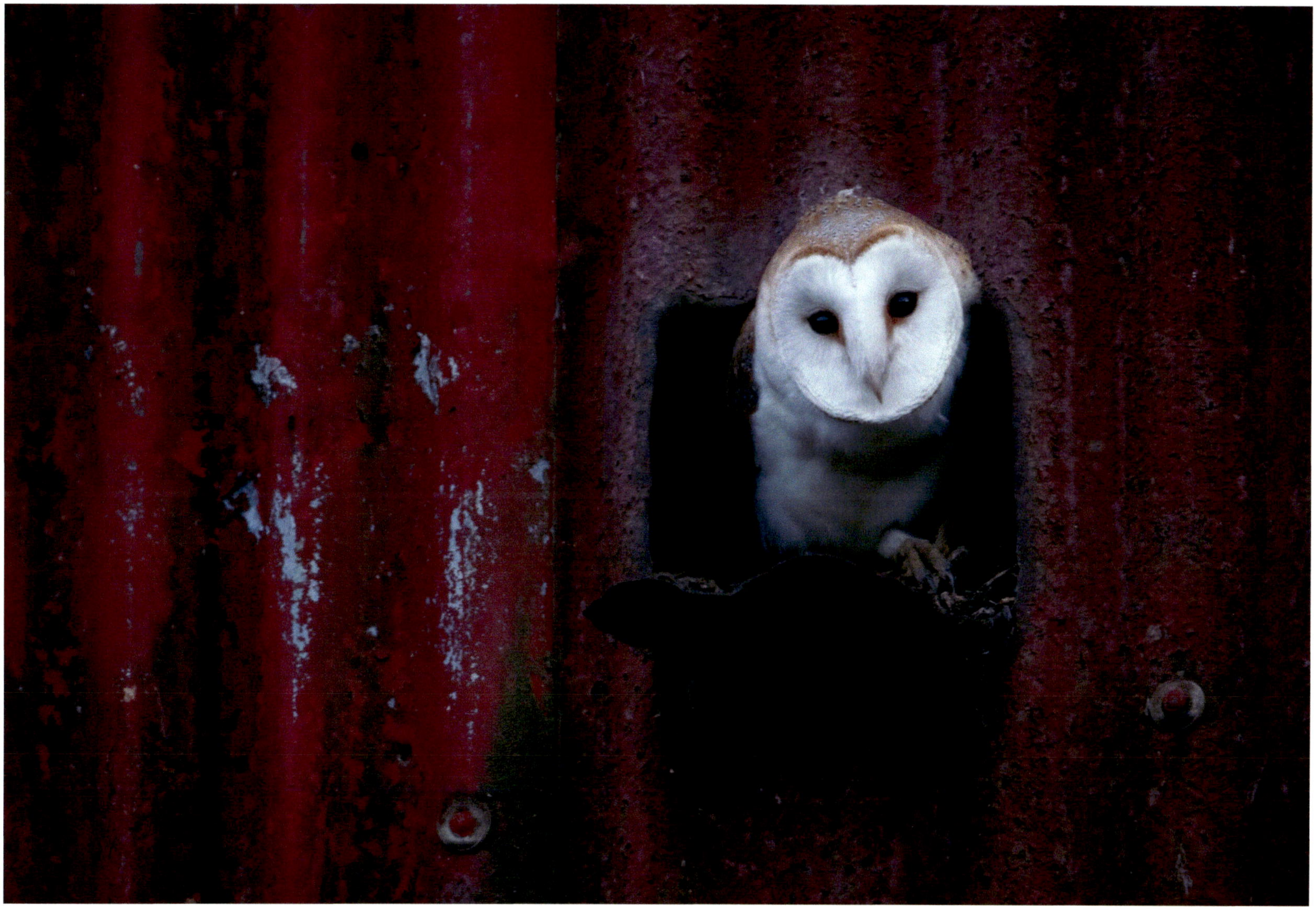

'...sets barn-owls mouse-hunting...'

CATOPTRICS

Dusklight weaves
Softer than silkworm
To cocoon the land;
Calls jack-snipe to drumming,
Sets barn-owls mouse-hunting,
Lures day-dreaming moths
To nuptial flight;
Unveils moon and stars,
Then glorious the night.

The Barn Owl holds a unique and mysterious allure for Irish people. It has dark, soul-piercing eyes. Its eerie territorial screech is largely responsible for the Irish legend of the Banshee. Even to this day ancient ruins are assumed to be haunted due to the strange hissing and snoring from the Barn Owl nest sites within. It is a magical spectacle to witness their silent, floating forms as the parents glide in with prey for the growing chicks. The snoring of the hungry chicks got much louder as an adult arrived at the nest. Barn Owls are nocturnal in Ireland. They are rarely seen during the day as they begin hunting about one hour after sunset and ending about one hour before sunrise. The invasive Greater White-toothed Shrew and the Bank Vole have had a positive effect on the Barn Owl population. As the shrew invades it is not such good news for the Pygmy Shrew or the Wood Mouse. However, there is increasing evidence that the range of the shrew as well as the greater provision of nest boxes is having a big impact on the breeding success of Barn Owls whose population has declined by around 50% in the past 25 years.

VOYAGER

Mending mackerel-torn nets,
Plying with whalebone needle,
The jerseyed fisherman explained
His craft, a cockle-shell curragh.

Putting out in it was hazardous,
Especially in the treacherous seas;
Disturbed waves showing white teeth,
Swallowing—maw ejecting flotsam.

Strong as was the ashen oar,
And muscular its rower,
Tideways could be turgid traps,
Overpowering in winter.

He would prefer a job inland,
Where no sea bird ever winged;
The soft lowing of cattle
Replacing the barking of seals.

Seals have a natural bark. A repertoire of barks, growls and groans helps seals recognize each other, establish and defend territories, and engage in other social interactions.

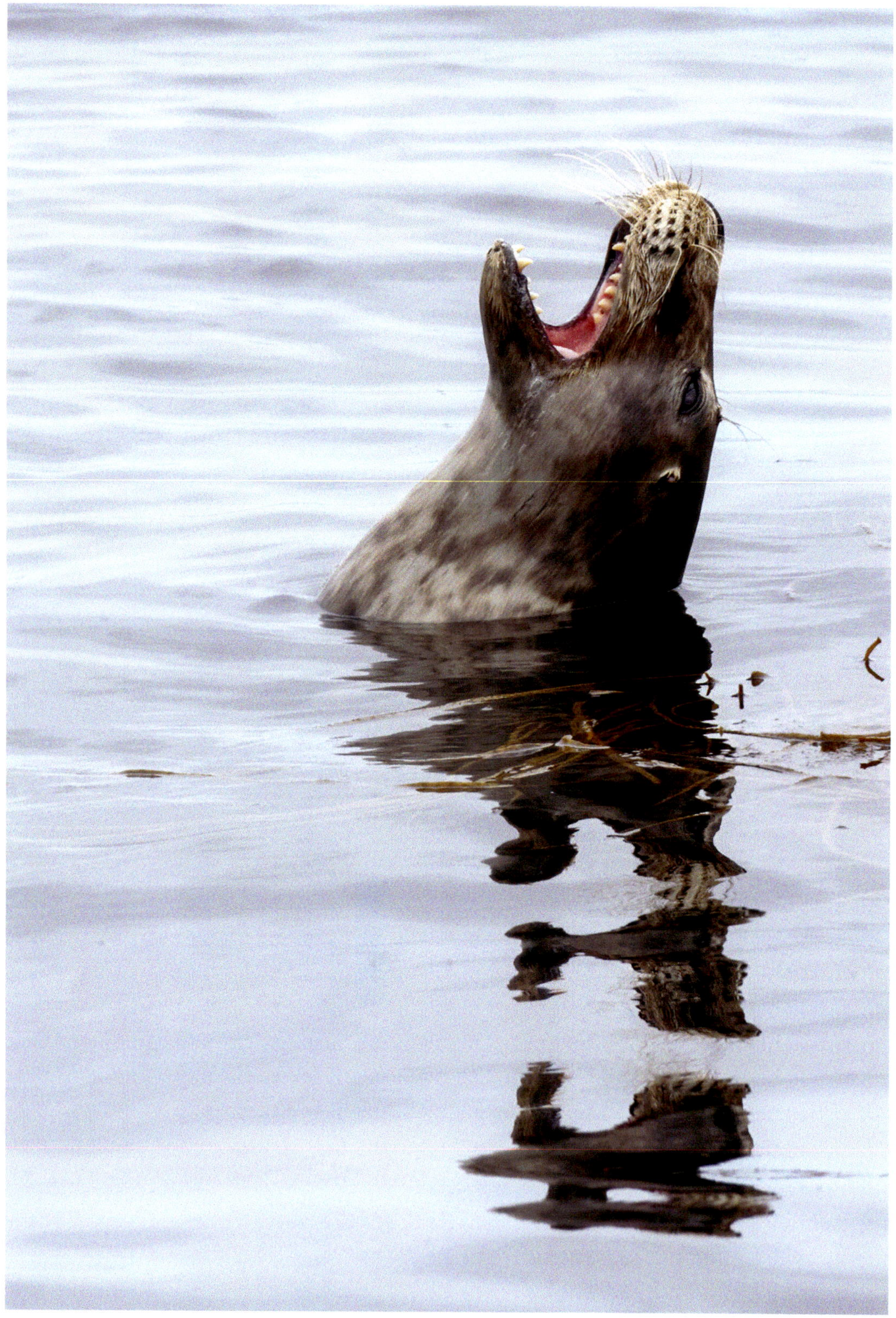

'...the barking of seals.'

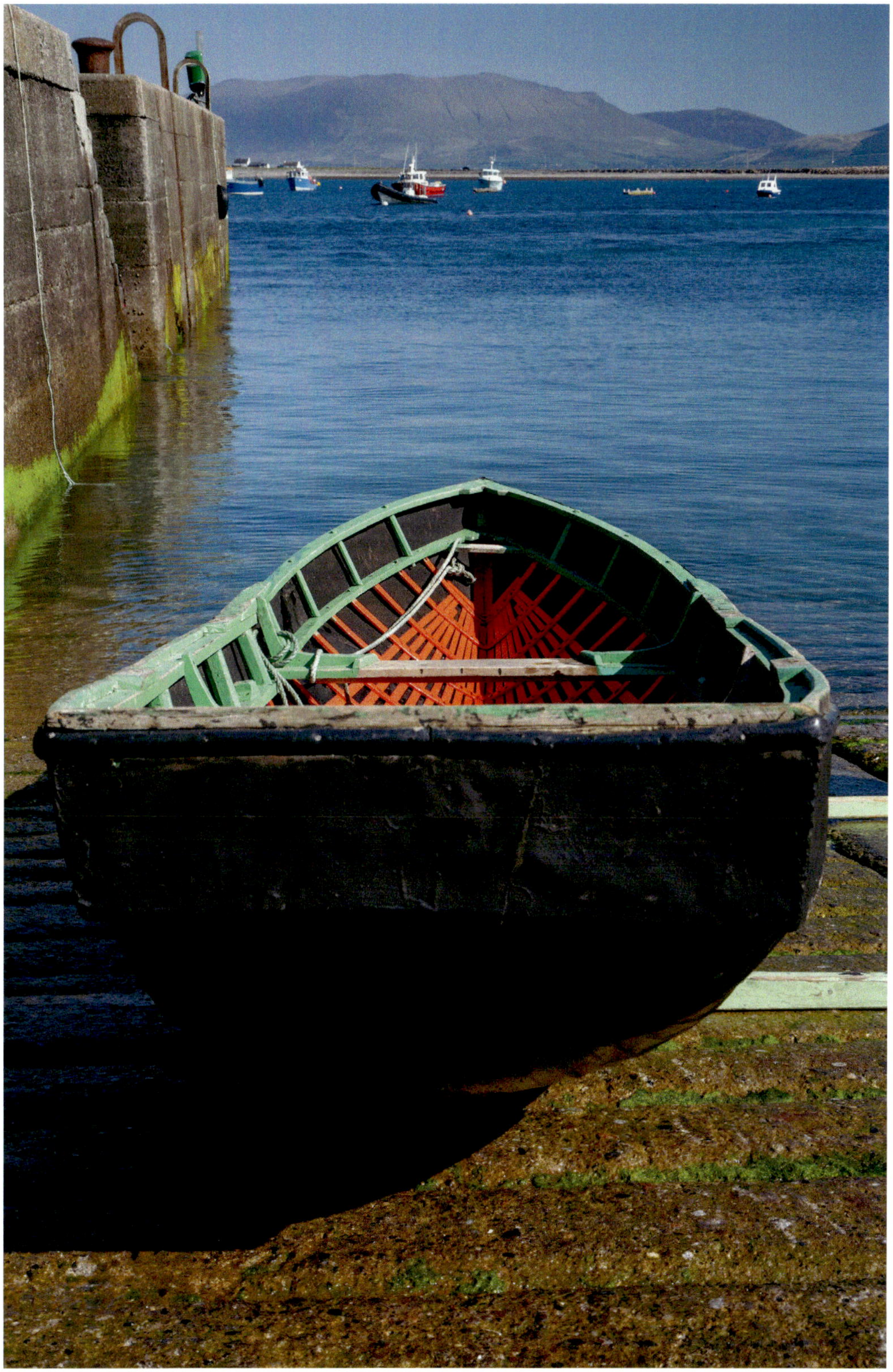

'...his craft, a cockle-shell curragh...'

The curragh, or currach, with its primitive design of a wooden frame and waterproof skin, is the best-known of all the Irish boats. Different forms of curraghs were made in different areas and ranged from the one-man paddling curragh of Donegal to two-, three- and four-man sized rowing curraghs. A three-man curragh or naomhóg was the norm in most areas for net fishing .

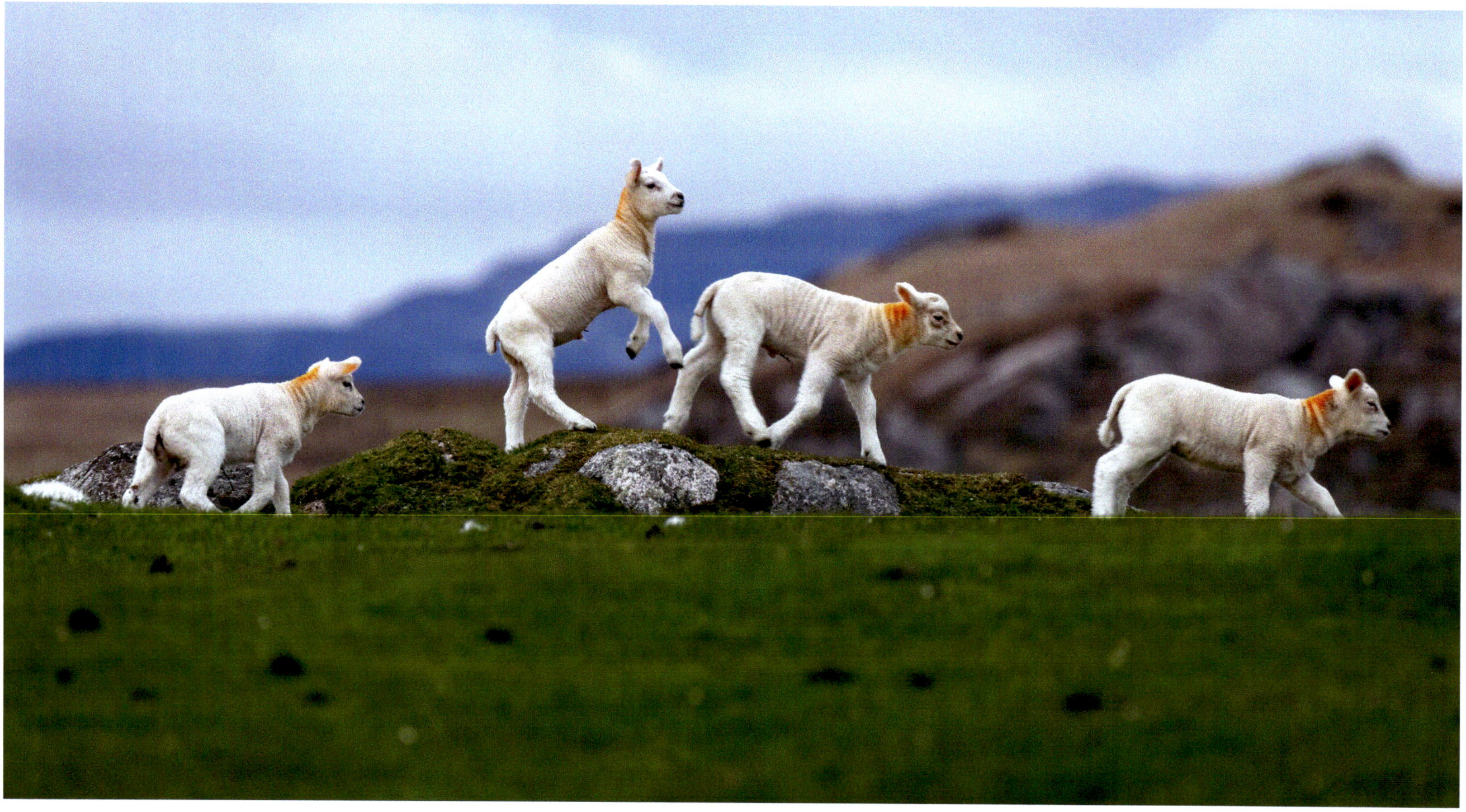

GOING TO THE FAIR

The O'Donnell brothers passed, herding hill sheep home;
With their trained collie-dogs, Dinky and Dora,
Watching the black-faced leader's every move—
A horned ram, now seven summers old.

He walked in front, continued on the road,
Not free to nibble at its grassy verge;
Sensing turnips and corn, with hay-strewn fold,
Would be his just reward at journey's end.

The collies ranged and turned, quick to harry
When stumbling laggards tried to break away;
To venture on the side paths, down the lanes,
Or into fields where bushes offered shade.

Afrighted ewes cavorted in confusion,
Urging their nervous lambkins into line;
With anxious bleatings called the foolish ones
From threatened dog-nips on their woolly rumps.

Each brother whistled; pointed with crooked staff;
Sent out the collies, then waved them back again;
And all in controlled disquiet travelled on,
Initial move for Brockagh Fair tomorrow.

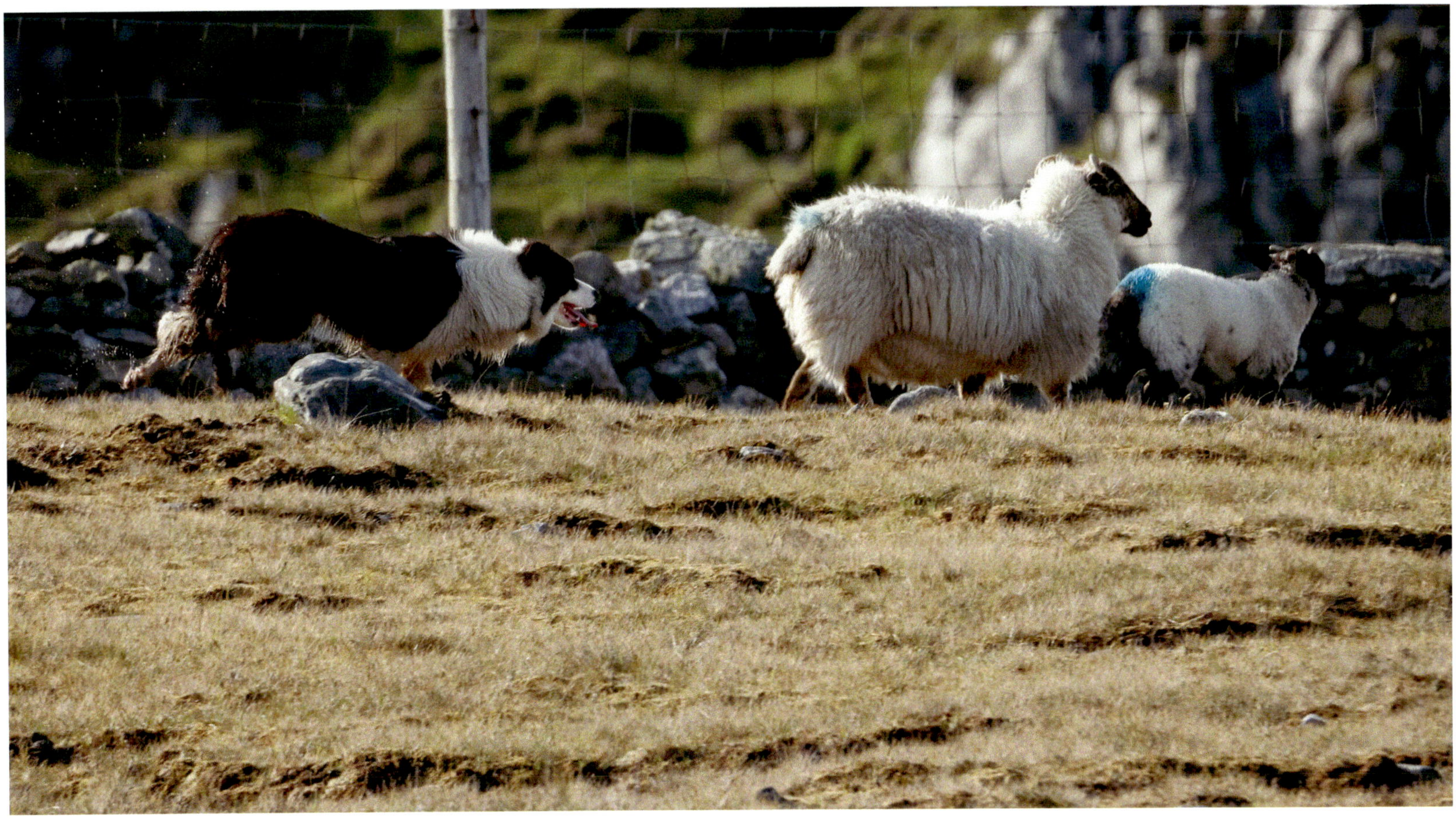

'Watching the black-faced leader's every move…'

The Border Collie is kept mostly as a working sheep-herding dog and is widely considered to be the most intelligent dog breed.

PENSIONER

Retired, he wondered where to go—
Back to the scenes of childhood?
The walnut tree, bright woodland stream,
Wrapped in aged mind, and endless dream...
Or stay beside his lighthouse?

In half-hooped sky, outlined the coast
Of rising hills, where curlew dwell
And lapwing scrape nests in the spring;
Where foxes prowl, and badger setts
Fern-hid, yawn in the bens.

The seasons passed, his doubts and hopes
Left him a wanderer on the slopes
Of Time; he floundered more and more.
The choice was his, he could not choose,
Then died, and only Heaven knew.

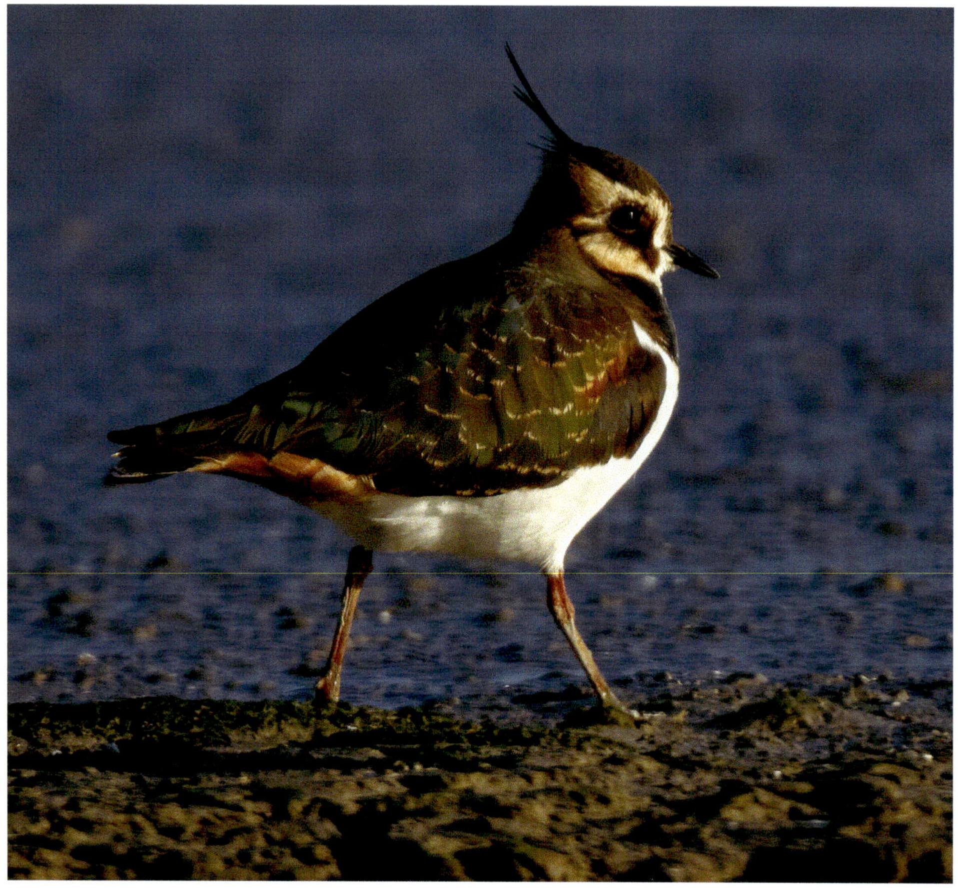

'And lapwing scrape nests in the spring; where foxes prowl, and badger setts fern-hid, yawn in the bens.'

The Lapwing's nest is a shallow scrape in the ground, into which the female lays three to four well camouflaged eggs. No other birds are allowed to encroach on the bird's nesting territory. This provides safety for the young who feed for themselves soon after they are hatched. It is different for birds that breed in colonies. In sea bird colonies the young don't need much space, as the parents bring food back from the sea.

Foxes are active throughout the year and do not hibernate. They do prowl in daytime in some areas but typically spend the day resting in cover.

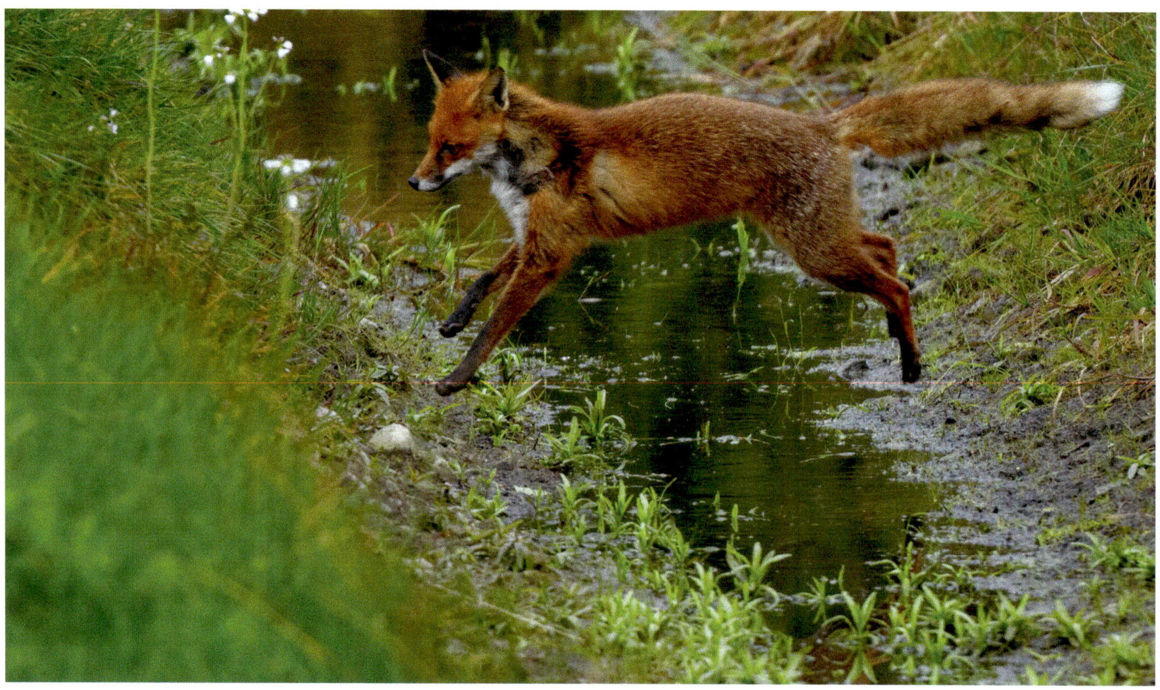

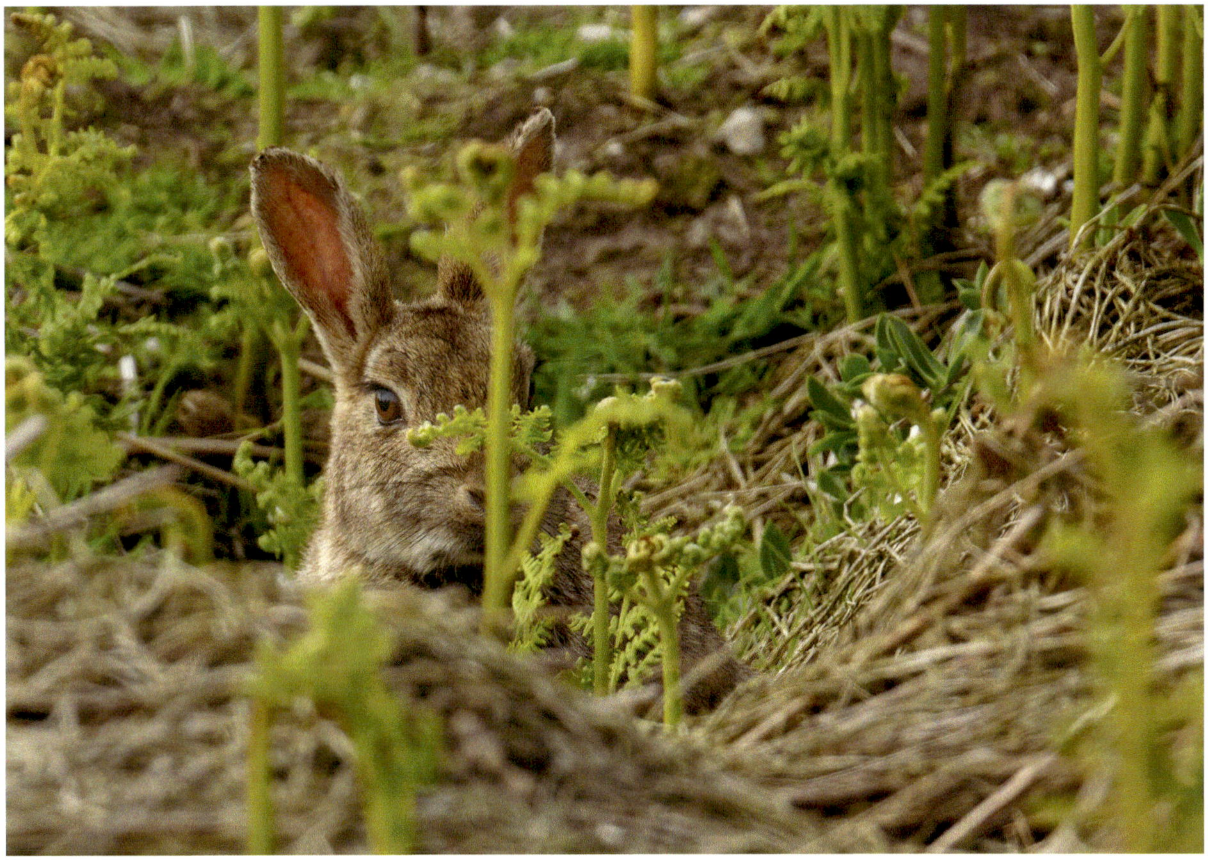

Springtime does provide the best weather conditions for the animals to give birth. One of the first signs of spring in Europe is the rabbits leaving their burrows. The young are alert and cautious.

'.And rabbit-youth comes out…'

THRONE OF TIME — SONG

When skies are deepest blue,
And the earth spreads below,
And sunset gleams a golden hue,
And moon shows silvery glow;
When beetles don their nuptial gloss,
And snails and glow-worms roam,
When birds build nests of laced moss,
Then Spring reigns on Time's Throne.

When haze half-veils each hill,
And rabbit-youth comes out,
And mavis of the golden bill
And cuckoo are about;
When froglets from the rushes peep,
And fruited is the rowan,
When salmon rivers sparkle deep,
Then Summer reigns on Time's Throne.

Then Summer reigns on Time's Throne,
And fruited is the rowan,
When salmon rivers sparkle deep,
Then Summer reigns on Time's Throne.

When sea-wrack lines each strand,
And salt-sprayed rocks shine hoar,
And fulmar-petrel leaves the land,
And seals come close inshore;
When fishermen haul high their boats,
And seaward, breakers foam,
When otters change their summer coats,
Then Autumn reigns on Time's Throne.

Then Autumn reigns on Time's Throne,
And seaward, breakers foam,
When otters change their summer coats
Then Autumn reigns on Time's Throne.

When gales blow o'er the sea,
And waves run mountain-high,
And gulls cower in the lee,
And clouds skud 'cross the sky;
When islanders share scanty fare,
And ships, battered, come home,
When spindrift fogs the icy air,
Then winter reigns on Time's Throne.

Then Winter reigns on Time's Throne,
And ships, battered, come home,
When spindrift fogs the icy air,
Then Winter reigns on Time's Throne.

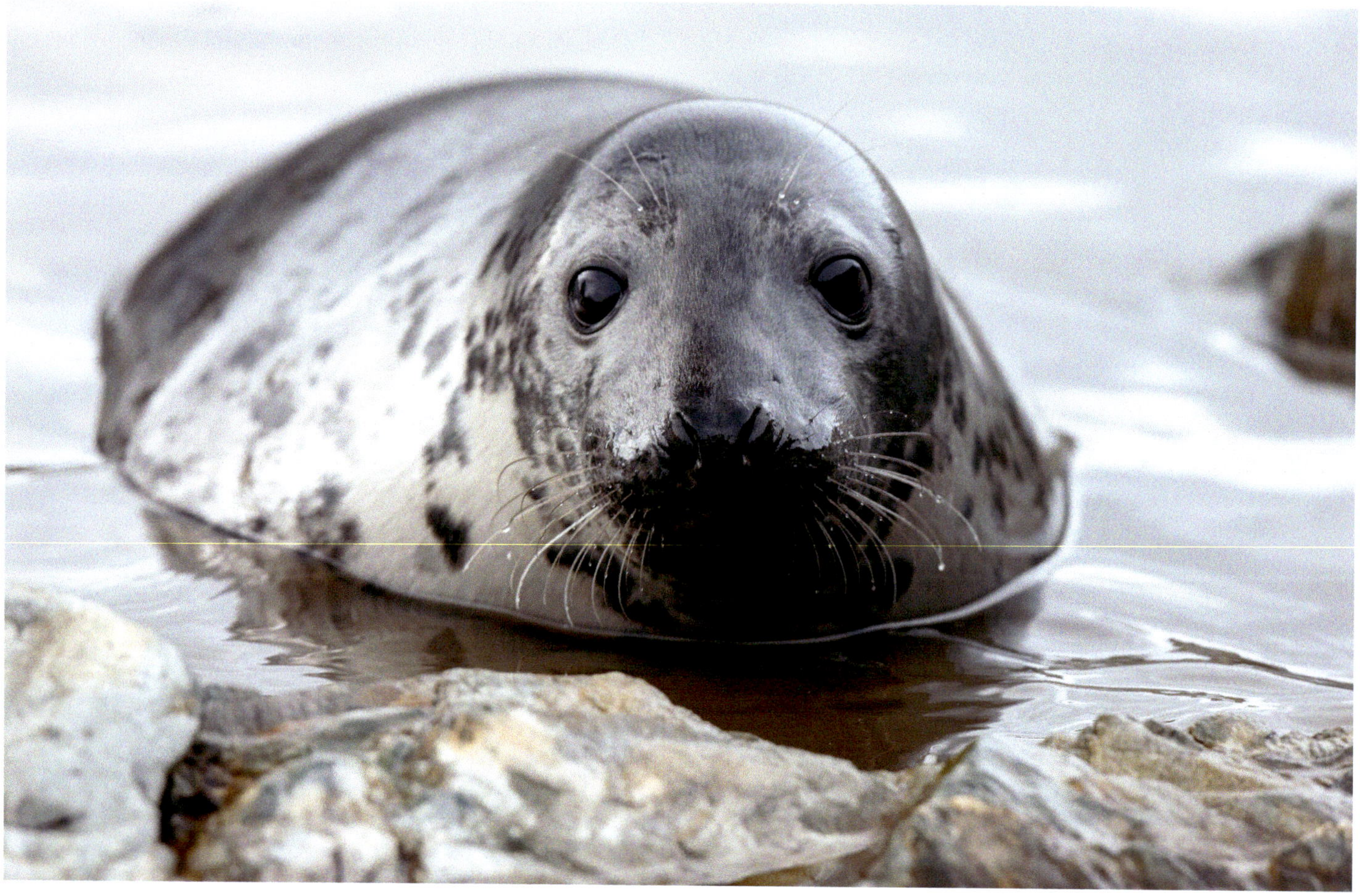

'And seals come close inshore…'

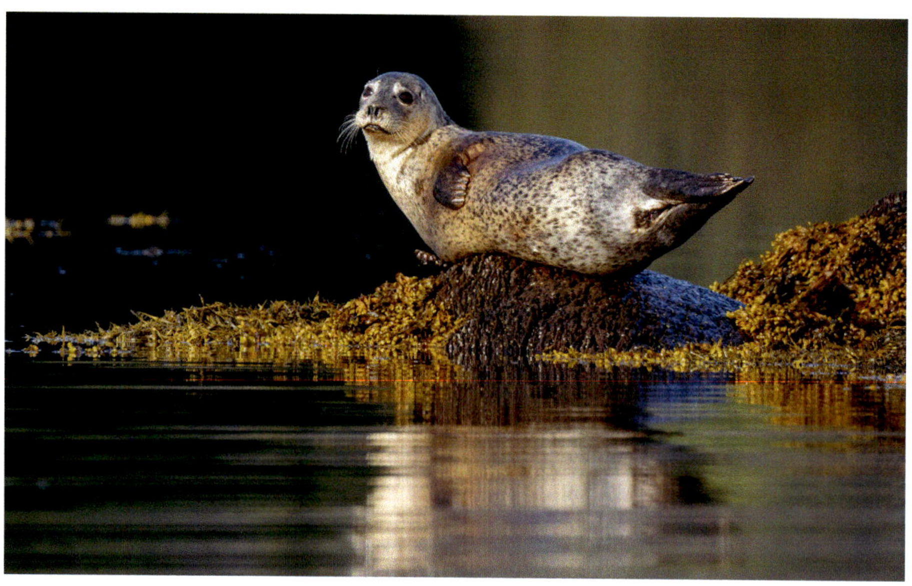

Common seal

The Common Seal (left) stays close to shore in June as after eleven months' gestation she gives birth to one single pup which can swim only a few hours later. The sheltered bay of Glengarriff in Co. Cork is home to a large colony of Common Seals where there are many rocky islets to haul out on to give birth.

Grey Seals (above) on the other hand generally give birth from September to December on remote and generally undisturbed areas, in particular offshore islands. Pups are born with a furry white coat and cling to the land for a few perilous weeks. The mother comes ashore to feed the pup on a diet of high-fat milk during which time it sheds its white coat and rapidly gains weight and size. After this it is abandoned to fend for itself and has to take to the water.

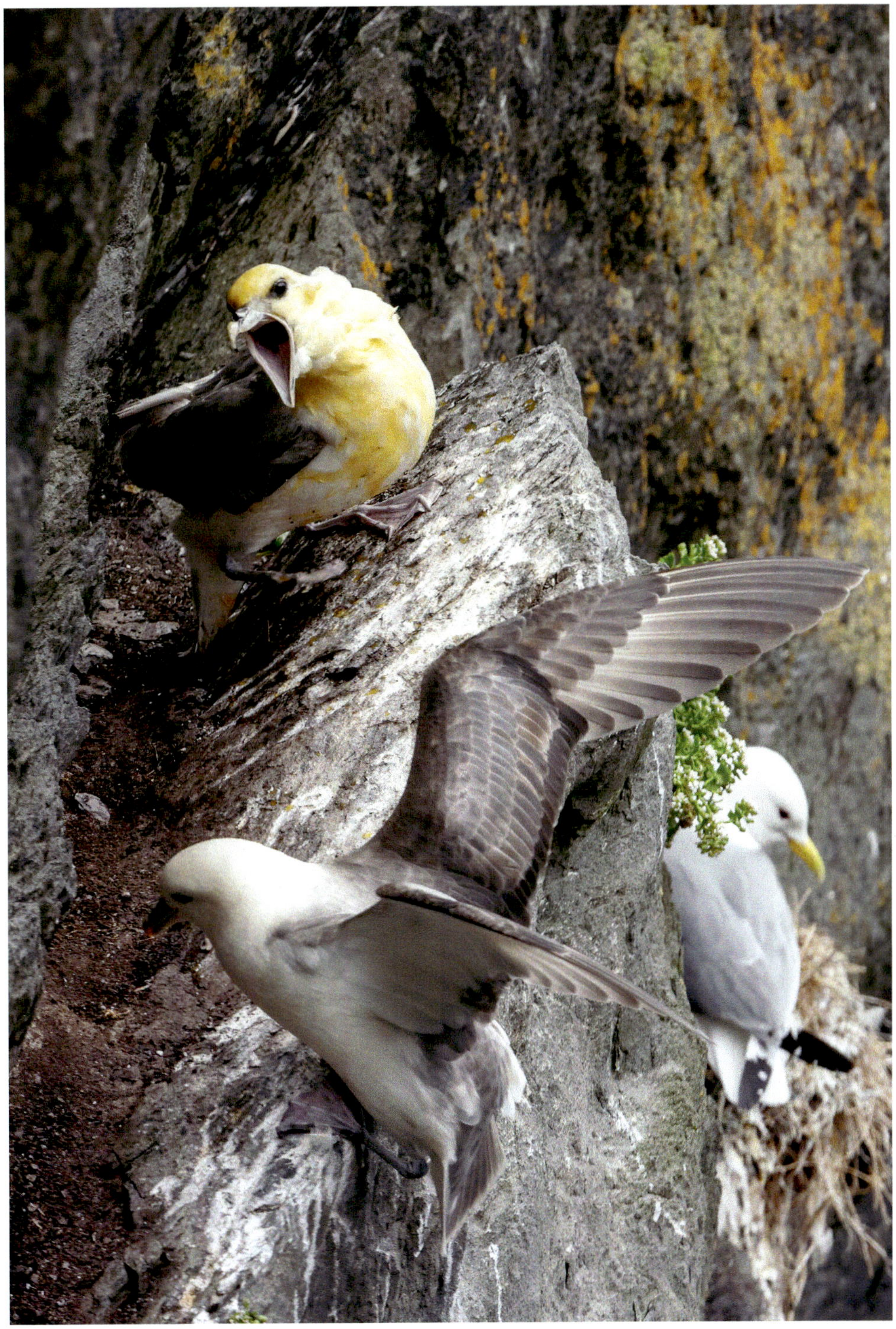

'And fulmar-petrel leaves the land...'

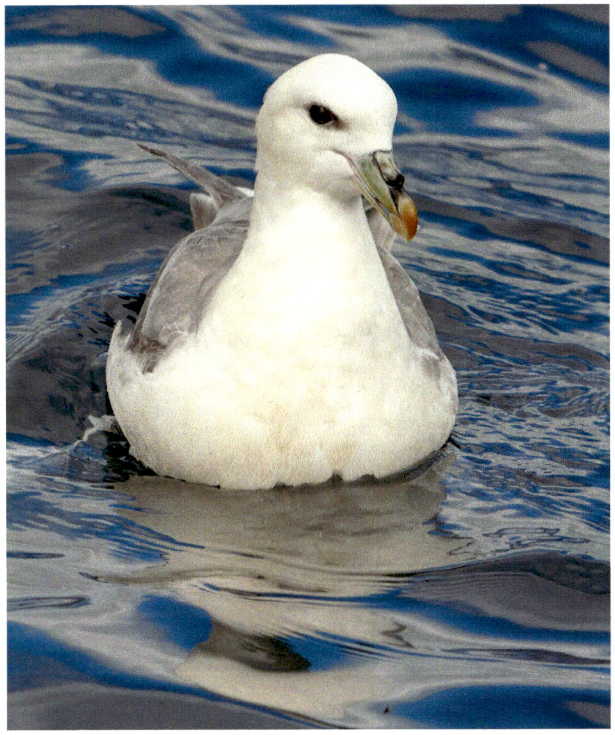

Fulmars are pelagic birds, meaning that they spend their entire life at sea apart from when breeding. Both the Fulmar and the Storm Petrel are easily distinguishable from the gull family with their stiff wings and tube noses. The birds imbibe a lot of seawater and have glands in their bill to extract the salt from the water which is then expelled through the tube in their beak.

They have a habit of spitting a foul smelling stomach oil as a defence mechanism when threatened. This oil coats the feathers of the predator inhibiting their ability to fly. The oil is very sticky, coats the feathers and is impossible to preen out. Oiled feathers then stick together so that the bird is no longer waterproof. This unfortunate fulmar has been spat on by another fulmar and may die.

CORMORANTS

In arrowed strings birds, bronze-black, fly
First light across a rainbowed sky;
Splash down beside wave-washed rock-stooks,
To food forage, molluscs and flukes.

Long necks full stretch, broad wings
outspread,
Small recurved crest adorns each head;
Some showing shield on either flank,
White summer badge of adult rank.

All turn to face the rising sun,
Like weather-cocks in eddy-run;
Then dive to leave the surface bare,
As if a bird was never there.

Now rise again—three, seven, eight—
One in hooked bill holding small skate;
Another, dressed in nuptial vest,
Becomes airborne, with wrack for nest.

Brown seaweed, dulse, and mermaid's-hair,
Transported in the mouth with care;
Entwined with rush, sea-rods and sedge,
Foundation laid on cliff-top ledge.

And so cormorants put in their day,
At fishing, nesting, courtship play;
Fulfilling cycle of their kind,
The edict of a Master Mind.

The Cormorant has a white thigh patch early in the breeding season, losing most of these white feathers during the summer. It has a sloping forehead that gives it a wedge-shaped profile. During the breeding season, there is a crest on the nape. Cormorants are closely related to pelicans, and their overall body shape is a very ancient one. Unlike other diving birds such as gannets, which dive by plunging into the water from the air, cormorants dive directly from the surface. Since they're so well adapted for swimming and finding fish underwater, cormorants are very successful hunters.

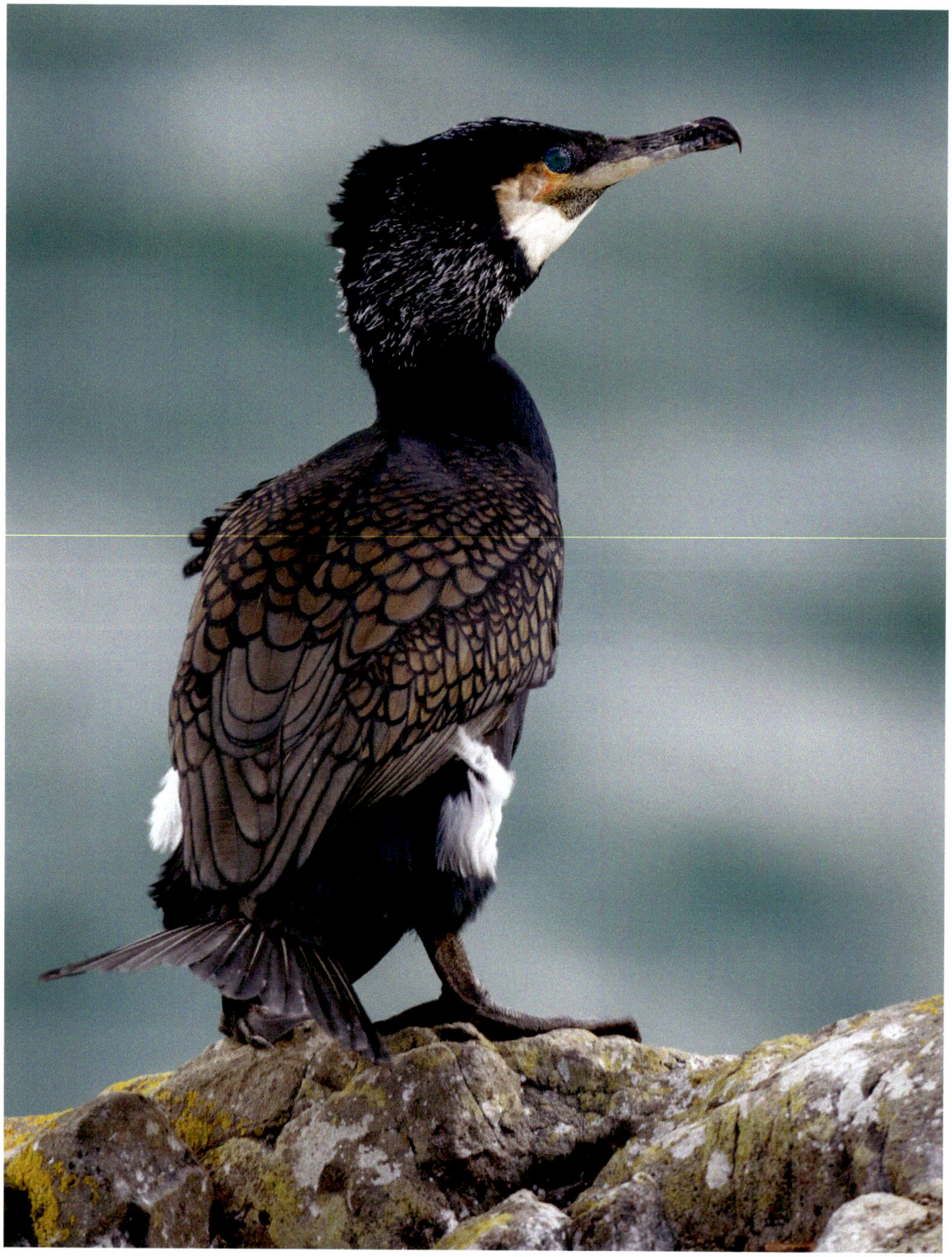

'Some showing shield on either flank, white summer badge of adult rank.'

JOURNEY INTO SPRING

In March, the gulls from winter rest,
Begin to move, pair and invest
In withered grass, club-moss and ling,
And glitters grey the flirting wing.

They go and come, fly far and wide,
Or bob across the plankton-tide;
All on food-foraging intent;
Sand-eel and prawn to pay the rent.

Occasionally burst into song
As nights shorten and days grow long;
The fishermen full weather-wise,
Unwraps his nets, hearing the noise.

He knows when gulls begin to sing.
Bleak winter's done, advances spring;
The cymbals in the feathered throat
Ringing its time to launch his boat.

Wide spread of tail and beak-uptwist
Are movements in the winter missed,
Apparent to his weather-eye,
Traced in outline against the sky.

But now retuned, they tell his world
Of nature's winding sheets unfurled;
He found a brown gull-chick today
As Patrick's sun bejewelled the bay.

The curragh is a light, buoyant and adaptable craft that can be launched and beached in the most exposed places. For many coastal and island dwellers of the Atlantic coast, it was the only boat they could afford and has been used successfully to fish, to transport animals and people, for harvesting seaweed and a variety of other purposes.

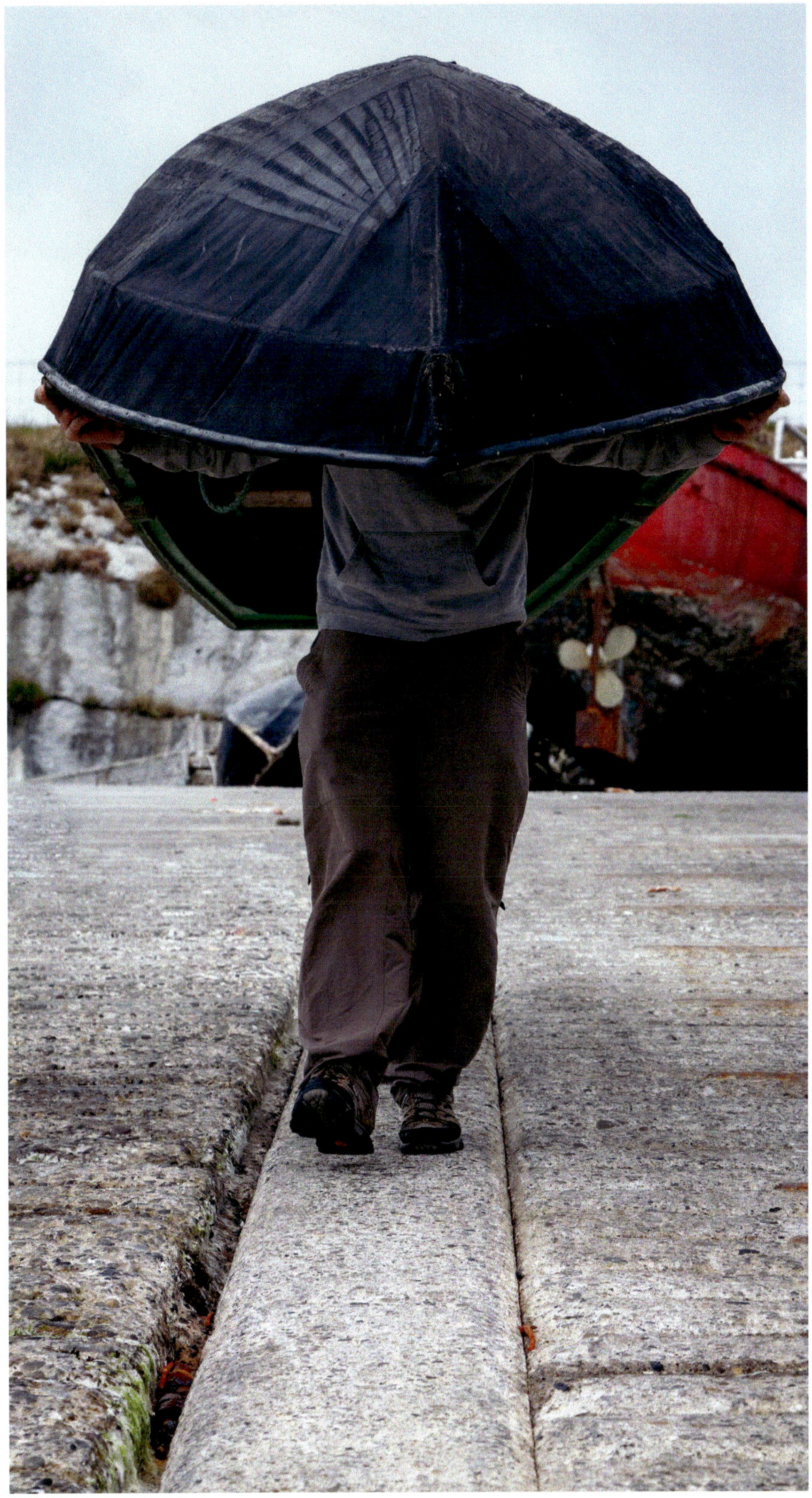

'The fisherman full weather-wise…'

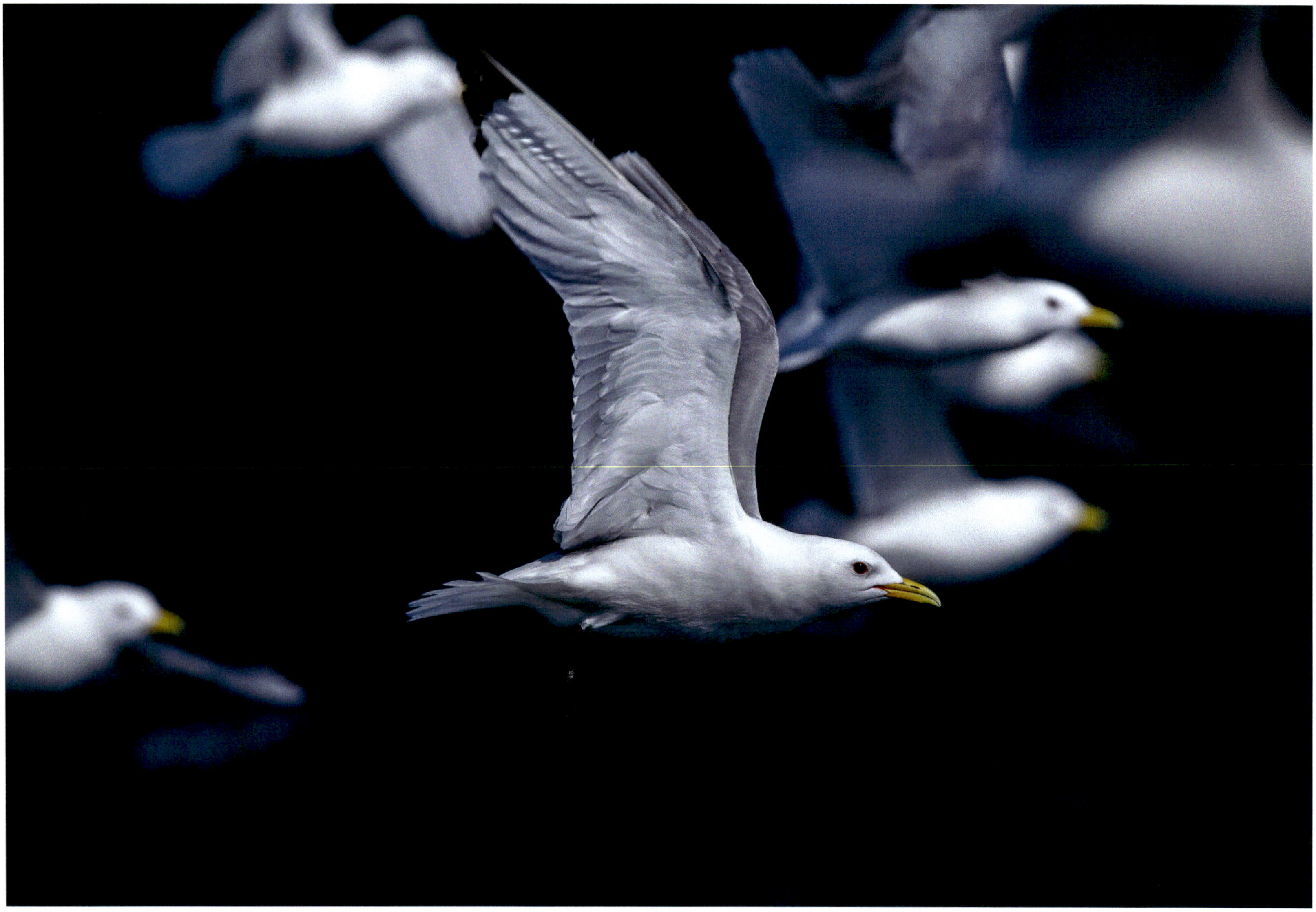

'...knows when gulls begin to sing, bleak winter's done, advances spring.'

With its graceful flight, the Kittiwake is our most sea-loving gull and is able to cover huge distances out of sight from the coast except during its breeding period. In flight, the jet black wing-tips show no white and look as if they have been dipped in ink. This beautiful bird feeds on the surface of the sea, unlike the puffin, which is adapted to dive up to 200 feet beneath the sea.

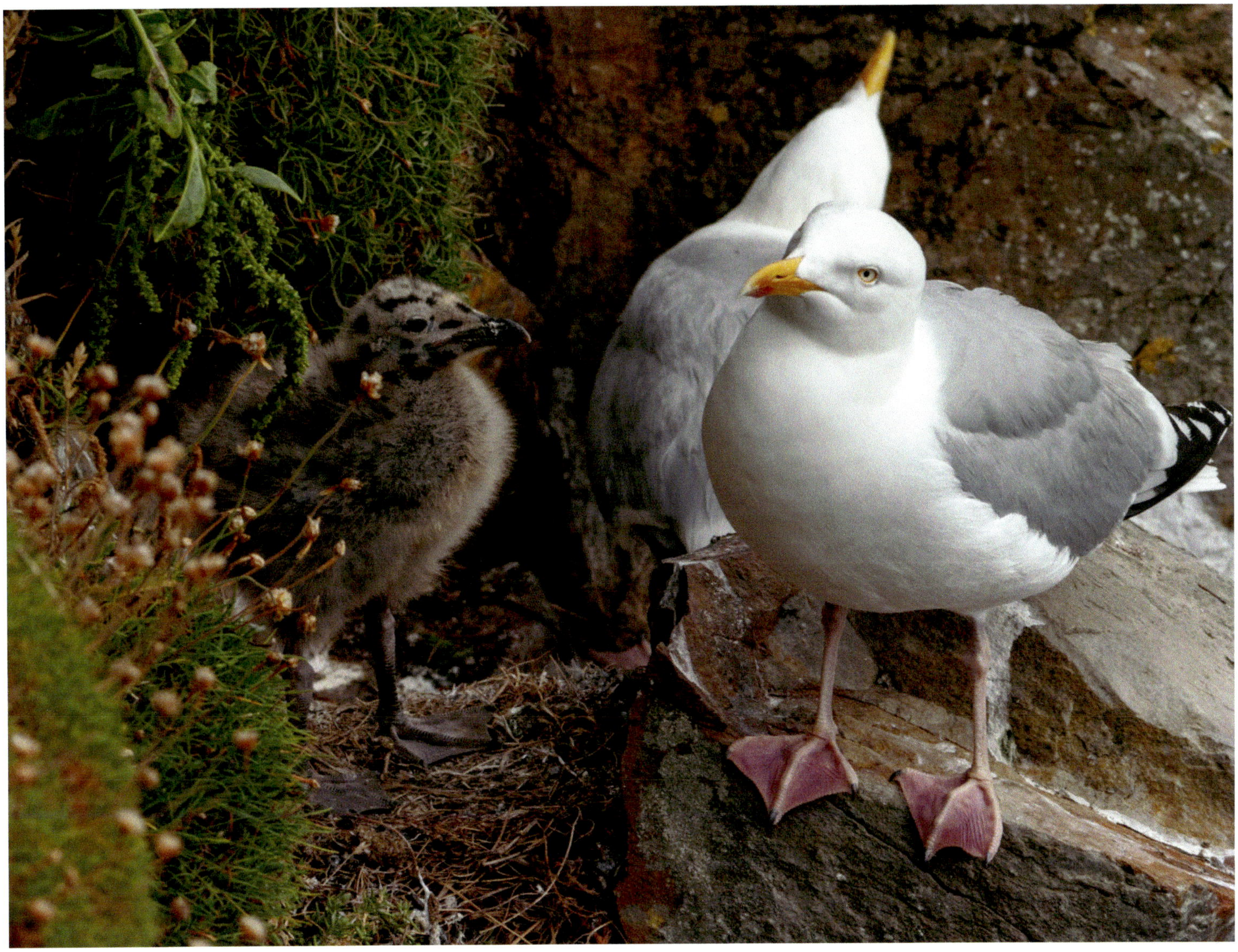

'He found a brown gull-chick today…'

The Herring Gull is probably our most familiar gull species. The legs are pink and the bill yellow with a red spot on the lower tip. The juvenile has a streaky brown appearance with a dark bill. It is thought the red spot is a target for the young chick to peck at, stimulating the adult to regurgitate food.

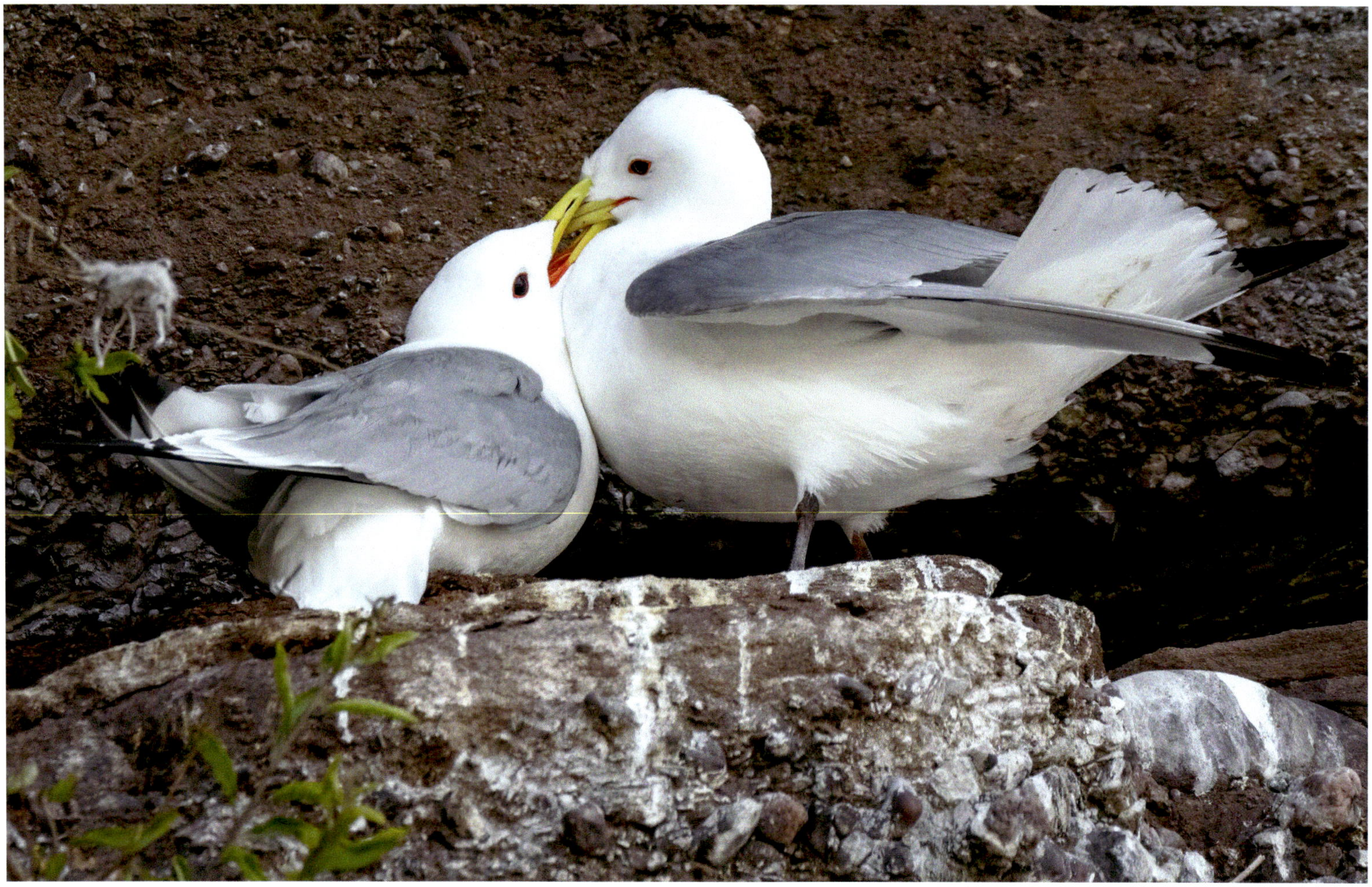

'In March the gulls from winter rest, begin to move, pair and invest…'

The Kittiwake, our smallest gull, is a beautiful mainly white bird with deep black eyes and jet black wing tips. Monogamous pairs nest in colonies from May to September, where they can be found nesting on the sheerest sea cliffs. To seduce the female, the male will feed them at their nest site. The inside of its mouth is also a characteristic feature of the species due to its rich red colour. It will also jerk its head up and down, gradually opening its bill, to attract a female.

Ground nesting birds tend to wander about. However, young Kittiwakes born on cliff edges have an innate fear of falling over the edge until they can fledge.

LITTLE SILVER FISH

The gulls on trembling feathers cleave the sky
With turn and twist, long tail-rudders spread out,
Or swim with breast to breast of oiled ocean,
Ochreous vermilion-tipp'd beaks a-dipping
In search of little silver fish
That glitter in the moonlight.

And men in fragile craft are anchored near,
Only a one-ply plank twixt them and death,
Watching the long brown line of seaborne corks
Above the thousand tiny squares of thread
In search of little silver fish
That glitter in the moonlight.

And where the boot-marked beach spreads to the
All brown and grey, and blue, with seething buzz
The sandhoppers that scavage, time unending,
Are out with putrid thirst and one-way minds
In search of little silver fish
That glitter in the moonlight.

The more graceful Lesser Black-backed Gull stands apart from other large gulls, such as the Herring and the Great Black-backed, by its smaller size. The Lesser Black-backed Gulls in the image are demonstrating their mid-air antics using their rather long, pointed wings which extend far beyond the tail when perched.

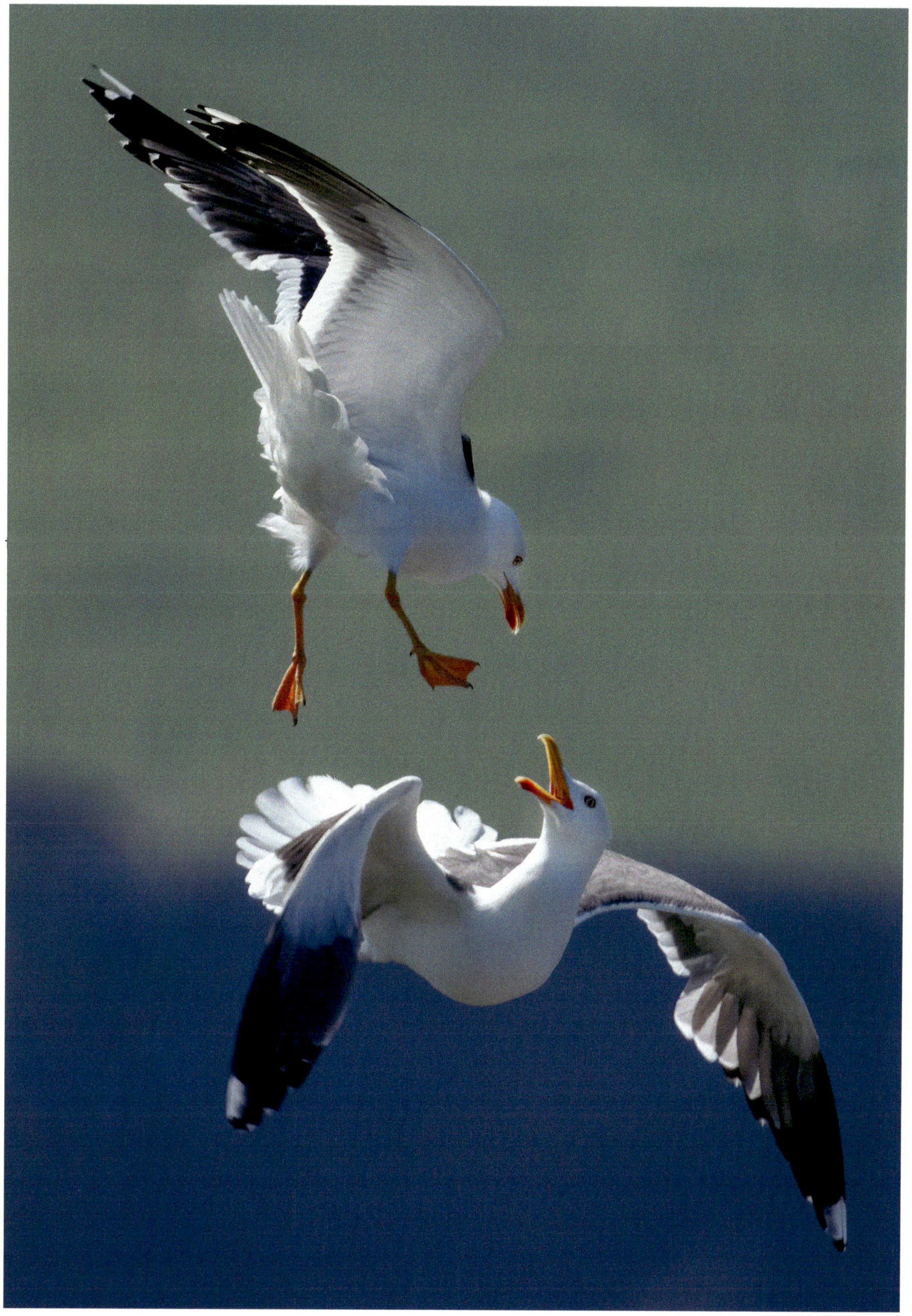

'...With turn and twist, long tail-rudders spread out...'

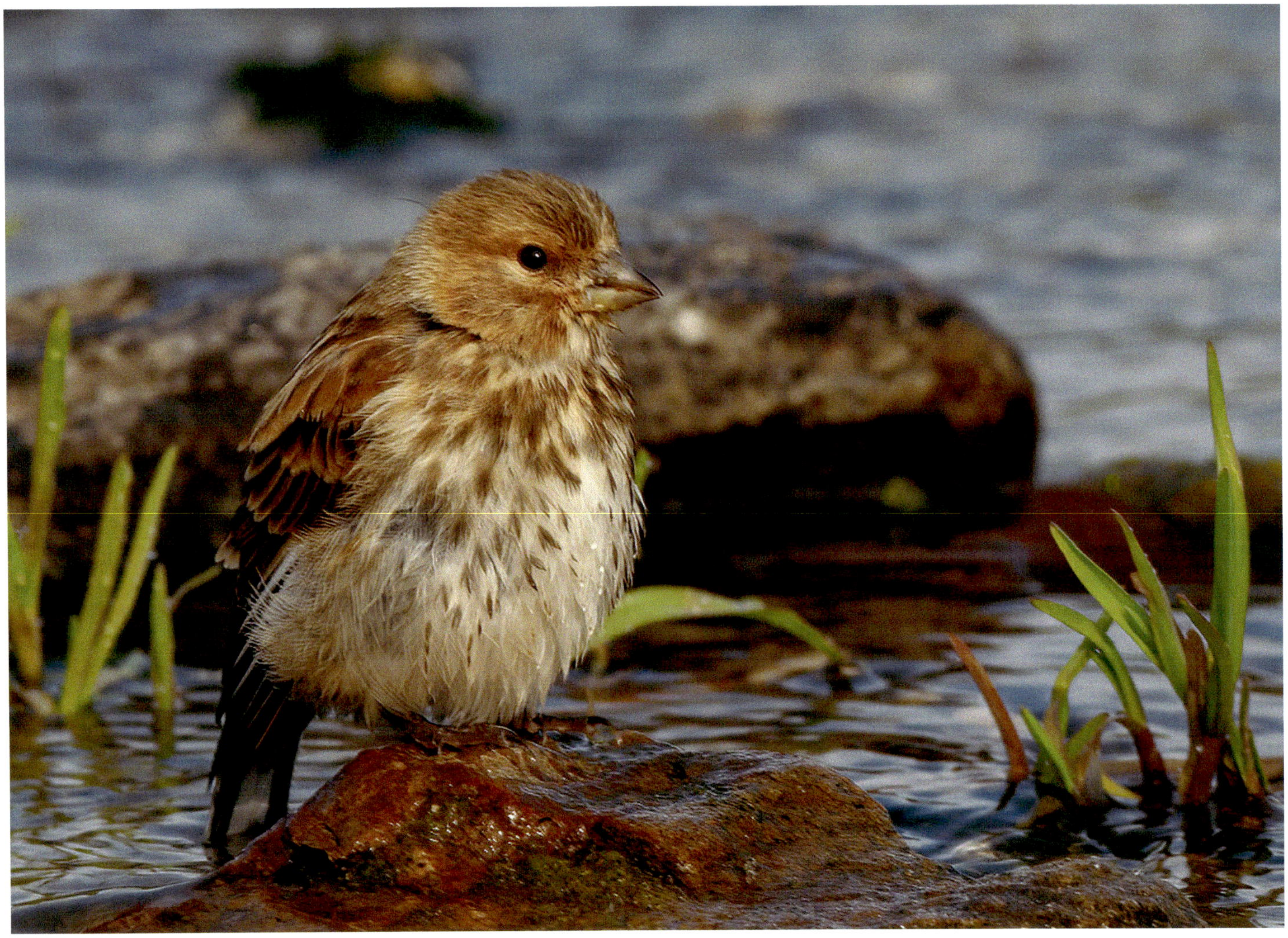

'I heard a litch-fowl and a linnet trilling sweetly in a bramble bower…'

BIRDSONG

I heard a litch-fowl and a linnet
Trilling sweetly in a bramble bower,
In reverie I stood and listened,
Borne heavenwards for one God-sent hour;

And soon around me gathered a throng
Gaping and asking, "What is it?"

"Only," I said, "two birdeens in song,
A litch-fowl and a mountain linnet!"

The Linnet is very vocal and sings all year and is widespread resident throughout Ireland. The female Linnet lacks the red markings of the male and their breasts are streaked buff. They are usually seen in pairs and stay close together throughout the Summer, feeding on the ground and low down in bushes. Outside the breeding season they can form large flocks.

THE SCRAW-CUTTER

Here's work for Island-man to do,
Cutting scraws on the turfy brugh;
From light to dark, thro' noon and eve,
With open shirt and roll'd sleeve.

Slaking thirst in the nearby spring,
Hearing the red-poled linties sing,
Seeing beetles break from the clay
To run, wee frightened things, away!

Building stacks on the stripp'd ground,
Like gallaun pillars, scattered 'round;
Then home to recoup strength in rest,
Unmindful of his wife's broad breast.

The Linnet is a small member of the finch family and is restless and active. The male is most easily recognisable by the crimson breast and crown during the breeding season. The song of the linnet is melodious and fluty containing fast trills and twitters.

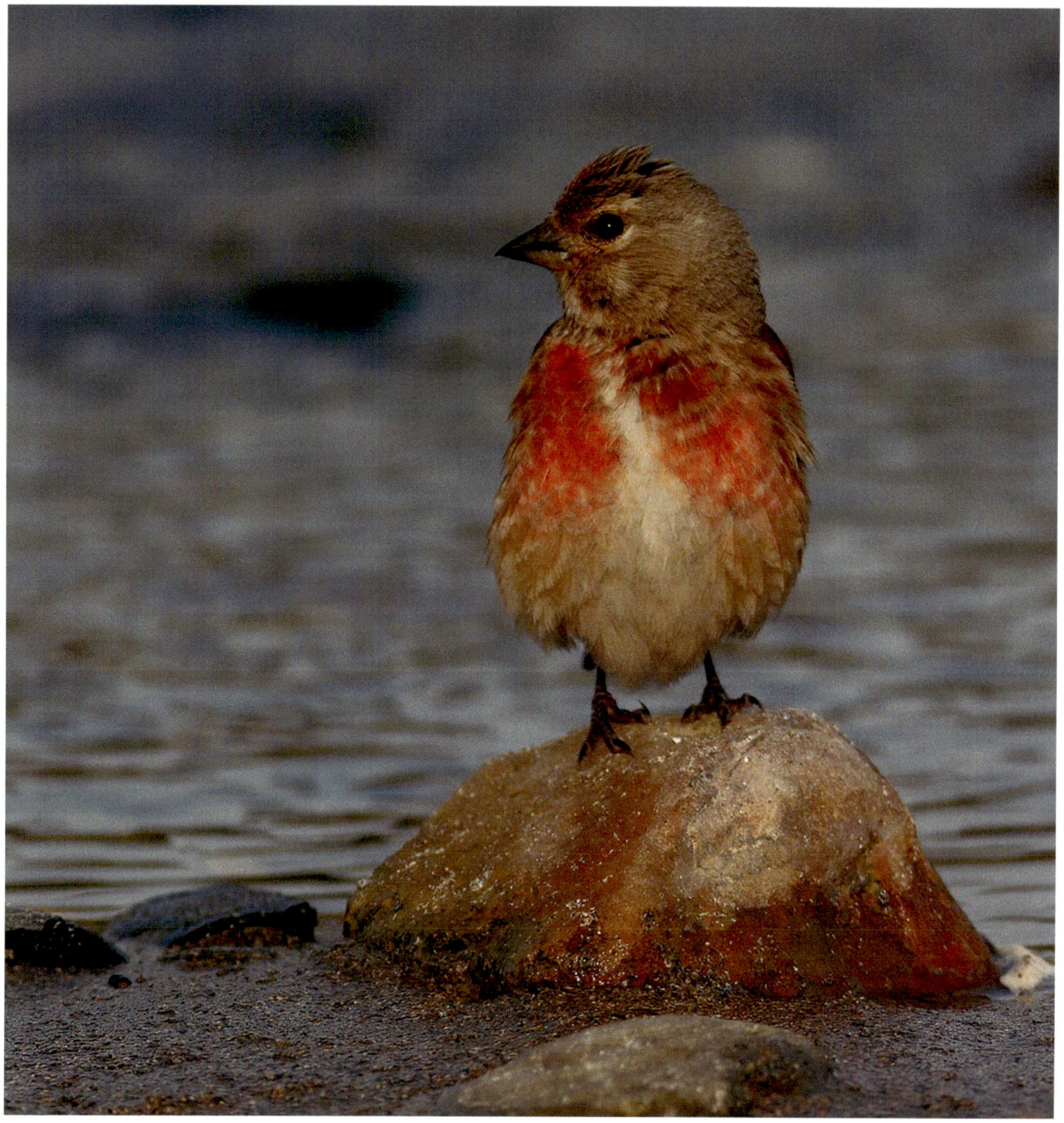

'...hearing the red-poled linties sing...'

PUFFIN

From nesting burrow
The puffin waddles out;
Looks around,
Spreads wings,
Becomes airborne,
Whirring:
Splashes down,
Paddles,
Dives,
Goes fishing.

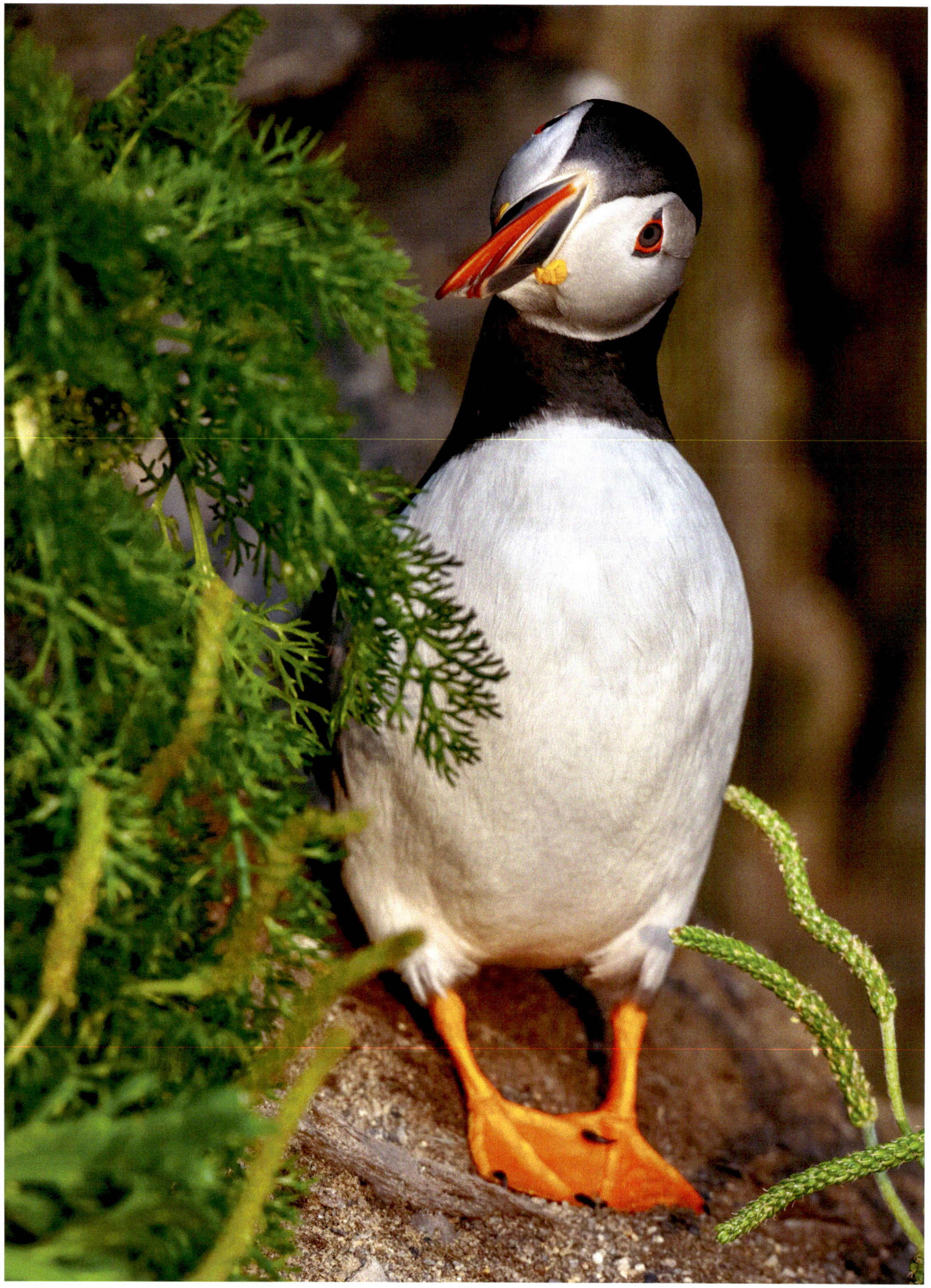

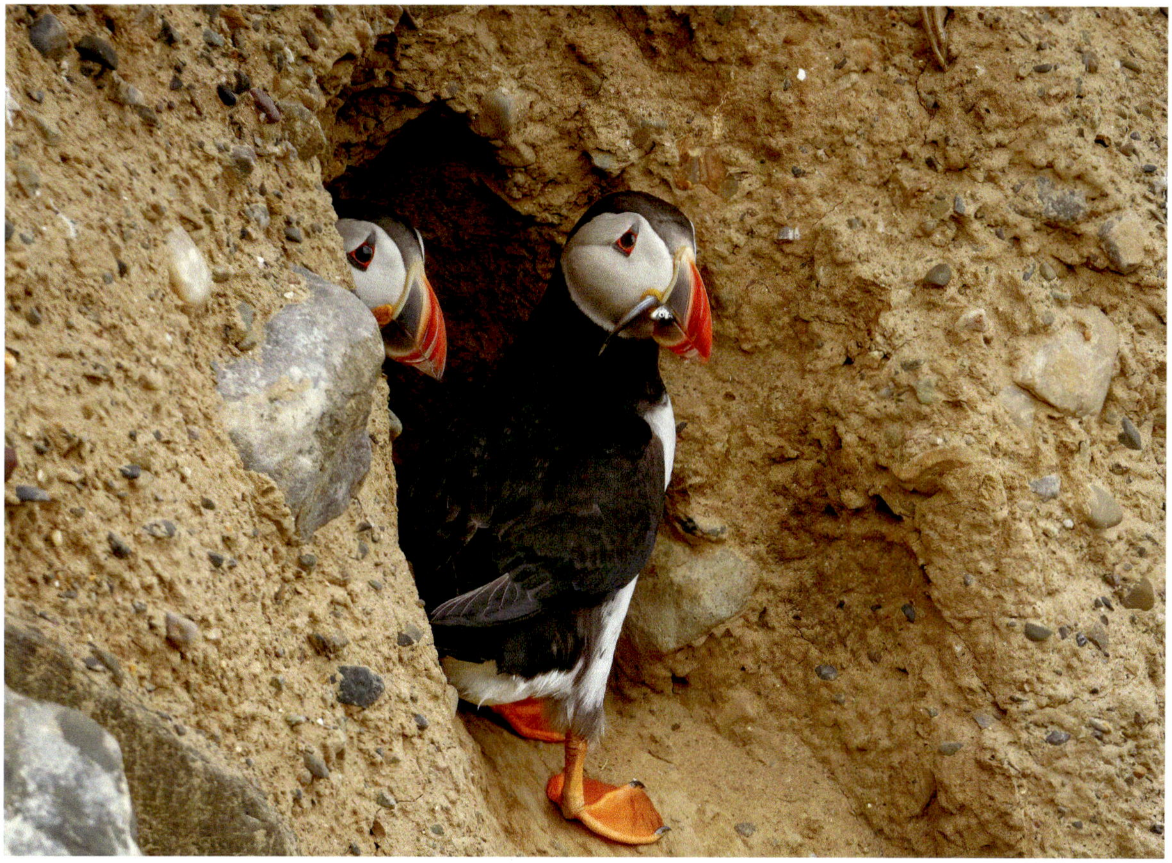

'From nesting burrow the Puffin waddles out.'

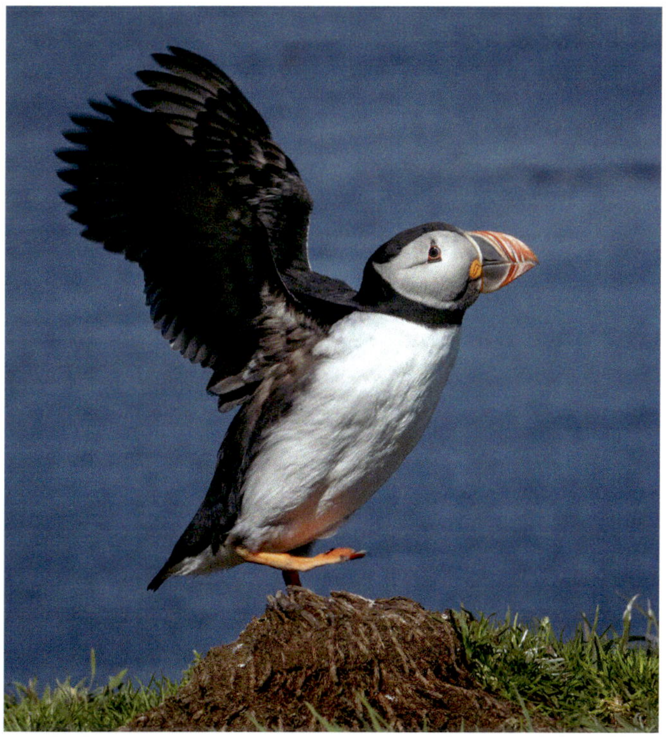

'Spreads wings…'

Skellig Michael , an island seven miles off the west coast of Ireland, is home to thousands of Atlantic Puffins for part of the year. Puffins spend the winter months at sea far from land where they moult and acquire new flight feathers in time for the summer. The increased light of spring releases hormones to bring changes to the body and brain, transforming the grey winter birds into colourful enigmatic sea birds ready to spend their summers on the island mating, breeding and fattening their chicks. The very orange bill, feet and legs come from pigments called carotenoids found in the fish they eat. This iconic species is also known as 'the clown of the sea' because of its multi-coloured bill, its large white patch on the face, and its comical flight. However, this elegant bird is no clown, being a survivor on both land and sea, covering large distances over water, known for being long-lived and monogamous, and burrowing holes on land to rear its young. The puffin mostly dives up to fifty feet to catch fish but is also capable of propelling itself using its short wings to a depth of 200 feet, lasting two minutes beneath the ocean. It has to beat its short wings very fast in order to stay airborne

MEMORIES

Having lived in a lighthouse
On a bare rock
Surrounded by sea
For most of my life
And now retired.

The thing I remember
Is dense fog clearing
At the turn of high tide;
And the stars coming out
Like primroses in the sky.

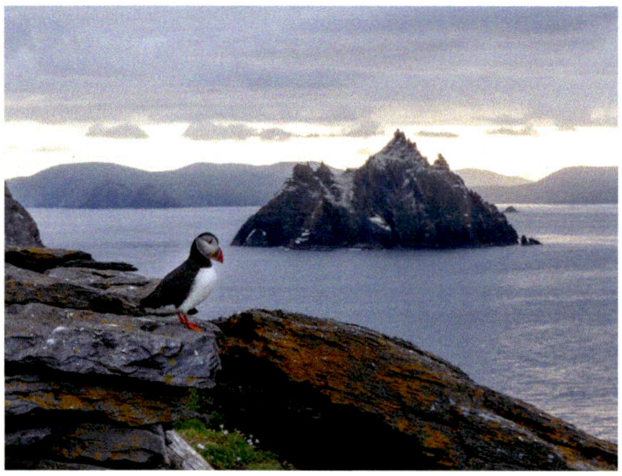

The Skellig Lighthouse located on the craggy island of Skellig Michael stands on the south western tip of Ireland and is a 12-metre high building isolated from the rest of the world.

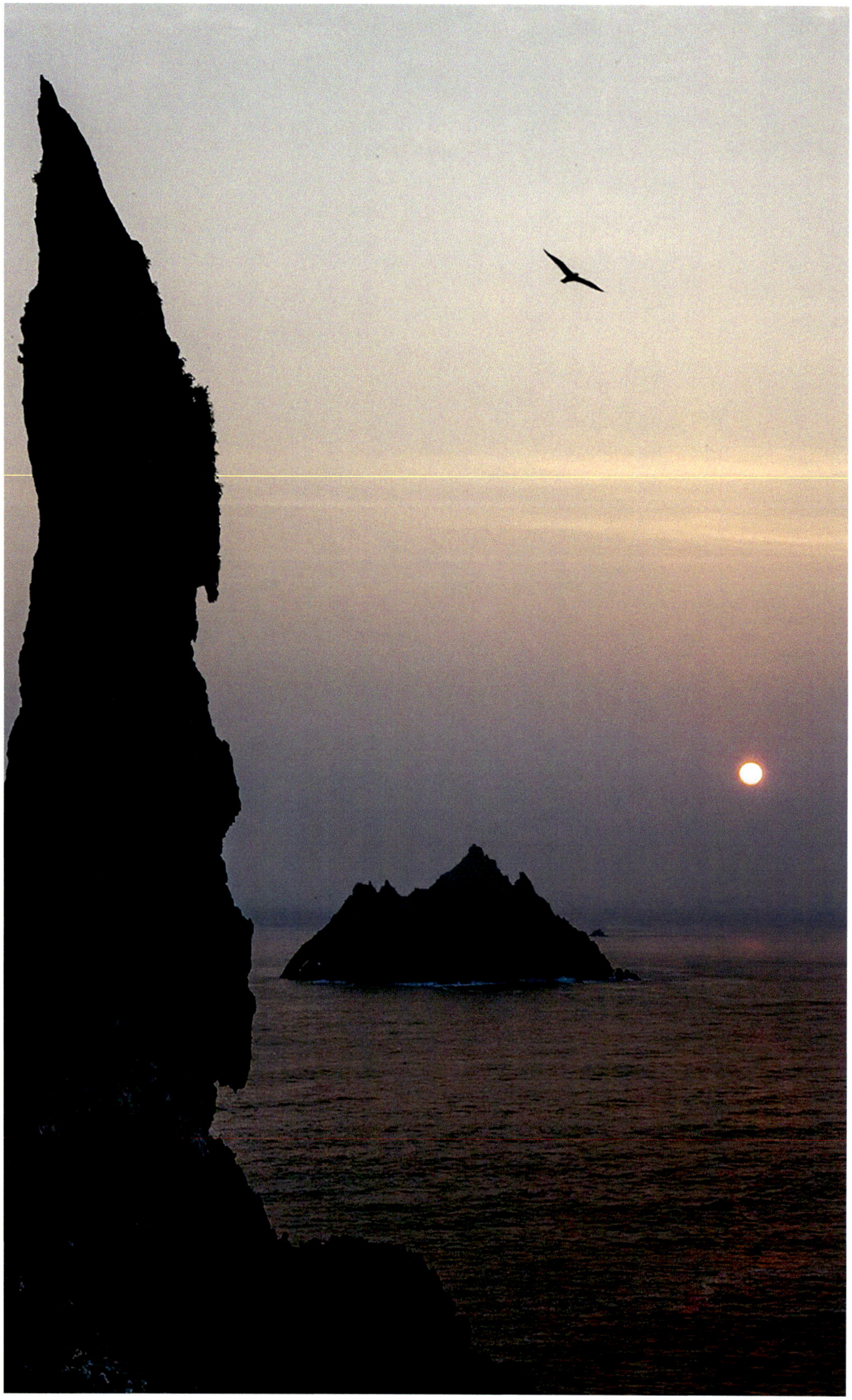

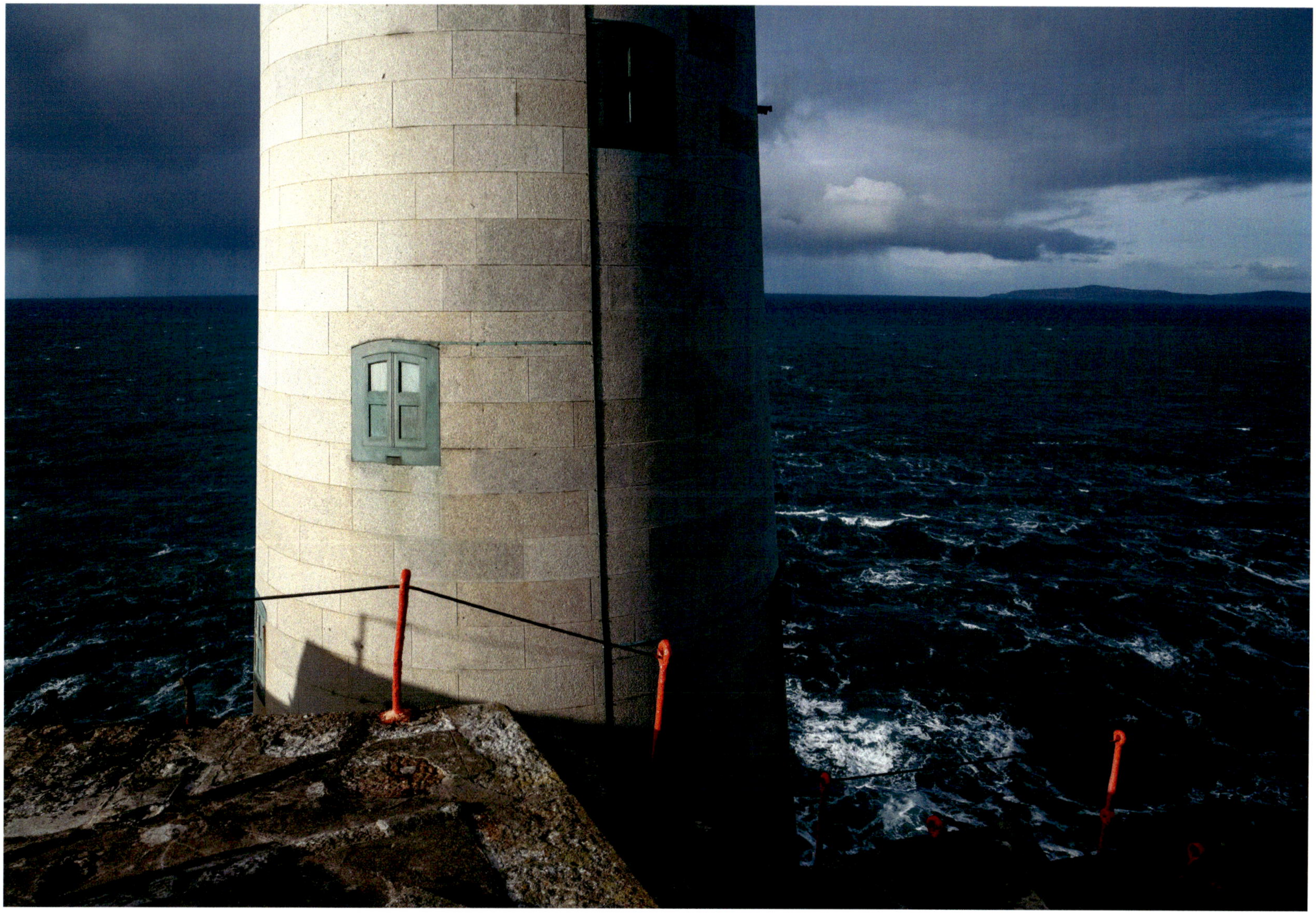

'On a bare rock surrounded by sea…'

Fastnet Lighthouse is a 54-metre-tall lighthouse (the tallest in Ireland) situated on the remote Fastnet Rock in the Atlantic Ocean. It is the most southerly point of Ireland and lies 8 miles off the mainland.

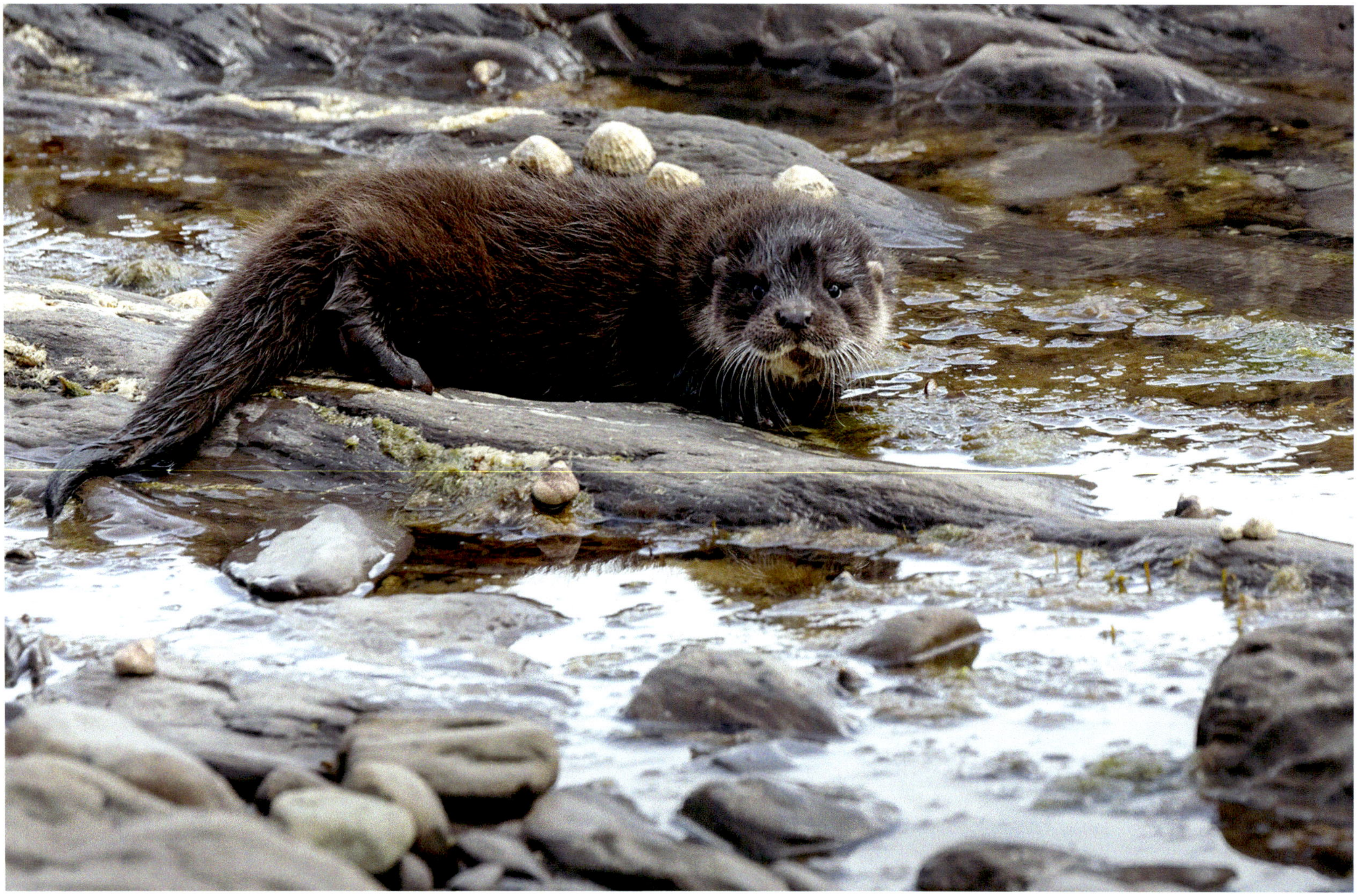

'Baby otters play beside the shore…'

NIGHTFALL IN INISHTRAHULL

The kittiwakes and cormorants go to sleep,
Puffins into their nesting burrows creep,
Grey seals in their harem caverns snore,
And baby otters play beside the shore.

Click-beetles sheathe their short translucent wings,
Young bees come home with pollen-laden slings,
Winged ants mate on the low sodden walls,
And garden worms come forth from tube-shaped halls.

The flowers close their petals for the night, ·
Daisy, violet, starwort and eyebright;
White clover folds and crinkles as if dead,
Whilst bedstraw to the zephyrus nods its head.

An oily patch marks herring in the bay,
Beside, migrating salmon leap in play,
Elvers climb the streamlet's pebbley rungs,
Where tadpoles rise to test their half-formed lungs.

Departing sunbeams linger on the tide,
Ensaffroning the wavelets far and wide,
Betwixt the clouds the moon is rising full,
Venus shines bright, night falls at Inishtrahull!

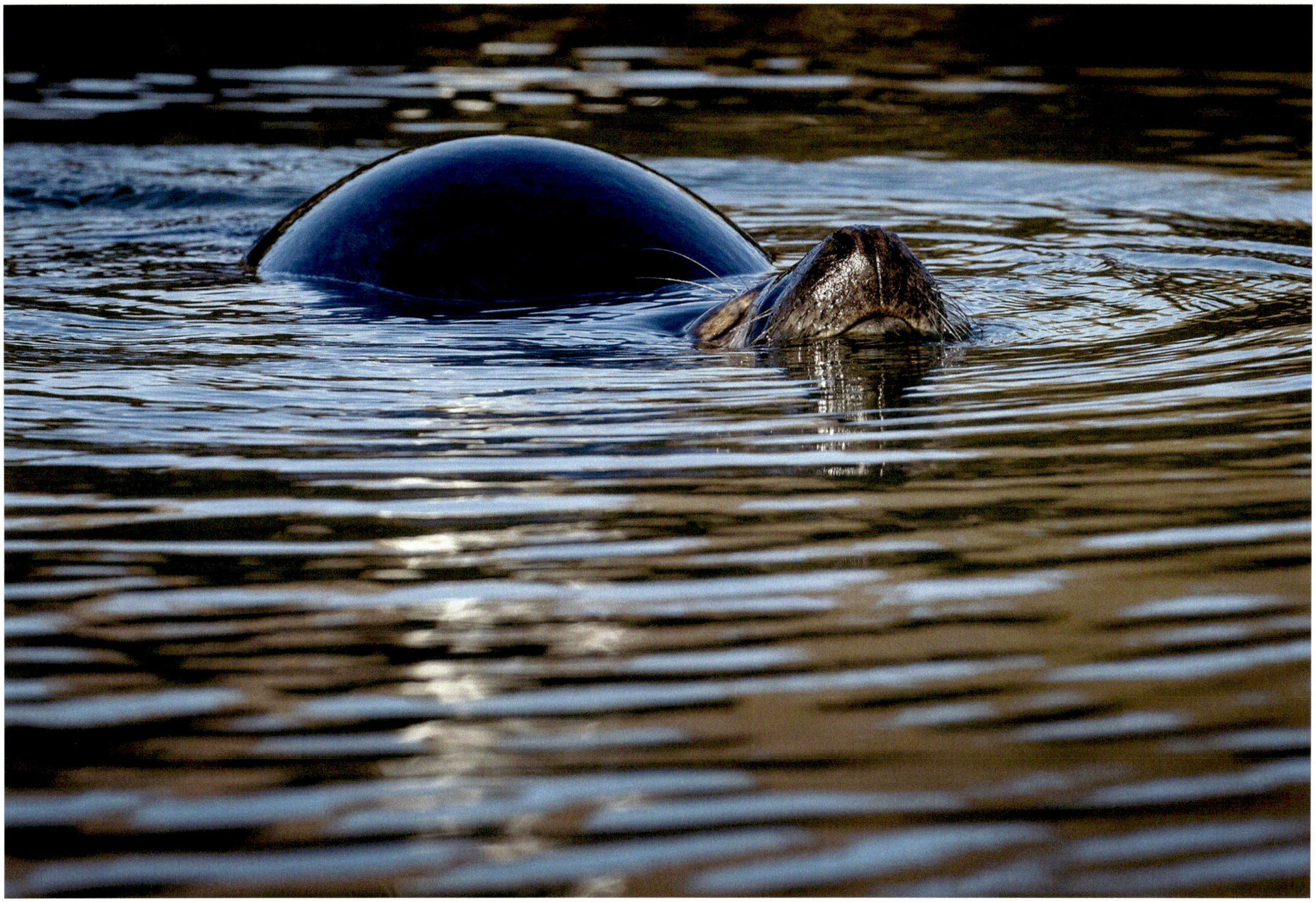

'Grey seals in their harem caverns snore…"

The Eurasian Otter (facing page) is found in a variety of aquatic habitats in Ireland such as lakes, rivers, streams, estuaries, marshland, canals and along the coast. It is regarded as one of Ireland's most charismatic native mammal species. The otter is usually born in early spring, though they can be born in any month of the year. The young otter doesn't enter the water until it is about 2 months old, is suckled for 6 months and remains dependent on the bitch for about a year and until at least as big as she is.

The Grey Seal (above) often relaxes and sleeps in the water, floating horizontally on the surface with their noses bobbing above the water.

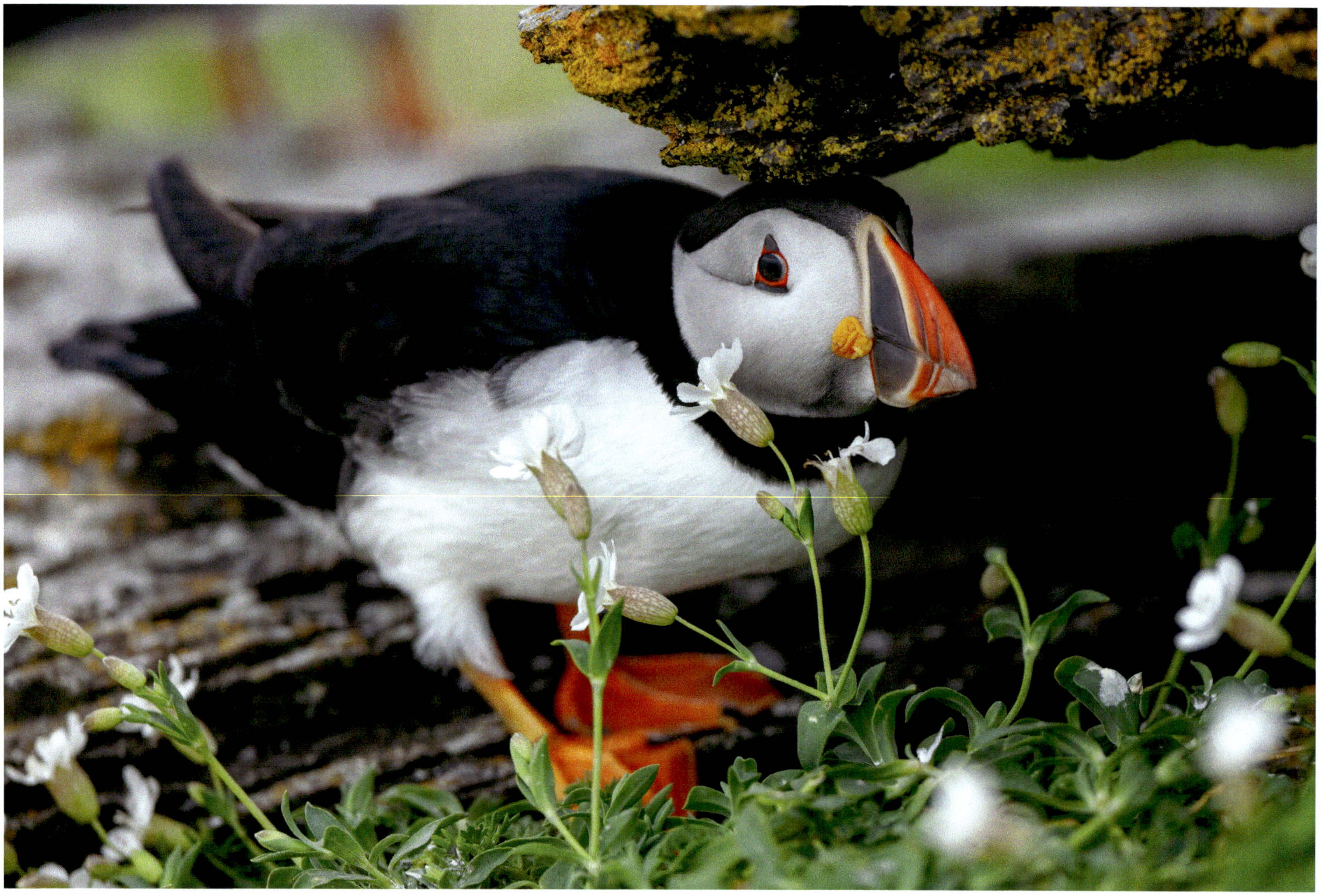

'Puffins into their nesting burrows creep…'

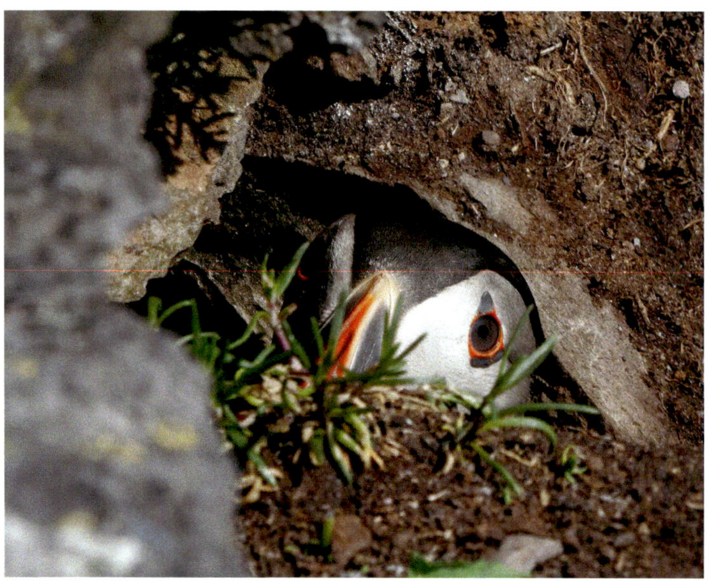

Atlantic Puffins nest underground in burrows they dig themselves or take over rabbit burrows. Where burrowing is not possible, they nest in crevices and cavities on rocky islands with short vegetation and on sea cliffs. They form long-term pair bonds with the male building the nest, the female laying a single egg and both parents taking turns to incubate the egg and feed the chick. Male puffins perform most of the work of clearing out the nest area, which is sometimes lined with grass, feathers or seaweed.

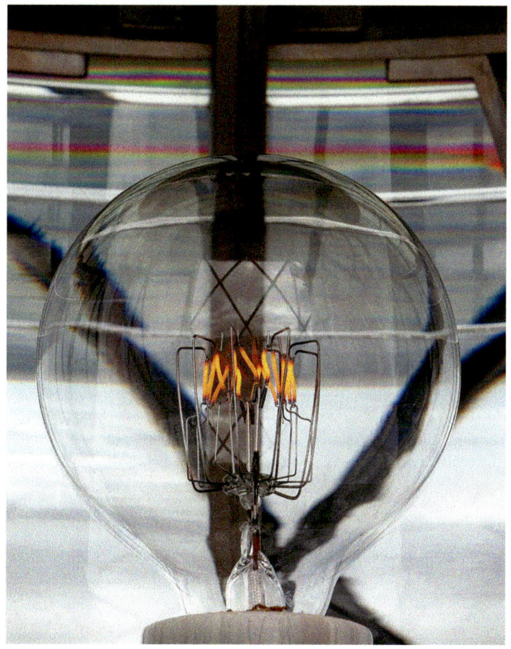

SOLILOQUY OF A LIGHTHOUSE-KEEPER

Out on this rock is a lonely place
Attending the lighthouse light,
Day after day I see no face,
Only the moon's by night;
At times the roaring sea is hushed
And mirrors the starry heavens above,
Or wavelets dance, Auroral flushed,
Bejewelling each wrack-strewn cove;
Aslant the dome steel fog-jibs sway
Out on this rock ....

Out on this rock in its mantle drab
Thick mist comes stealing 'round the tower,
Ships' sirens moan and gulls' cries stab
The air, as in the lee they cower;
Skies break: the sun's about to win ·
Through cloud, and beam on every side;
Lag basking-shark show dorsal fin,
Swim lazily against the west-going tide,
And fed, the otter comes to play
Out on this rock....

Out on this rock at sunset's glow,
White spindrift on the lantern-pane
Sparkles and glistens, and runs below
In rivulets of fire into the sea again.
A ghostly form comes floating down,
Alights upon the flagpole's stay,
Great saucer eyes and speckled gown,
An owl, bewildered by the ray;
And the lantern clock tocks time away
Out on this rock....

Out on this rock sweet moments come
When memory glides on swiftest wings
To my childhood cot; a bent-thatched home;
To an ivied church where a choir sings.
Then I kneel; and pray that when I grow old,
When the heavenly keeper my soul shall call,
He will knight me with a sword of gold,
And end my lonesomeness 'midst loved ones all;
No lighthouse light, in The Light's fulgent ray
Far from this rock....

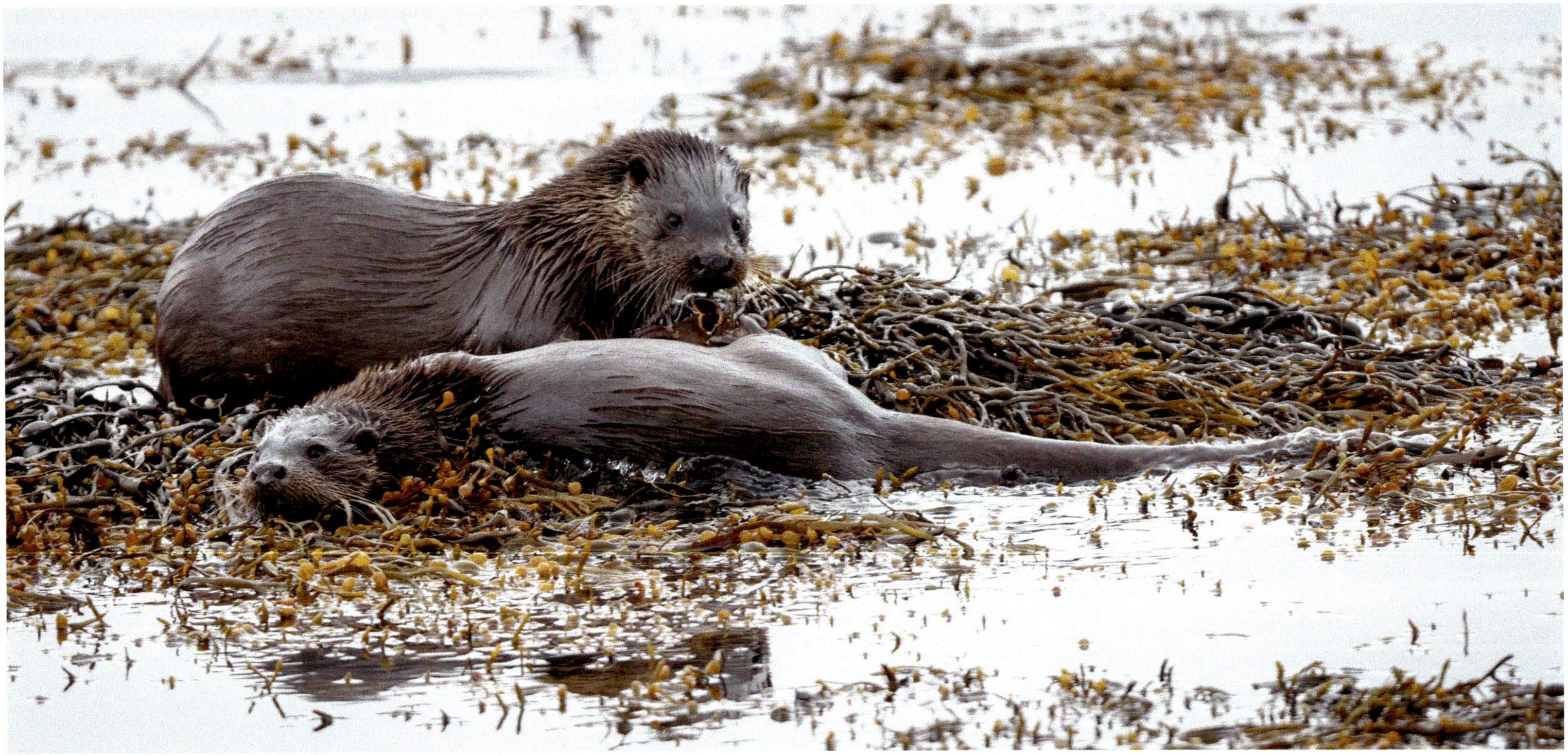

'And fed, the otter comes to play out on this rock…'

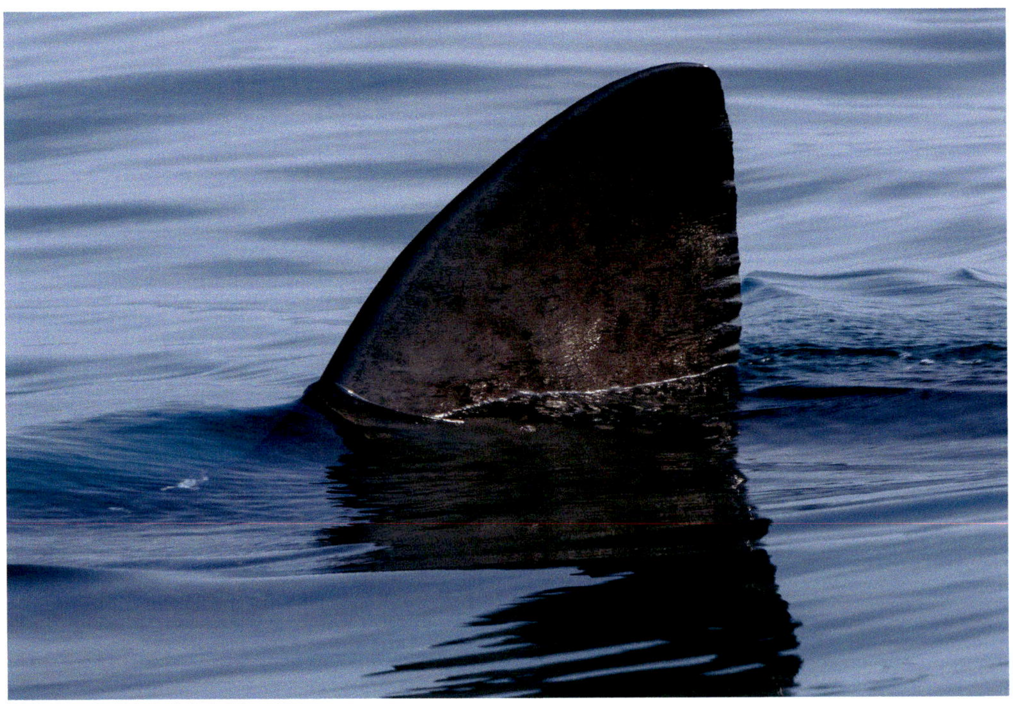

'Lag basking-shark show dorsal fin…'

Male Eurasian Otters are entirely solitary and only come into contact with females to mate with much splashing and playing. They are very mobile (spending much time travelling its long territory), social, and playful but also a territorial animal prone to sudden aggression. Where a group of otters are seen together, it is undoubtedly a female with cubs. Cubs do play with each other and this may be important in helping them develop their hunting skills and social bonds. Although territorial spraint-marking may warn away intruding otters, it does not prevent fights and the large amount of bacteria in their bite can result in death.

The Basking Shark is the second largest living shark found in all the world's temperate oceans and is known to move and migrate through the Irish Sea, feeding on the nutrient-rich waters. The shark takes its name from its feeding habit of slowly cruising below the surface of the water as a harmless filter feeder. It follows plankton concentrations in the water column and is therefore often visible at the surface and often close to land.

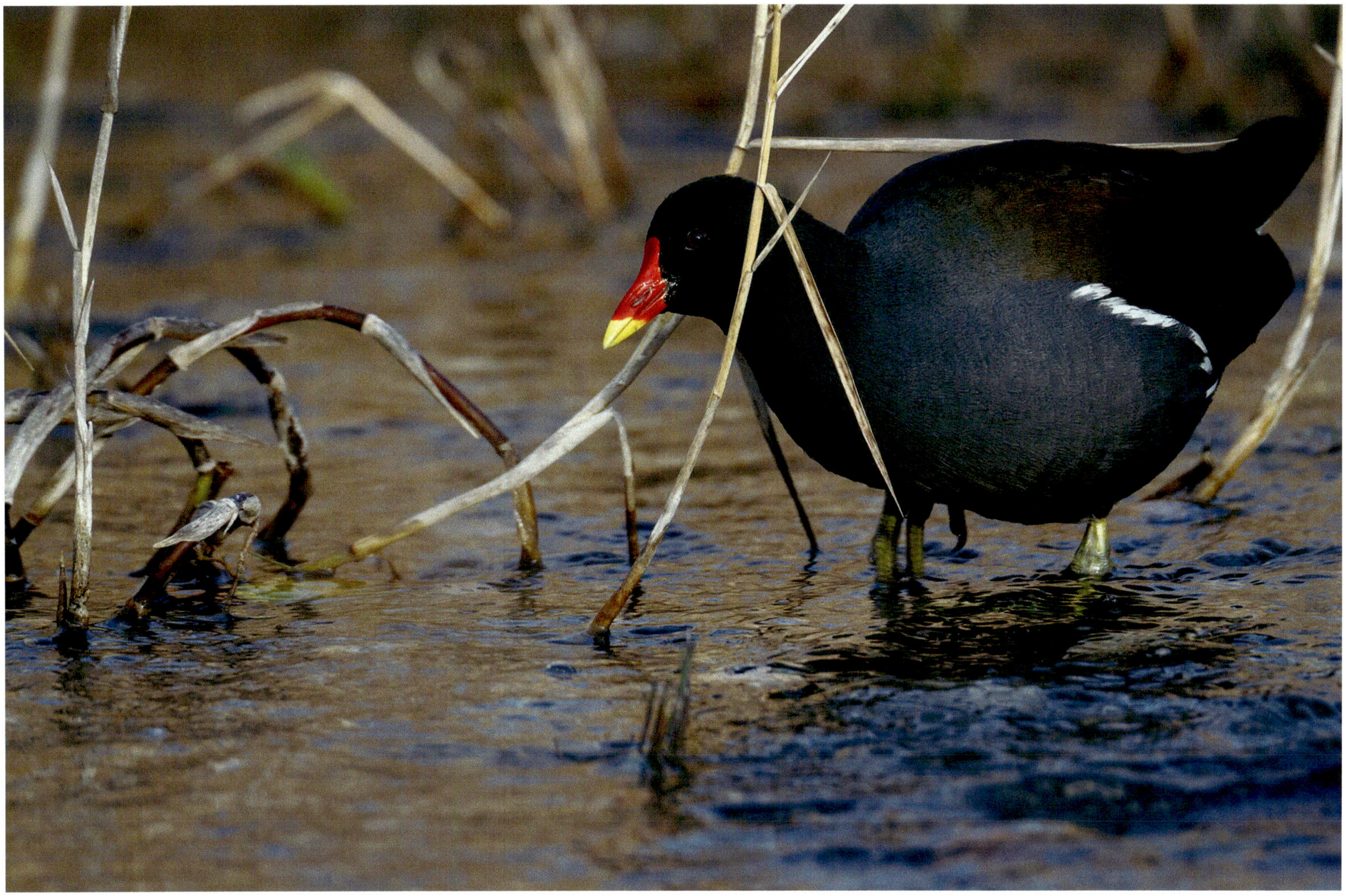

'...clucking water-hens.'

LITTLE BLACK BEETLE.

DOWN by the river one sunny May day
A little black beetle came out to play;
He ran through the mosses, climbed over stones,
And crawled up the pipe-stems of dead frogs' bones.

The little black beetle looked trim and neat,
His wing-cases gleamed in the blazing heat,
A humorous twinkle was in his eye,
And he joked with the red-ants passing by.

Down to the stream came a thirsty young thrush,
The little black beetle dived 'neath a rush,
Sagacious of safety he lay there awhile,
Then out again with a dare-devil smile.

Sat on a cushion of smooth meadow-grass
Watching the bumble-bees pass and repass,
Saw gnats emerging from pupal-skin boats, ·
A host of nymph-earwigs changing their coats.

Saw spiders weave webby concentric rings,
Heard grasshoppers tuning their fiddley-wings,
The swish of a trout as he jumped to the fly,
The squeaks of a vole with a stoat in full cry.

Heard husky moss-cheepers and wee willow-wrens,
Green linnets, a redpoll, clucking water-hens;
That little black beetle who came out to play,
Down by the river one sunny May day.

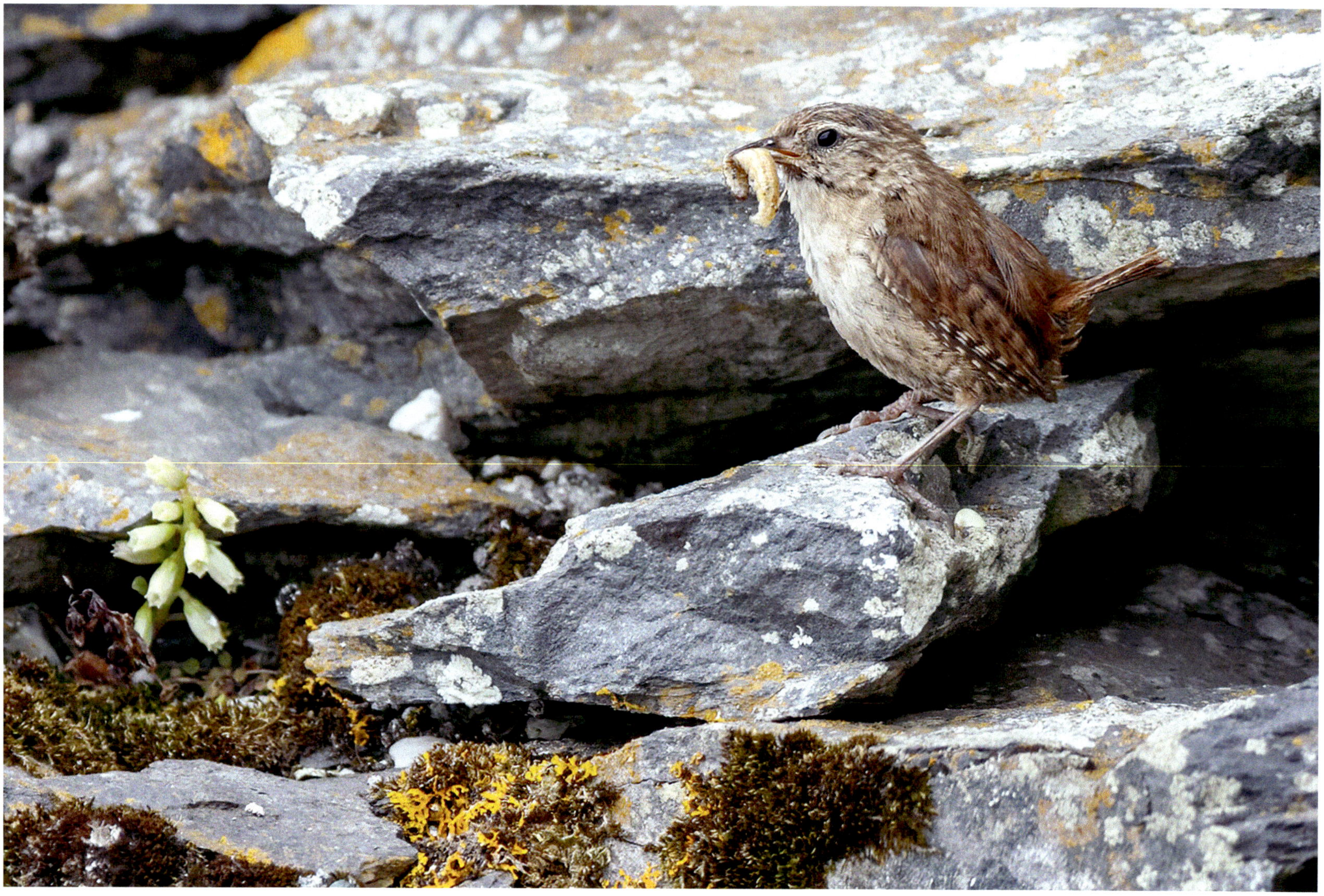

'…Heard husky moss-cheepers and wee willow-wrens, green linnets, a redpoll, clucking water-hens…'

In Ireland the Moorhen (previous page) is known in many districts by the nickname Waterhen. The Moorhen is usually quite secretive and feeds on both plants and animals. Its long unwebbed toes have flaps of skin which open for swimming purposes. The call is short and explosive and given from dense vegetation.

The Wren (above) is a tiny bird with incredibly loud voice. Its familiar song is delivered with such gusto as if it is trying to burst its lungs. On very cold nights these very small birds seek each other, huddling together in an old nest or bird box to stay warm and maintain energy.

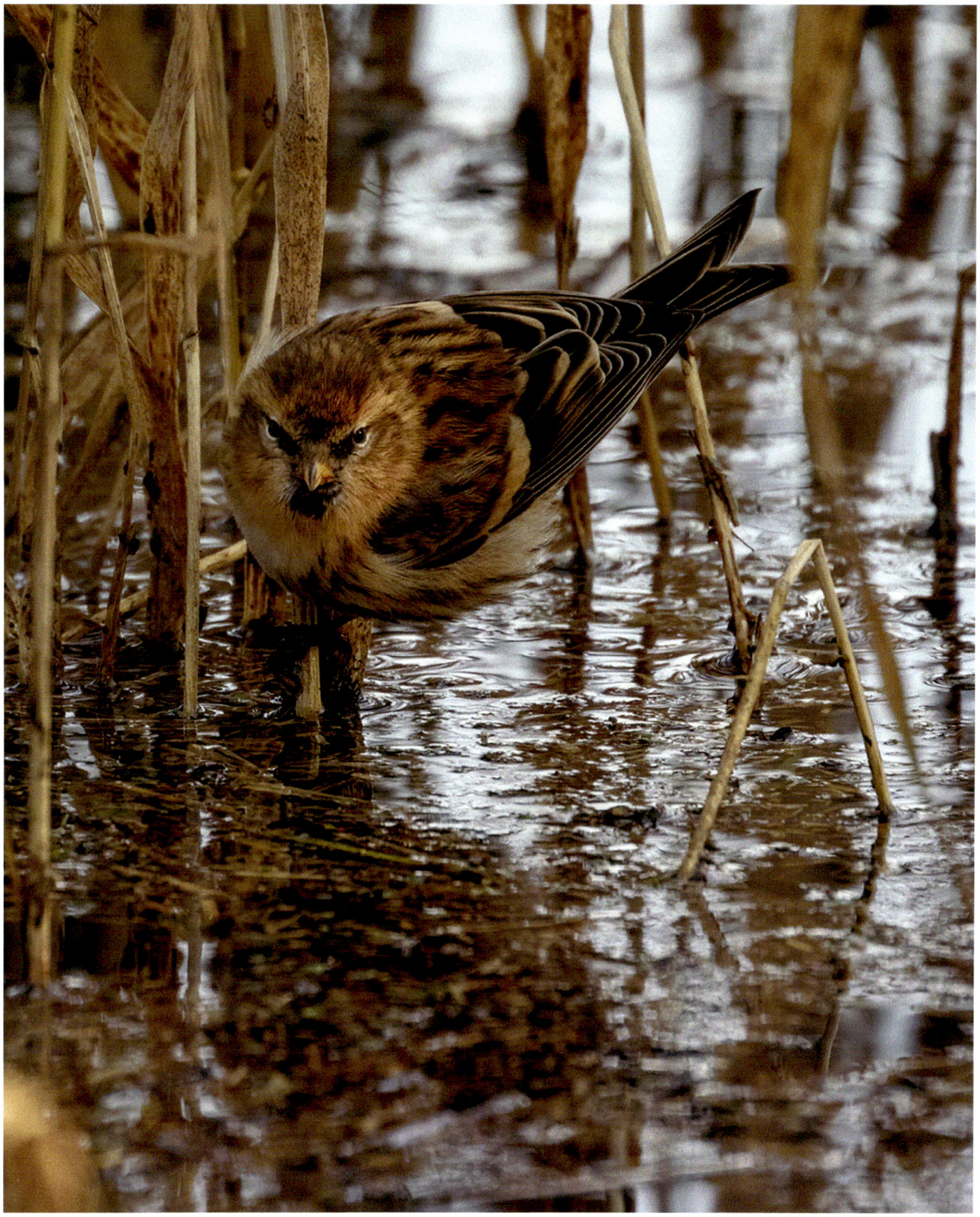

Redpolls are small charismatic finches that form vocal chattering flocks. The adult male Redpoll has a reddish forehead . It is mobile and restless and can acrobatically cling or hang upside-down on cones or perch nimbly on vertical and bent twigs.

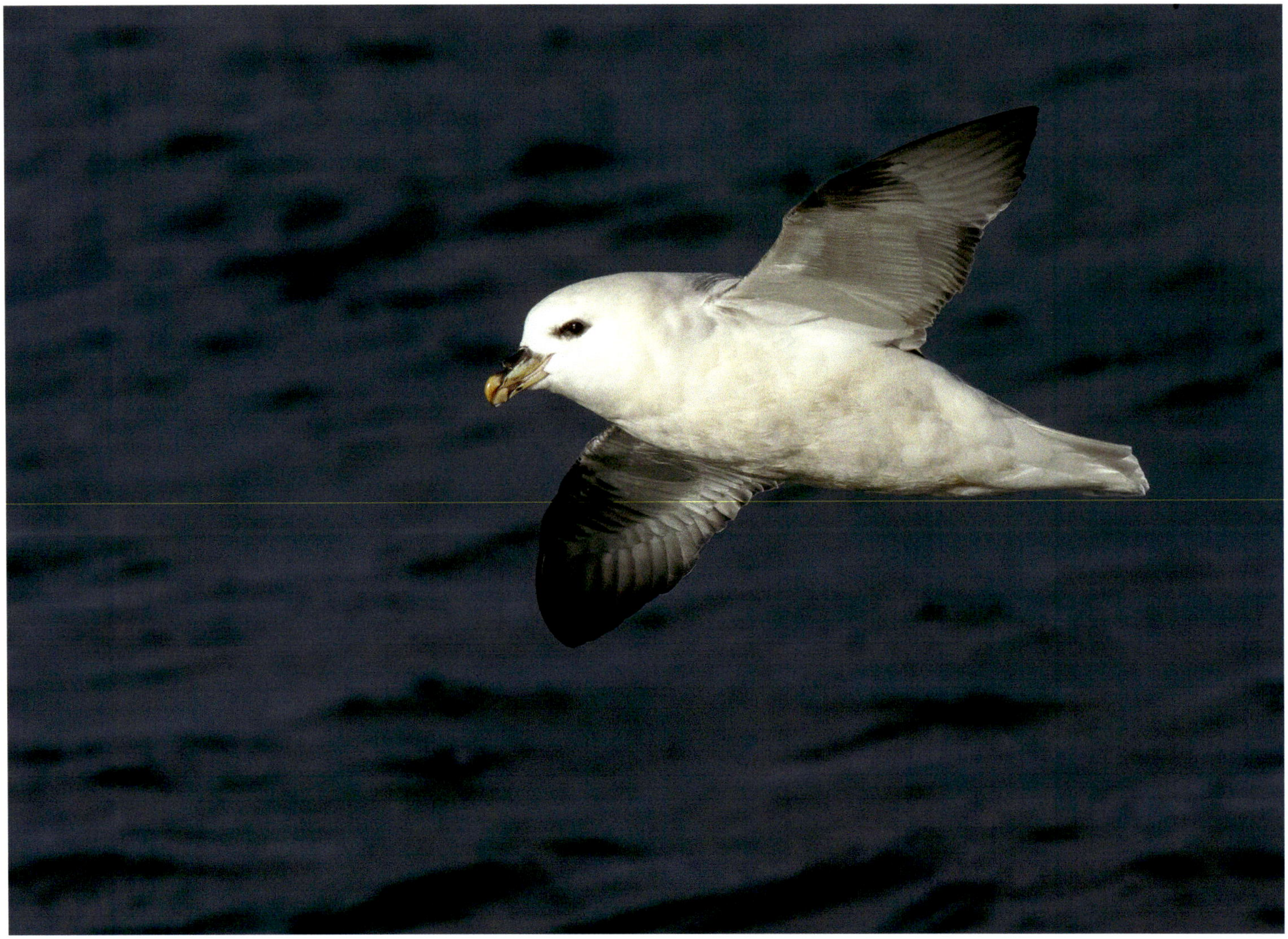

'Where surf denotes the harbour bar a tube-billed fulmar petrel wings.'

NIGHTFALL

The sea threads restlessly afar,
Grey home for hidden fishy things;
Where surf denotes the harbour bar
A tube-billed fulmar-petrel wings.

From weed-veiled rocks, with croaking talk
The old rooks wrench the dog-winkles ;
Jet kilted legs at stalking walk,
Brown beady eyes gay rogue twinkles.

Resplendent in the spume-fed nooks,
Scottish Lavage and Scurvy Grass ;
Ripe Cleaver's recurved prickle hooks
Like red hail, shower each glabrous mass.

Now sewin leap from tide to air,
Albescent in the amber light,
And otter coming from his lair
Yikkers at this finned fulgent sight.

The sun sinks low, the moon hangs high
On horns that point the Milky-Way;
A meteor falls down the sky—
Blue night enfolds the views of day!

Fulmars superficially resemble gulls but are readily distinguished by their soaring flight on stiff wings perfectly at home in strong winds and by their well-developed tails and tube noses. The Fulmar can smell its prey and see it with his large dark eyes. They can drink saltwater or freshwater as, like many sea birds, they have nasal glands that excreted excess salt. Fulmars, unlike gulls, are unable to stand except for a fleeting second, so they sit down the instant they land.

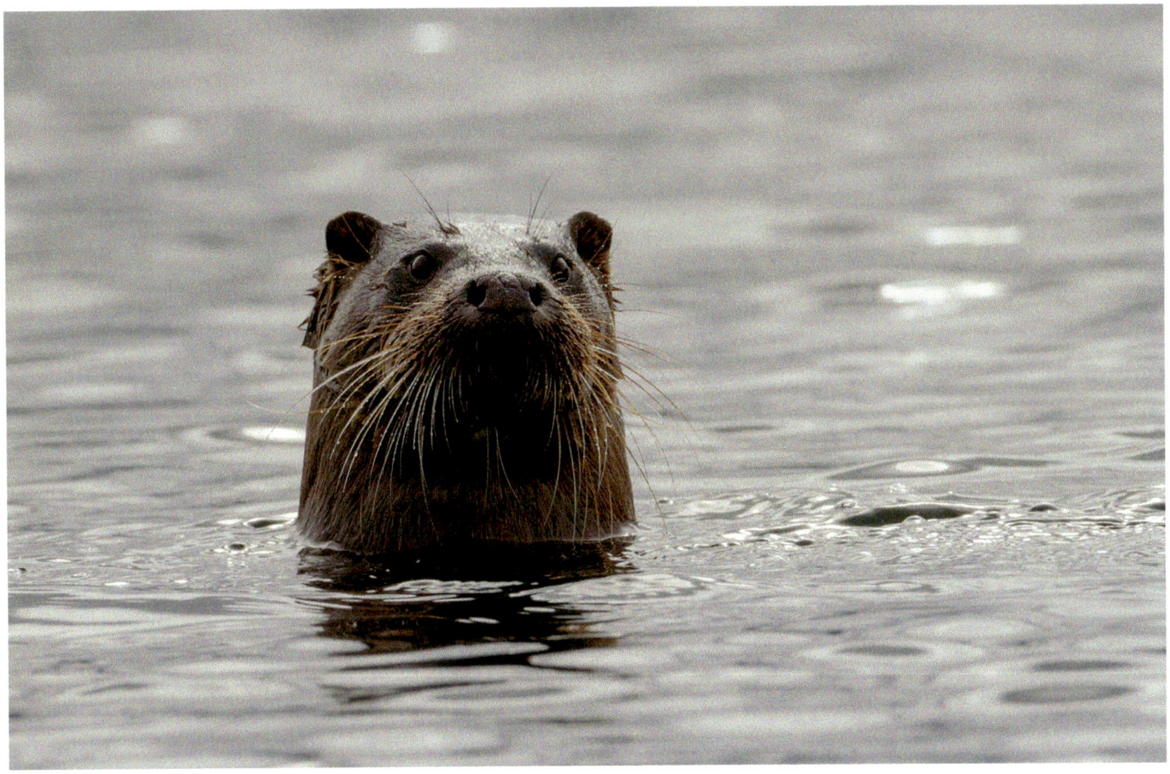

'And otter coming from his lair…'

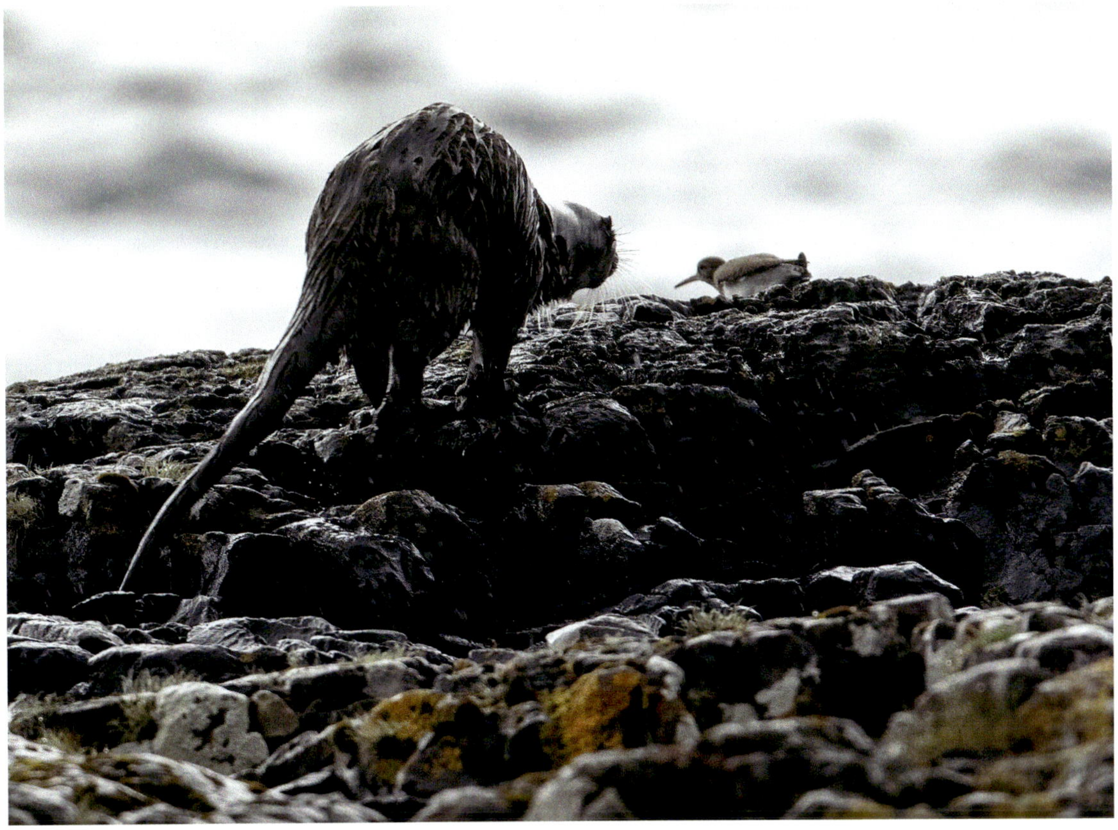

An otter's lair, called a holt, is used for sleeping and resting. The most common type of holt is a hole leading to a cavity under the roots of a tree which is dry and has space to sleep in. Otters also enjoy warmth and sunlight so frequently curl up to sleep the day away above ground. They inhabit both freshwater rivers and lakes as well as coastal areas. Coastal dwelling otters must be close to a fresh water source to enable them to rid their fur of salt. They have a double layer of coat to keep them warm which is so important in this streamlined, active animal which spends much time fishing in cold water. Their ears and nostrils are closed when swimming under water and the bubbles seen on the surface are caused by pressure forcing air bubbles from the otter's coat. In dark or muddy waters their extravagant whiskers are used to detect movement. They have large webbed paws but much of their power comes from a long flexible back and muscular tail. The length of its back makes the otter a poor jumper but it can climb well.

The otter feeds mainly on fish such as salmon and trout, as well as eels and small fish. They will however feed on a range of prey when available and the remains of birds and small mammals have also been found in sprint. The otter in the image on the left is stalking a Redshank, but the lucky bird escaped.

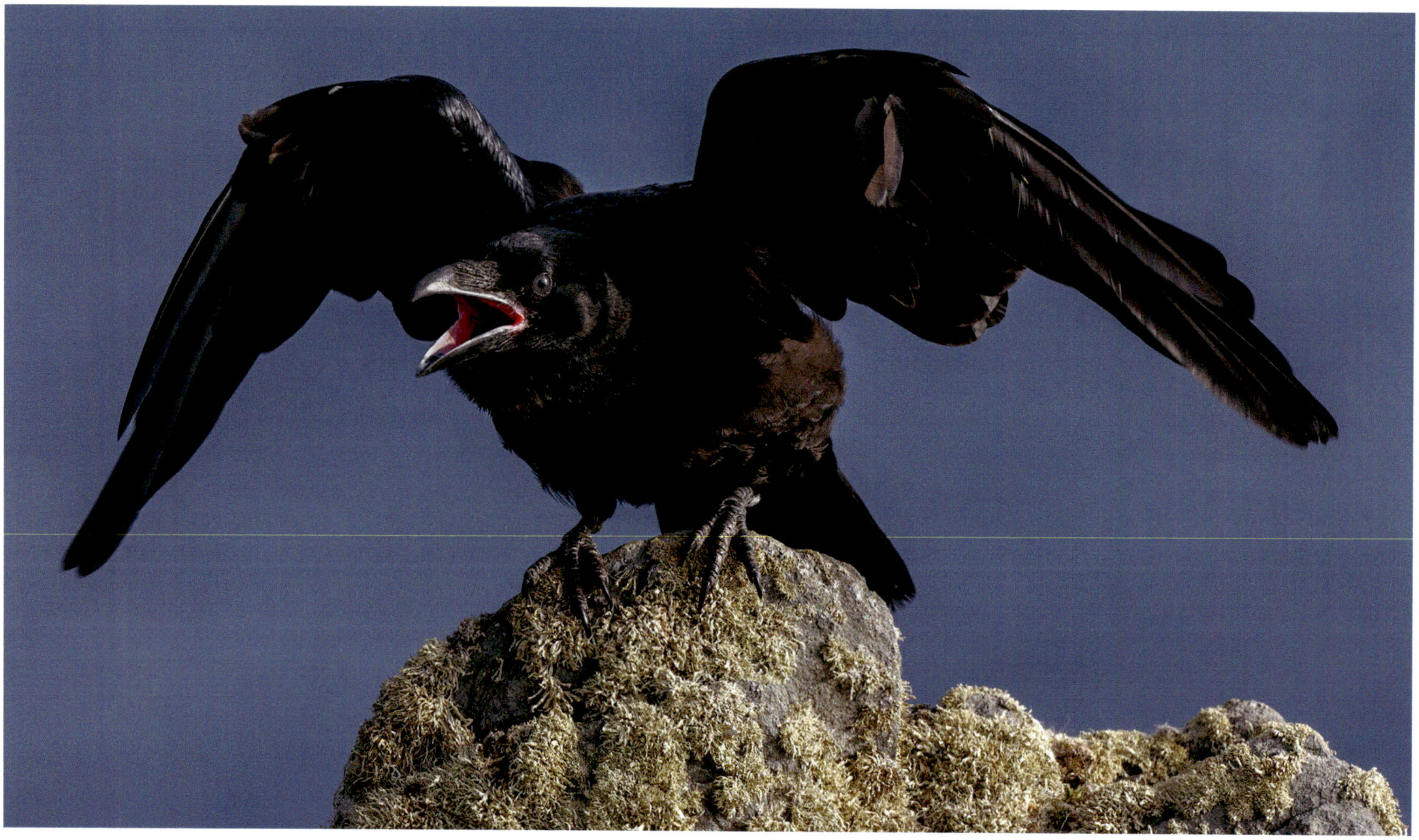

'The old rooks wrench the dog-winkles …'

The Rook has ruffled drooping belly feathers which distinguish it from other crows. They are gregarious in all their habits, building together in trees and being together in search of food. They are intelligent and resourceful birds, and there is a sense that there is much more to them than meets the eye.

HIKERS IN DONEGAL

The fields are full of flowers as we pass,
Primrose, coltsfoot daisy, and knot-grass;
Carpets of mosaic patterns smelling sweet
And glistering in the sun's life-giving heat.

Buds and leaflets deck the greening trees.
Whose sapless old limbs creak to the wafting breeze,
And woodlarks on the topmost skiey branches
Pipe their liquid nuptial songs in snatches.

Hark to the thrush, the thieving jackdaws call,
The wheatears chattering on the old stone wall;
Voices so pleasing to traffic-deafened ears
Our faces brighten, each drops the mask it wears.

A football-jerseyed bee is buzzing by,
Next comes a nectar-seeking butterfly;
On a mushroom feasts aspersa the snail,
A silvery slip-stream oozing from his tail.

At distance by the haze-embroidedr'd hill
Two hunting falcons soar, then stoop to kill;
Wild goats on the lofty toothéd ridges lie
Silhouetted on the wide brocaded sky.

Hikers in Donegal, we stroll along,
Finding peace in Nature and in Her song.

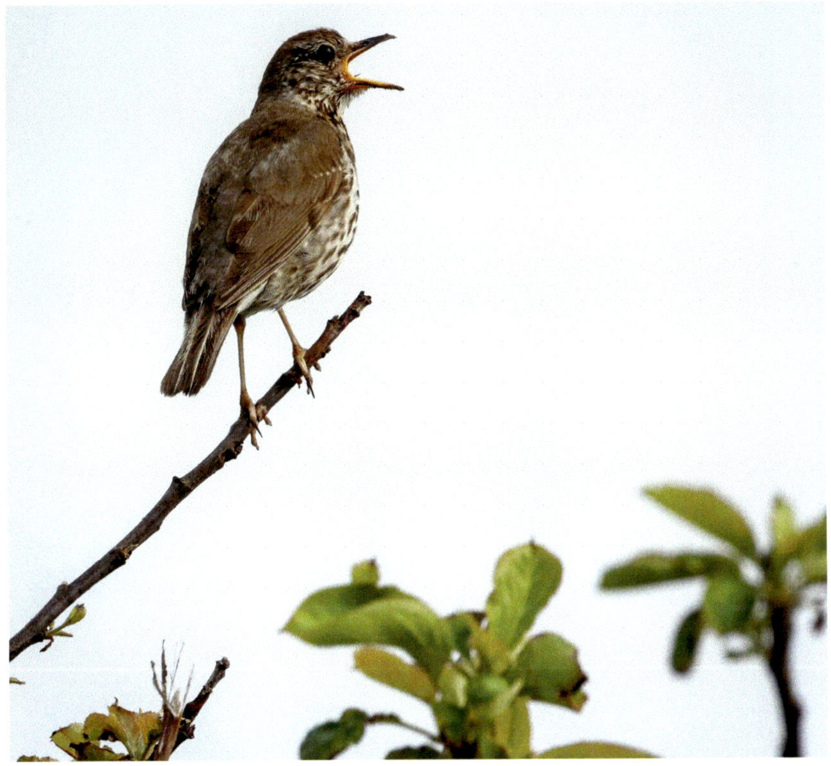

'Hark to the thrush…'

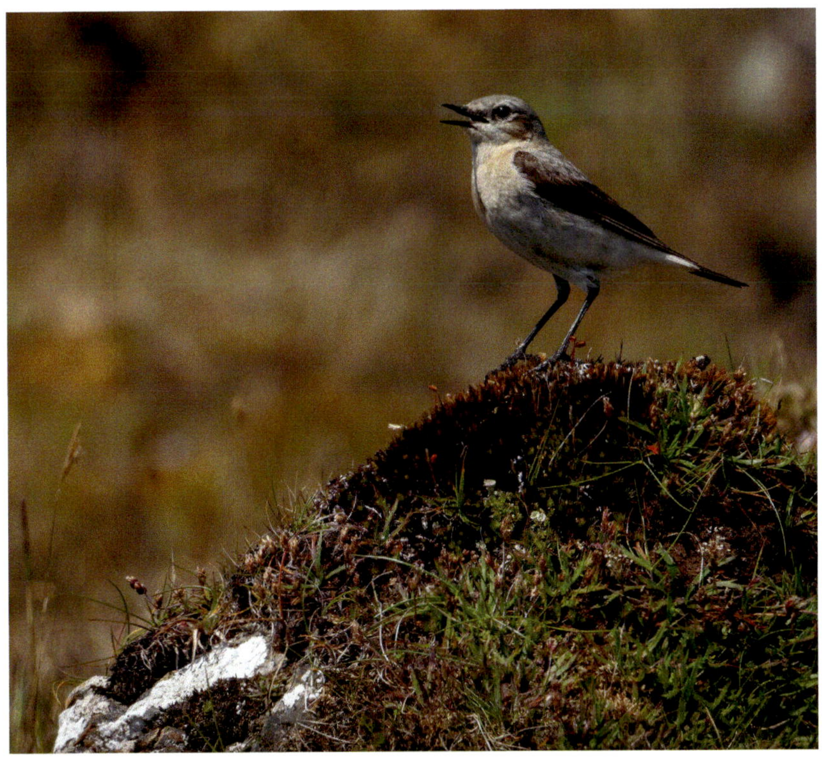

'The wheatears chattering on the old stone wall…'

The Song Thrush's distinctive melodious song has frequently been referred to in poetry. They sing mainly in the morning and evening, usually from the top of live conifers.

Wheatears can be seen running or hopping along the ground and walls. Its jumbled-sounding song is quite variable, often including whistles, trills, and mimicry.

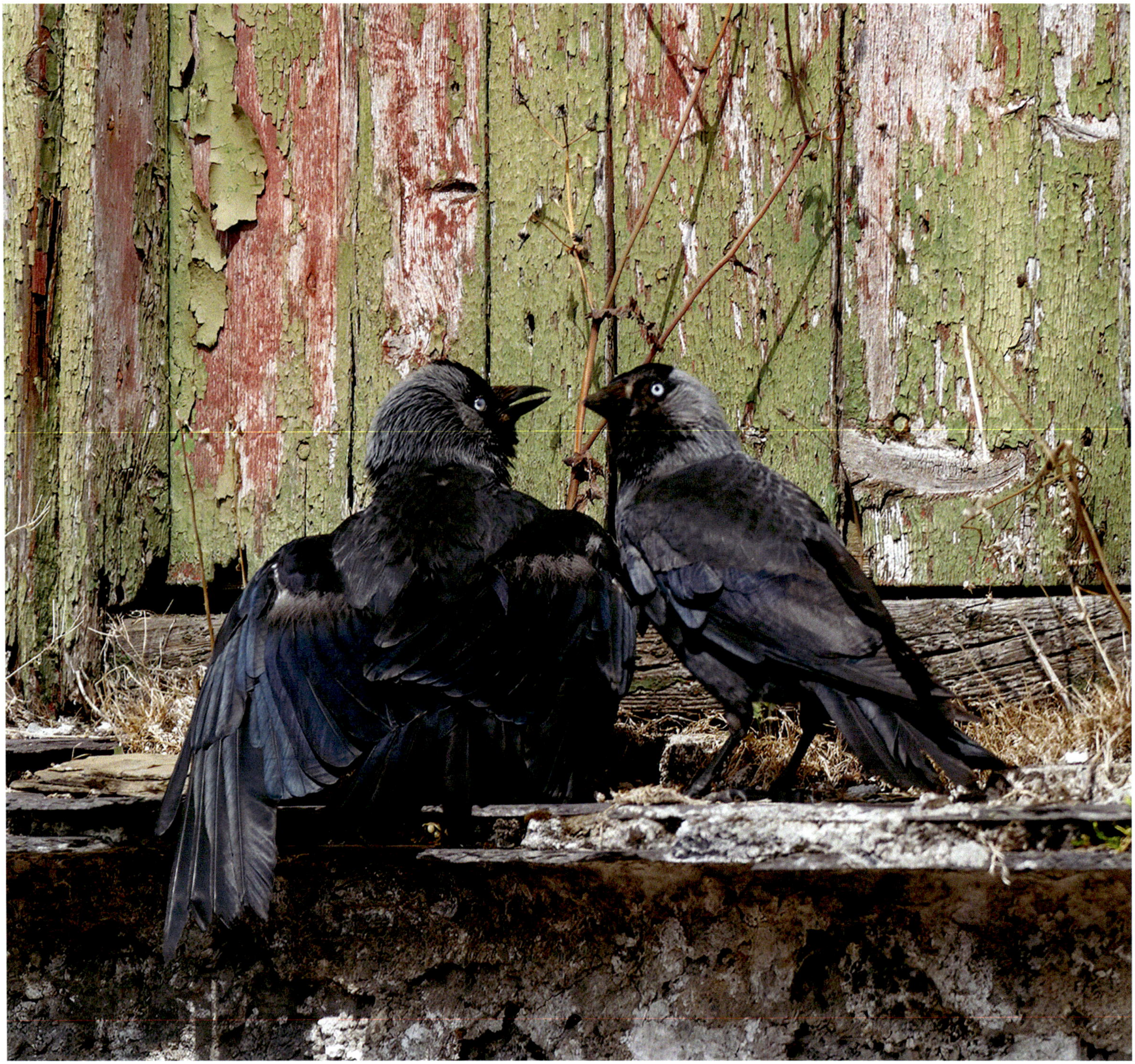

'Hark to the Thrush, the thieving jackdaws call…'

Whilst scavenging for food, Jackdaws keep a sharp look-out for bright, glittering objects which it loves to collect and take back to its untidy nest. This clever bird has a useful habit of ridding sheep of parasites and eating harmful insects.

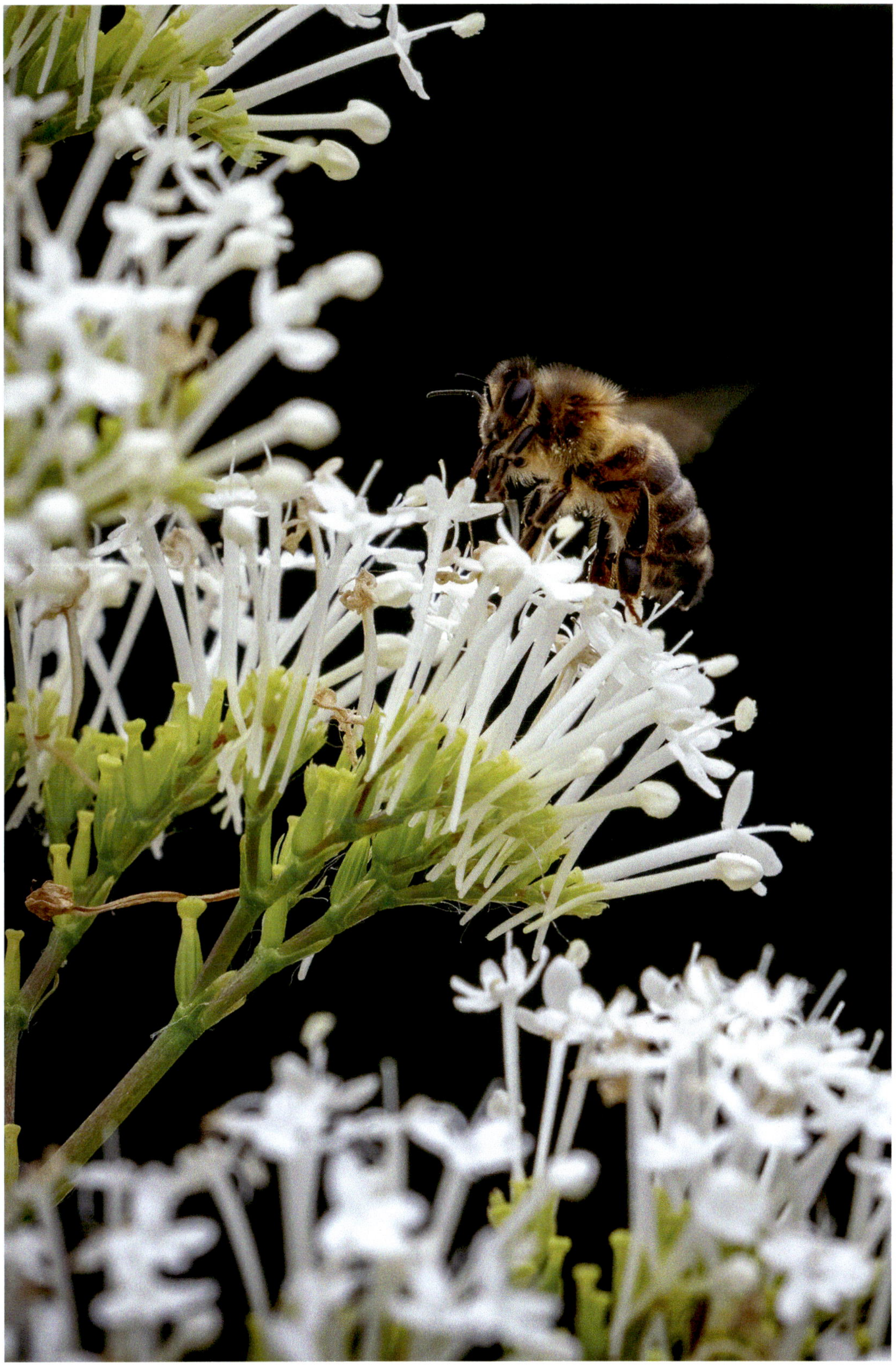

'A football-jerseyed bee is buzzing by...'

The Honey Bee is popular around the world due to their characteristics of highly effective pollination and nectar collection. There are over 100 bee species native to Ireland but only the honey bee gives honey. Some bees act as scouts and when they have found the right kind of bloom they perform a dance which indicates to the rest of the bees in the hive the exact direction and distance of the pollen bearing plants they have discovered.

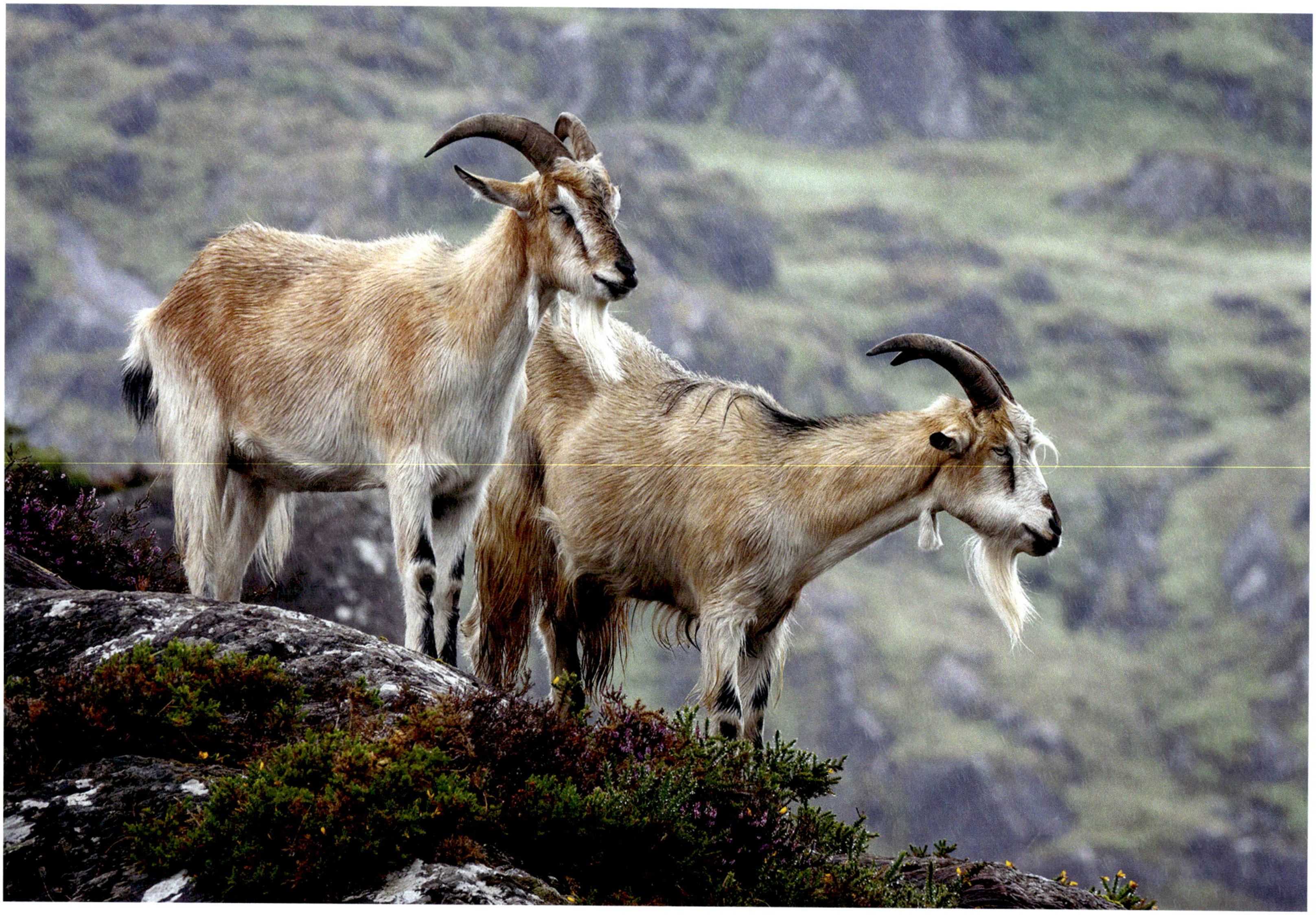

'Wild goats on the lofty toothéd ridges lie sillhouetted on the wide brocaded sky.'

Herds of wild goats are established in the west of the country where they roam isolated areas since escaping from the domestic herds of early Irish settlers. The feral goats at Malin and Mizen live in loosely associated groups of up to a dozen females with one or more males. Their split hooves allow them to climb rocky upland areas where even sheep struggle to graze.

MYSELF

Oftimes I sit beside the sunlit sea
And listen to the murmur of its waves,
Watching the fishing boats with sails full-free,
And kittiwakes love-nesting in ledged caves.

For in the whisperings of the white lipp'd foam
My heart is wafted up, dull care away;
I rise, a worker knowing life's a poem,
And happiness pervades my simple day.

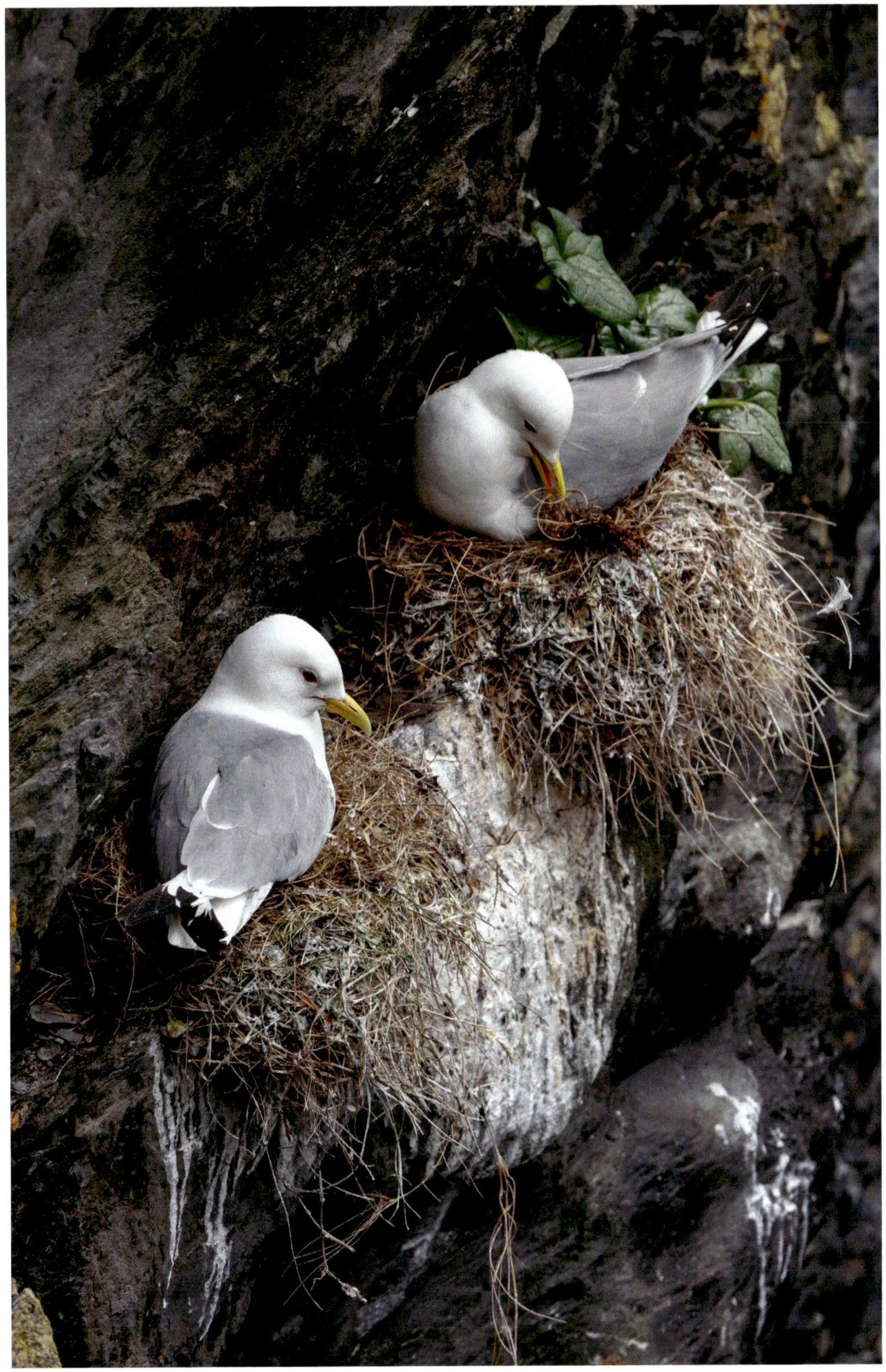

'And kittiwakes love-nesting in ledged caves.'

Kittiwakes winter at sea and are rarely seen over land. They breed in colonies on steep sea cliffs where they build nesting platforms on the most vertical and sometimes improbably steep areas. Building the nest in order to welcome their fragile eggs is a tedious task and requires time and energy. The parents begin the nest with a layer of mud and grass with a higher rim around the edge in order to keep the eggs from rolling out. It is lined with soft and dry material such as moss, grass or seaweed. Once the eggs are laid, the parents will take turns and incubate their clutch. Birds pick food from the surface of the sea in flight or settle on the water and then shallow dive. They may also plunge from a height like a tern.

Ground-nesting birds tend to wander about. However, young Kittiwakes born on cliff edges have an innate fear of falling over the edge until they can fledge. If food is in short supply, the chick that has hatched first and is stronger will dominate the younger chick and eventually push it over the edge to a certain death.

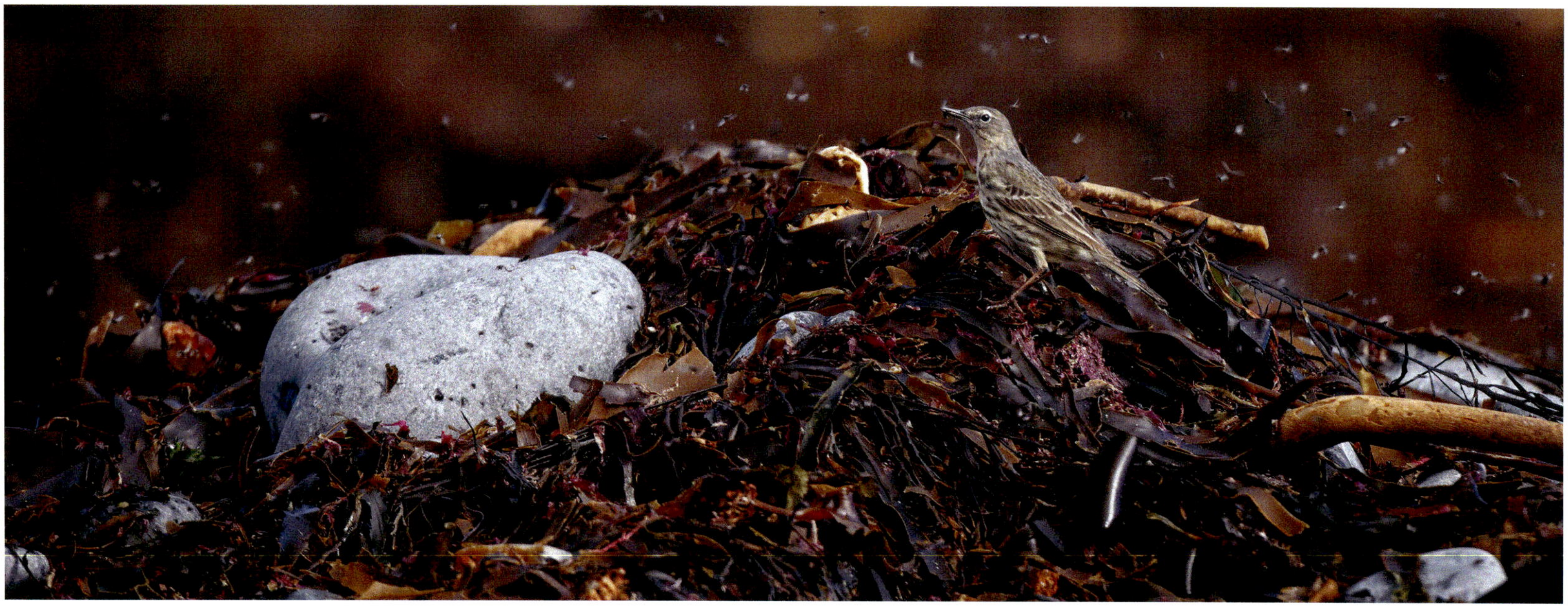

'Rock-pipits ebbed to stardust skies…'

SANDPORT

The earwigs cowered in their nests
Beneath us on the sandy brugh,
And meadow-moths with mottled vests
Drank sea-campion's saline dew.

Grey ghost-gulls gyred above sea
With hungry raucous mewing cries
Green-plover trilled their courting glee,
Rock-pipits ebbed to stardust skies.

About a foot or two away
The snail italia stretchéd out,
His shell-house banded silver-grey
Balanced behind his hornéd snout.

Wee weevils gleaming golden green
Eat leaflets off a nettle-stem,
Maternally a wild wasp-queen
Foraged the waste-land's tangled hem.

And as we stood there, left and right
Two skylarks rose on feathered floats,
To fill our hearts with wild delight,
Sweet music bubbling from their throats.

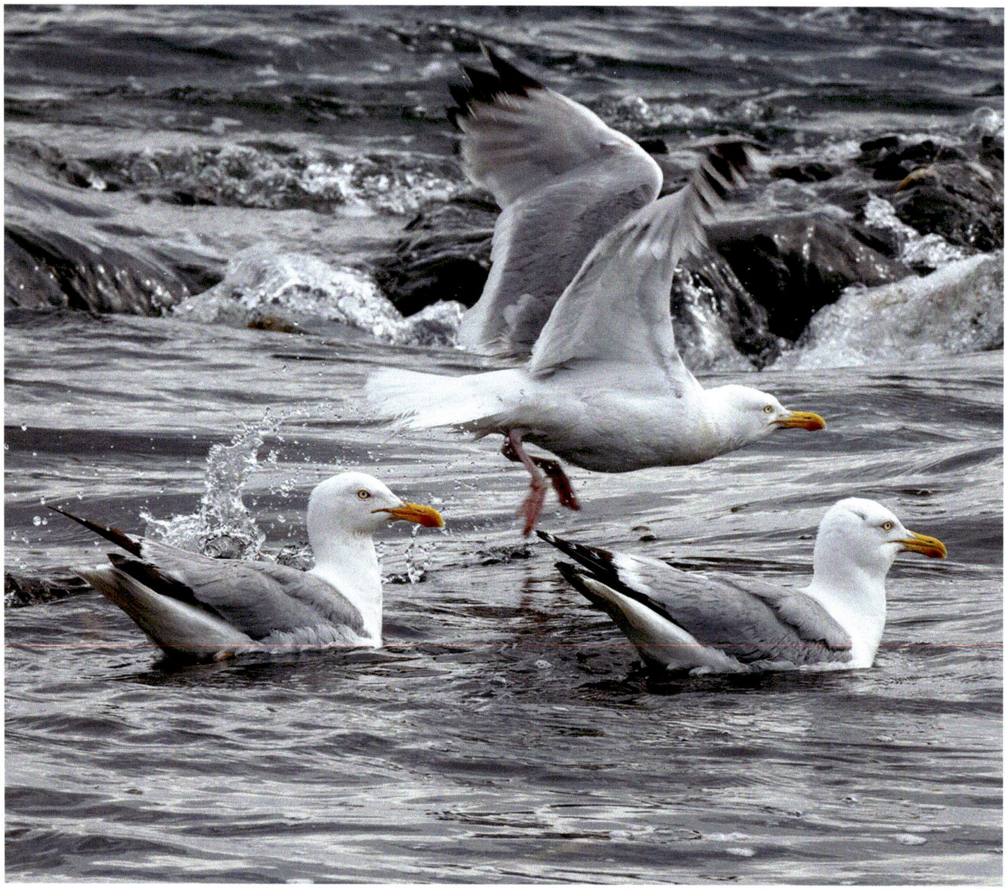

'Grey ghost-gulls gyred above sea with hungry raucous mewing cries…'

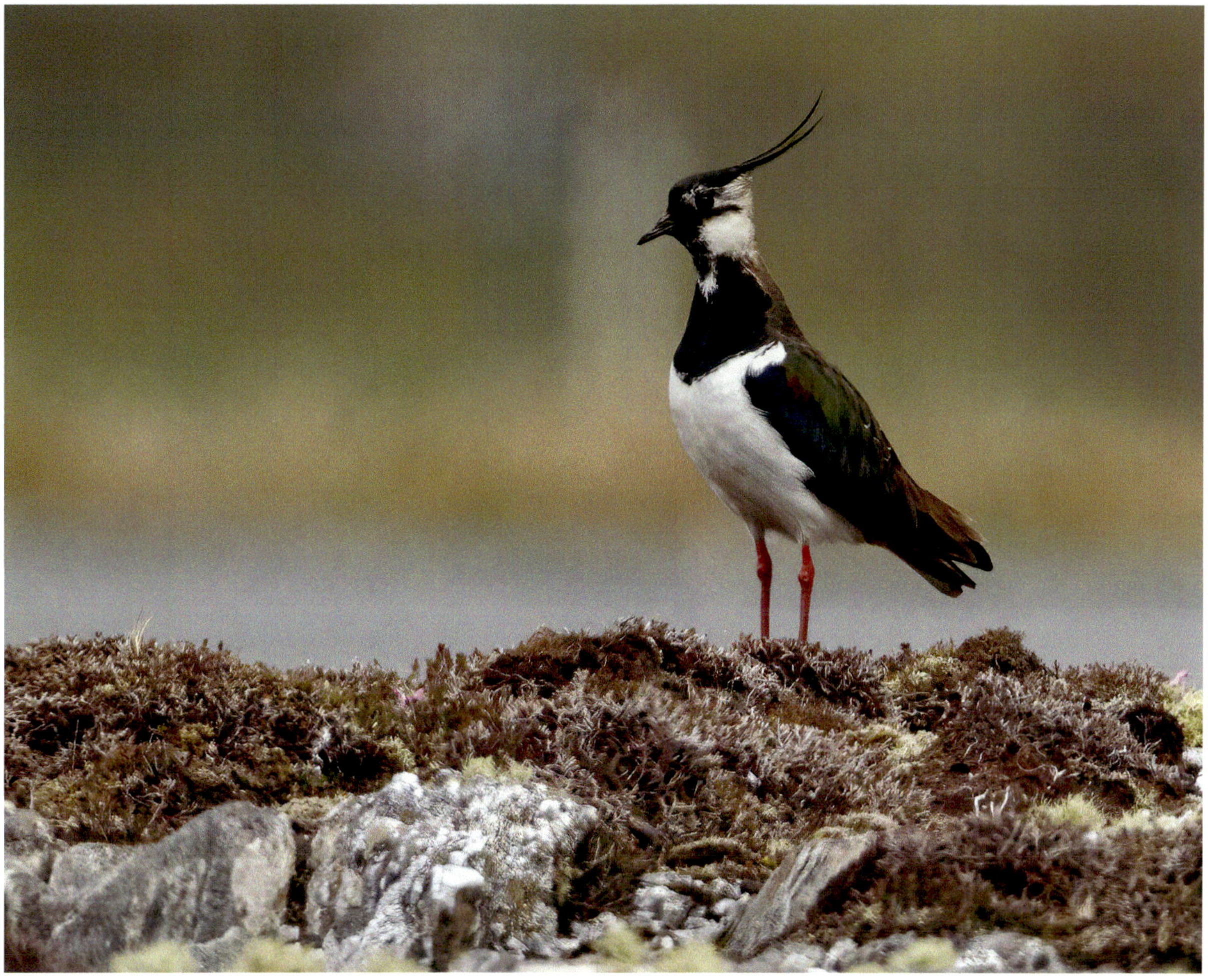

'Green-plover trilled their courting glee…'

The Rock Pipit (previous page, top) seeks out much of its prey on foot eating insects, beetles, small fish, small shellfish and seeds. It would have been easy to miss the frenzied feeding activity of the rock pipit as she was so well camouflaged against the seaweed.

Herring Gulls (previous page, bottom) are easily distinguished from black-backed gulls by their much paler grey backs.

The "pee-wit" call of the Green Plover or Lapwing leads to its alternative name of Peewit.

The snail's funny horns are its olfactory organs, which give it a very keen sense of smell. The number of spirals on the snail's shell indicates its minimum age. As the snail gets older the shell grows and gains more rings by the addition of calcium carbonate to the edge of the shell aperture.

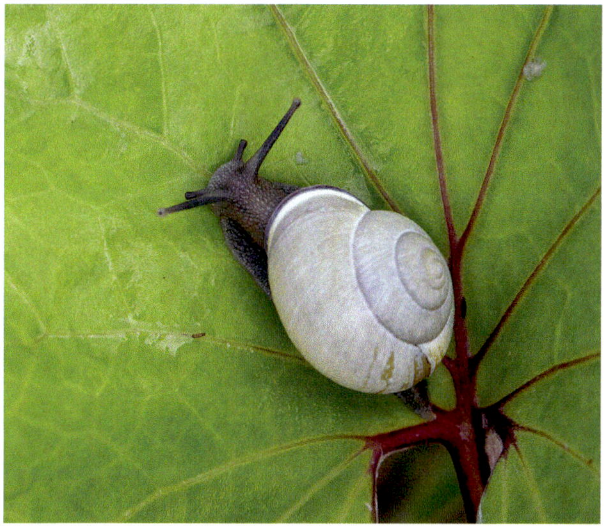

'The snail italia stretchéd out, his shell-house banded silver-gray…'

LANDRAIL

Crake
In the creaking corn
Shuttling.
Raucous
In search of love.

The Corncrake (also known as a Landrail) is a shy, secretive bird of hay meadows. It spends most of its time hidden in tall vegetation, its presence only betrayed by its rasping call which was once so dear to many and kept others awake on still, summer nights. Corncrakes were once numerous in Ireland but are now confined to islands such as Tory Island and Inishbofin. When hayfields were cut by hand, the breeding birds could escape and the nest left untouched by selective use of the scythe. The decline may be because the grass is mown by mechanical cutters destroying the nests and the young.

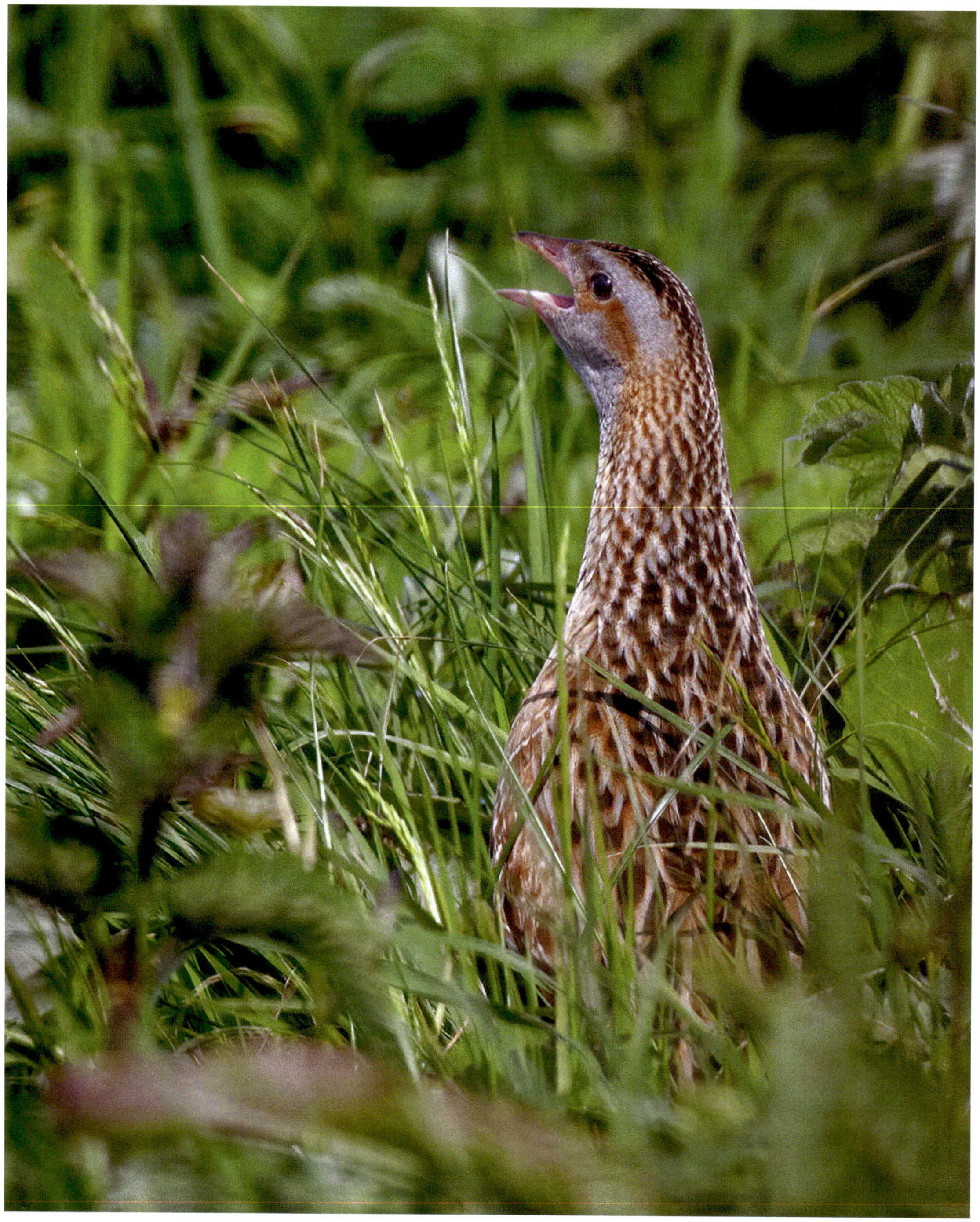

'At close of day when he awakes, he listen to the brown corncrakes...'

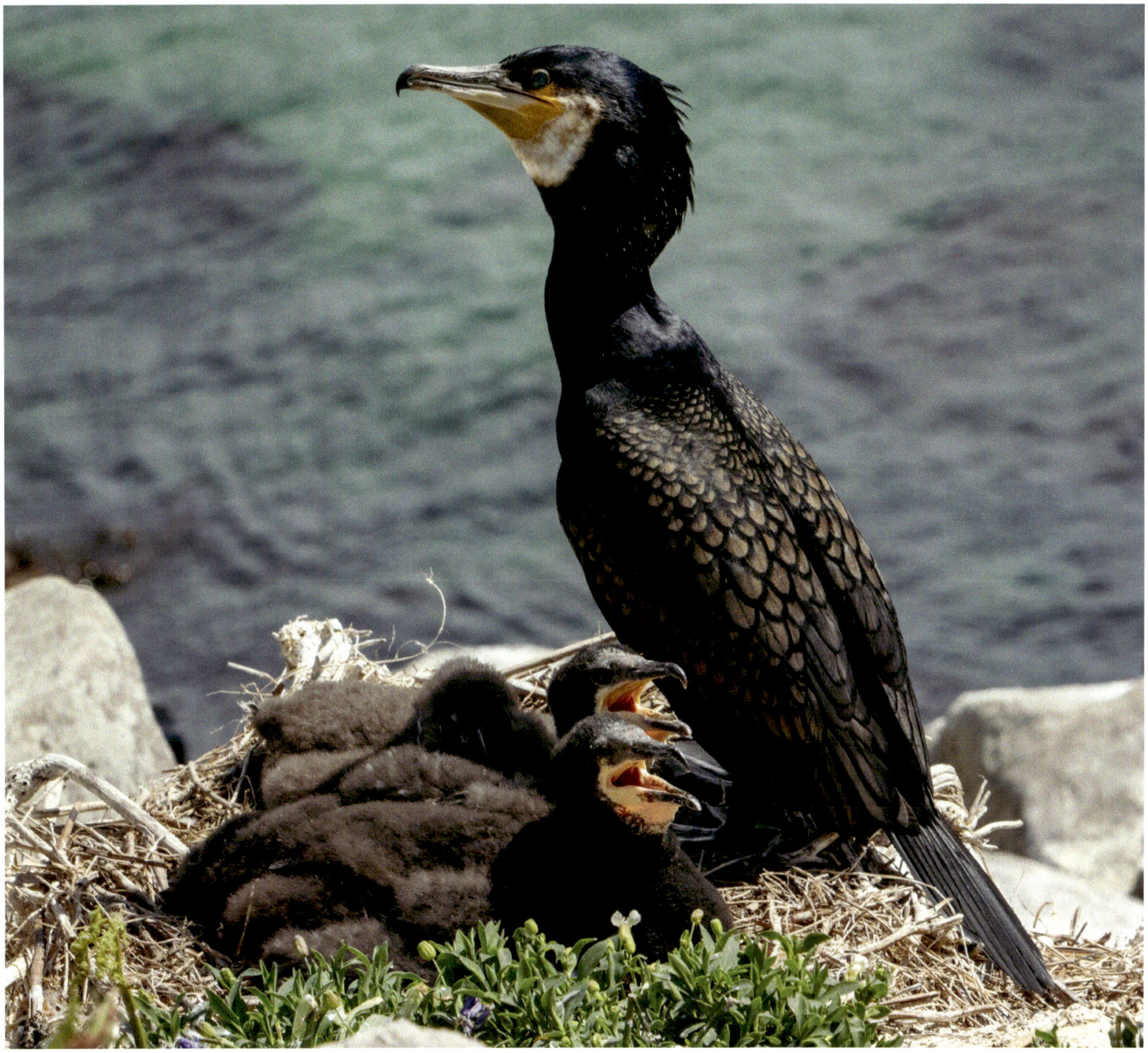

'See! the cormorant takes his stand, reverend like, as if to preach.'

The Cormorant (facing page) has a long body and neck and a long strong hooked bill. The adult breeding bird is black with a green, bronze and blue gloss to its plumage. It has startling bright green eyes and yellow-orange faces. The Cormorant breeds very successfully on Lambay Island.

SEASCAPE

Were the rough rocks gird the land
Near the sud-besieged brown beach,
See! the cormorant takes his stand,
Reverend like, as if to preach.

On the unseen tides of air
Silently three terns pass by,
To their young in grassy lair
Puffins fly with herring fry.

From the cave ethereal sounds
As the fissured wind frets through,
Sunbeams, glinting sea-pink mound,
Gull wings dappled-adust, blue!

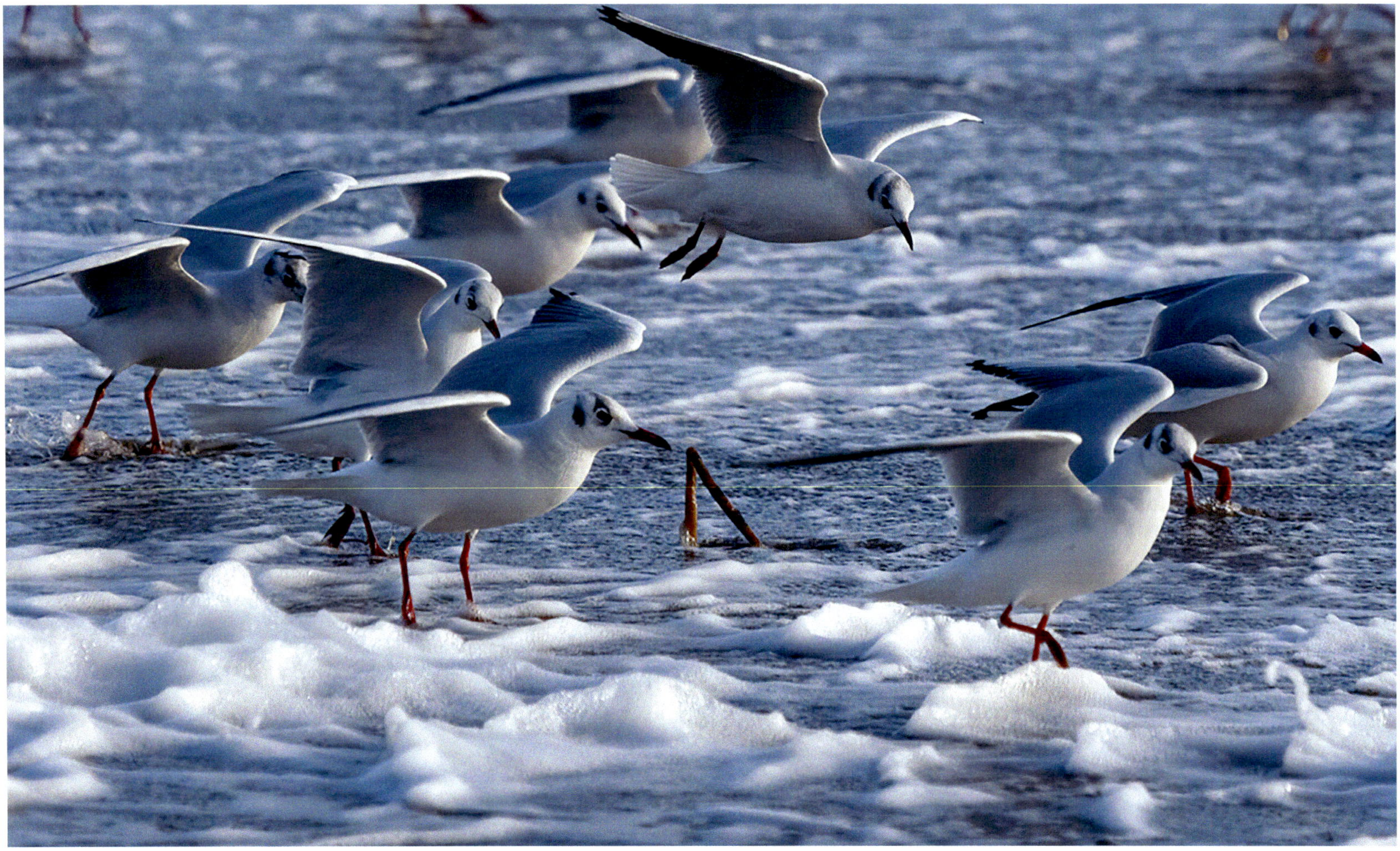

'Gull wings dappled-adust, blue!'

The Black-headed Gull is resident along all Irish coasts. Adults have red legs, and in summer plumage, a dark brown hood on the head. In this winter shot the hood in absent and is replaced by a dark spot behind the eye.

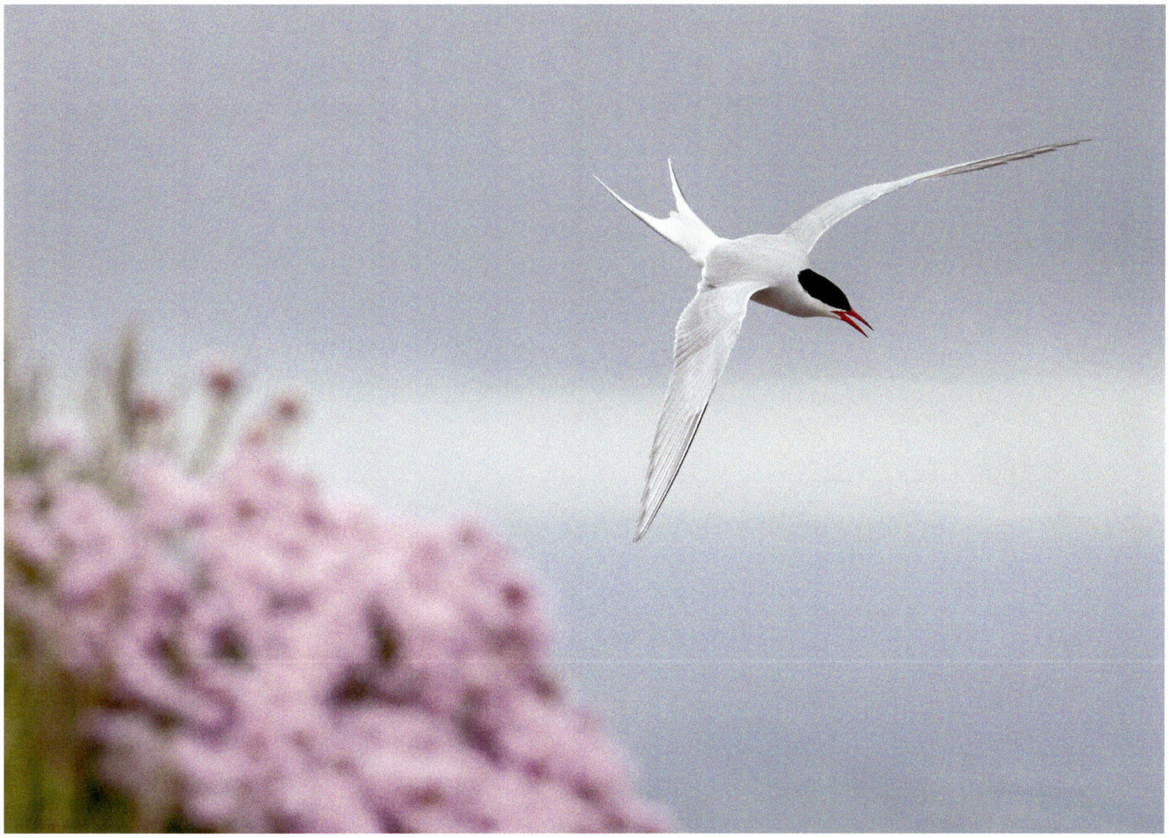

'On the unseen tides of air…'

The Arctic Tern with its long tail streamers is a summer visitor from March to September to all Irish coasts, nesting on beaches and offshore islands where the Sea Pinks or Thrift grow in dense tufts of papery, pink flowers. The Arctic Tern holds the record for the longest migration of any animal in the world, moving continually between the Arctic summer and the Antarctic summer. Before it is 6 months old, a young Arctic Tern, the size of a blackbird, will fly 20,000 kilometres to the Antarctic at the other end of the world. These birds are so lightweight they can glide through the skies on a breeze, swoop low over the sea and then climb back into the air. Its black cap, blood-red bill and its outstretched swallow tail all add to the beauty and grace of this remarkable bird. The Arctic Tern in the image shows the all-red bill and narrow black border to the wings which separate it from the common tern.

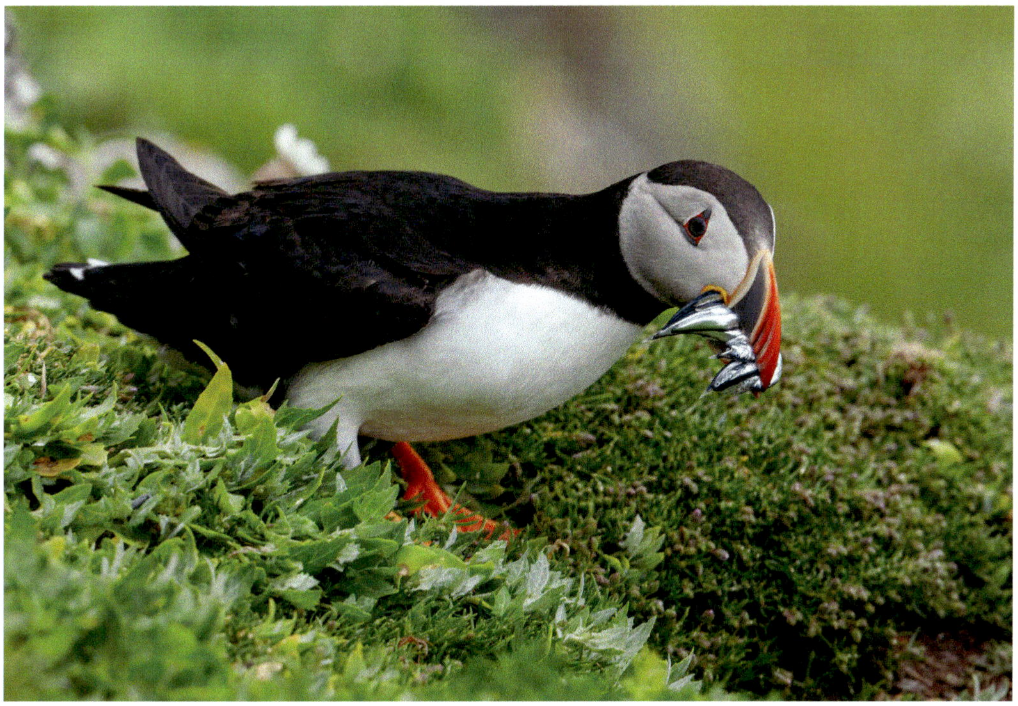

'To their young in grassy lair puffins fly with herring fry.'

An adult Puffin returns with his beak full of sand eels, which are energy-rich, to feed the single young chick. The Puffin's large beak and mouth has backward pointing spikes which enable it to catch many small fish in one dive without swallowing them. Only when the bill is full does the Puffin fly back to the nest. At 6 weeks, the Puffin cannot yet fly, but from the moment they enter the sea, they can swim and dive. Only after several more weeks can they actually fly up into the air..

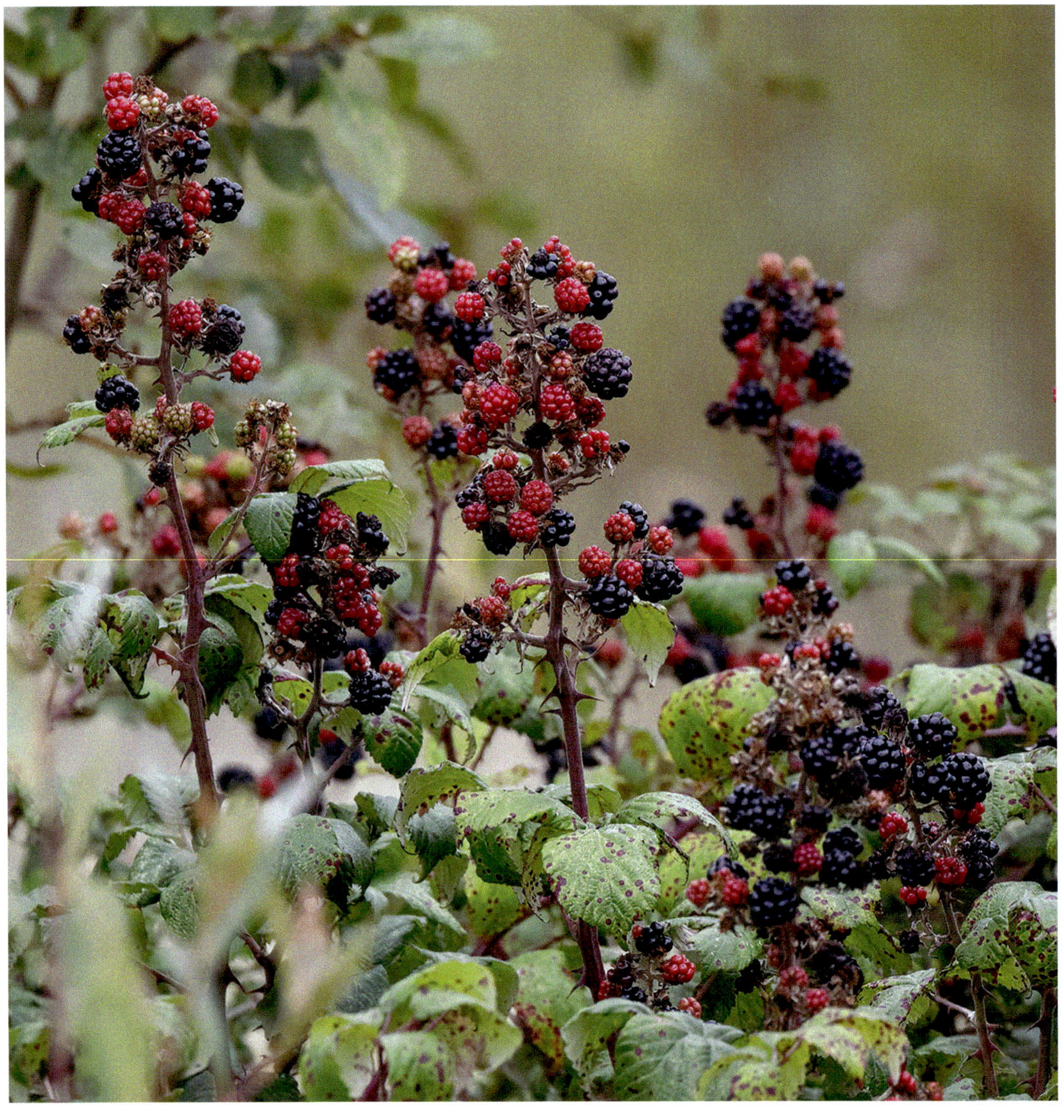

'The air is fumed by fragrant flowers, blackberries squint from thorny bowers…'

Blackberries have been part of our diet for centuries due to their delicious taste and availability, growing by the roadside all over Ireland

FALL-TIME

The sun beams in a quiet sky,
Outside their sett, cub badgers lie,
An ousel on the hillock's peak
Breathes oven-heat through open beak.

The mower whets his blunted scythe,
It twinkle-winks the lambent light,
Ripe wheaten straws already cut
Lie in a gorgeous golden swath.

Goose-feathers on the water's face
Are tiny white-sailed yachts in race,
Across the pond they lightly skim
To tack again at zephyr's whim.

The wild wasp-queen hunts in the wood,
Her late-born spins its silken hood,
Young meadow-browns dance o'er the lea
Where cats-ear clocks are flying free.

By cryptic crevice that he loves
The tiny red rock-spider roves, ·
A beetle from a bunch of grass
Comes out to sun his jet cuirass.

The air is fumed by fragrant flowers,
Blackberries squint from thorny bowers,
And brown ants building nests in clay
Hear throstles thrill 'Fine day, fine day.'

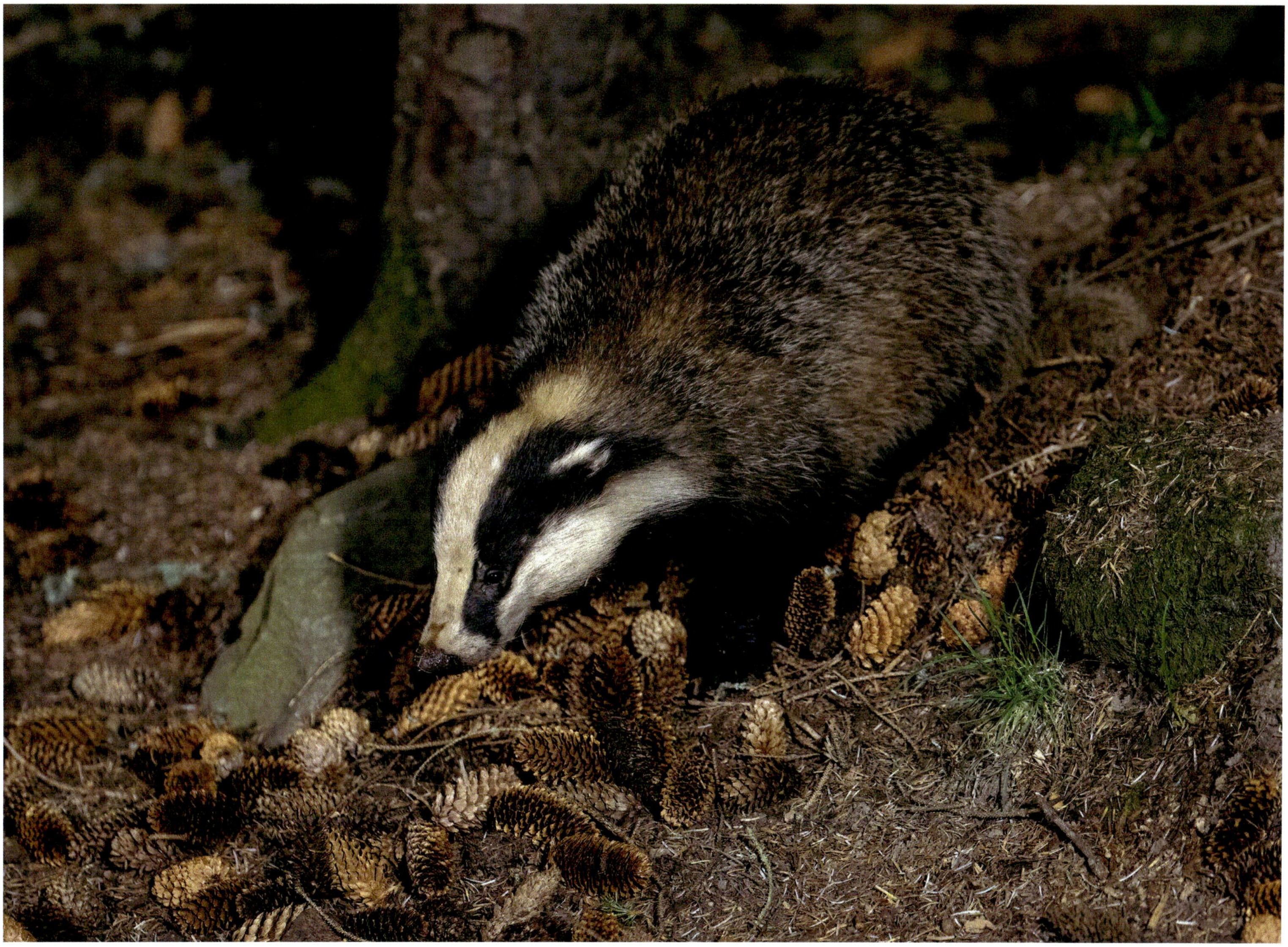

'Outside their sett, cub badgers lie…'

Badgers are secretive and principally nocturnal, and are seldom encountered in the wild. They have no natural predators in Ireland and they cause little damage to agricultural crops. They don't hibernate but they can slow down and go into a deep sleep for days if the weather is harsh. Interchange between badger groups hardly ever occurs and monitoring has shown that they normally travel only about one kilometre from their setts.

Badgers and their setts are a protected species by Irish and European law (under the Wildlife Act 1976, Wildlife Amendment Act 2000). There is no conclusive proof that badgers are to blame for the spread of TB, and the main source of transmission is from cattle to cattle. In Ireland in 2011 nearly 7,000 badgers were slaughtered at huge expense, and in 2012 only 55 fewer cattle were diagnosed with bovine TB. It has been demonstrated both in Ireland and the United Kingdom that killing badgers does not solve the problem and is totally inefficient in the elimination of bovine TB. Vaccination of badgers with oral bait costs less than culling and vaccination trials in Ireland indicate that bovine TB can be wiped from badger populations.

SPORTSMAN

I saw a wild duck by a lake,
A throstle in a tree,
A robin on a garden rake,
A whinchat on a fencing stake,
And a wren so wee, so wee,
And a wren so wee.

I saw a wagtail near a dam,
A tern skim o'er the blue sea,
A raven chase a weakling lamb,
A nesting jackdaw wool a ram,
And a skylark in the lea, the lea,
And a skylark in the lea.

I saw a sportsman with a gun,
He fired with fiendish glee;
He shot the birdeens one by one,
Then laughed to see what he had done,
And sorrow came to me, to me,
Black sorrow came to me.

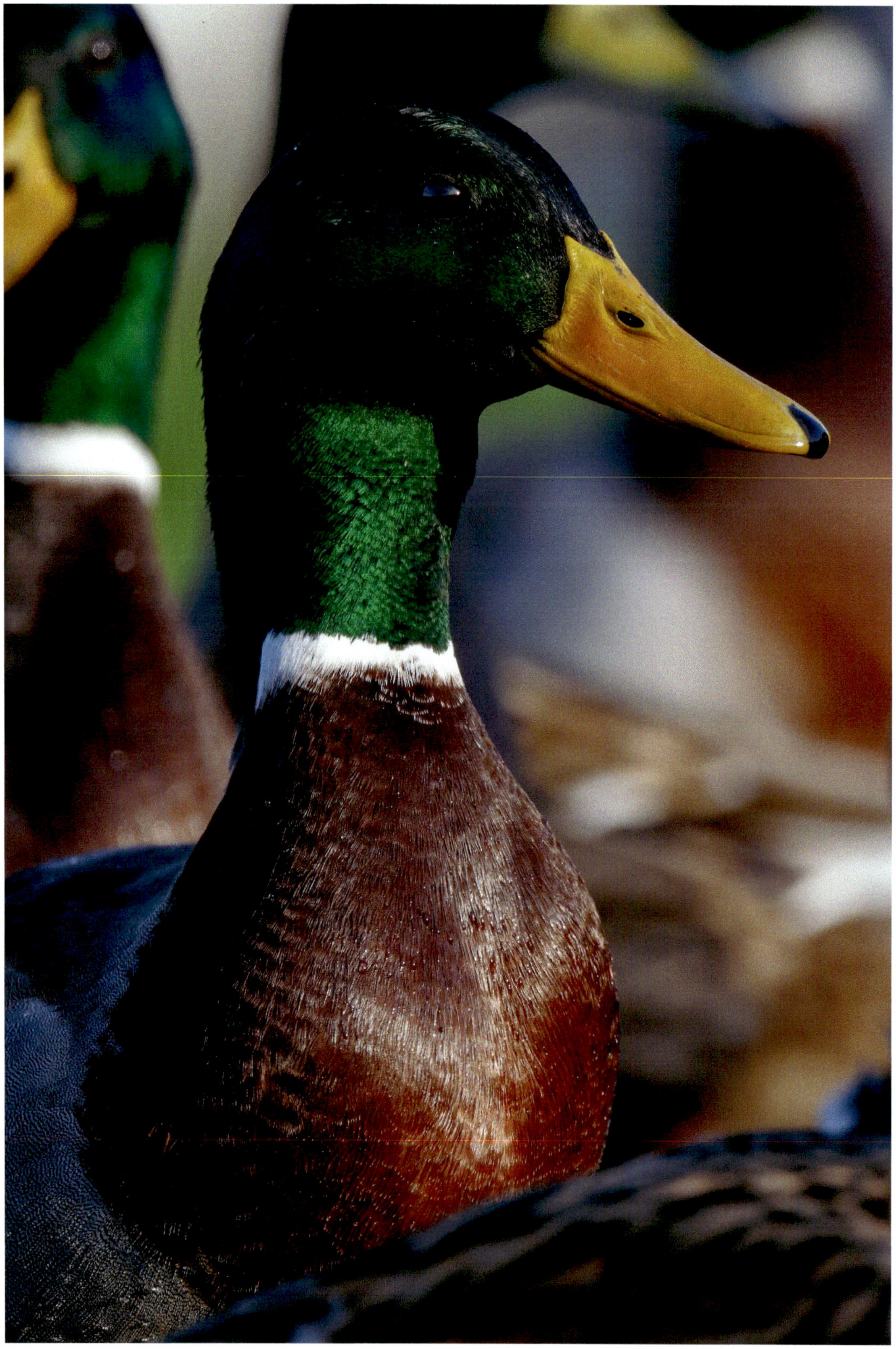
'I saw a wild duck by a lake…'

The Mallard or Wild Duck is widespread throughout Ireland. The males have a striking green head, yellow bill, and white ring around the neck with grey underparts. It is devastating to think that these beautiful birds as well as numerous other species of geese and duck were needlessly exploited for sport and shot in vast numbers in the past. The National Association of Regional Game Councils records that 23,810 Mallard alone were shot in Ireland in 1983. Many species must surely have been further endangered by shooting to kill as well as causing gross disturbance for feeding birds and a loss of habitat. Many of our declining species are now protected by law, and shooters of permitted species are encouraged to remember that it is not the size of the bag that counts.

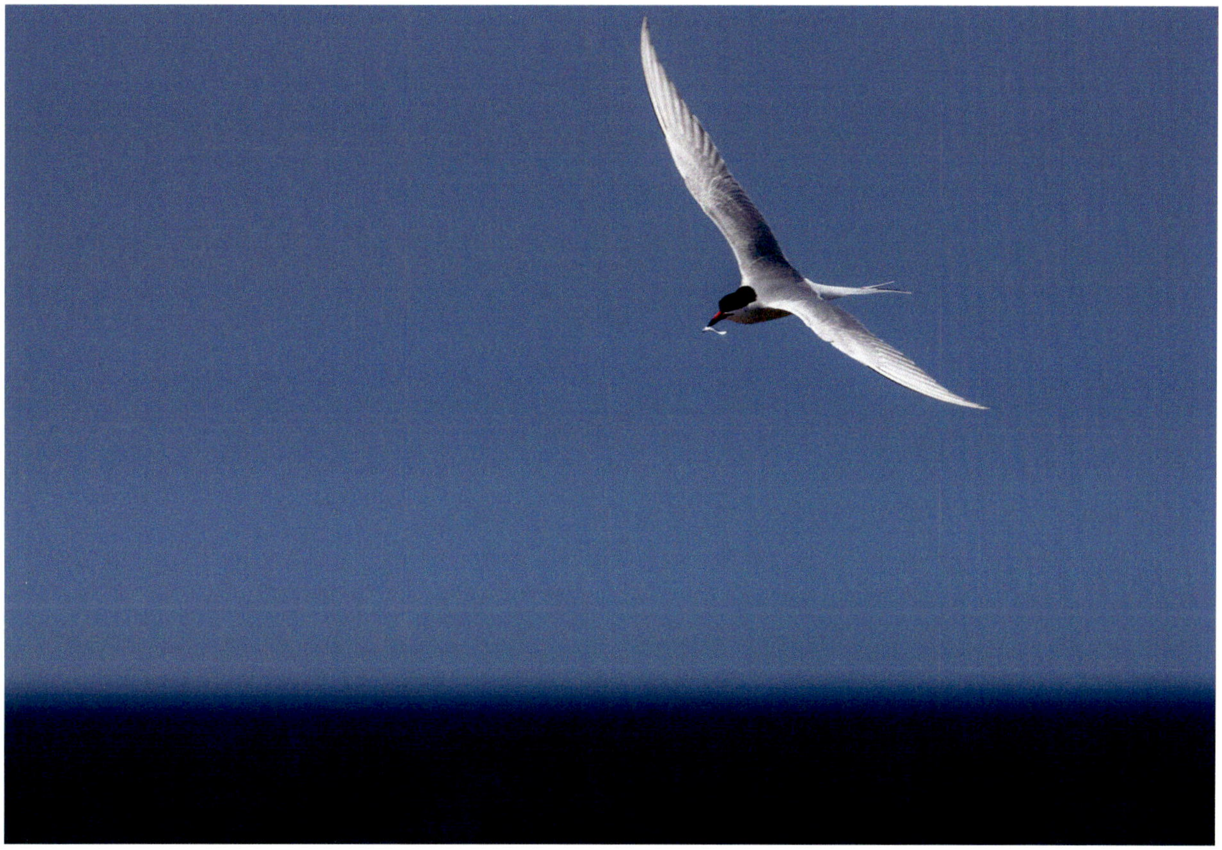

'A tern skim o'er the blue sea…'

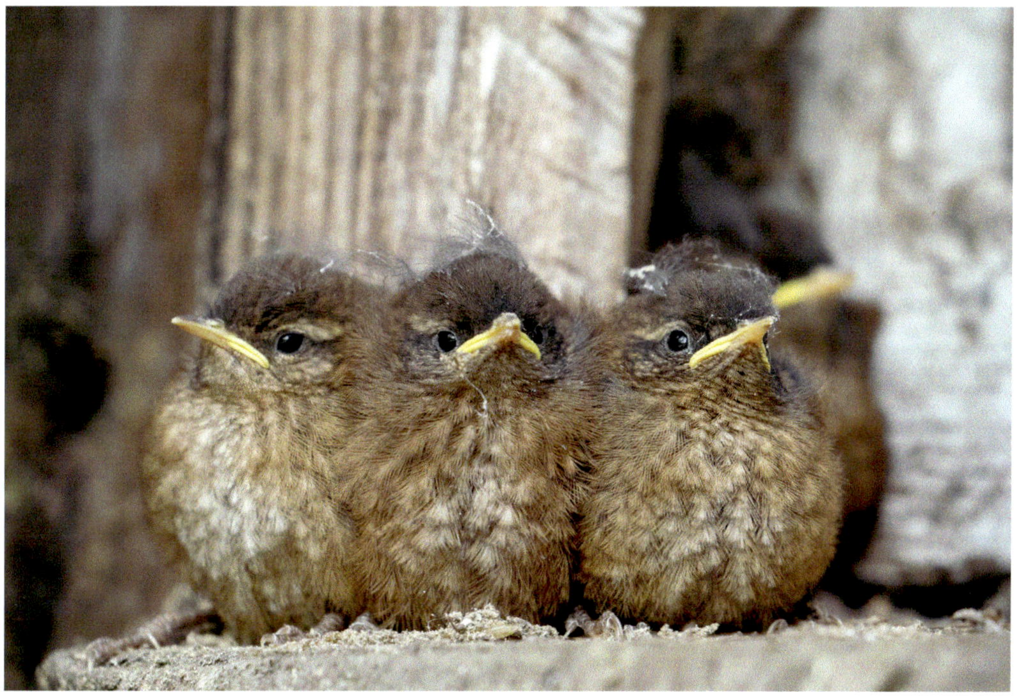

'And a wren so wee, so wee…'

The Common Tern (left) with a fish in its orange-red bill with black tip. Common Terns have shorter tail streamers than the Arctic Tern, which do not extend beyond the wing tips.

Wrens (below) are the second-smallest bird in Ireland, the smallest being the Goldcrest. For such a small bird, the Wren's songs are long and amazingly loud. These tiny baby wrens have just fledged.

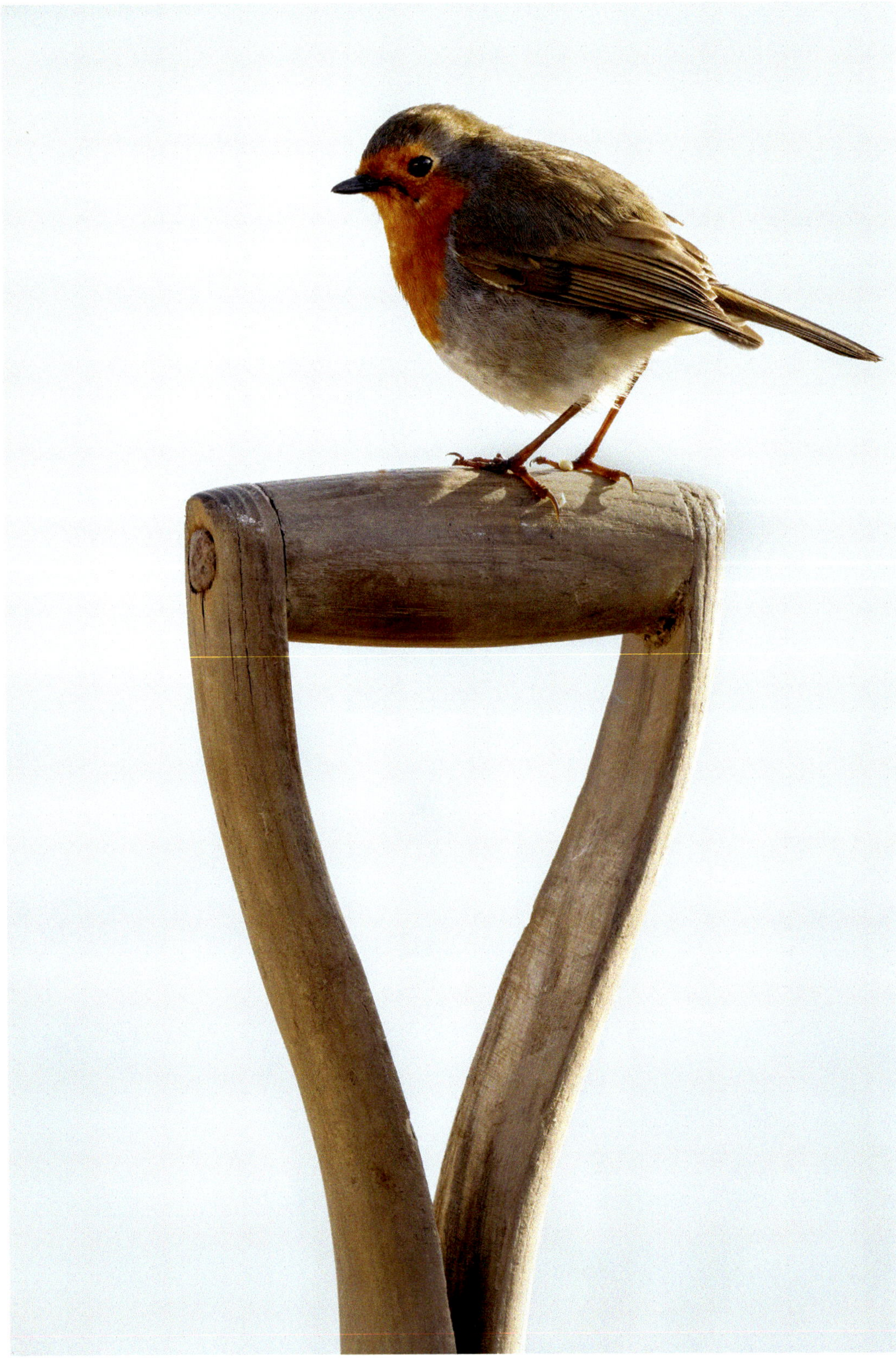

'A robin on a garden rake…'

The Robin is one of Ireland's favourite birds and is not afraid of people at all. For centuries it has been the symbol of good luck, happiness, and rebirth.

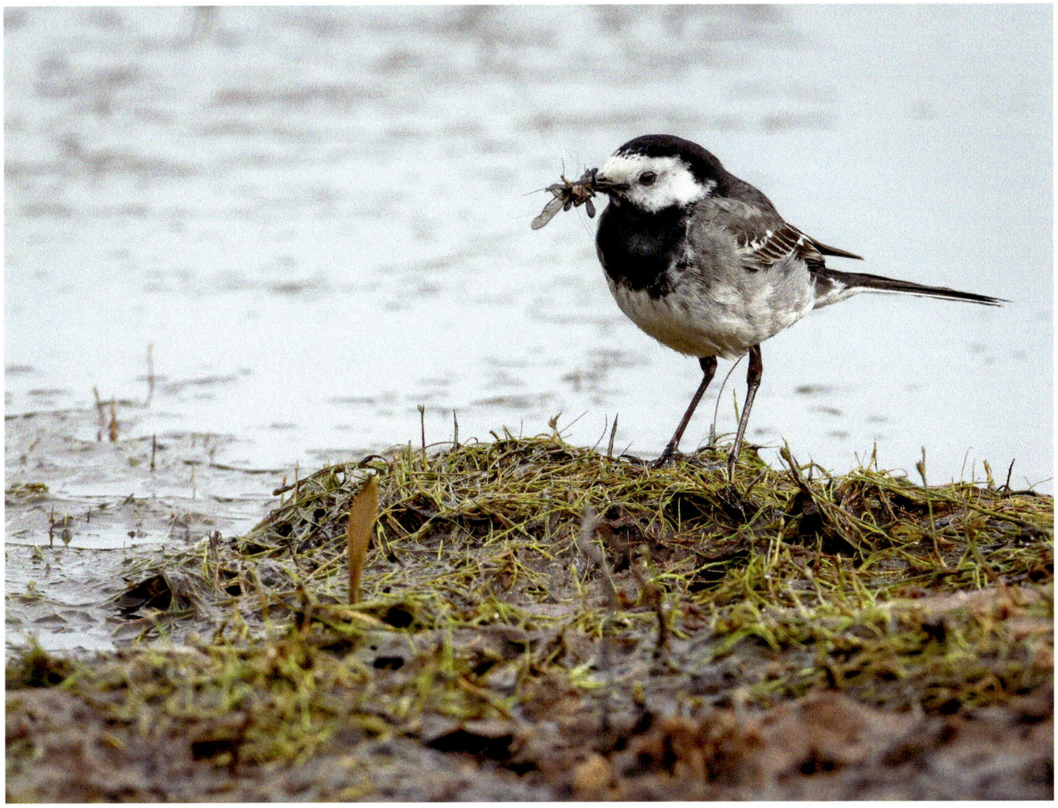

The Pied Wagtail is a common and widespread resident throughout Ireland. When it's not standing and frantically wagging its tail up and down, it can be seen dashing about over lawns or car parks in search of food.

'I saw a wagtail near a dam…'

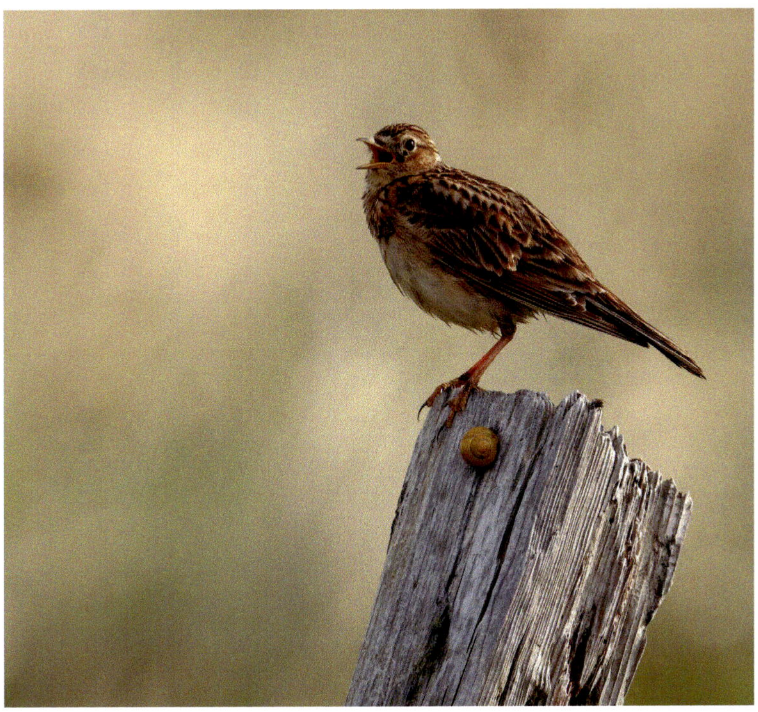

The male Skylark is particularly noted for its rich, sustained song. It sings often at dawn from a perch but is more usually seen in the air climbing higher and higher on fluttering wings. They hover effortlessly in one spot before parachuting back down to earth singing unceasingly until they land.

'And a skylark in the lea, the lea…'

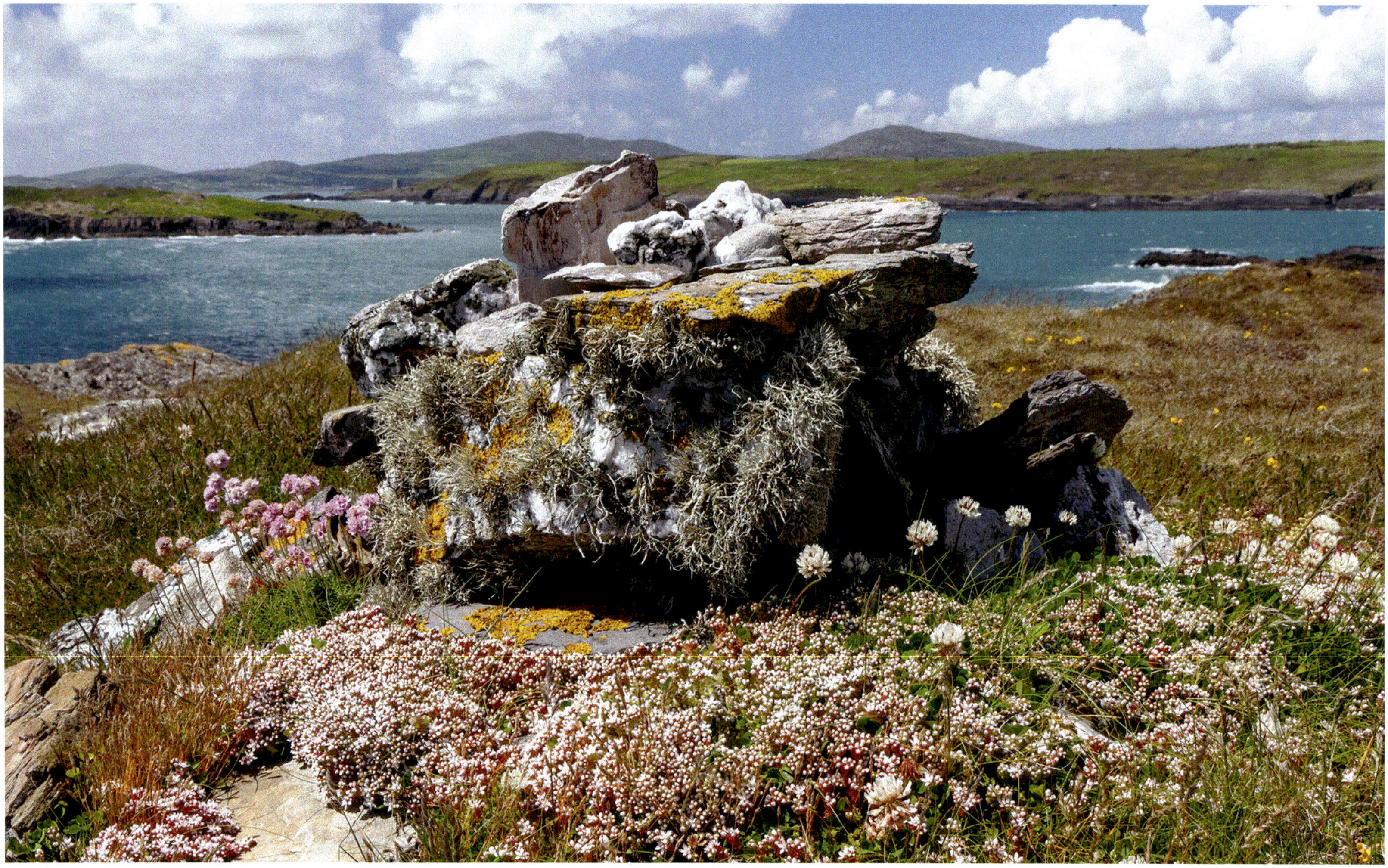

'And lichens yellow, silver-grey, adorn the scarred rocks beside…'

LATE EVENING

THE pale sea-pinks are gymped with spray,
Thrown by the dancing breeze-swept tide ;
And lichens yellow, silver-grey,
Adorn the scarred rocks beside.
Wee white-faced glabrous chickweeds hold
With threadlike rootlets to their beds,
Tall cats-ear flowering purest gold
Nods its several branched heads.
The sunset-wheel illumes the sky
With spokes of stippled amber-light,
We hear a sentry curlew's cry;
Thee limestone cliffs glint ghostly white!.

This possible prehistoric wedge tomb on Long Island in West Cork is adorned with colourful lichens and surrounded by Sea Pinks and English Stonecrop.

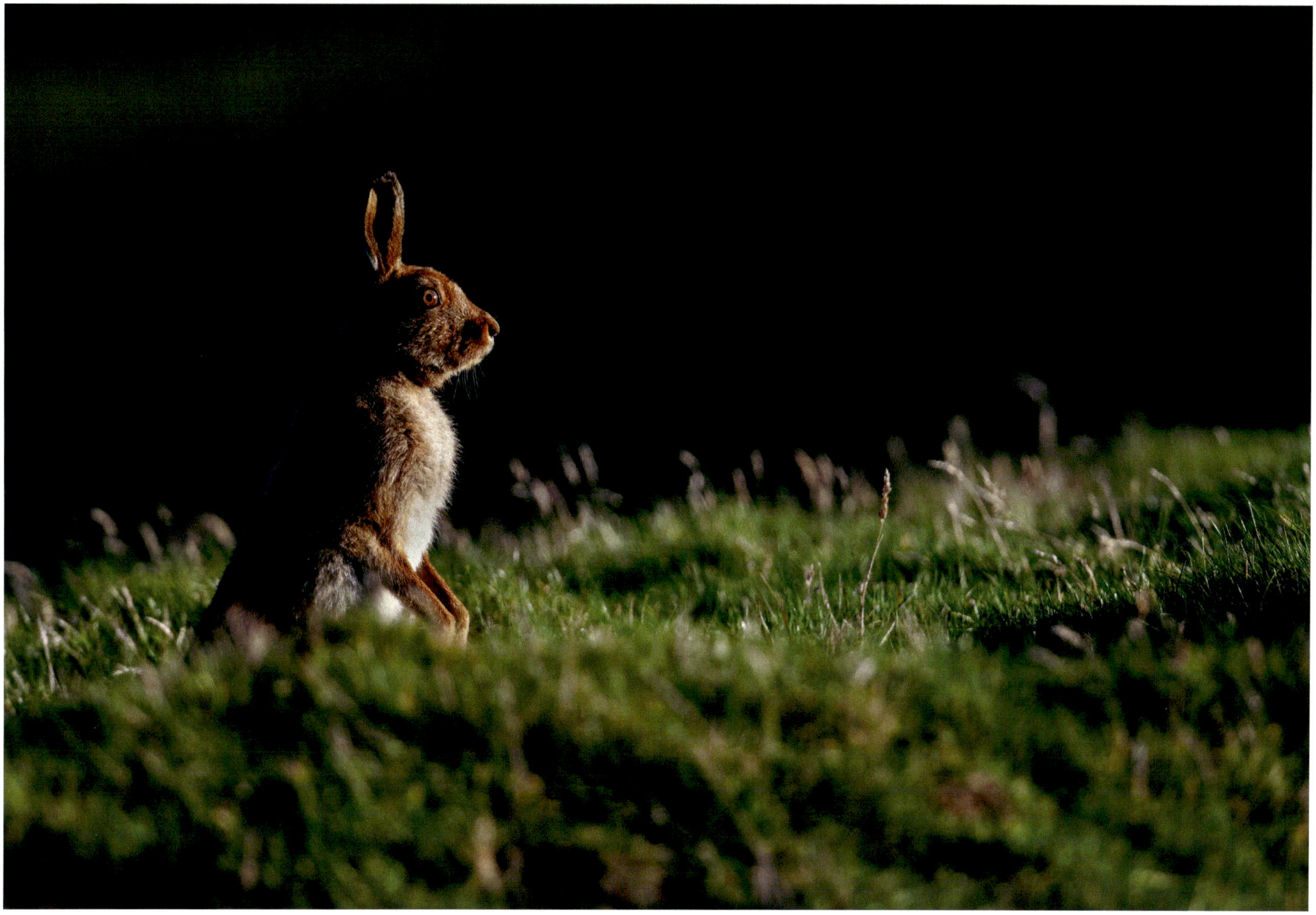

'And where the hill-hare makes his seat…'

JANUARY

The scurvy-grass creeps down the strand
Unfolding petals puce,
Red-throated divers off the land
Replace the solan-goose,
Wild storm'd seas do loudly roar,
With white teeth chew the wrack-strewn shore.

Brown curlew congregate in flocks
Where plashy is the clay,
Crumpled crape-lichens drape the rocks
Bright yellow, blue and grey,
Buff throstles in the thickets hide
From wispy winds that woosh outside.

The badger in his sett's asleep,
And snails attached to walls;
Betimes black beetles take a peep
From cryptic crevassed halls,
And where the hill-hare makes his seat
Green plover cry: "Pee-weet, pee-weet!"

The Irish Hare does not hibernate, and the breeding season extends from January to November. When alarmed, a hare will run for about 50 yards and then stop, ears pricked, and almost always side-on to you so they can watch you. A hare sees much better sideways.

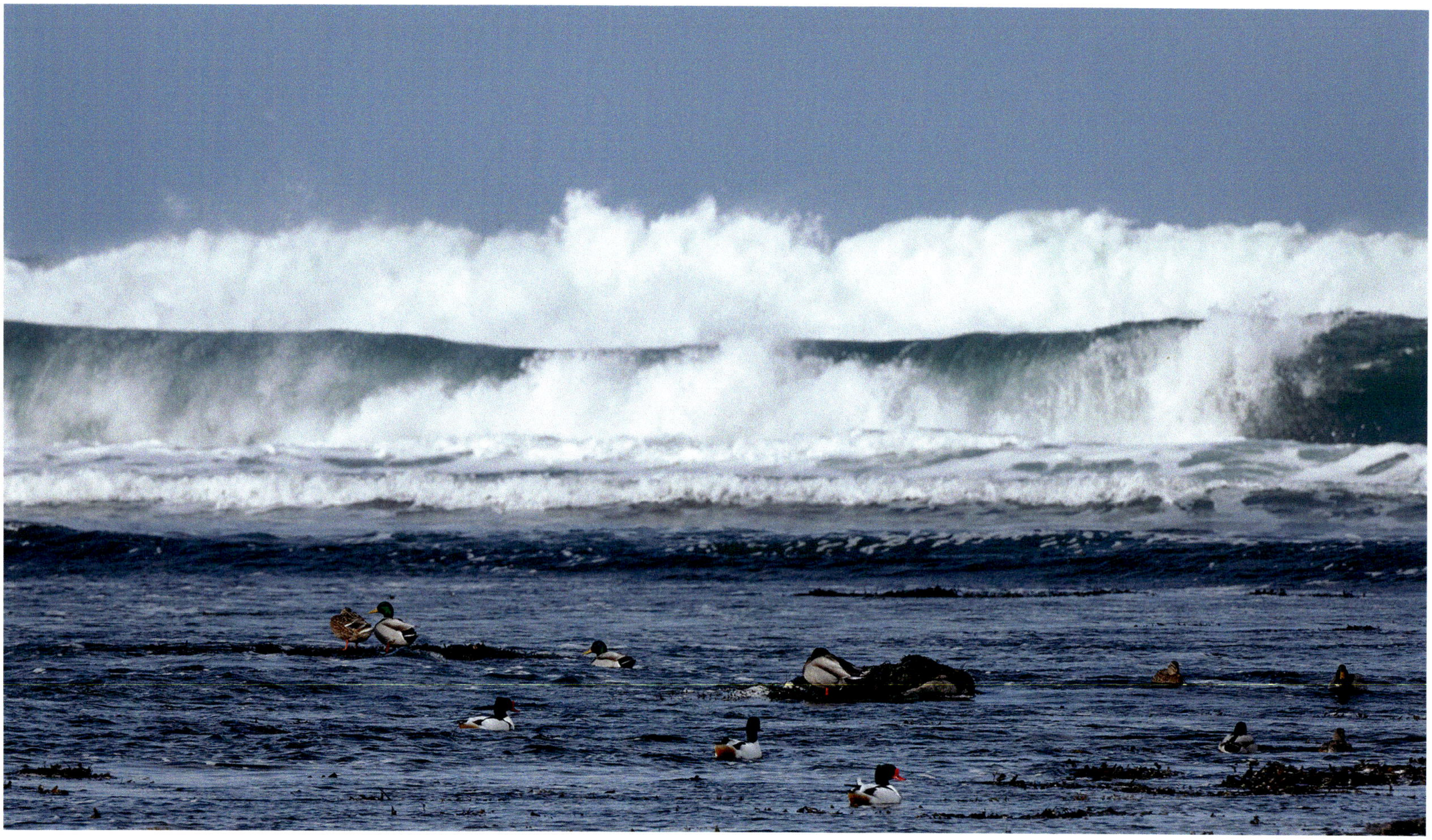

'Wild storm'd seas so loudly roar...'

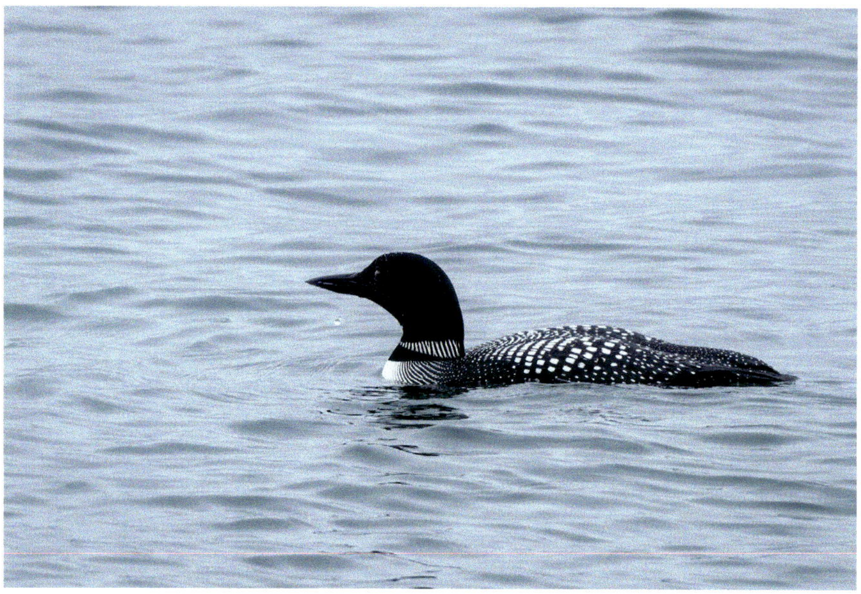

'Red-throated divers off the land...'

The flocks of Mallard and Shelduck are completely at ease in the wild seas of the Aran Islands' Inishmore. The Shelduck is strikingly beautiful, with its black-and-white plumage, orange breast band, and dark green head.

The image on the left shows a Great Northern Diver. This and the Red-throated Diver are visitors to Ireland from September to April.

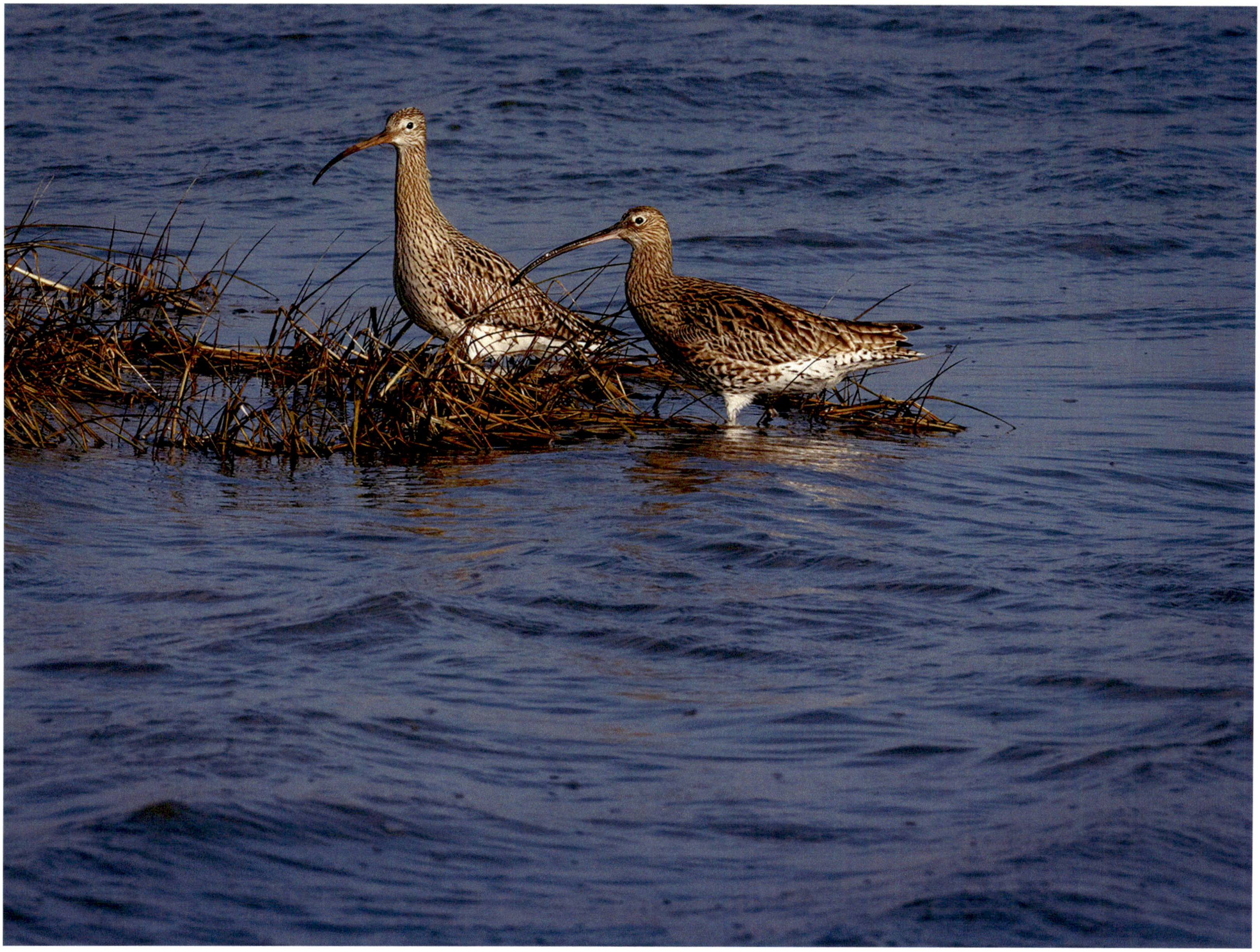

'Brown curlew congregate in flocks Where plashy is the clay…'

The Eurasian Curlew is declining throughout its range, and the severity of the decline in Ireland has been especially acute. Their numbers are supplemented by winter visitors. They have a plaintive, haunting call, which was a definitive sound of Ireland on land and coast. Its long, curved beak is used to catch prey living in vertical burrows. The tip of the beak makes a wide arc, searching the sediment below and probing its full length of 15 centimetres in the soft mud of an estuary to reach worms and shellfish living too deep for other shorebirds to obtain.

SEPTEMBER

The cot's paint-blebbéd ivied eaves
A-glimmer with sun-dancing dyes,
Pied wagtails chase deciduous leaves,
Mistaking them for butterflies,
And martins cleave blue-breasted skies.

June cuckoo's twin-flex'd mocking song
Thrice magnified in nook-notched glen
Re-echoes not the rocks among;
Each field that's lea-stubble again
Is ranged by the grain-picking hen.

Beneath the fruited orchard trees,
Bruised windfalls' ruby-emeral heaps
Are added to by every breeze,
To hidey-hole the hedgehog creeps,
Half comatose a fool-frog leaps.

And by the tinkling drinking-well,
Obscure in its tenebrous light,
The brown-black sprinkled whorléd shell—
A wall-snail's—snuggled to water-tight
Against dog winter's gelid bite.

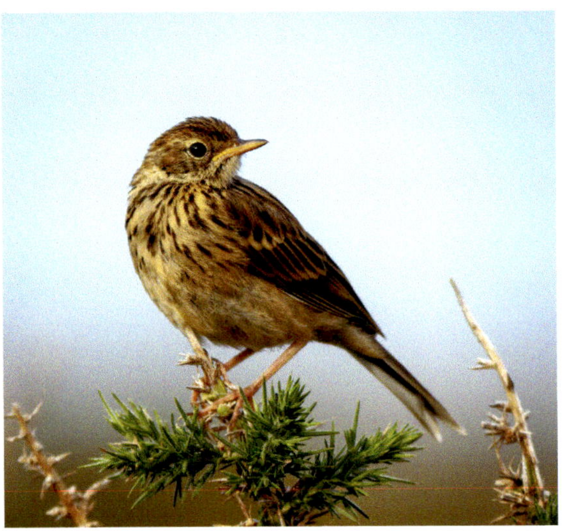

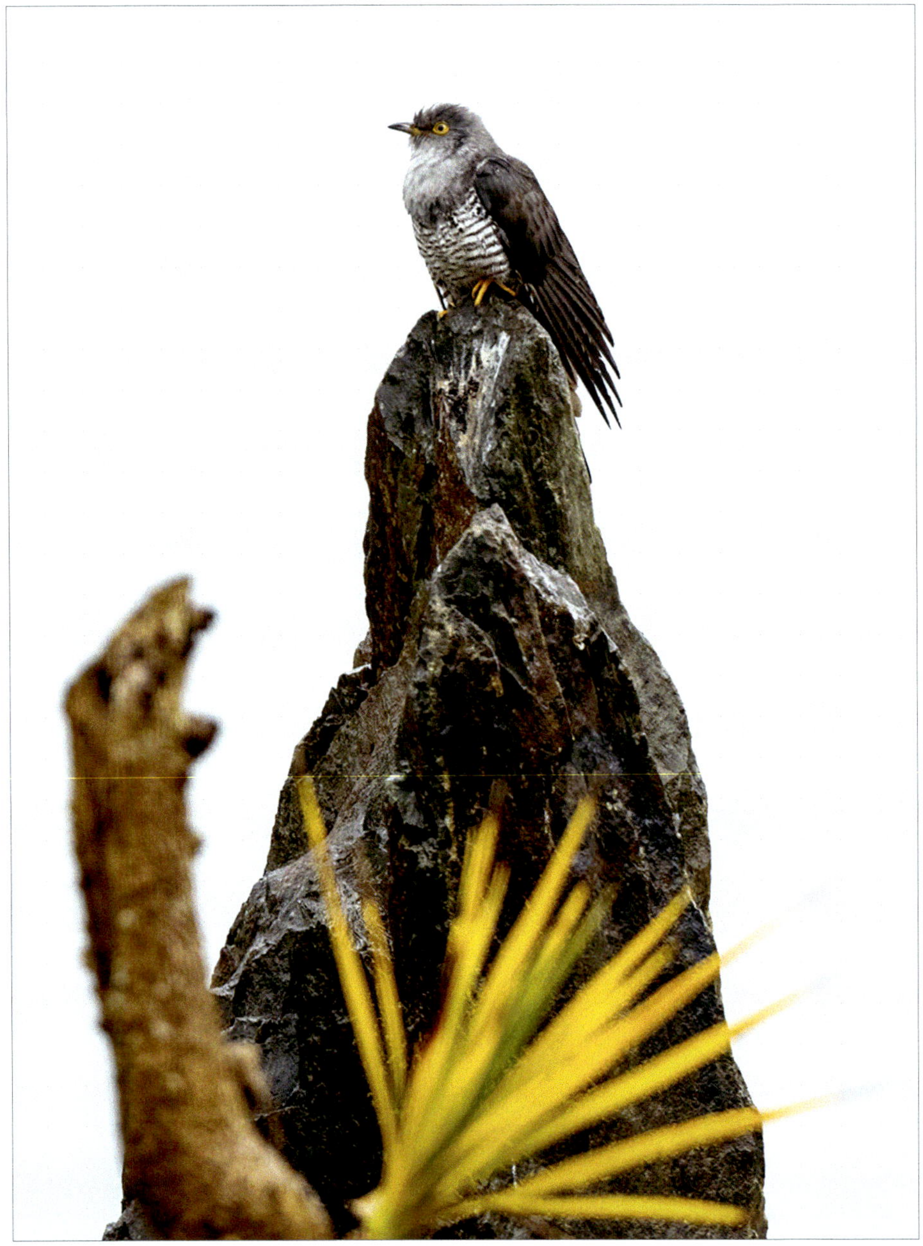

'June cuckoo's twin -flex'd mocking song…'

The Cuckoo's song is probably one of the most recognisable and well-known of all Irish migratory bird species. Despite its obvious song, which is heard from late April to late June, it is infrequently seen. Sightings are easier on islands with a lack of trees or shrubs, such as Long Island in Co. Cork, and where the Cuckoo targets the nest of the ground-nesting Meadow Pipits (left) to deposit its own egg. One male may have several mates, each of which lays from 6 to 20 eggs in the nests of small birds. After hatching, the blind, naked young Cuckoo instinctively pushes any egg or young bird out of the nest with its strong wing stumps. Only the huge gape of its beak remains to stimulate the foster parent to bring food. The Cuckoo's eggshell often resembles the eggs of the birds whose nests have been invaded.

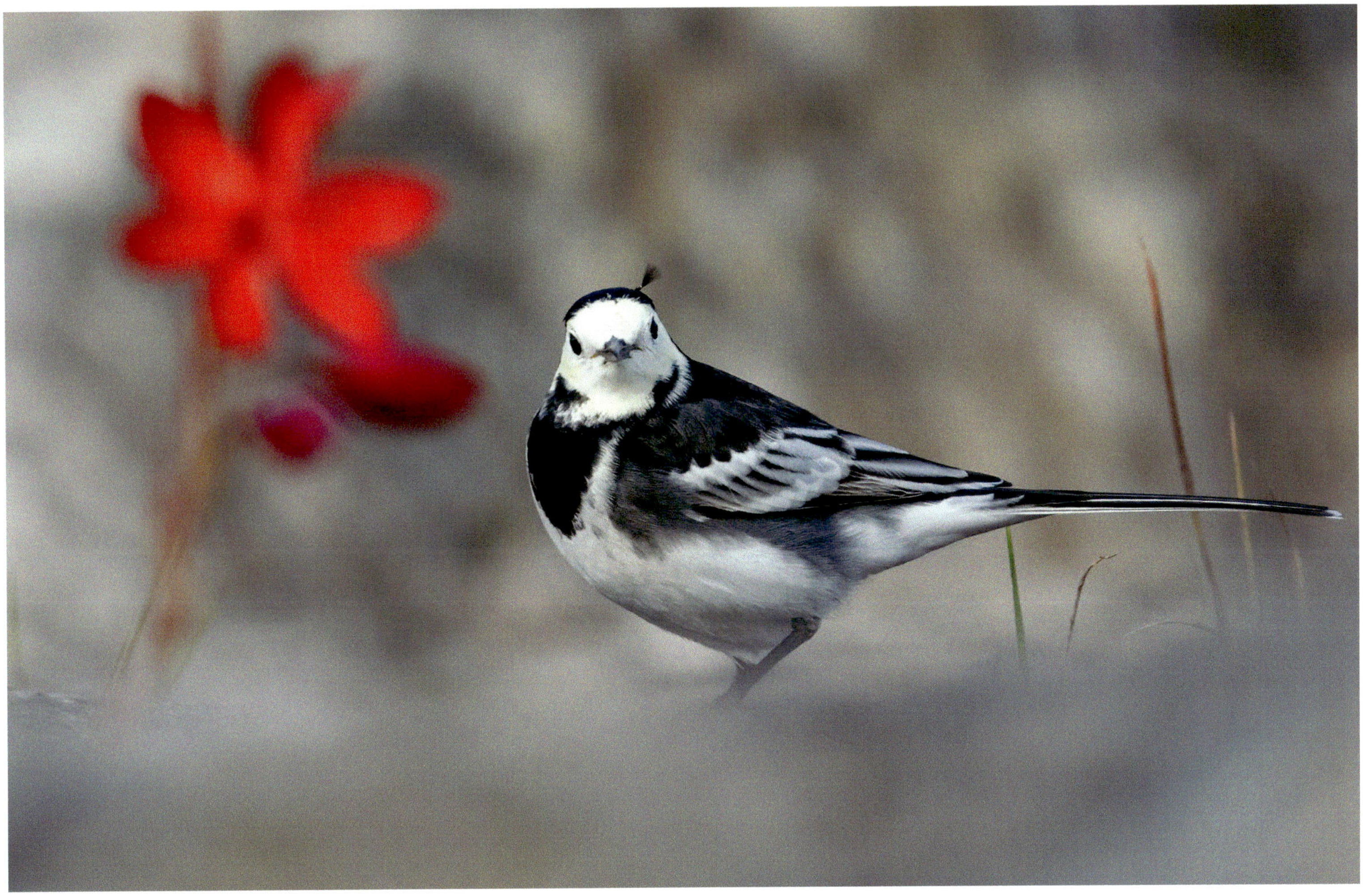

'Pied wagtails chase deciduous leaves, mistaking them for butterflies…'

The Pied Wagtail is a wonderful agile little bird constantly wagging its tail and dashing around in search of insects.

JUNE

As I walked through the fruitful fields
Sweet June was enthronéd there,
Red roses sprigged her vert kirtél,
White hawthorn deck'd her hair.

Brown birds sang on each budding bough,
Grey carpet-moths took wing,
Around a gnarled crab-apple tree
Flashed fair a fairy-ring.

The buzz of bees was in the air,
The lilt of bubbling brooks,
Ze-zipping tunes of grasshoppers
Came from the ferny nooks.

Where spiders climbed the bearded grass
Jewelled lady-birds came down,
Lymph cuckoo-whisks were on the flowers,
Aphids in the ant town.

The hillside glowed to amethyst,
Like gold each quartzite dune;
Out of the earth she smiled at me,
Glad happiness-giving June.

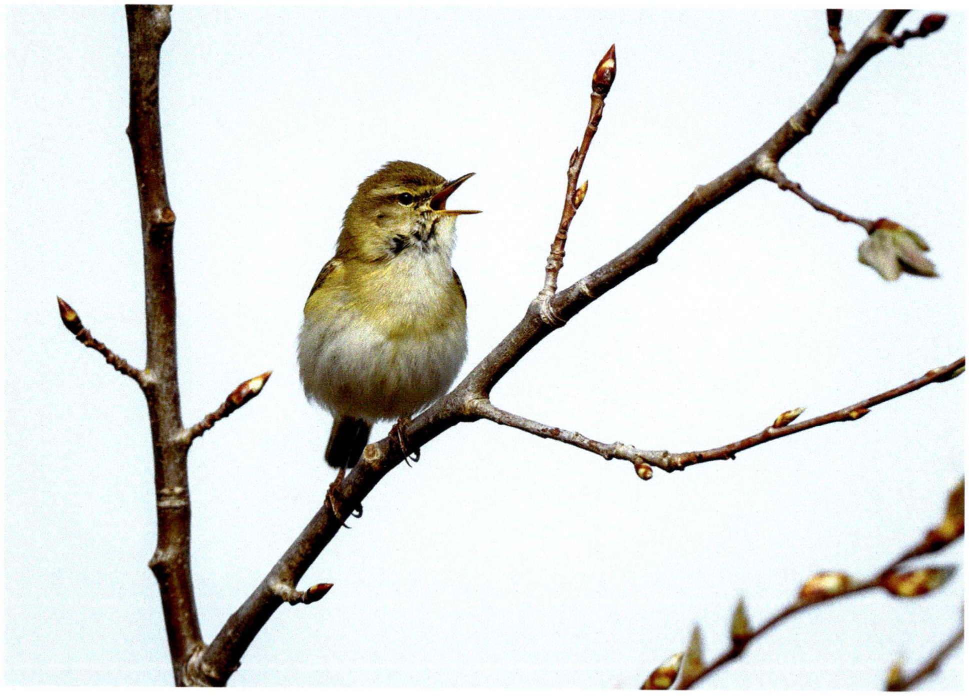

'Brown birds sang on each budding bough…'

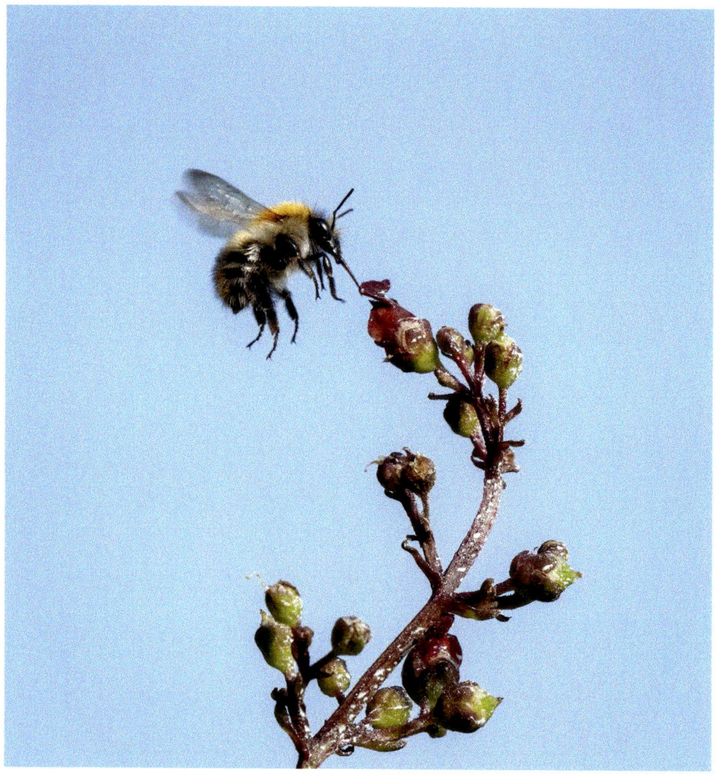

'The buzz of bees was in the air…'

The Chiffchaff is usually the first of the immigrant warblers to arrive back in Ireland in March and April. It is sometimes confused with the willow warbler, but the Chiffchaff is usually browner with darker legs. This small, active bird can be very vocal, singing its characteristic 'chiff-chaff' song. It is a restless little bird and easier to see when the trees are in bud.

There are 100 bee species in Ireland, of which twenty-one are native garden bumblebees, including the Carder Bee seen in the image. The bumblebee live in colonies with a queen but they don't make honey like Honeybees. They can travel up to 5km to feed but commonly forage within 1km of their nest.

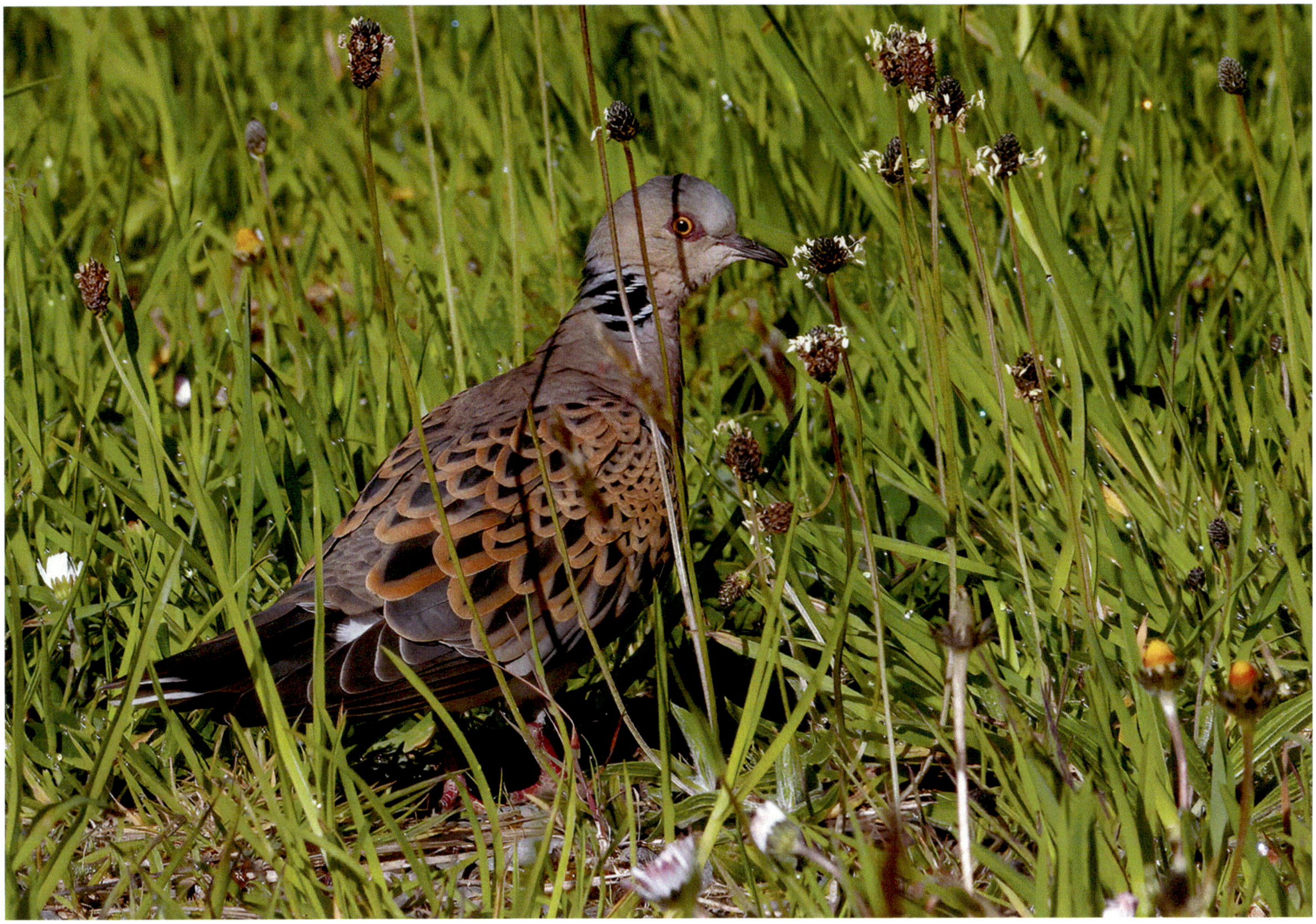

'The place where blue breeched beetles rove, and coos each mating turtle-dove.'

NOCTURNE

Aspersa leaves a silvery trail
As he glides out at fall of night,
His shell, like a spendrift spray'd sail
Glitters in the half-lidded light,
And telescopic eye-stalks bright.

At rendezvous, where faery-ring
Is born of sporing fungus leads;
He gluttons like a starvéd thing
On little lawny mushroom beads,
And quaffs pellucid dew-drop meads.

Always and always in the dusk
That purple-shades the leafy groove,
When moschatel embalms with muck
The place where blue breeched beetles rove,
And coos each mating turtle-dove.

The Turtle Dove's gentle purr has become increasingly rare following population declines. The distinctive band of colour gives the dove its name as it looks like it can draw its head into the neck like a turtle. It feeds on seeds and berries as well as caterpillars and other larvae.

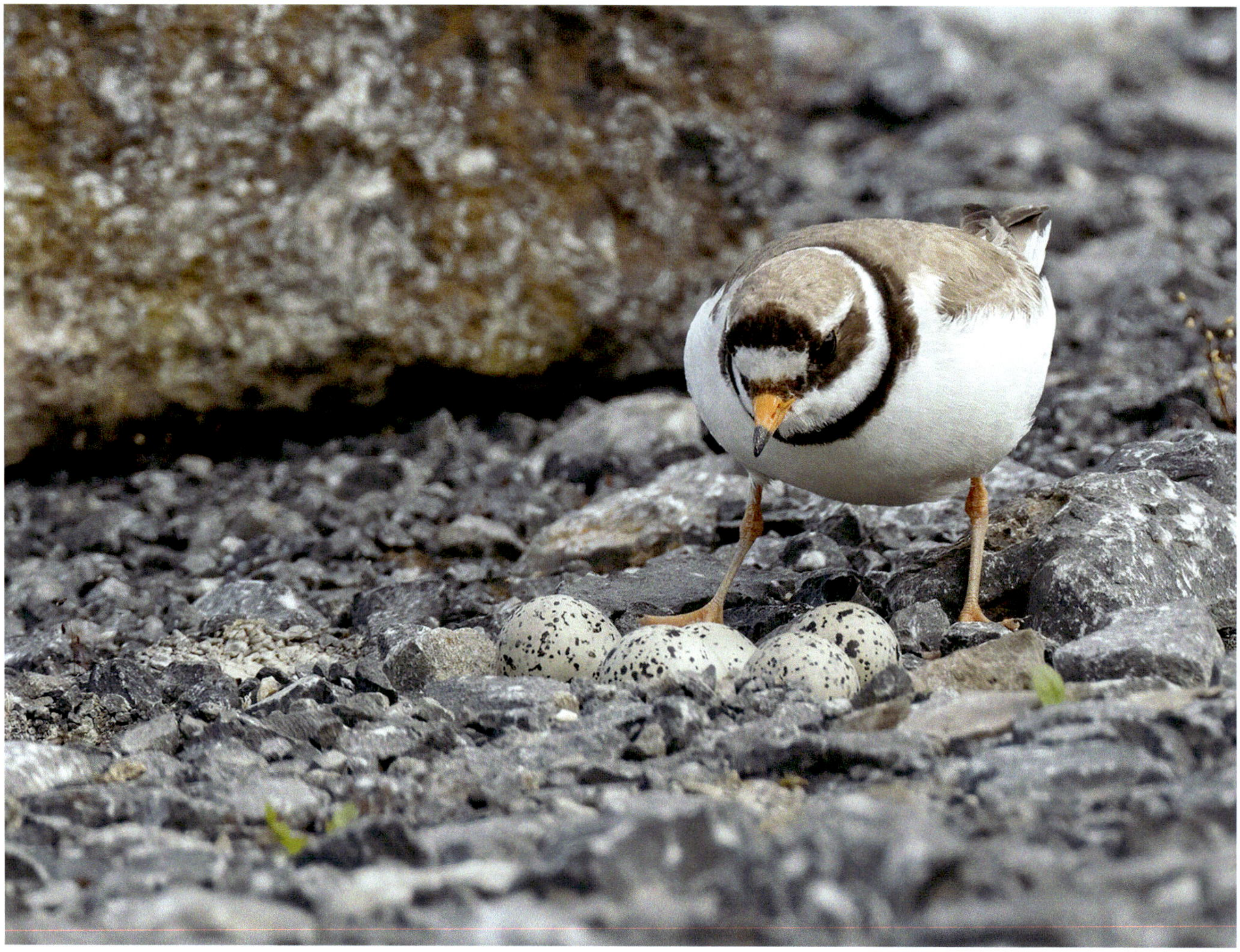

The Ringed Plover's eggs are perfectly camouflaged in the quiet part of an active quarry. If a potential predator approaches the nest, the adult will walk away, calling to attract the intruder and feigning a broken wing. They normally breed on beaches around the coast on exposed wide sandy or shingle beaches.

RINGED PLOVER

"Tu-li, tu-li-tu," the ringed plover cry,
As I near the place where their four eggs lie,
Well camouflaged with speck'd pebbles around,
Almost invisible on the shore ground.
"Tu-li, tu-li-tu," in fear pipes the hen,
Faking side tumbles all down the big ben;
Where cock trails his wings as if badly hurt,
Then sidles away as I put on a spurt
To catch up with him—pretending assistance—
But wary enough he keeps out of distance,
Leading me onward when I hesitate,
Fluffed up his wings and drunken his gait,
Cricked his neck, head screwed to one side,
Beady eyes blinking and beak open wide.
Over the eggs a wee sun-beetle crawls,
Underneath them the black ants make their halls,
And *arion ater*, the ribbed black slug,
Followed by plant-feeding brown-backed shield bug,
Travel nearby at slow funeral speed;
Yet, the two birdeens to them pay no heed!
All the details in their elegant plan
Of wounded pretensions is to deceive man.
Rolling and bowing, and shaking with fear,
Pouted white breasts ducking in the grass near.
Shame on my teasing, I'll go on my way;
"Tu-li, tu-li-tu,"the ringed plover say!

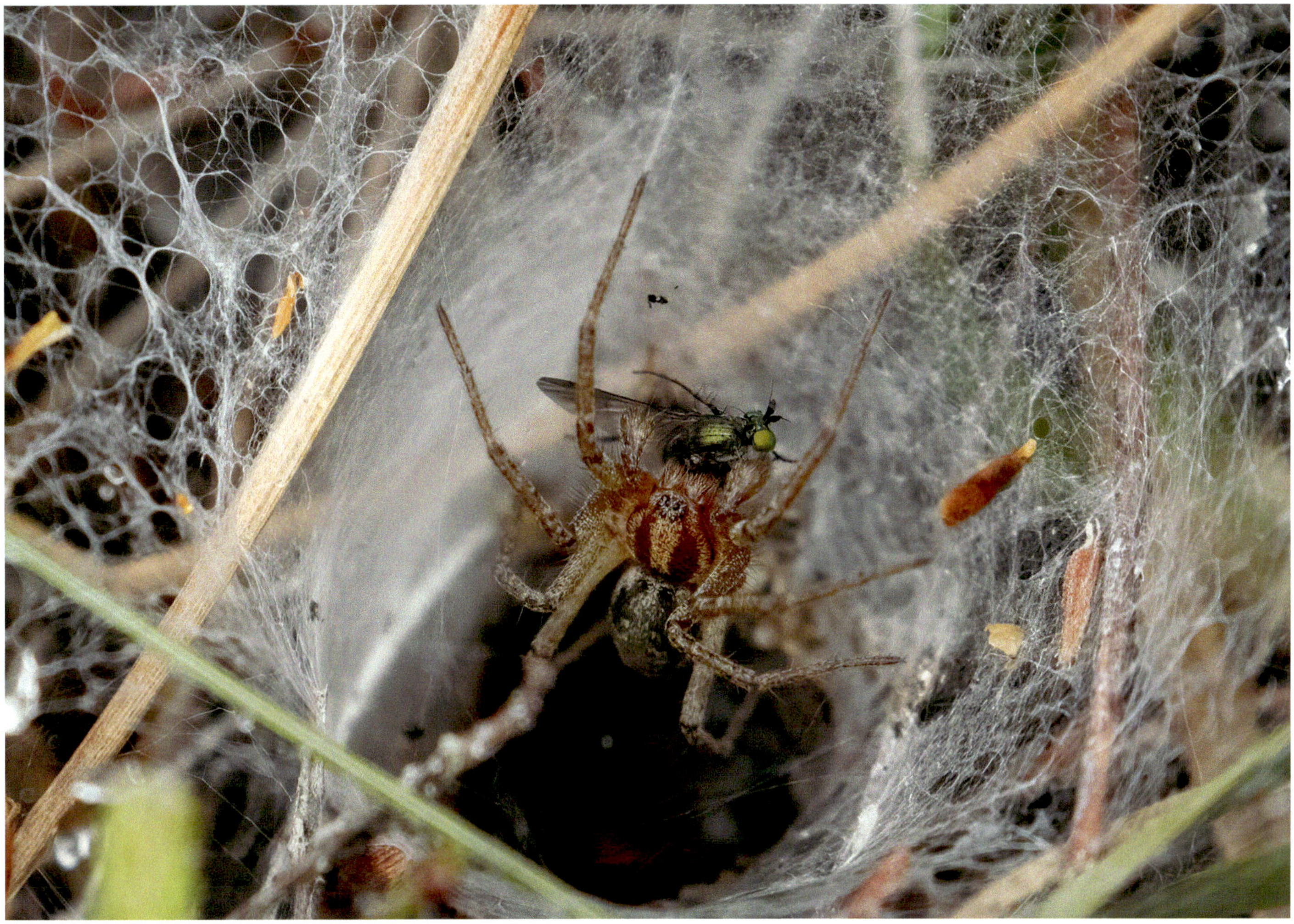

'The web so finely dangled, The fly was soon entangled…'

THE TRAP

Bejewelling the summer sky
A cobweb, and a dancing fly.
The web so finely dangled,
The fly was soon entangled.
Ensnared in silvery viscid skein
The captive struggled might and main.
Until the spider came to light
To end her labouring with a bite.
Another bite: then one and one,
Now thorax, legs and wings are gone
Bejewelling the summer sky
A cobweb—but not dancing fly.

This funnel-shaped web has been made by the Domestic House Spider (*tegenaria domestica*). The spider sits at the back
of the funnel shape, waiting for prey to disturb the web. When the silk threads in the web are disturbed, in this case by a Common Greenbottle fly, vibrations are sent to the spider, notifying the spider there is prey at the mouth of the funnel.

THE KILL

The stars were bright as polished gold,
Pale moonbeams glanced across the wold,
Sweet peace and joy reigned everywhere,
Rich floral scents embalmed the air.
Dor-beetles droned in harvest flight,
A glow-worm showed her green tail-light,
The badger cubs played in the glade
Beside the sett their parents made;
Then from the bole of a tall tree
A little owl came quietly,
With saucer eyes probed the haw-hedge
That straggled 'round the lake's brown edge;
Saw roosting there a white-faced coot;
Twice gave a fearsome hunting hoot,
Took wing across the winding stream,
Stooped low: I heard a vole's death-scream!

Barn Owls don't hoot the way most owls do but make a long, harsh scream that lasts about 2 seconds. They have excellent hearing and night vision for capturing prey at night. Their already keen hearing is made more acute by tufts of feathers on the ears which absorb sound. They can hunt by sound alone and are able to catch mice even in a pitch-black environment. The Barn Owl has a huge white facial disc, which is formed by the flattening of the face, and they can turn their heads through 270 degrees to see behind.

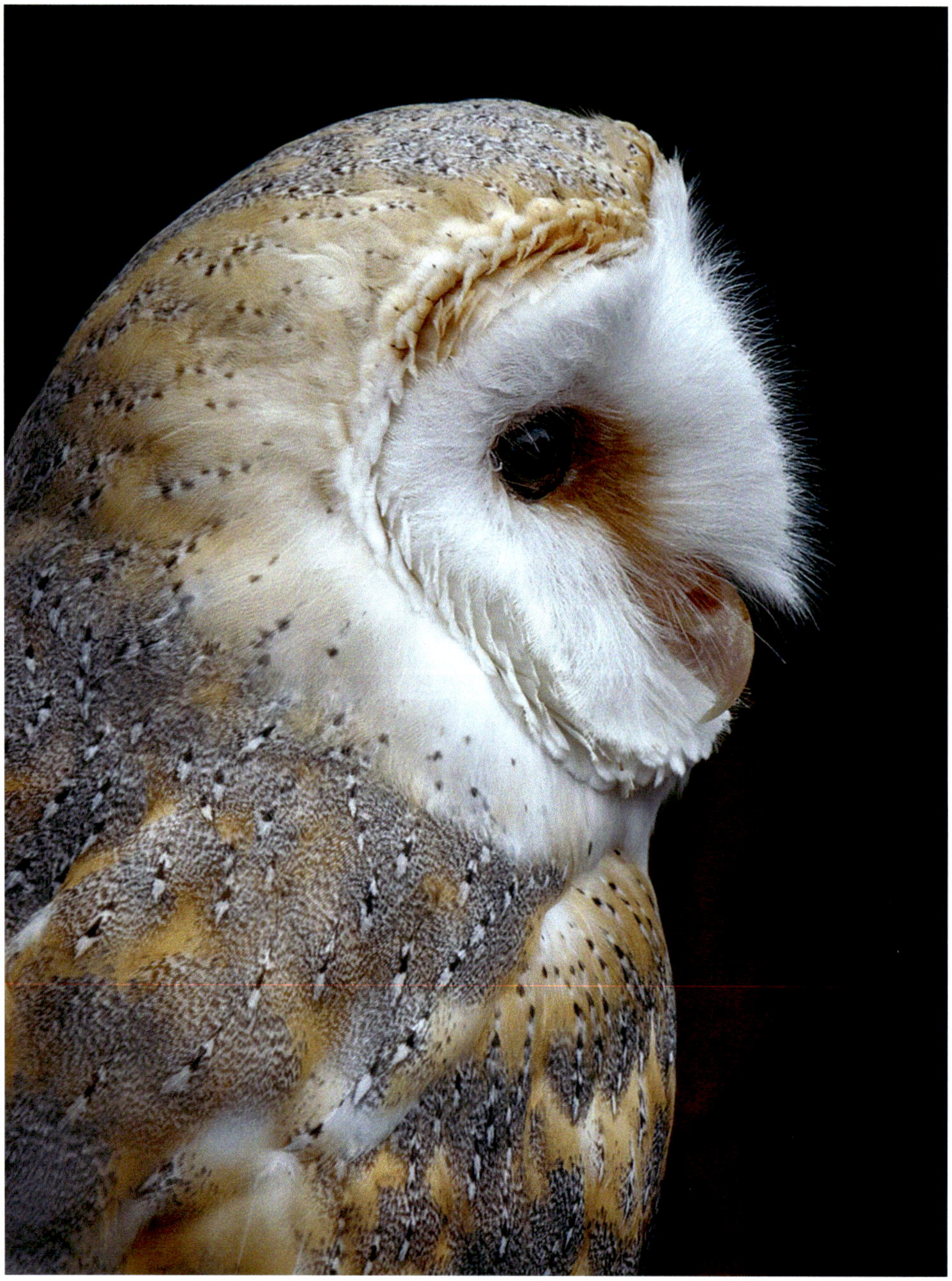

'Then from the bole of a tall tree a little owl came quietly…'

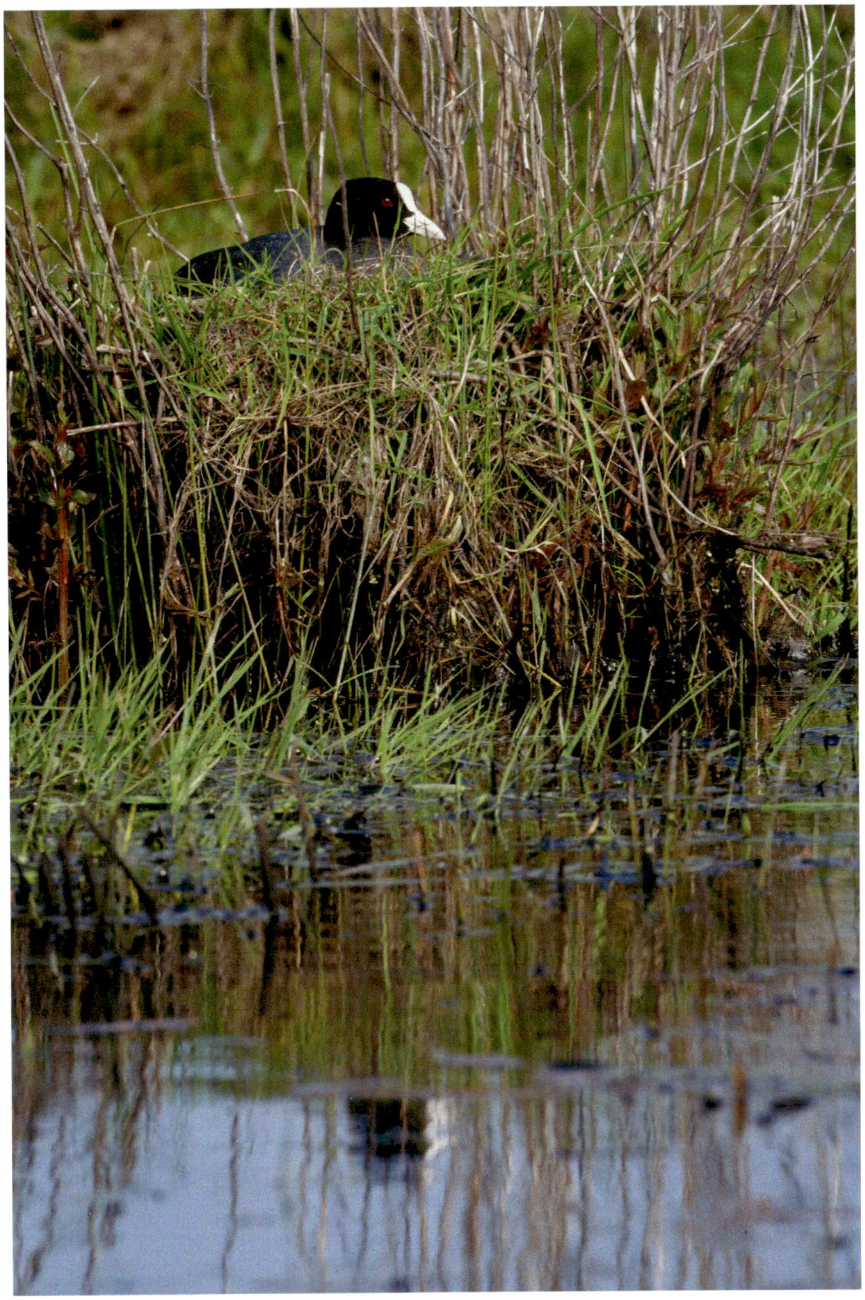

'Saw roosting there a white-faced coot...'

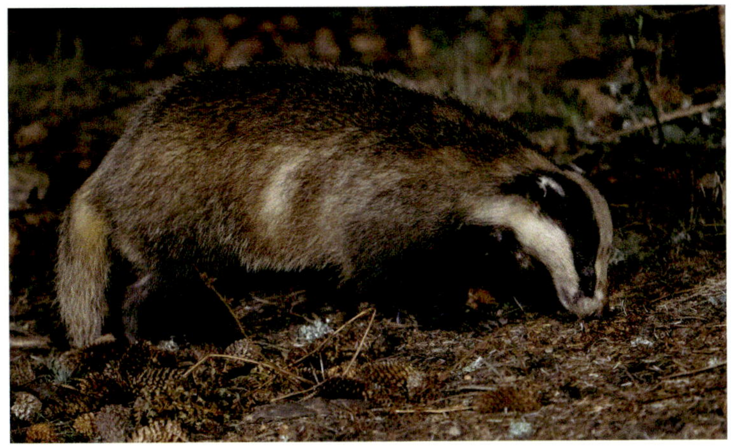

'The badger cubs played in the glade...'

Badgers are widespread throughout Ireland, living in social groups each of which has its own territory and is headed by a dominant male and female. They live in burrow systems known as setts, which can extend for more than 30 yards, and some setts have survived for hundreds of years. They are sociable and playful and live together in family groups known as clans. Cubs are born between January and March. They spend approximately the first eight weeks of life underground, emerging in late April or early May. Badgers have a particularly keen sense of smell. Their vision does not enable them to see much detail, and the cubs, in particular, are very short-sighted.

The white forehead and bill of the Coot (left) give it the appearance of baldness, and hence the term 'bald as a coot'.

QUINTET

November, the month of wild geese
Browsing over the bogland;
Unexpectedly a bittern booms
Alarming his quagmire congeners,
And in the disturbed darkness
A water-rail, heron and coot,
Are suddenly calling.

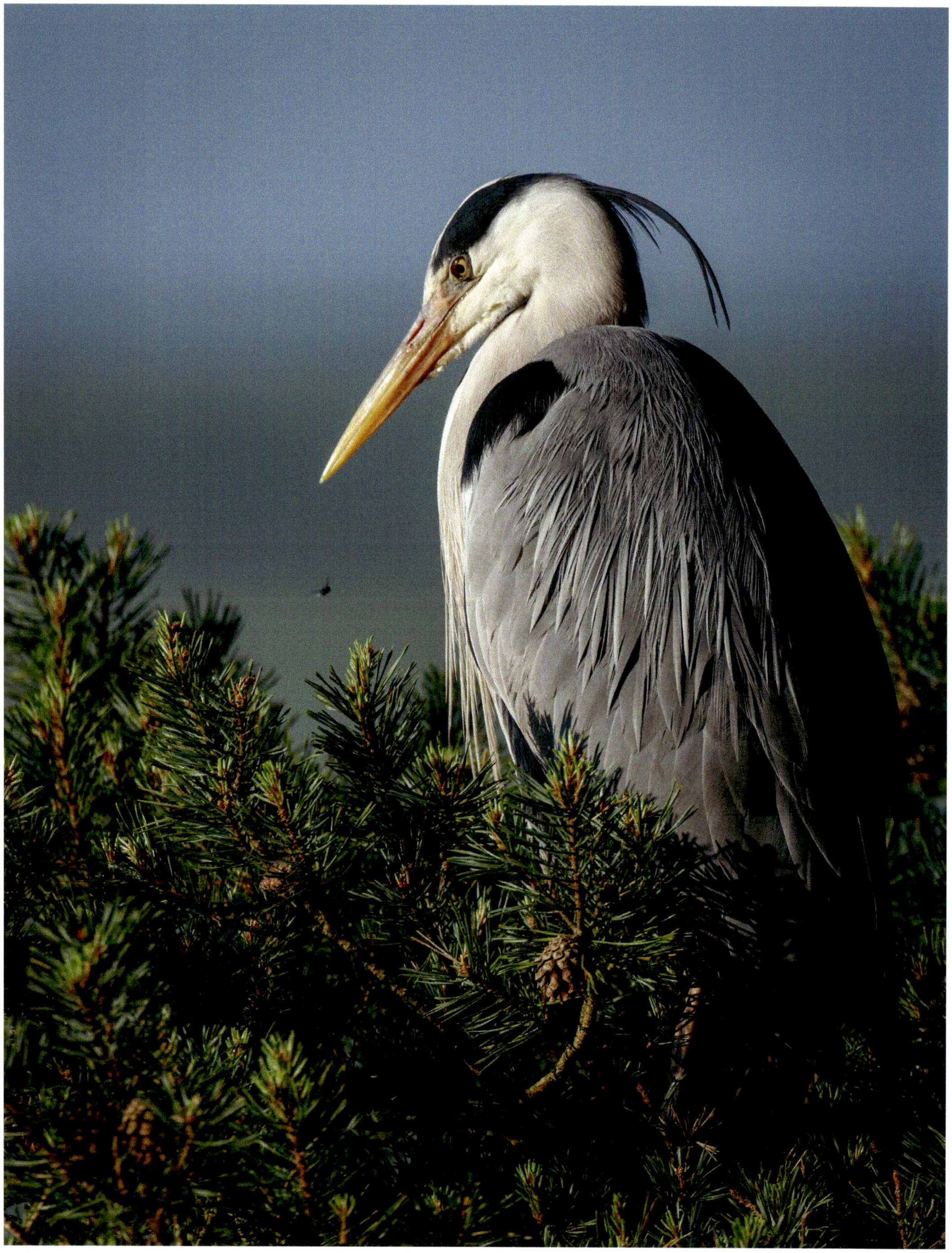

'...in the disturbed darkness a...heron ...'

The Grey Heron is the largest common bird in Ireland next to the Mute Swan. This wading bird is quite vocal, with a variety of calls depending on behaviour. It is often seen peering intently into the water and waiting for an unwary fish to come within striking distance of its dagger-like bill. It is also opportunistic, which means it is very unlikely to pass up the chance of an easy meal, even flies.

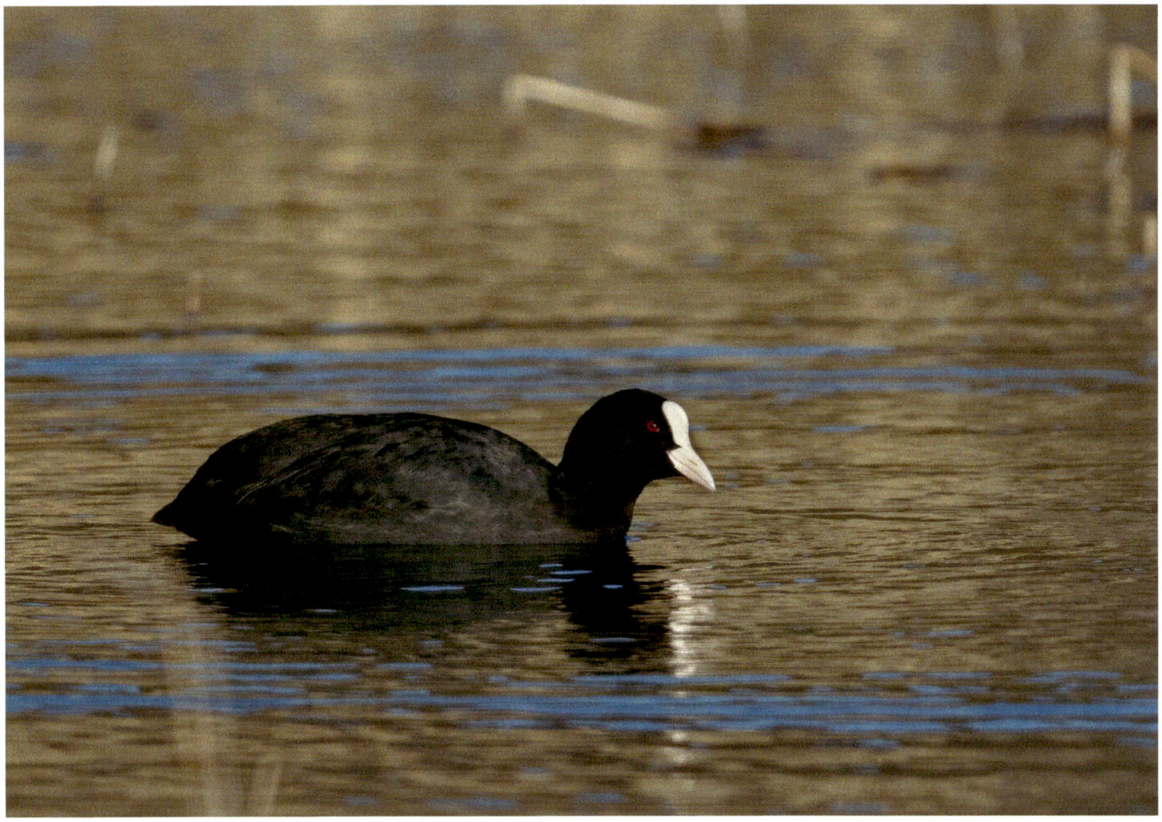

'...a water-rail...and coot are suddenly calling...'

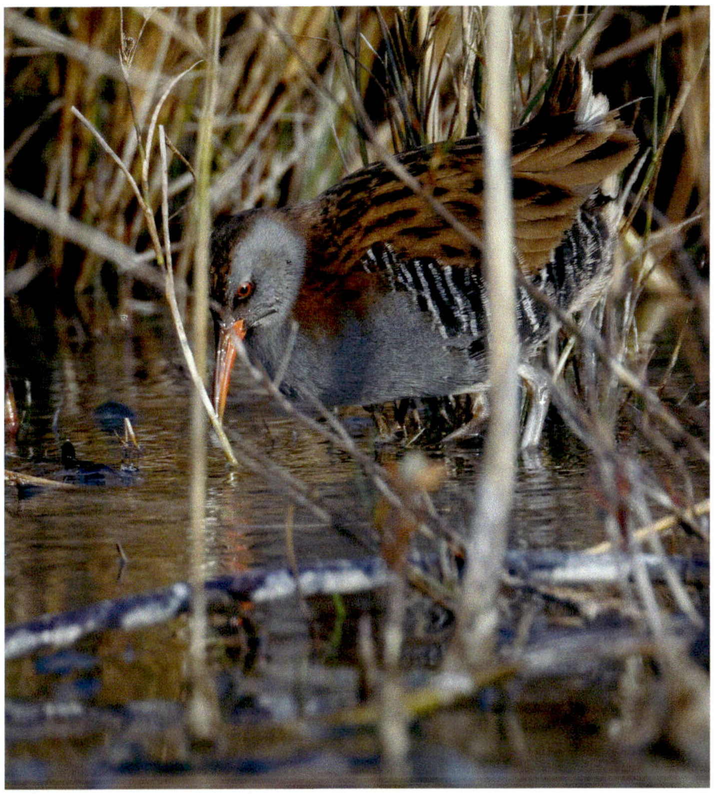

The Coot defends its territory fiercely and will charge intruders.. The call sounds like striking a stone with a metal bar.

The Water Rail (left) is a highly secretive and skulking species living in freshwater wetlands. They are more often heard than seen, as they are so well hidden by vegetation that you can be looking right at the source of the call and still not see them.

The Greenland White-fronted Goose (following page), a subspecies of the greater white-fronted goose, is one of Europe's rarest geese. It was once numerous and widespread throughout the bogs and marshes of Ireland. They first appeared on the Wexford Slobs in 1912, which has, over the course of the 20th century, become their stronghold in Ireland, hosting up to 10,000 birds arriving in October after a journey of about 3,000 km. Migration appears to have more to do with the availability of food than discomfort with weather. As plant life in Greenland becomes dormant for the winter, the geese make their way to milder climes in search of other food sources. This goose has a white forehead and irregular black bars on the belly, with pink or orange bills and orange legs.

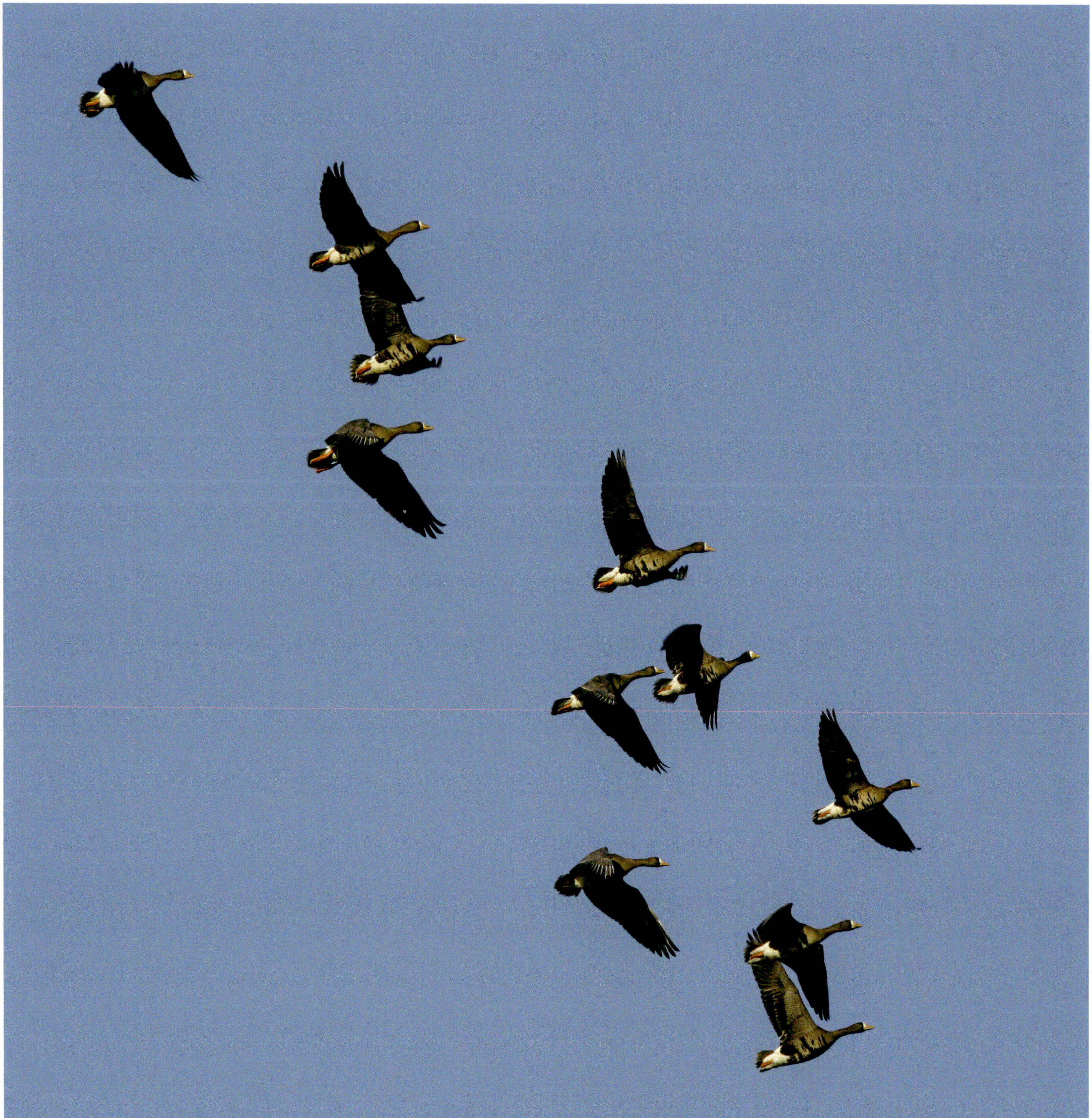

'November, the month of wild geese…'

GRASSHOPPERS

Visiting a sun-drenched meadow
Inhabited by grasshoppers
One feels utterly bewildered
Hearing their ventriloquial chirps.

Walk, all become graveyard silent;
Halt; they are as noisy as corncrakes:
There must be an intelligence
Linking their insect world with ours?

Listen, grasshoppers, as you dance,
Perhaps we could communicate,
Build a bridge to affinity,
Bestride the primordial earth?

Grasshoppers are among what is possibly the most ancient living group of chewing herbivorous insects, dating back to the Early Triassic epoch around 250 million years ago. They make chirping noises by rubbing a row of pegs on their hind legs against the edges of the forewings (stridulation) as a means of communication. Male grasshoppers spend much of the day stridulating to express reproductive maturity. The song of the male Common Green Grasshopper is penetrating, fast and continuous. That of the Common Field Grasshopper consists of a series of short chirps.

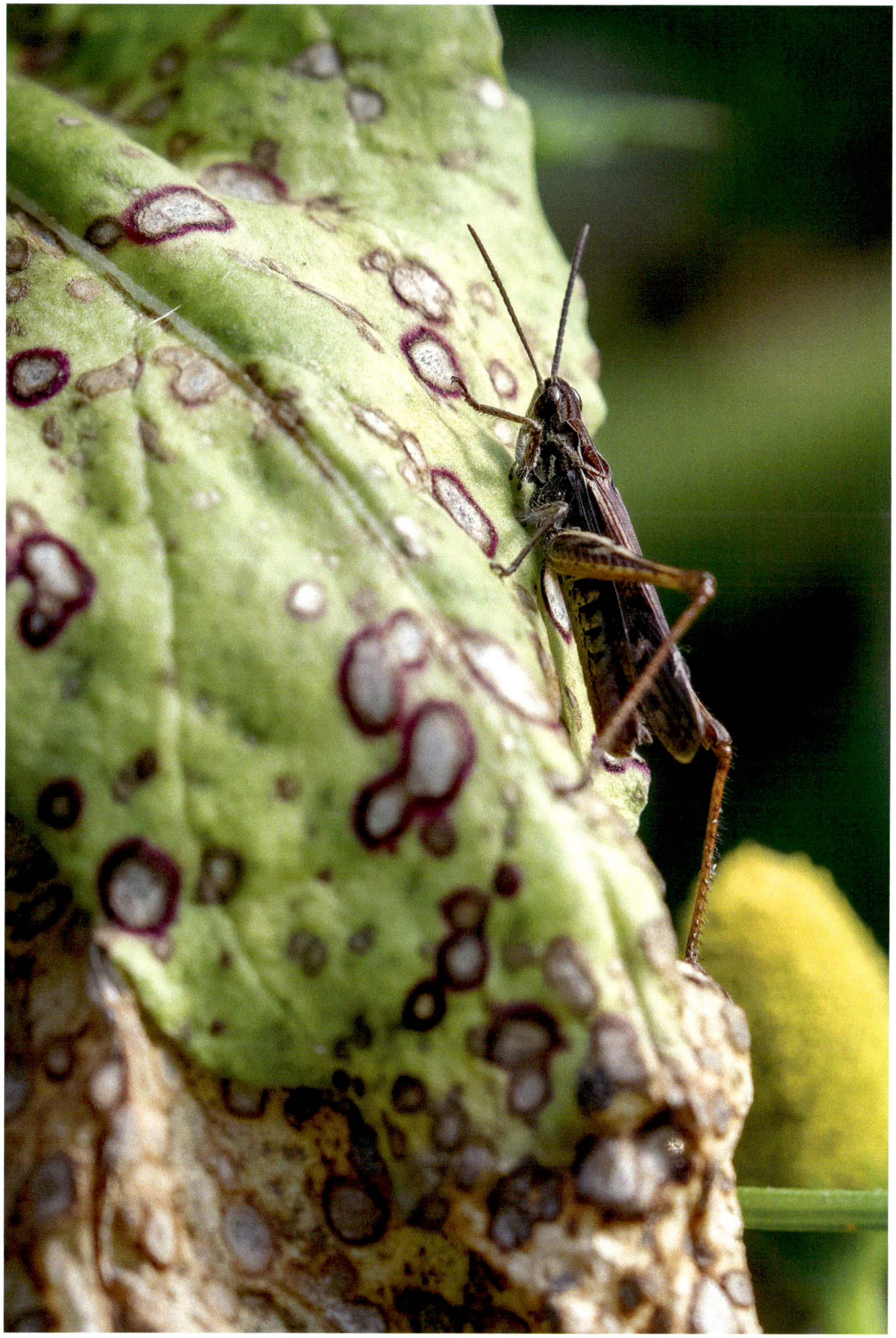

'Listen, grasshoppers, as you dance...'

WHEN SPRING COMES DANCING

When Spring comes dancing o'er the lea
Each plant begins to dress,
The bramble and the buttercup,
The lowly watercress;
The pimpernel, the heatherbell,
the campion by the sea;
The tormentil, the daffodil,
When Spring comes dancing o'er the lea.

When Spring comes dancing o'er the lea
The insect world is seen,
The red-ant and the grasshopper,
The beetle, jacket green;
The whirligig, the brown earwig,
The flick'ring flying flea;
The field aphis, the pond caddis,
When Spring comes dancing o'er the lea.

When Spring comes dancing o'er the lea.
The feathered tribe make love,
The siskin and the redpoll,
The pale blue turtle-dove;
the sanderling, the shy lapwing,
The creeper of the tree;
The crested tit, the rock-pipit,
When Spring comes dancing o'er the lea.

When Spring comes dancing o'er the lea.
The animals all play,
The rabbit and the lesser shrew,
The badger blueish-grey;
The otter dog, thea armed hedgehog,
The hare near his settee;
The marten-cat, the long-eared bat,
When Spring comes dancing o'er the lea.

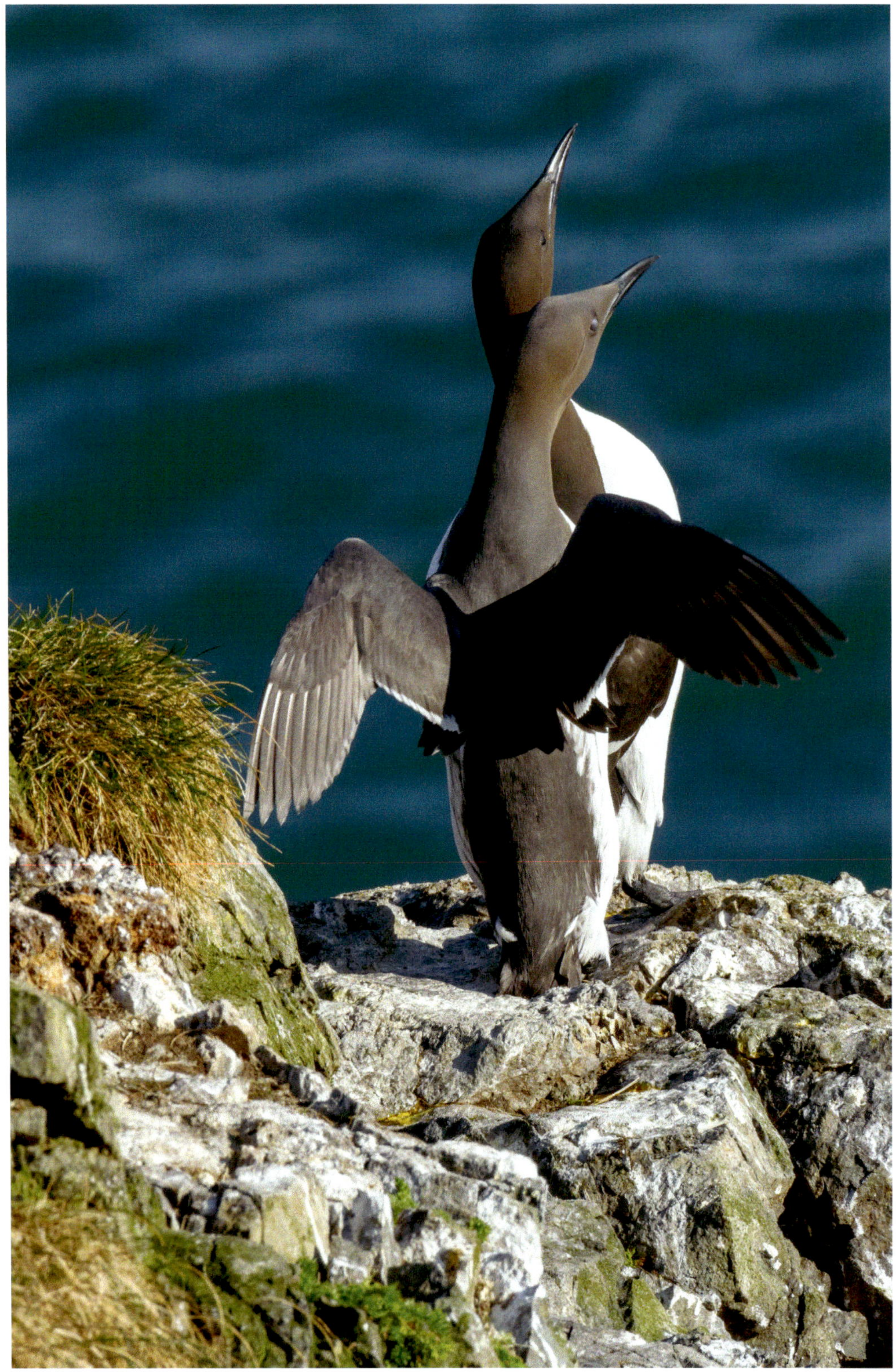

Guillemots: 'When Spring comes dancing o'er the lea, the feathered tribe make love…'

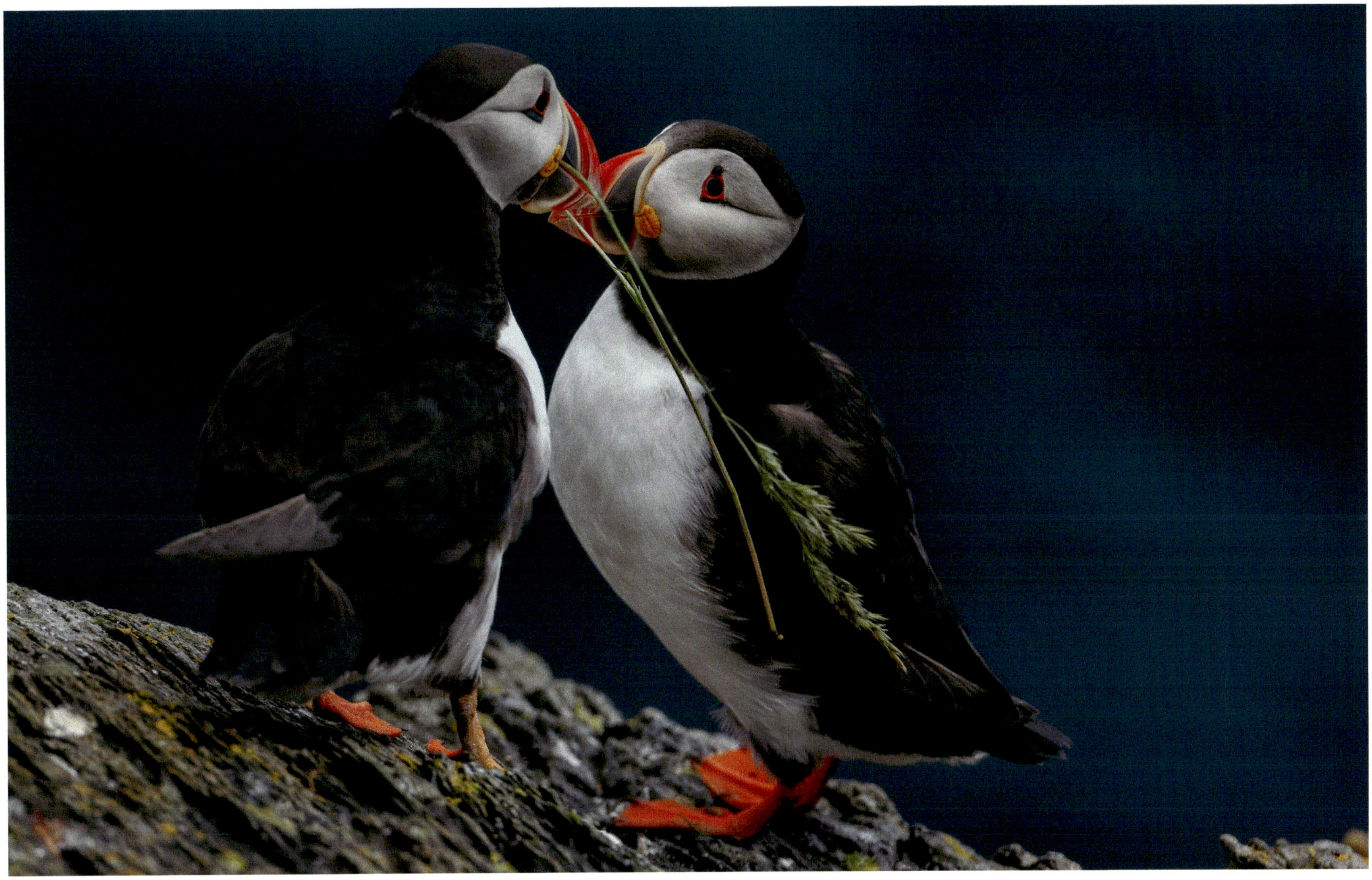

Puffins: '...the feathered tribe make love...'

All sea birds are monogamous and most mate for life. Guillemots, puffins and Razorbills are collectively known as Auks. They resemble penguins with their plumage colouring and upright stance. They are also expert divers and swimmers under water, using their wings to propel themselves in pursuit of sand eels and sprat.

On the previous page, two Guillemots standing on a cliff ledge begin courtship near the same site that they return to each year. In the breeding season, head and neck are completely dark brown. They build no nest but place their single conical egg on steep coastal cliffs. The egg's pear shape makes it roll in an arc, minimising the risk of it falling over the edge. The birds breed in colonies, living close together and facing the cliffs to protect the eggs and chicks from bad weather and predatory gulls. The chick is always with at least one parent while the other goes off fishing, diving a couple of hundred feet down and staying under water for over four minutes.

Atlantic Puffins (above) form long-term bonds, with the male building the nest in a burrow about a yard long, the female laying a large single egg, and both parents taking turns to incubate the egg and feed the chick. The characteristic bright orange bill plates grow before the breeding season and are shed after breeding. Their bills are used in courtship ritual called 'billing' when they rub their beaks together. Also here, the male has collected some nest material.

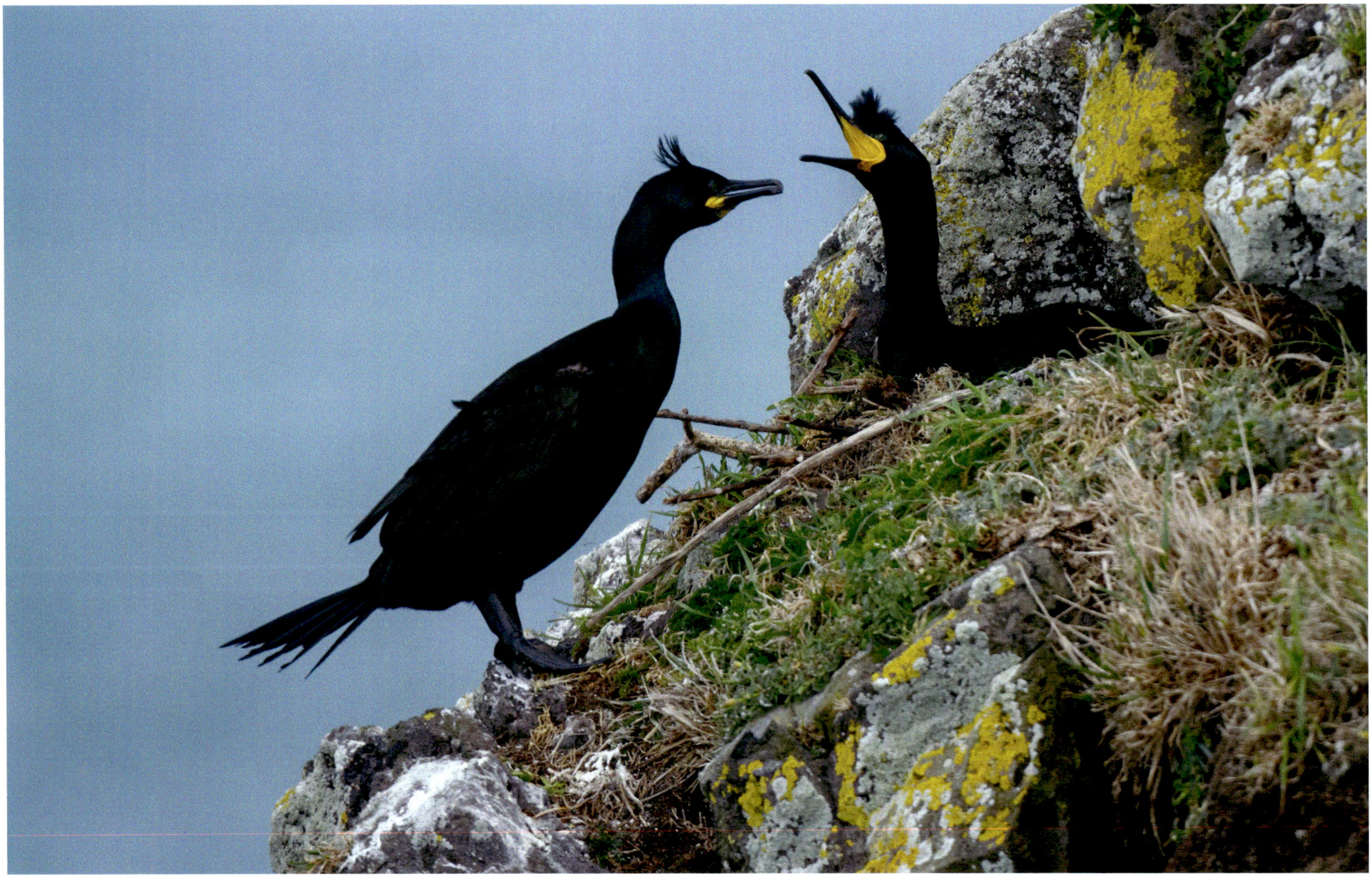

Shags – '...the feathered tribe make love...'

The strong, straight bill of the Shag is yellowish in non-breeding season and black during courtship. During the breeding season, the plumage acquires a green gloss and a large tuft of elongated feathers forms a conspicuous crest in the centre of the crown. Male Shags attract mates by performing the dart-gape, in which they point their heads towards the sky, moving it upward and forward with their bills open. Unlike the Puffin and Fulmar, the Shag lays many eggs.

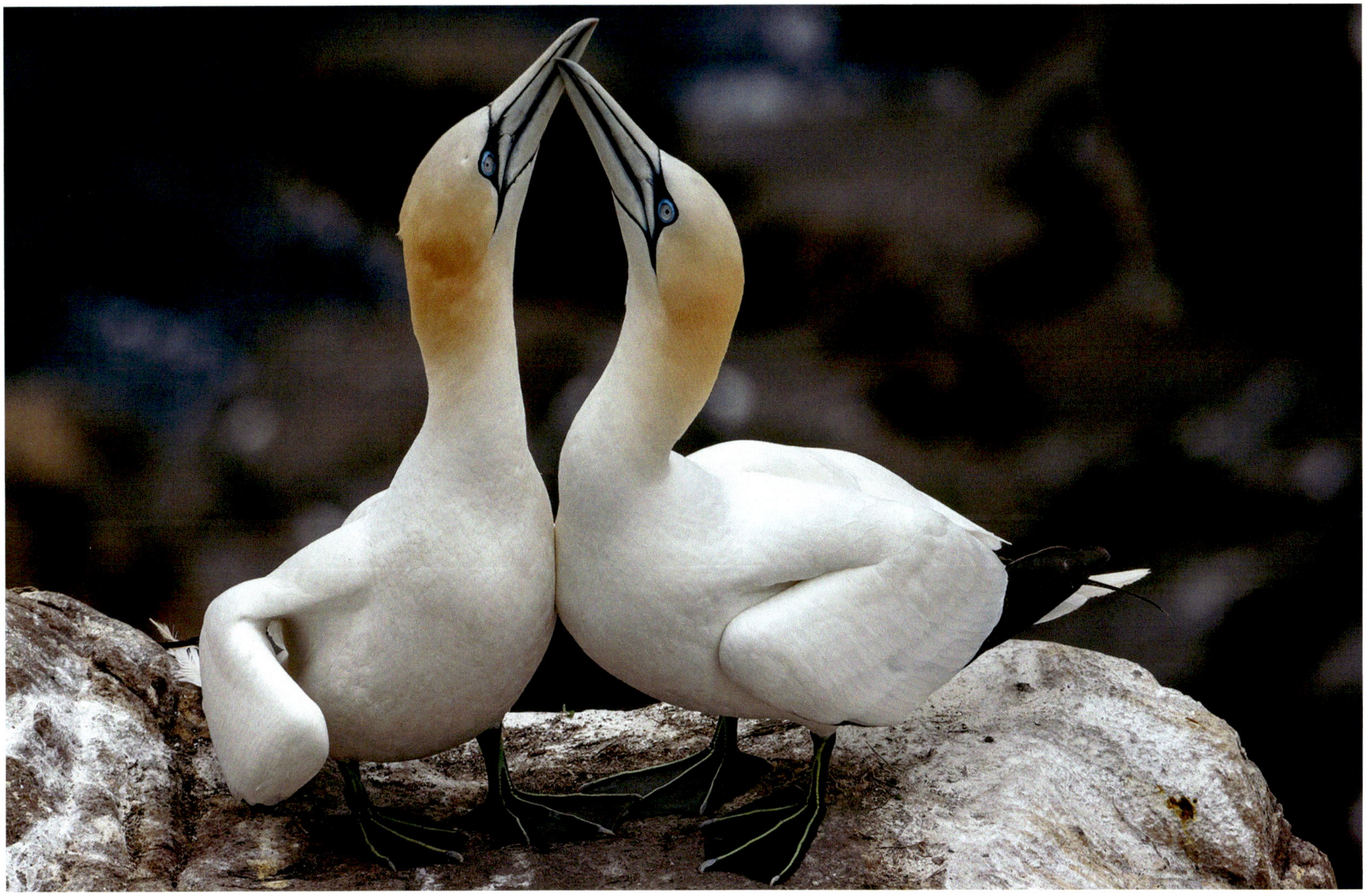

Gannets – '...the feathered tribe make love...'

There are five Gannet colonies off the coast of Ireland but Little Skellig is the second largest gannet colony in the world. Gannets conduct a distinctive mating display using their beaks to show affection. The two birds face each other, bowing, pointing their heads skywards, shaking their heads side to side with their bills held high and knocking against each together, breasts touching, and finally preening each other's neck. They fish by plunging into shoals, the great beak forming the arrowhead of a body with wings folded back and offering no resistance to the water.

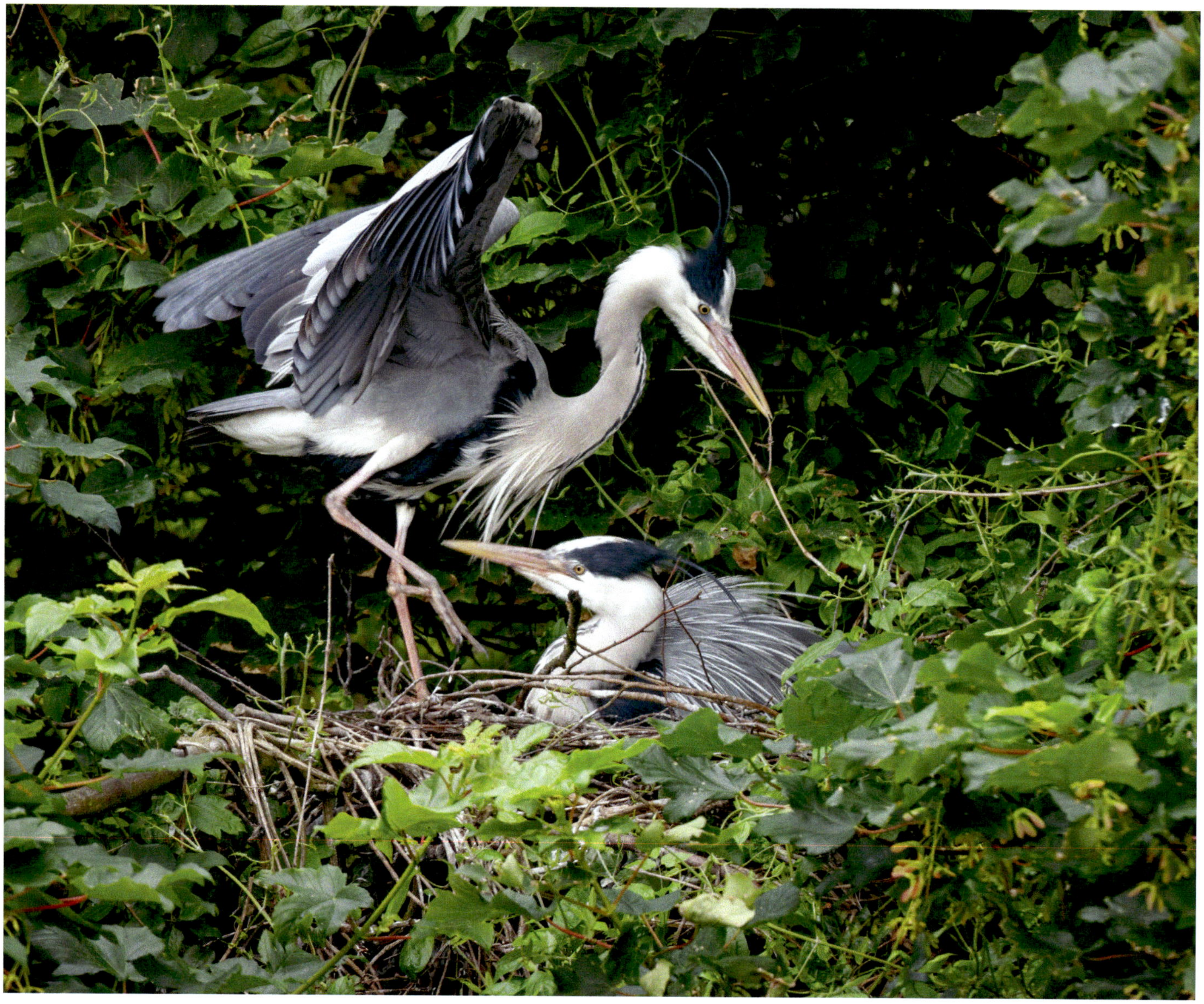

Herons – '...the feathered tribe make love...'

Perched high in the sycamore trees in Kinsale, Co. Cork, is a well-established Grey Heron colony. The breeding season begins as early as February and continues through May or June. The male selects the nest site, which may be on the site of an old nest. He selects a suitable female by displaying, and during courtship they engage in bill clapping and preening each other. At this time the yellow bill and legs change from yellow to deep orange and the crest becomes more developed. If he allows her to stay, they begin the nest building. He collects the nest material, finding twigs in the dense undergrowth, which is not easy for a large wading bird with long legs. Each stick is always transferred beak to beak to the female who tirelessly works the material to construct the nest . They then take turns to incubate the eggs.

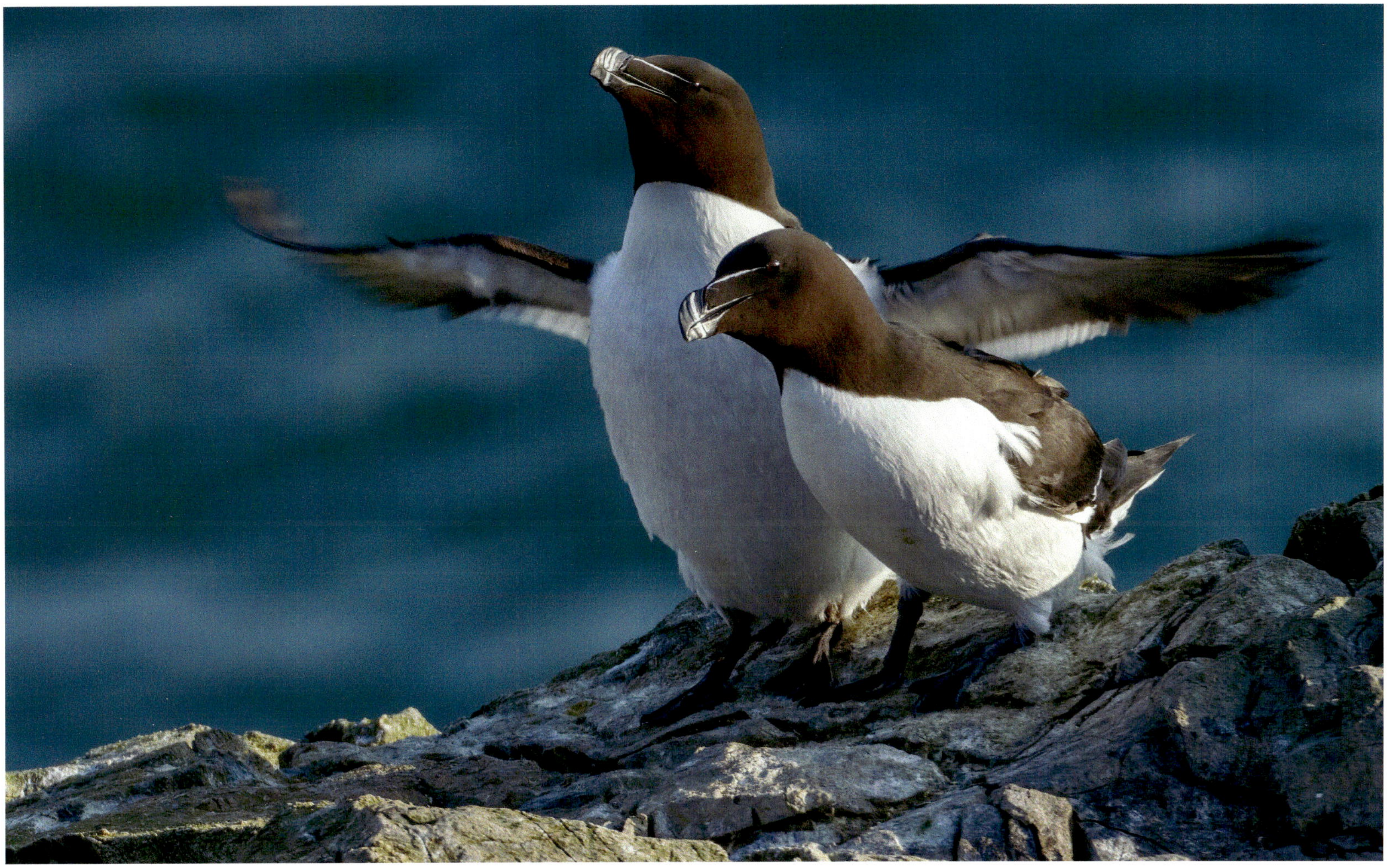

Razorbills – '…the feathered tribe make love…'

Razorbills court several times during breeding periods to strengthen their bond. The female lays one egg a year and both parents spend equal amounts of time incubating. Once the chick has hatched, the parents take turns foraging and sometimes fly long distances for prey. When puffins leave the nest they have to fend for themselves. However, the Razorbill chick is persuaded to leave at a younger stage by the father, who remains with it until it can fend for itself.

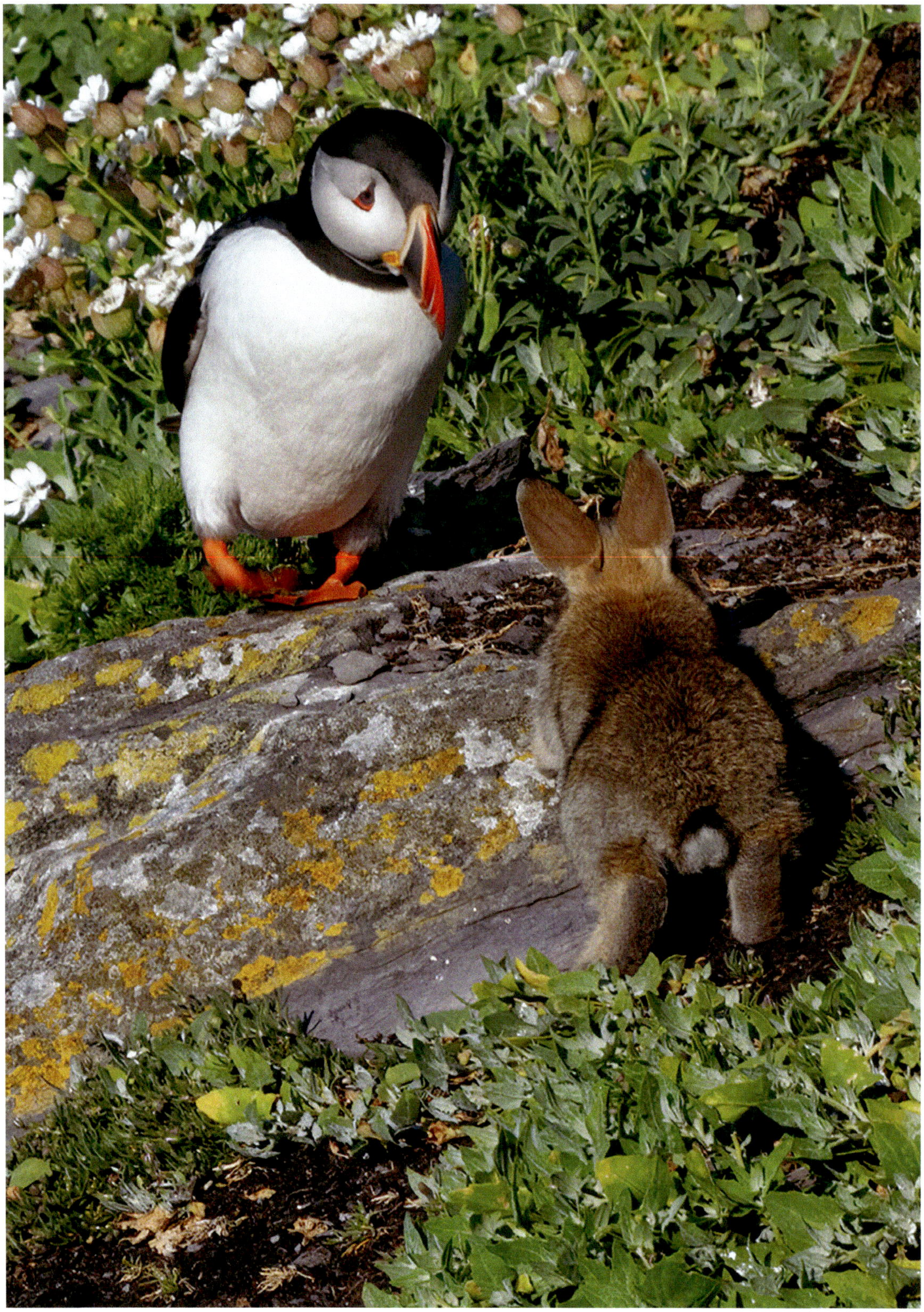

'The animals all play...'

Puffins have to share their burrows with the rabbit population on Skellig Michael. The baby rabbit is naturally inquisitive and playful, no doubt attracted by the puffin's claws and brightly coloured bill. Sea campion are at their finest from late May, which coincides wonderfully with the arrival of puffins.

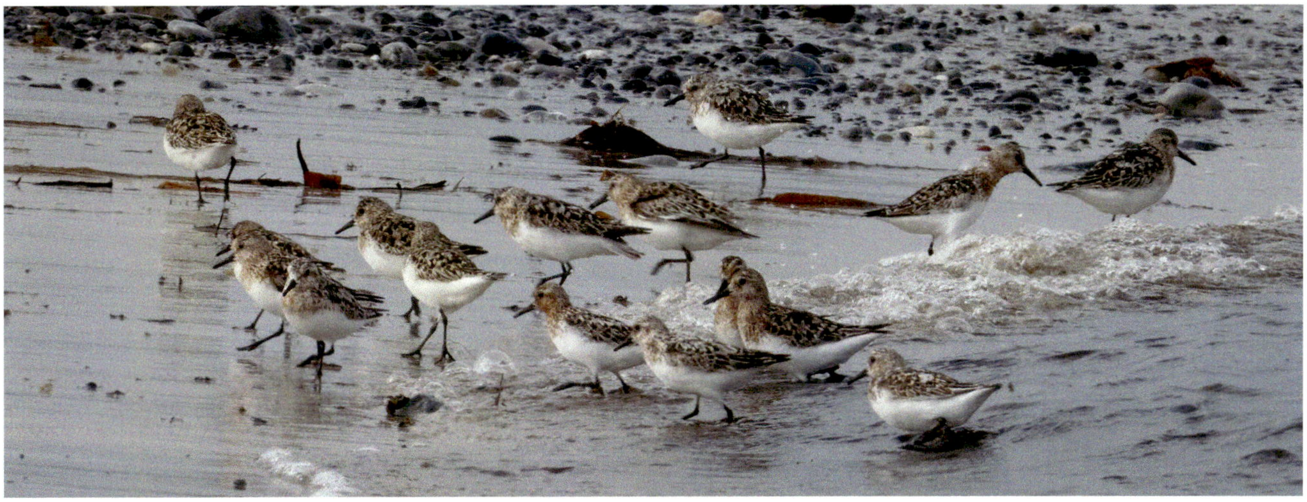

The Sanderling is a medium-sized sandpiper. It has a highly characteristic feeding technique of scampering back and forth in small flocks after the waves looking for insects, crustaceans, and worms.

'...the sanderling...'

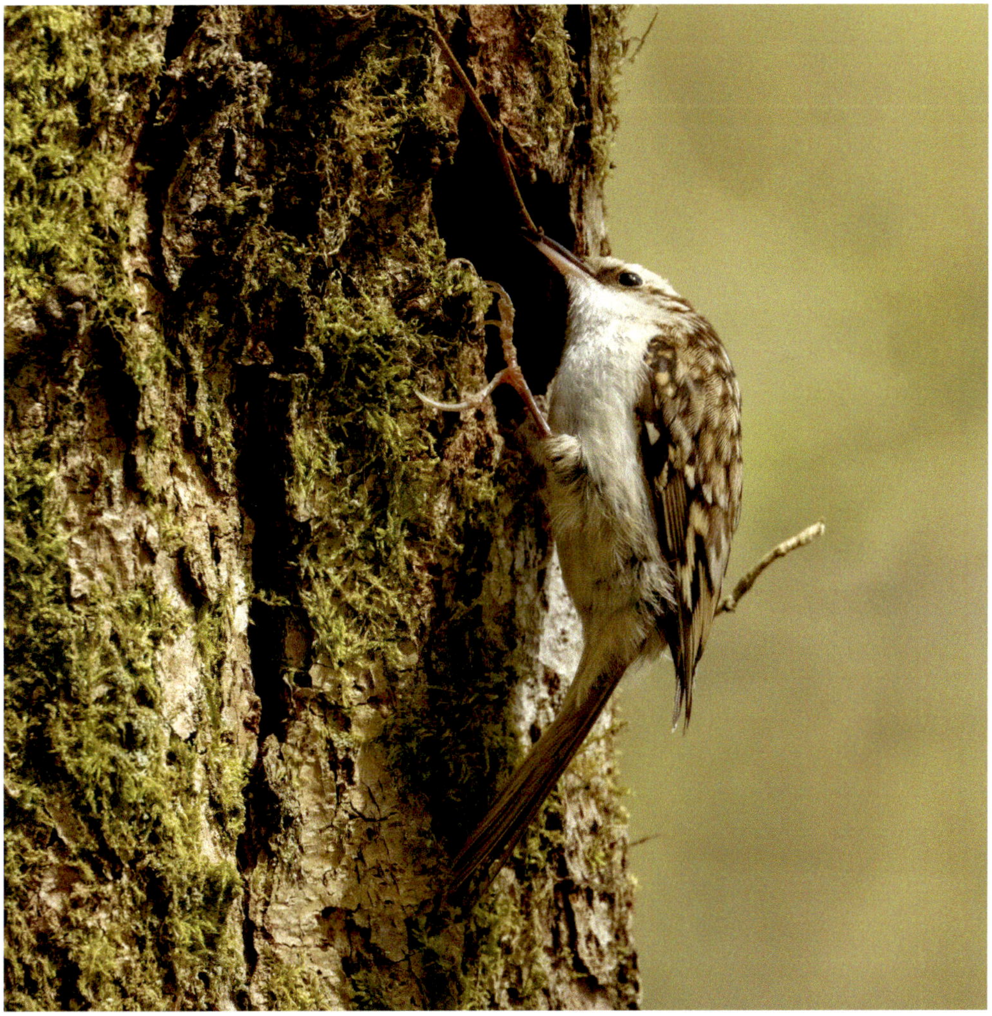

The Tree Creeper (above) scurries up tree trunks and on reaching the top flies to the base of another tree. They nest in narrow gaps and clefts or behind the loose bark in mature trees. Tree Creepers are hard to spot but it is the movement that gives them away.

'...the creeper of the tree...'

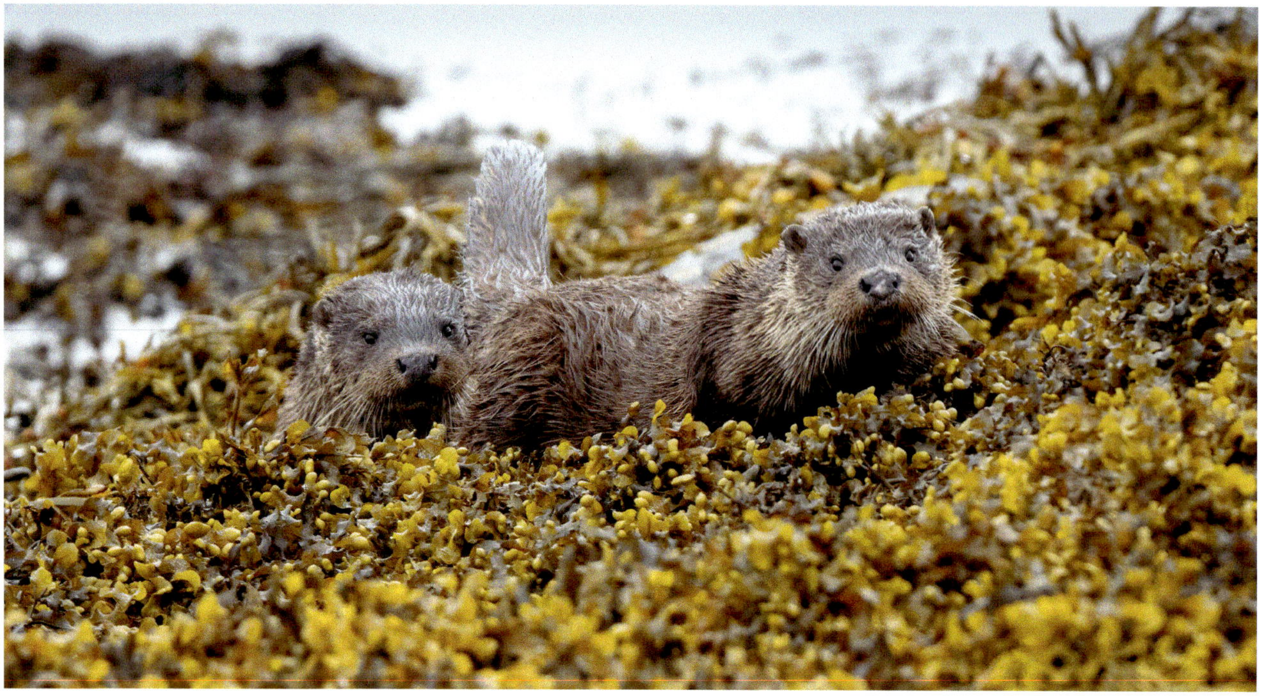

Although otters are nocturnal, carnivorous hunters, the coastal dwelling individuals are generally more active in the daytime compared to those who occupy freshwater habitats

'…the otter dog…'

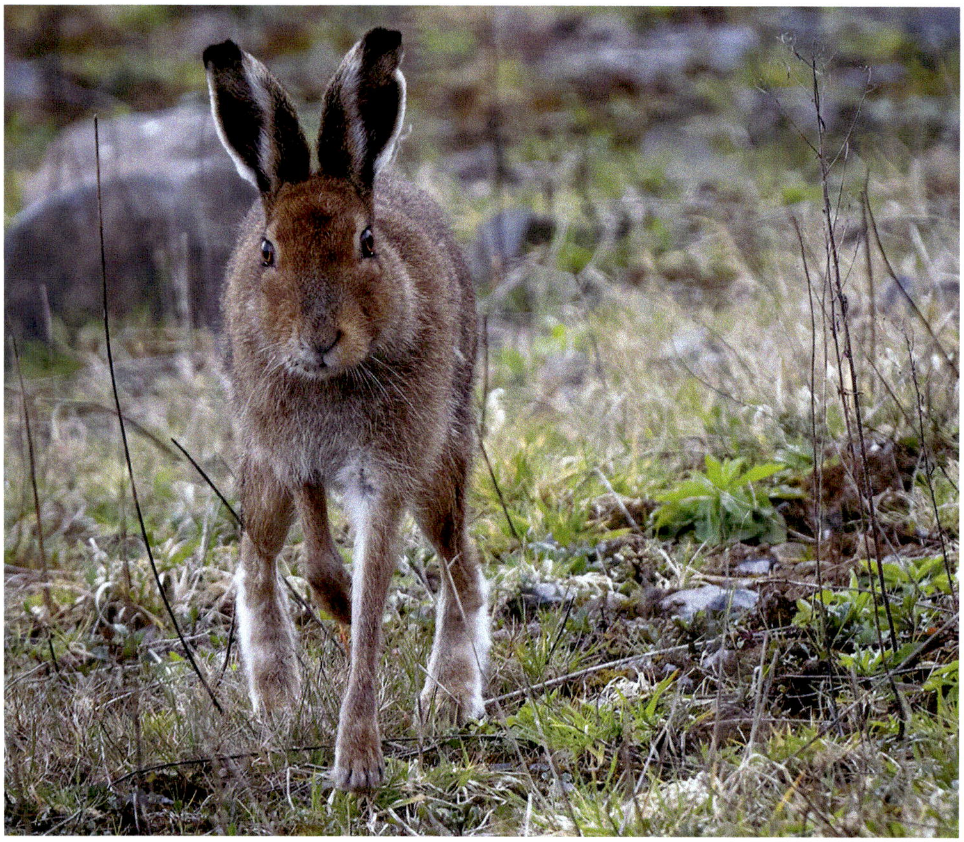

The Irish Hare is unique to Ireland and is arguably our oldest surviving mammal. The Irish Hare is larger than the Mountain Hare found in Scotland, which is also a sub-species of the Arctic Hare, but smaller than the Common Brown Hare, which arrived from southern Europe and has longer limbs than both species. The long hind legs propel the hare at phenomenal speed over short distances, reaching up to 30mph and jumping heights of around 2 metres. The all-white tail of the Irish Hare is perhaps its most characteristic feature along with its relatively short ears and elongated head. It is among the most graceful of our mammals.

'The hare near his settee…'

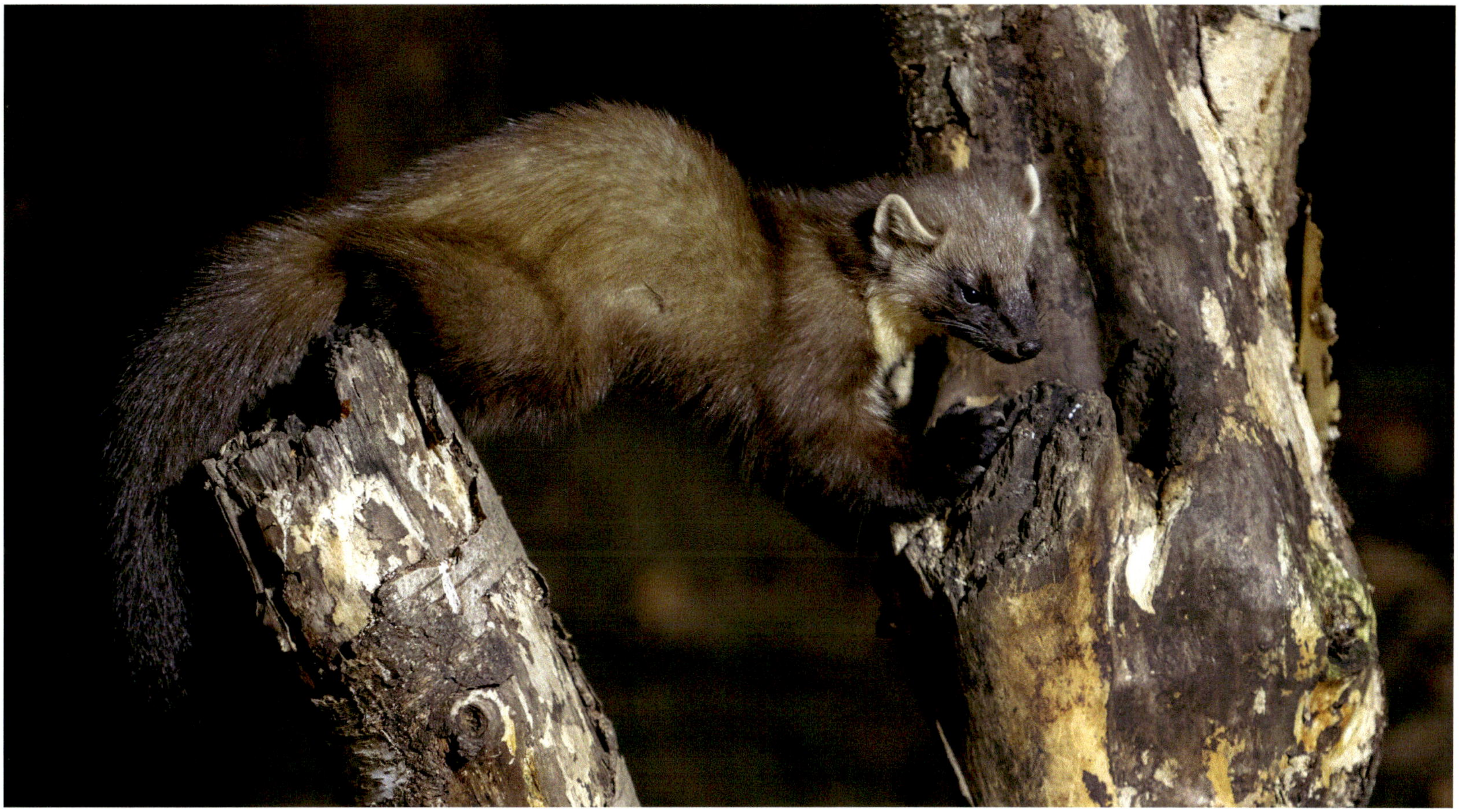

'…the marten-cat…'

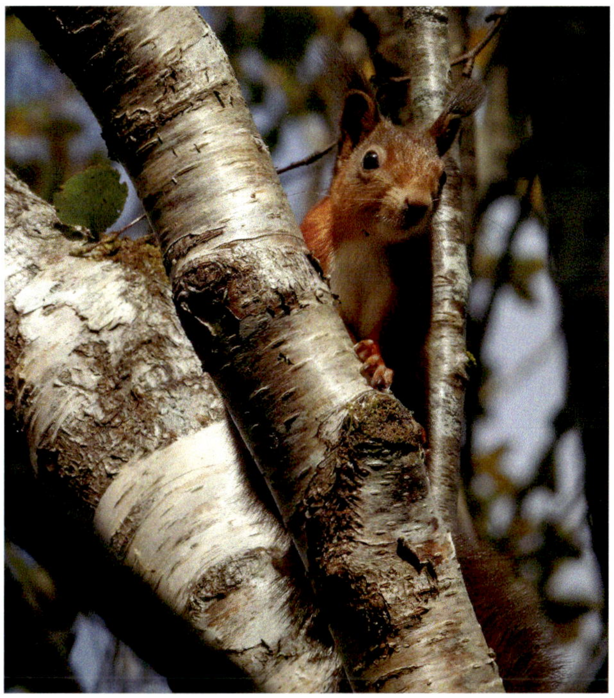

The Pine Marten is Ireland's most elusive wild animal and is credited with reducing the population of the invasive Grey Squirrel. It was once widely distributed throughout the country until the 17th century when the clearance of many native forests as well as hunting the animal for its pelt caused a drastic decline in numbers. By the 1970s it had become the rarest of all the Irish mammals but has been legally protected since 1976, and with enlightened attitudes and the planting of new forests their numbers have increased.

It has been discovered that Red Squirrels (left) can coexist with pine martens but Grey Squirrels cannot. The Pine Marten is the size of a domestic cat with a rich fur coat, a very long tail, a distinguishing creamy-yellow throat patch and is adept at climbing trees. The Grey Squirrel is twice the size of the native red squirrel and is possibly slower and more easily hunted by the carnivorous pine marten. Its introduction to Ireland led to a displacement of the charismatic Red Squirrel partly due to competition for food and space but also due to a disease carried by the Grey Squirrel called squirrel pox virus, which was fatal to the native species.

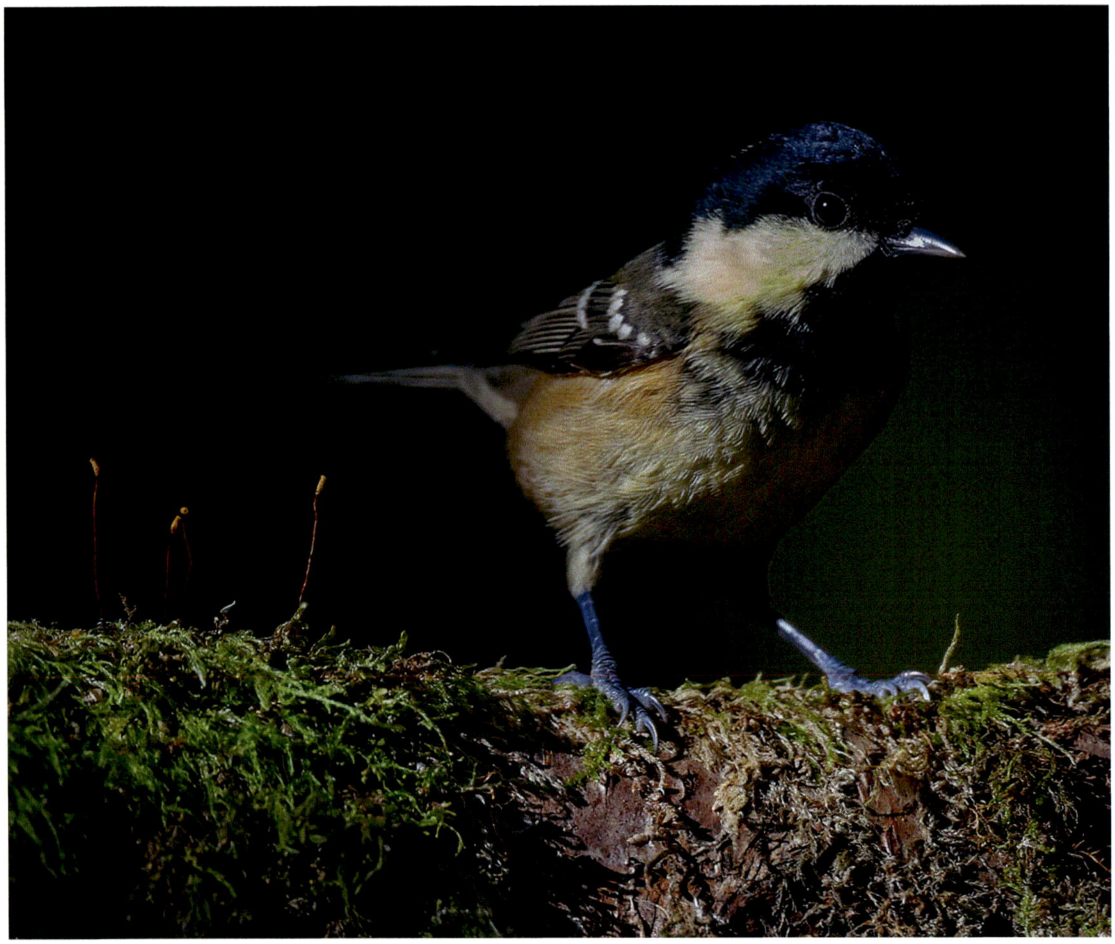

'…the crested tit…'

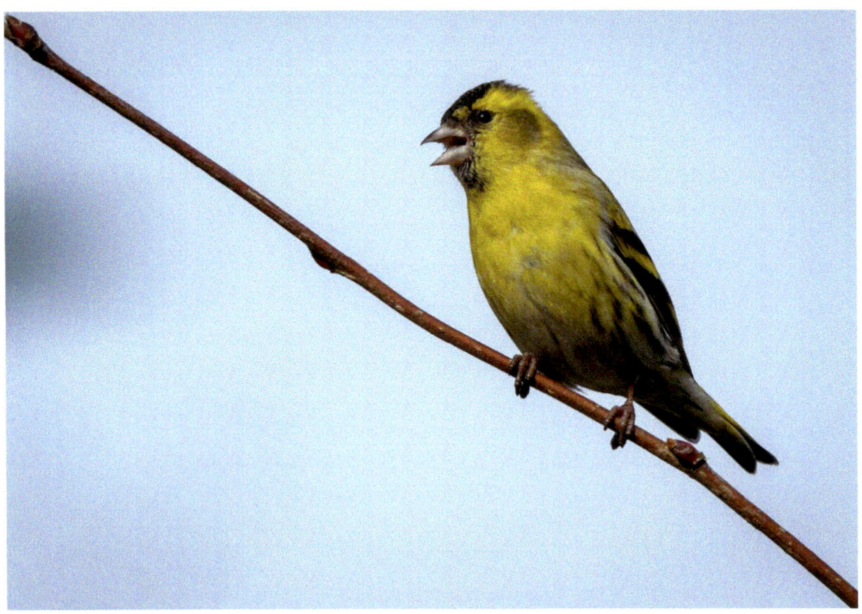

'…the siskin…'

There are no Crested Tits in Ireland only in the highlands of Scotland. The poem's reference may be to the Coal Tit (above) which is resident in Ireland and often show a tiny crest.

Come the spring, the beautiful yellow-green female Siskin will build her nest high in the cover of a conifer tree.

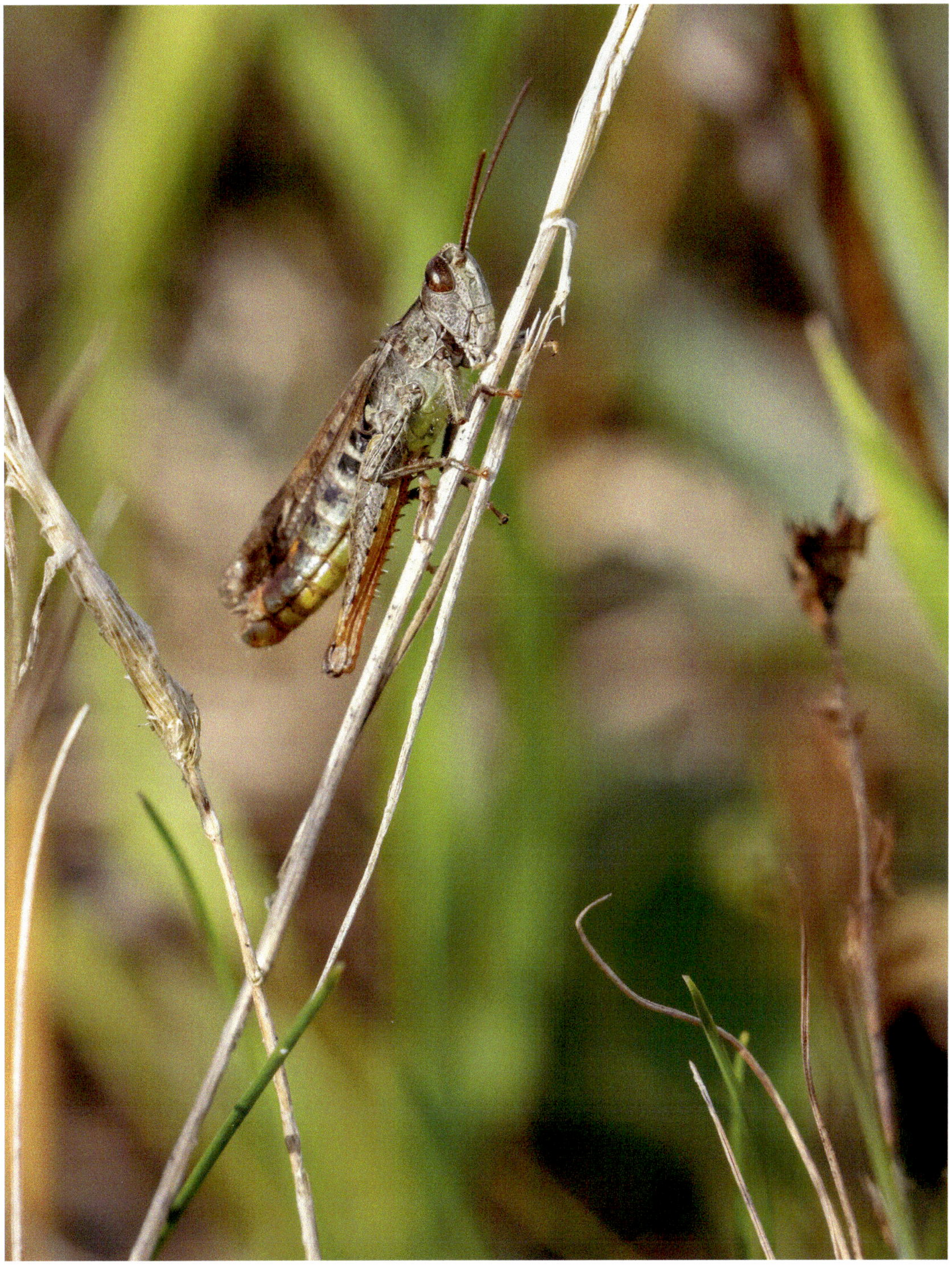

"OH COULD I BE A GREEN GRASSHOPPER"

I list to the chirps of the grasshopper
As he flies from blade to blade,
And never comes a cropper,
For hopping is his trade,
And he does it unafraid.

Oh! could I be like a green
grasshopper,
My love, I would fly to thee;
Dress'd as a princeling, dapper,
Joyful as melody,
But a pauper, Love, I be.

Grasshoppers are typically ground-dwelling insects with powerful hind legs that allow them to escape from threats by leaping vigorously, usually flying for only a short distance. The Common Field Grasshopper shows great variation in colour. Normally, the adults range through several shades of brown, with the most common varieties striped, semi-mottled and mottled. The female Common Green Grasshopper is always green. The male is either green or brown with a certain amount of green on the face. The Common Field Grasshopper prefers dry habitats, whereas the Common Green Grasshopper is a moisture lover and prefers lush vegetation.

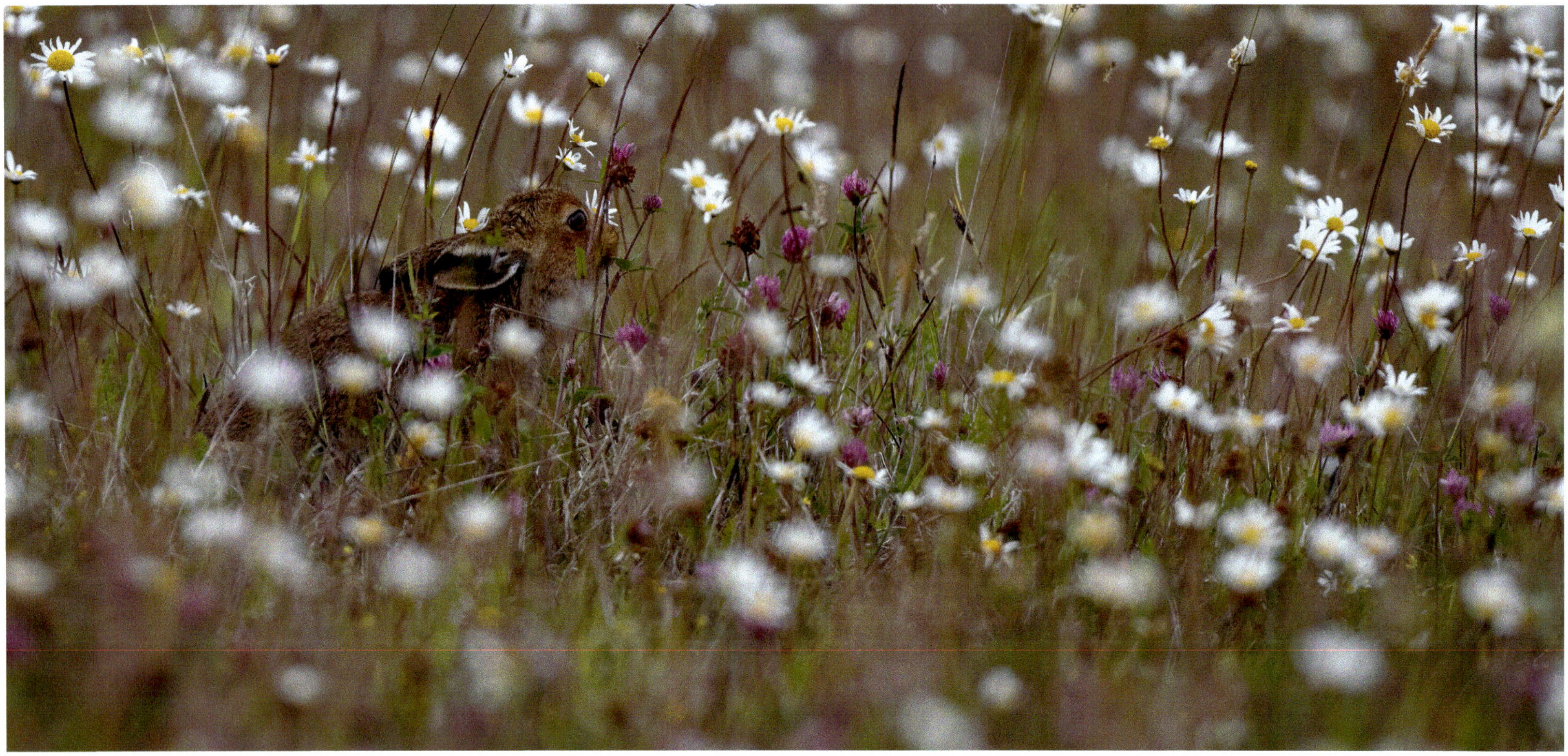

'...daisies dressing everywhere...'

MAY-TIME

May is in the fragrant air,
The goldfinches are singing,
Daisies dressing everywhere,
And busy brown bees winging.

Glitter the glum-grasses green,
Algae on the wishing-well,
Spider webs wove in between,
And the wall-snail's mottled shell.

Hedgehogs are awake again,
Burnets floating o'er the thorn,
Stoats in the shadowy lane,
Mice through the ascending corn.

Comfrey, coltsfoot and red clover,
All sweet nature is awake,
Icy winter-time is over,
The wild geese have left the lake.

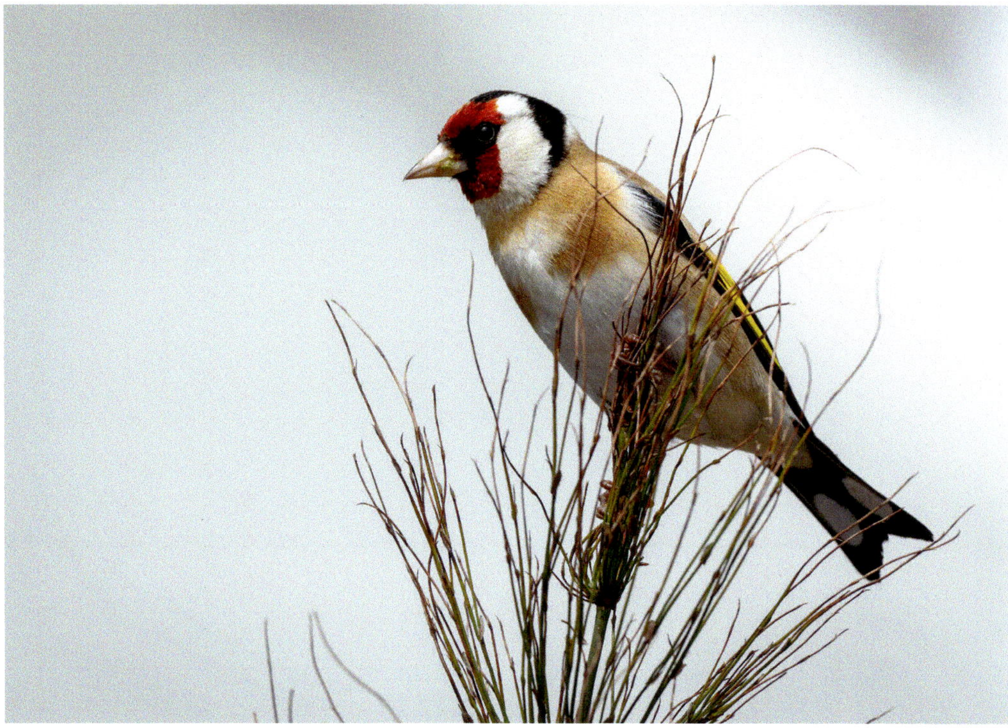

'...the goldfinches are singing...'

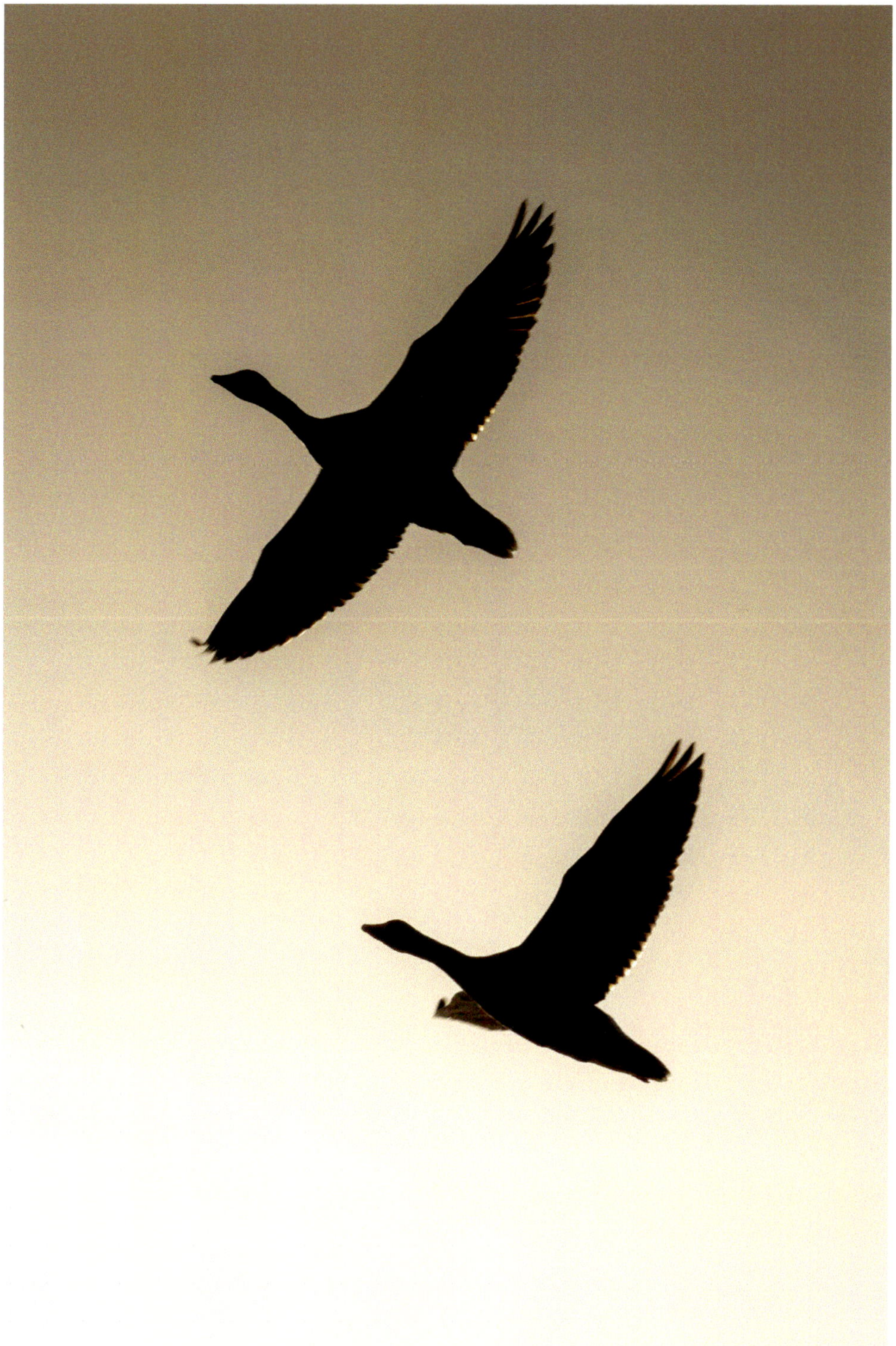

'...the wild geese have left the lake...'

The Oxeye Daisy (previous page) is a native wildflower. The flower has white petals and yellow central florets. It is perfect for pollinators and in this case a good hiding place for a leveret.

The Goldfinch (bottom, facing page) is one of Ireland's most widespread and colourful small birds.

Thousands of geese and swans migrate from Iceland, Greenland and Canada to spend the winter in Ireland. Around October, Icelandic Greylags (cousins of the Greenland White-fronts) are among the many species that fly 1,300km directly across the ocean to Ireland, returning to Iceland to breed in April. Day length tells the birds it is time to move north, and when the wind feels right, an impulse travels through the flock.

The Six-spot Burnet Moth (below) is a day-flying moth that flies with a slow, fluttering pattern and is very abundant on some coastal sites. Because the burnets' antennae gradually thicken towards the tip and they fly in sunshine, they could be mistaken for butterflies. The green caterpillar of the Six-spot Burnet hibernates in winter and, in spring, crawls up a stem to make its cocoon.

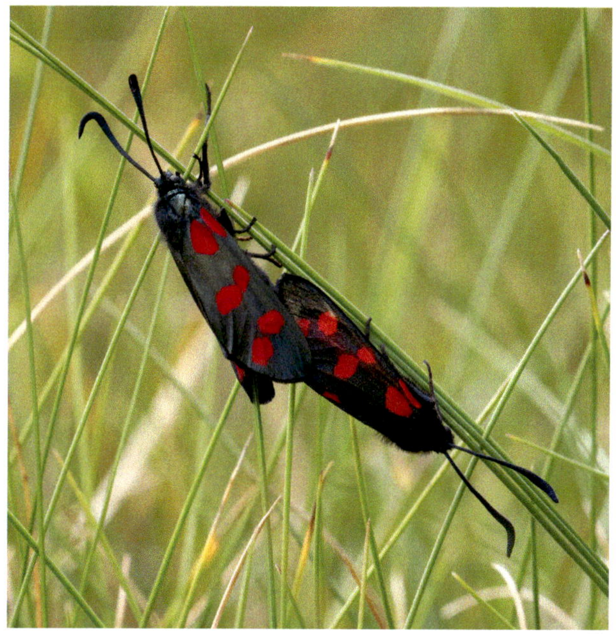

'Burnets floating o'er the thorn...'

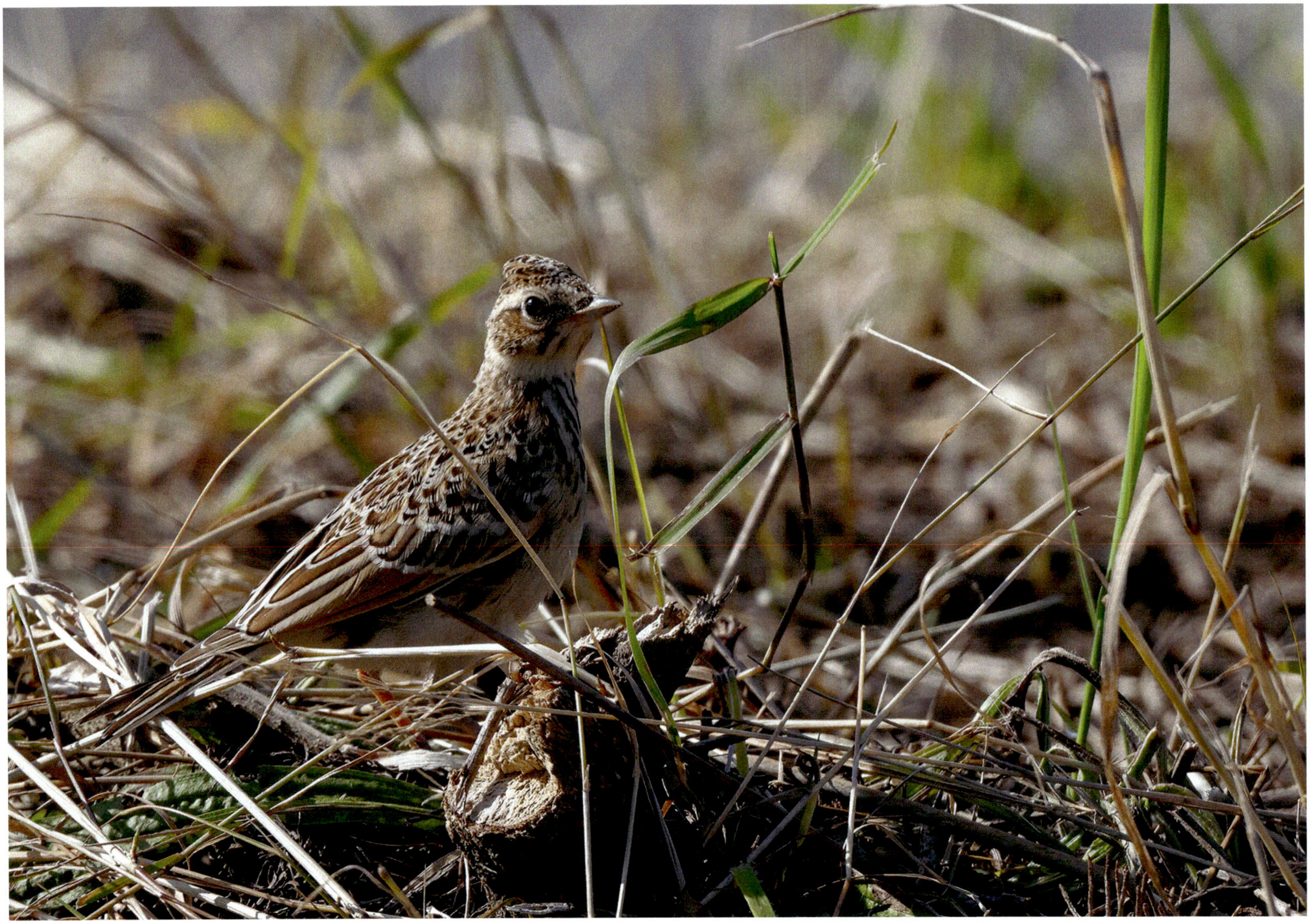

'...and silent is the wee brown lark...'

NIGHT-TIME

This is the time when snails creep out
And you and I go home:
When glimm'ring glow worms rove about
And the mischievous gnome:
And the pollock gobble the pink prawn fry,
And the sleepy milch cow's teats are dry,
And kestrels to the cliff eyrie fly,
And you and I go home.

This is the time when beetles meet
And you and I go home:
When Shannon's power bejewels the street
And ghost moths come:
And pools and lakes twink in the dark,
And mushrooms grow in the big sheep-park,
And silent is the wee brown lark,
And the hillside fox is heard to bark,
And you and I go home.

The Skylark sings from late winter until midsummer , from first light until evening. At the end of its song flight the Skylark descends while singing, and then falls to the ground with folded wings. It is then silent and very difficult to detect.

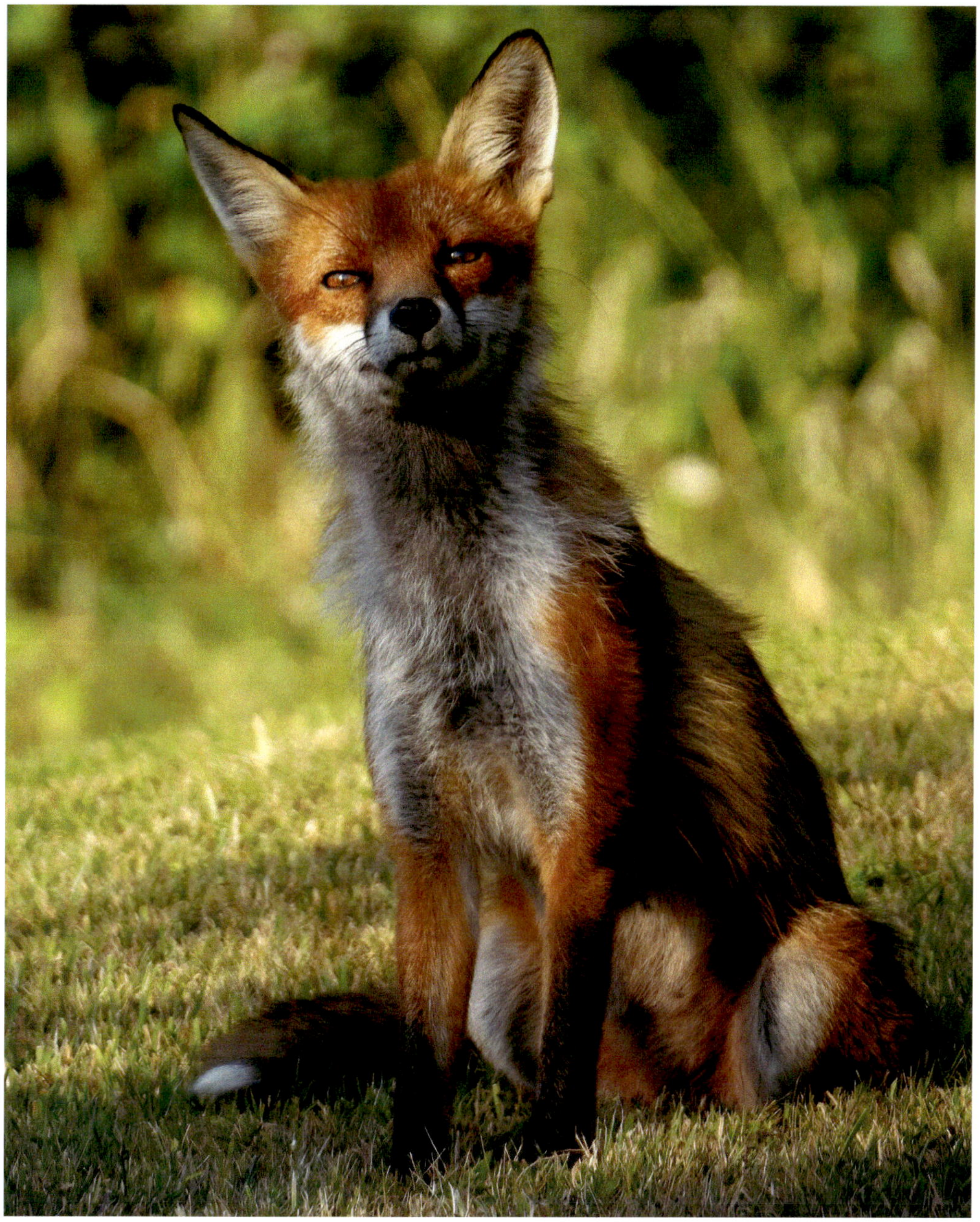

'...and the hillside fox is heard to bark...'

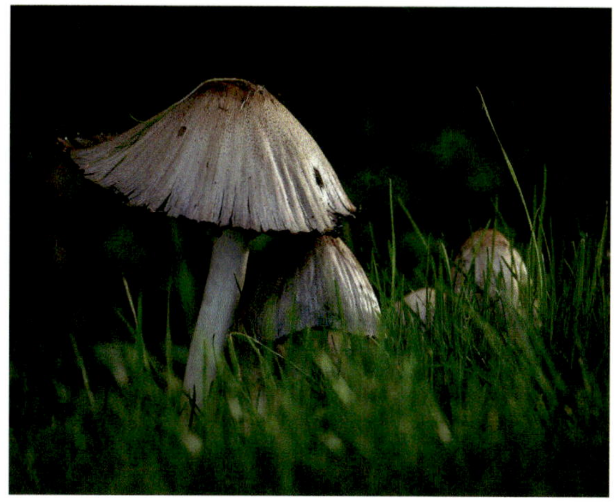

'...and mushrooms grow in the big sheep-park...'

The Lawyer's Wig or Shaggy Inkcap is an unmistakable fungus that occurs in meadows, woods and roadside verges. It displays a tall, narrow, cylindrical cap that is white and very 'shaggy' with 'scales' over its surface. The cap gradually opens out to a bell shape and is only is edible when young.

Foxes may make barking sounds when they feel threatened or when they want to communicate with other foxes. A female fox or vixen lets a male or dog fox know that she is ready to mate by making a cry like a scream. These screams are often answered by the bark of the dog fox.

SPRINGTIME IN INISHTRAHULL

The honey bees stir in the hive,
Red ants within their earthy keep,
Moth chrysalids become alive,
And snails awake from winter sleep.

The cushat coos unto her love,
Cock-robin dons his marriage vest,
The pilgrim birds are on the move
Feeling the ingrained urge to mate.

No plant but bears a leafy bud,
The ivy green its rocky stair,
Bog pimpernel peeps through the mud,
With spearwort and the gilly fair.

The haze of heat dims the lake shore,
Calmed in the mighty ocean's swell,
Rivers in torrents are seen no more,
Or catspaws sweeping the drinking well.

The winds are hushed, the sky is peaceful,
And Springtime reigns o'er Inishtrahull.

Whooper Swans are migrants. Having overwintered in Ireland to avail of our milder climate and ability to feed on water plants from the bottom of shallow lakes, they return northwards to the tundra in Iceland to breed and feed the shores of an Arctic lake. The distance from Inch Wildfowl Reserve to Inishtrahull is 25 miles. With 6,000 birds on average over-wintering at the reserve, it is possible that D. J. O'Sullivan saw Whooper Swans when he recorded an unspecified species of swan fly over Inishtrahull for the *Irish Naturalists' Journal*. The gentle bugling of these birds is an unmistakable sound, but unlike the Mute Swan, the sound of their wings in flight is silent. This image of Whooper Swans was taken in May on Inishbofin. This pair had not followed the rest of the flock to the breeding grounds in Iceland in April. Maybe they had not yet decided to leave, although some have been reported as residents in Ireland in the summer.

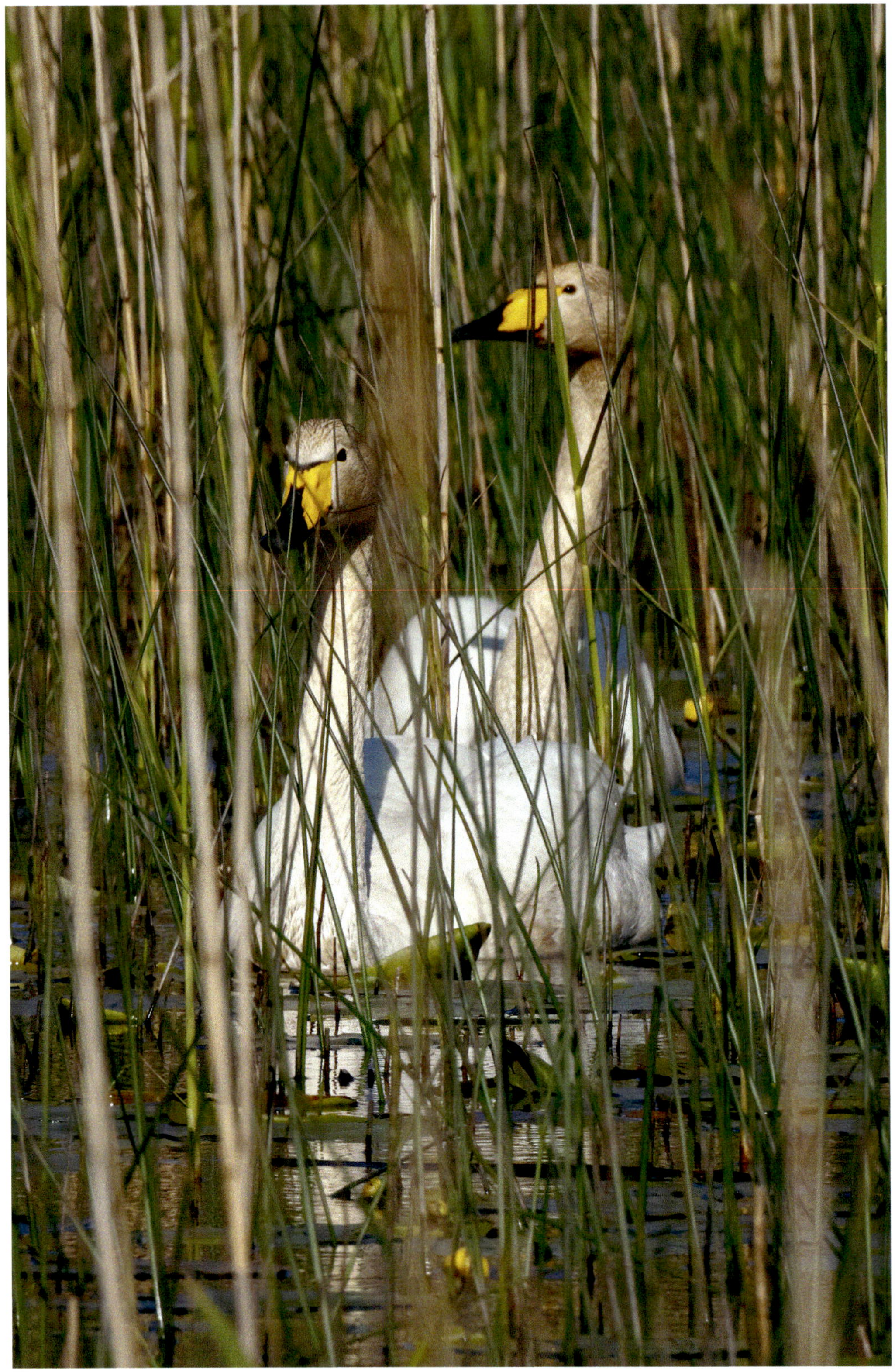

Whooper swans – '...the pilgrim birds are on the move...'

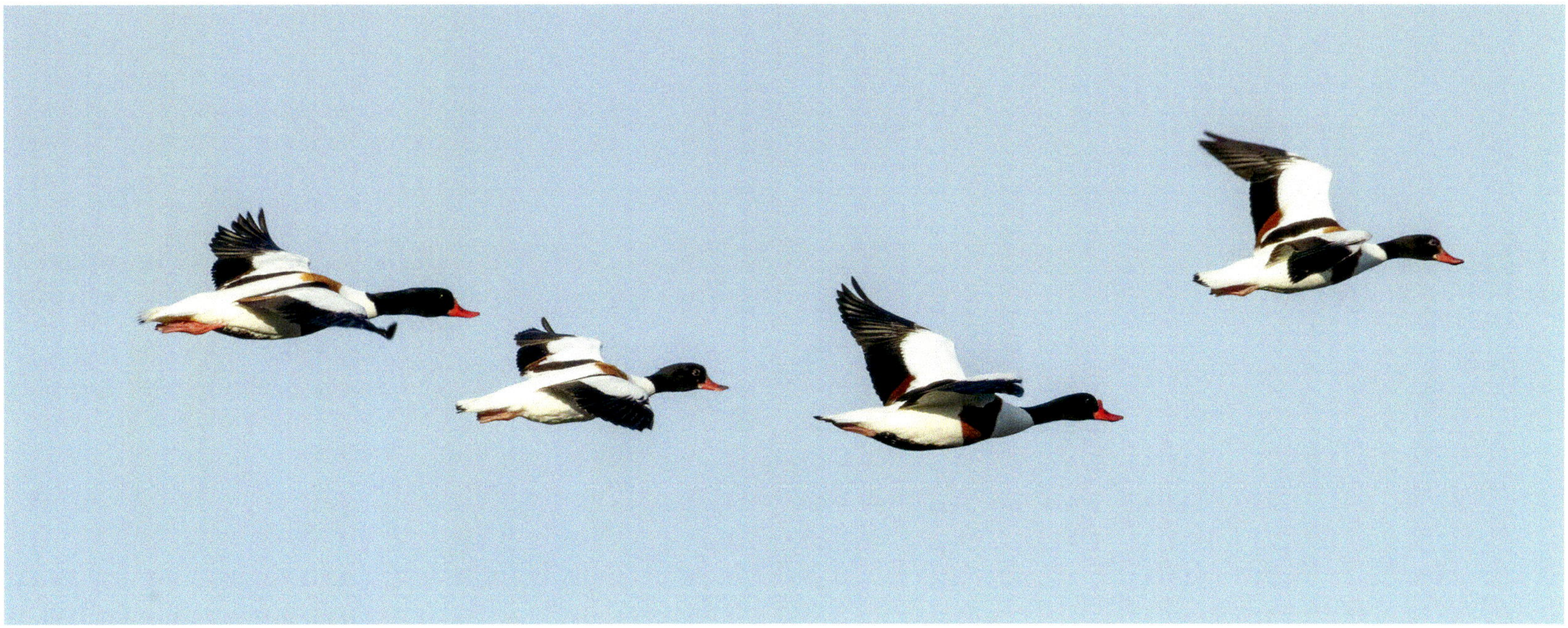

'...feeling the ingrained urge to mate.'

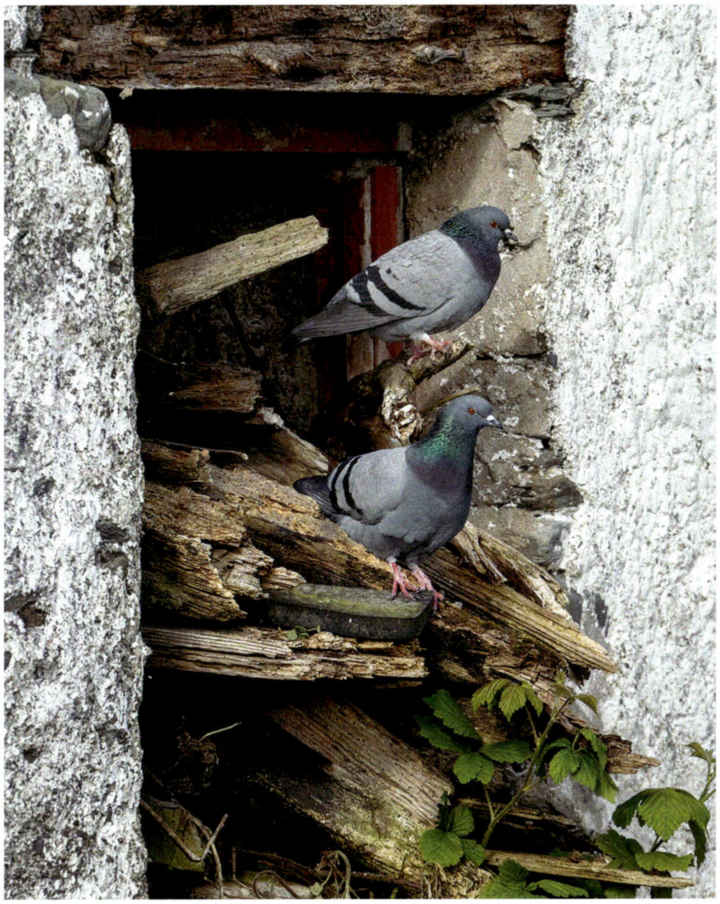

...the cushat coos unto her love,...'

Inishtrahull, the most northerly bird colony in the country, provides a wintering ground for Shelduck (above) before they move to their breeding grounds in the spring. It is one of the very few species of duck that habitually breeds underground, normally making use of an existing burrow. The drake keeps watch for potential danger while the female is brooding and warns her with a special alarm whistle. Every year in late summer, the majority of Irish Shelduck leave all the ducklings in the care of two or three females to depart for the sanctuary of the extensive mudflats of the Wadden Sea. There, they moult their flight and tail feathers and regrow their plumage; when they can fly again, they return home to their wintering grounds.

The Cushat refers to a Pigeon, Wood Pigeon or Ring Dove. The wild, 'pure' Rock Dove is the ancestor of all domesticated and feral pigeons. It is now only found around rocky sites and cliffs in remote areas of Mayo, Galway, Kerry and Cork .

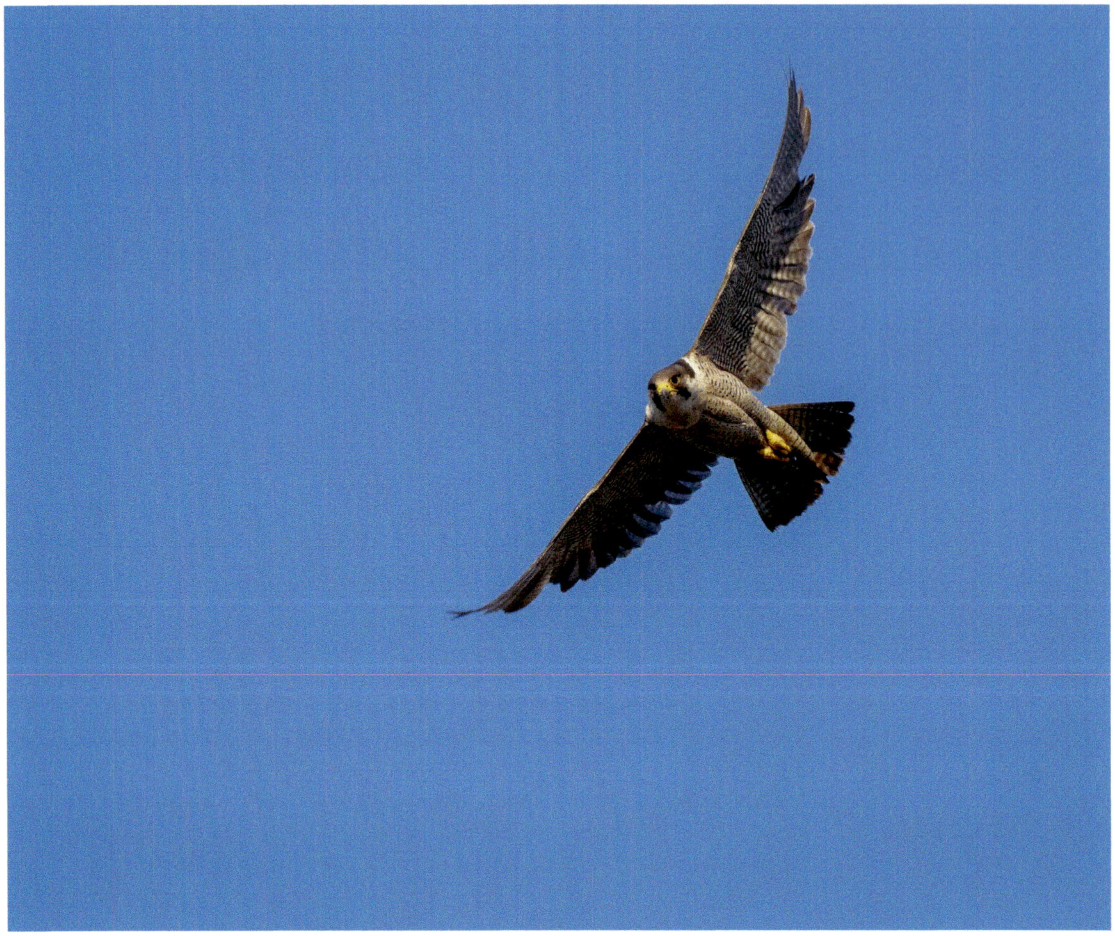

Peregrine falcon– '…the pilgrim birds are on the move…'

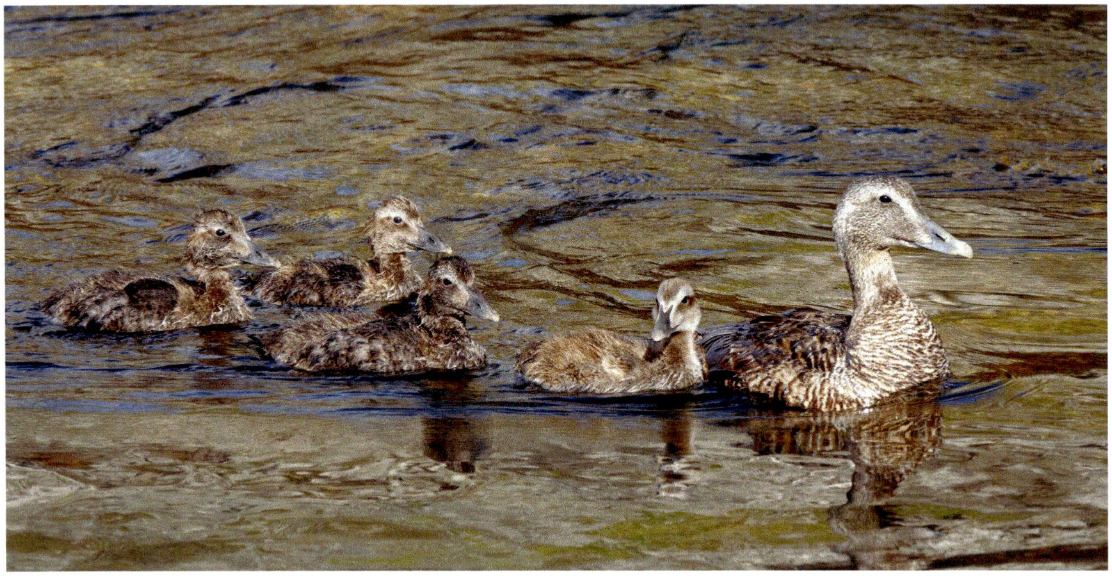

Eider ducks – '…the pigrim birds are on the move…'

The name Peregrine Falcon comes from the Latin word *peregrinus*, which means 'wanderer' or 'pilgrim'. It is so named because outside of the breeding season, these birds travel widely, including visits to Inishtrahull. They prey on many kinds of birds as well as mice, young hares and rabbits. In flight, it frequently soars following swift wing beats and is the fastest bird on earth. It kills its prey by diving from a great height at speed, striking feet first in the air. Such dives have been timed at over 200 miles per hour.

Irish breeding Eider Ducks are at the southern edge of a wider breeding range. Our individuals make relatively short movements outside of the breeding season to shallow, inshore coastal waters near estuary mouths, reducing their exposure to the elements. Common Eiders are resident and nest very successfully in large colonies on Inishtrahull, greatly preferring salt water to inland waters. Their bulky down keeps them warm and dry. This is the duck from which the famous eiderdown is obtained in the Arctic where they breed in large colonies. The brown female plucks it from her breast to provide a soft and warm lining for her nest. The farmer later harvests the down from the empty nest.

CARROWTRASNA

This old bog road, I know it well,
With tiny stream on either side;
And place where in the twiggy dell
The greenfinch serenades his bride
With twitting notes in summer sun.
I know the pad where jet snails glide
Through gleaming grass when night's begun;
Each faery ring on mossy fell,
The meadow-sweet and pimpernel,
Where lizards through the brackens run.
Here flies come to the thistle top
To sip the nectar it exudes,
The grey crow with replenished crop
Cries caw! this peacefulness interludes,
And then away, away, away.
Deep toned, the bells in steeples ring
The Angelus, how sweet they sound.
And harebells on long thin stems swing—
Their puce heads nearly touch the ground
Then waft-kiss'd come erect again.
Such tiny rock spiders abound!
Across the heath a bow of rain—
A lintie nigh the pink-tinged ling
Utters his twee-kreck twittering
And then his mad ramping refrain.
Now Eily with her milking pail
Comes tripping o'er the stubble-lea,
Is heard the craking call of rail
As Eily calls "Hallo" to me,
And my heart pulses lovingly.

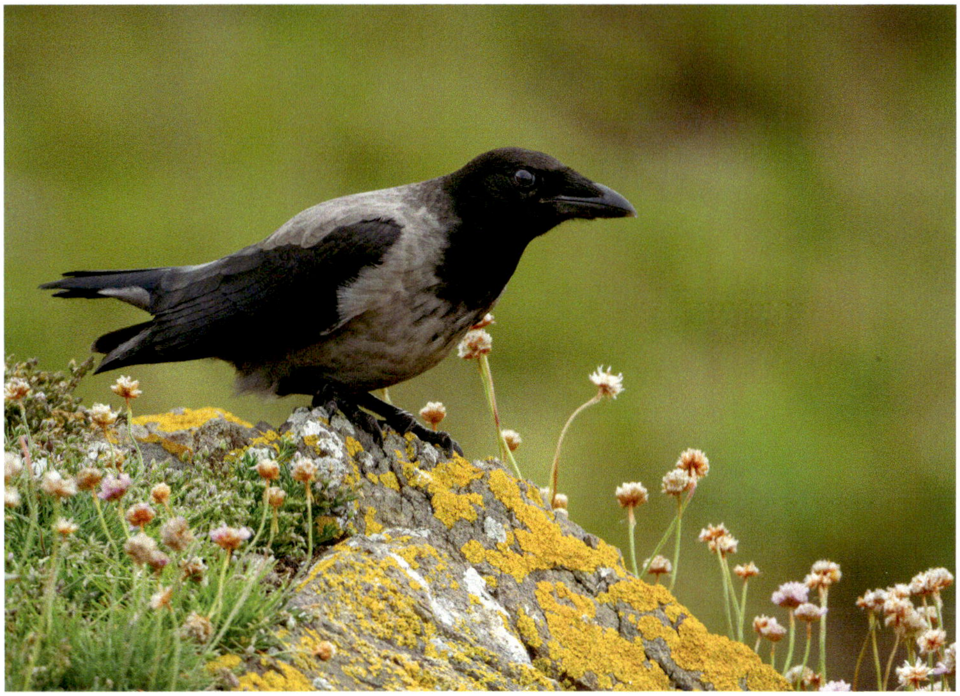

'...the grey crow with replenished crop...'

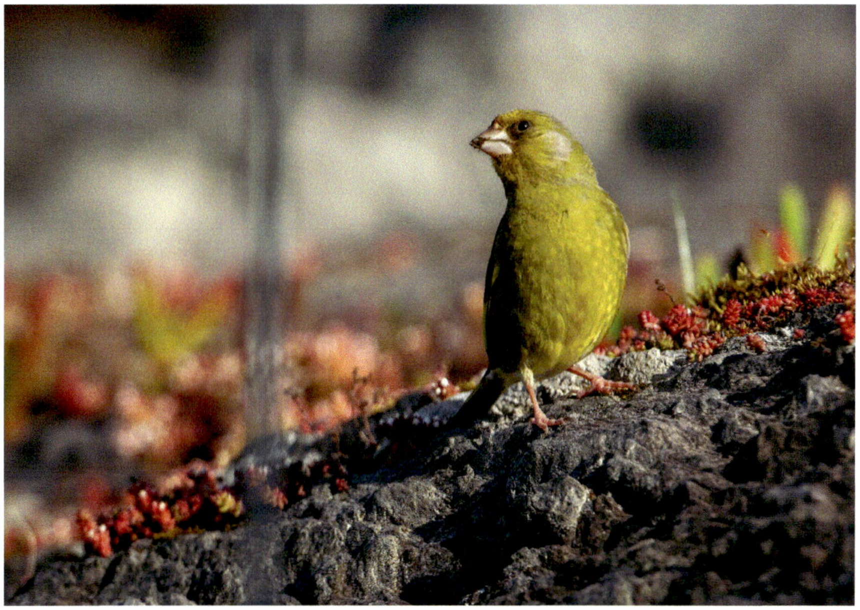

'...the greenfinch serenades his bride...'

The Hooded Crow is also known as the Grey Crow and has brains, strong claws, and a razor-sharp beak. It can be equally at home on the coast, in the mountains, or in city centres.

Greenfinches are large, chunky finches that are mostly olive-green, but with a yellow patch on the wings and tail. Females are grey-green with less yellow. The Greenfinch song, a jumble of bubbly notes and trills is most often delivered from the top of a small tree or bush, though in spring a male may utter a lengthy song whilst in flight.

MISTAKEN IDENTITY

A ring ouzel met a mistle thrush
Food-foraging 'neath a bramble bush:
"Good day to you," the ring ouzel said,
"How many eggs have you this year laid?"

The thrush turned 'round, winked a merry eye,
With full-throated laughter filed the sky:
"How many eggs have I this year laid?...
I'm a cock, you silly old fool," he said.

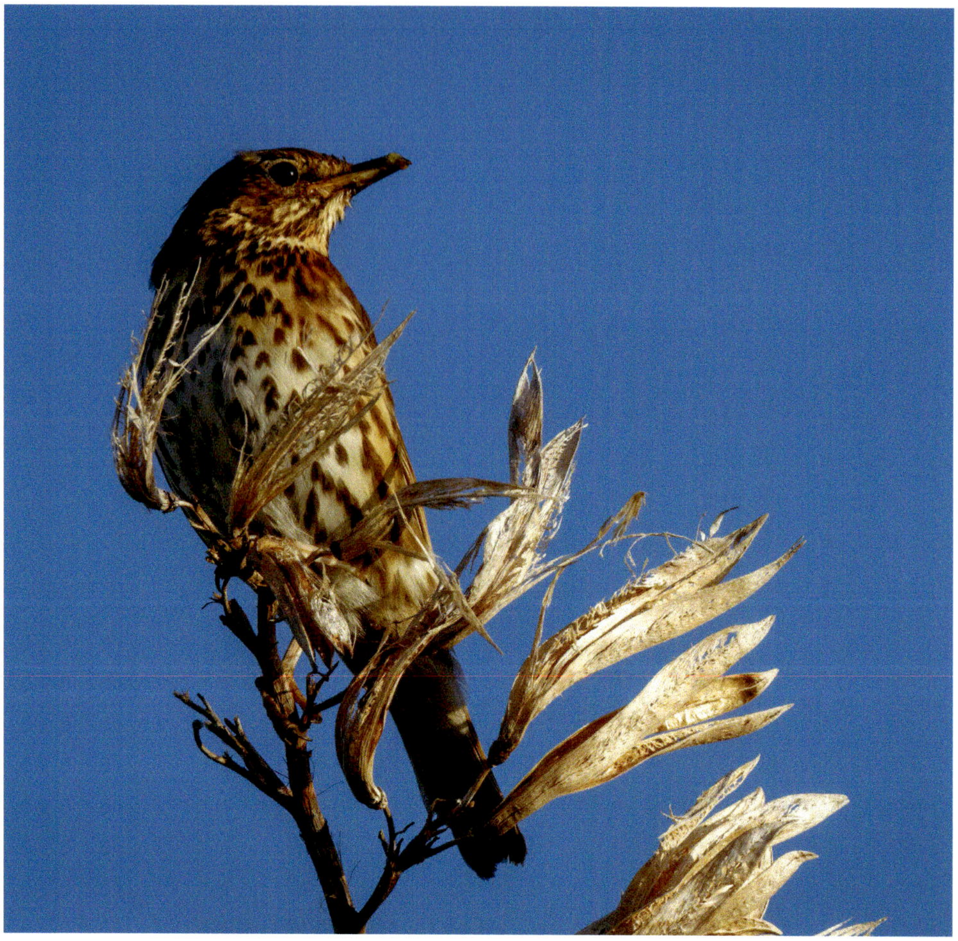

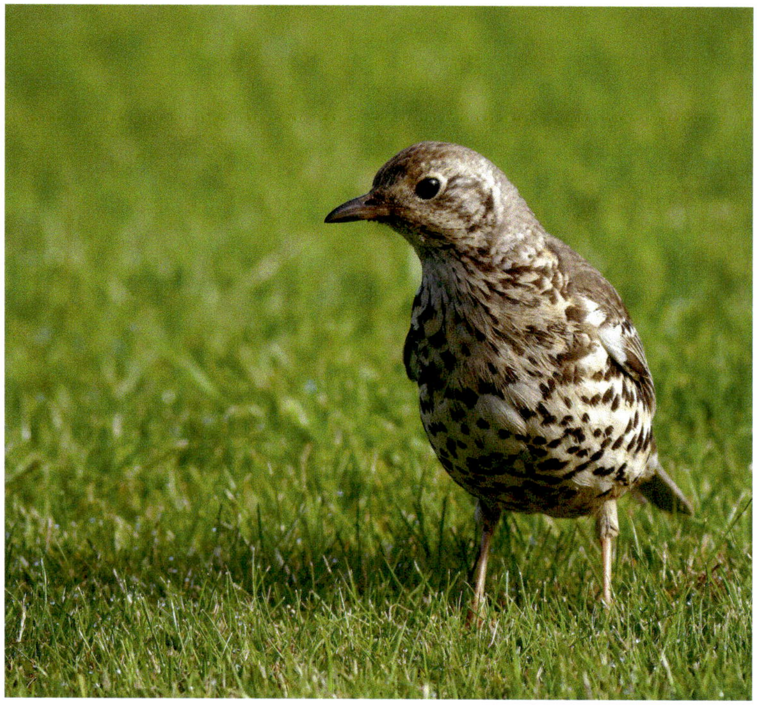

There is no obvious difference between the male and female thrush. It is also difficult to identify the differences between the Song Thrush (above) and the Mistle Thrush (right). One of the main differences is the arrowhead spots or upside-down hearts on the chest of the Song Thrush compared to the rounded black spots of the Mistle Thrush. The Song Thrush has a chestnut brown tinge on the upper breast, and its belly is white with fewer spots. Its song, with more sustained and sweeter notes, is also different from the unvarying whistles of the Mistle Thrush.

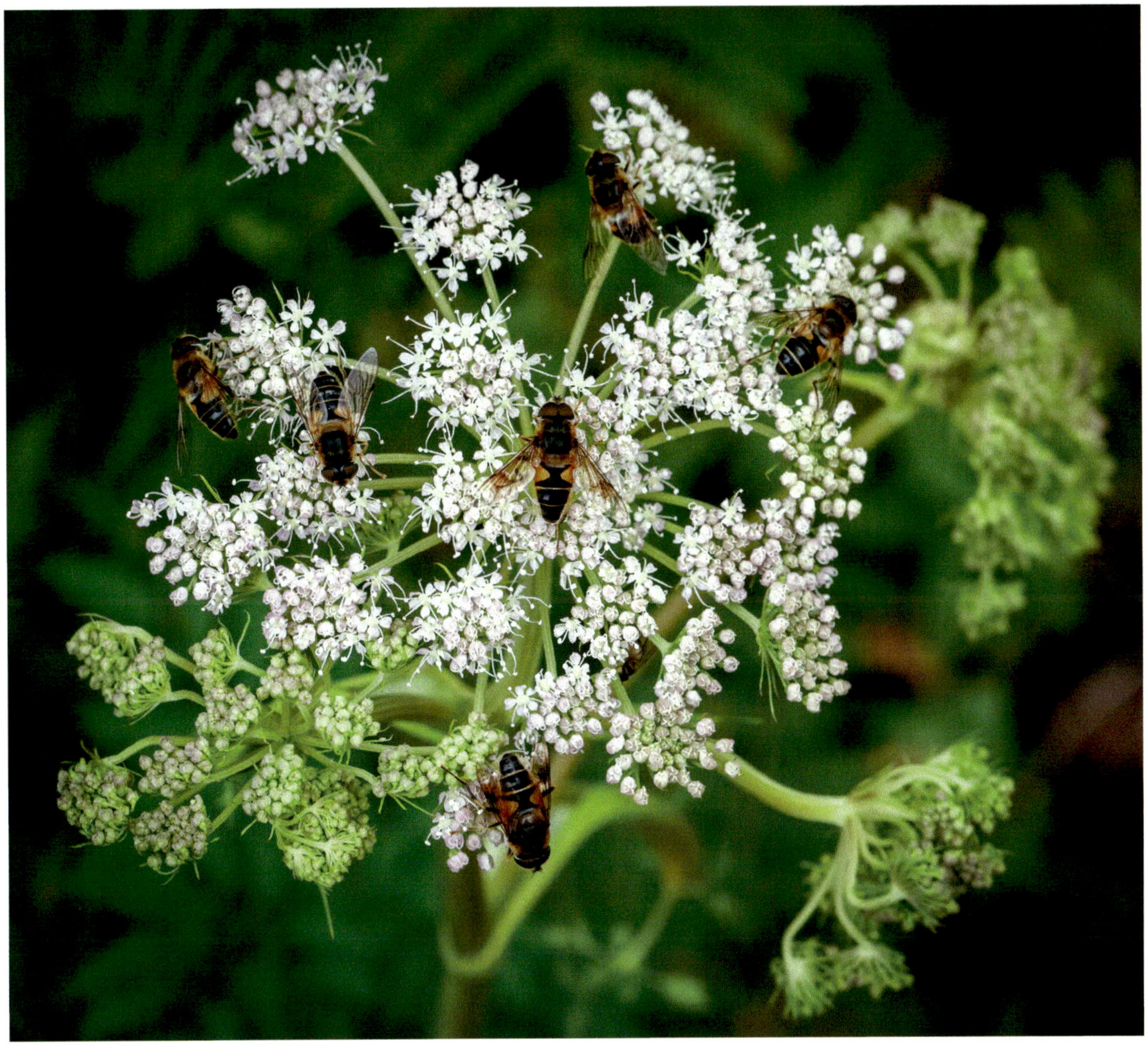

'The insect tribe takes wing…'

TIME CHANGE

This April dawn is fine,
Appointed for the buds
Of ash to show black toes,
And frog-hoppers make suds.
Air drinkable as wine,
Plough clay ready for hoes,
And burgeoning the sloes.
Awakening everywhere
The insect tribe takes wing,
Amid the flowery dells
Eyebright is blossoming;
Bee nectar-seekers stare
Into corolla-wells
Of purple heather-bells.
The clamour-cock of life
Crows loud on every hand,
By wind-kiss'd waterside
Grey dunlin takes his stand
To serenade his wife:
Love-warmth is spreading wide,
Spring surges to full tide.

Eristalis nemorum is a species of hoverfly. Several species are known as drone flies because they bear a resemblance to the Honeybee Drone. Adults often visit flowers from April to October, as seen here on sweet-scented wild Angelica.

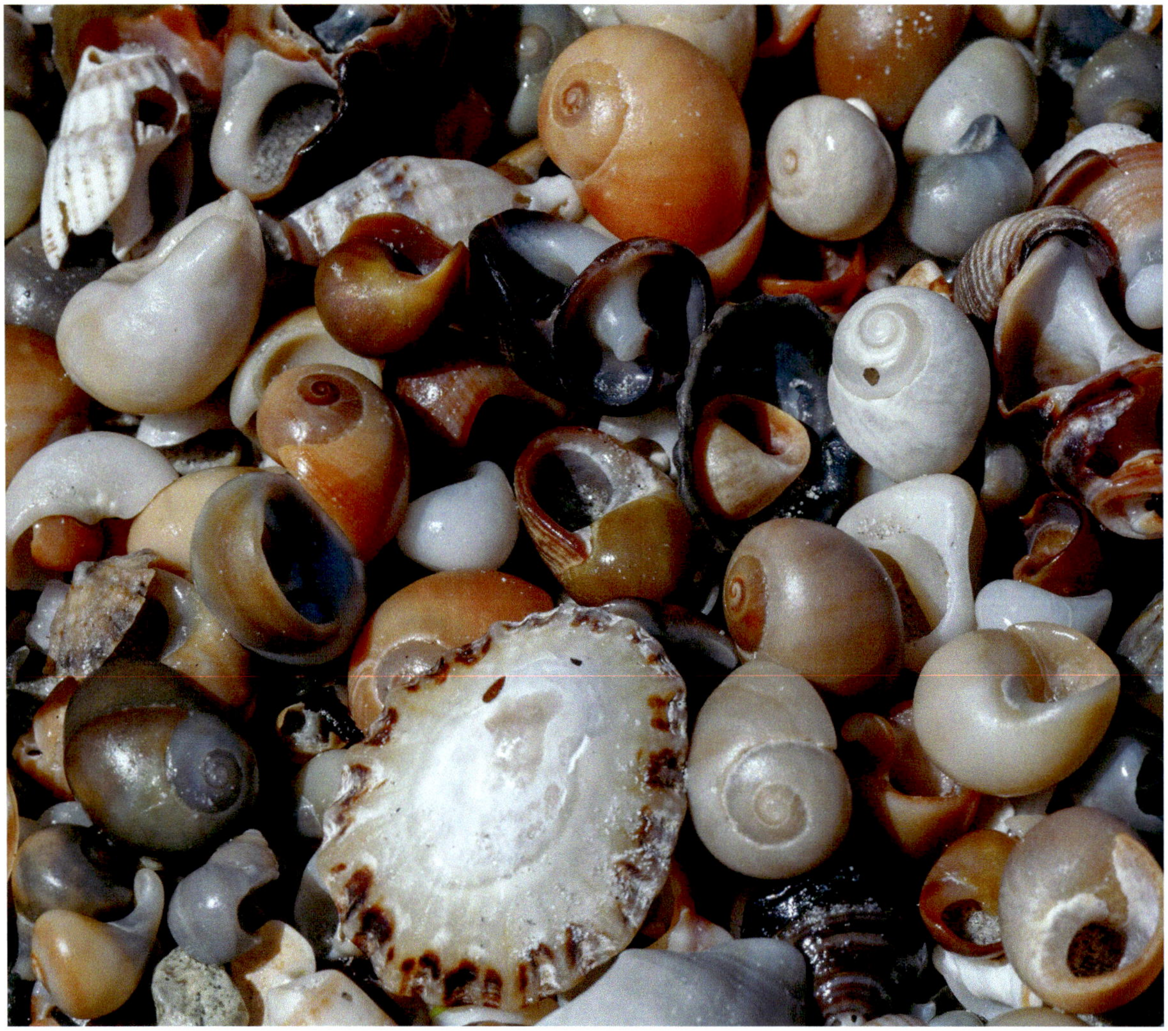

ENDOWMENT

When I was your lover
We travelled the byways, birdwatching.

When I was you lover
We beachcombed for painted topshells.

When I was your lover
We watched diadem spiders web-weaving.

Then came the delights of orange-blossom.

Home-making replaced the byways and beaches,
Children the attercop-artisans—

And I am still your lover.

The views along our coastline are unparalleled and you would be forgiven for spending the majority of your time gazing out to sea. As you crunch over the sand, shells and pebbles it is with looking at the beauty and detail beneath your feet.

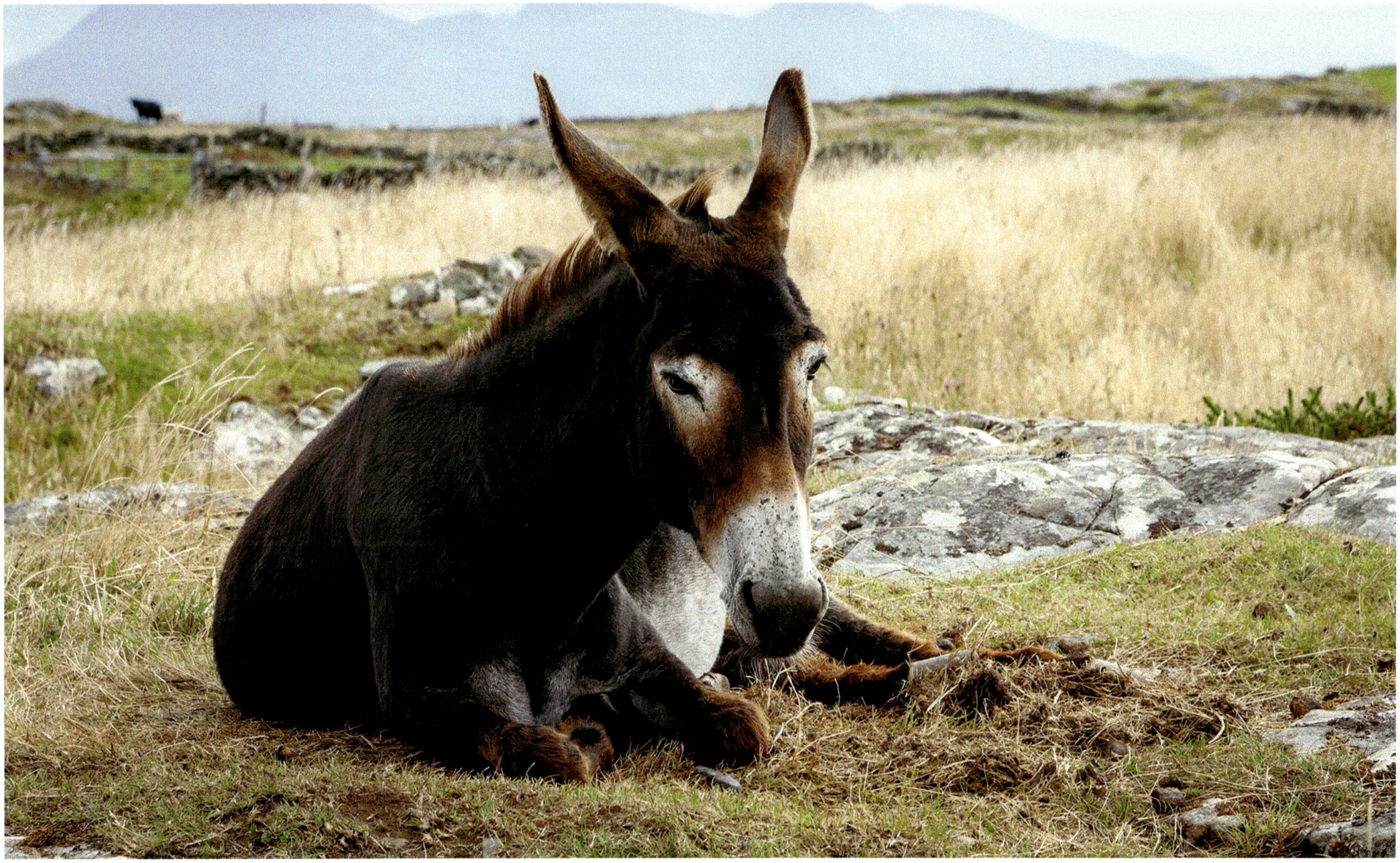

'The sunning ass, upon the edge…'

ARRANMORE

Bright sunbeams gleam 'twixt flouncing waves,
The Jew's-harp beetle sparkles blue:
Where gnarléd gorse shows armour'd leaves
A spider's net is dinked with dew.
The mist-bow o'er the stream glints red,
A brassy, brazen, brilliant tone
That flickers ochresous to lead,
Becomes nimbused, then nimbly gone.
Roan heifer noses through the hedge
Sweet honeysuckle bordering near;
The sunning ass, upon the edge,
Half wakes to twitch flies from her ear.

Brown bees are pulsing flower to flower,
To gilly comes the green-veined white,
This female's had her nuptial hour
As tatter'd wings denote in flight.
Ringed plover "tu-li-tu" around,
Show trailing wings and drunken legs,
Pretending hurt—fall to the ground,
A ruse to hide their "scrape" of eggs.
The wood-rush rustles faery tunes,
The cushat coos in elder tree,
And all along the ribb'd sand-dunes
Blue harebells dance in ecstasy.

Donkeys were introduced to Ireland to do the farm work carrying turf, milk, seaweed and flax. In 1897 there were 247,000 donkeys in Ireland, most of them working on farms and in villages. Estimated figures in 2017 suggest that there are now fewer than 5,000.

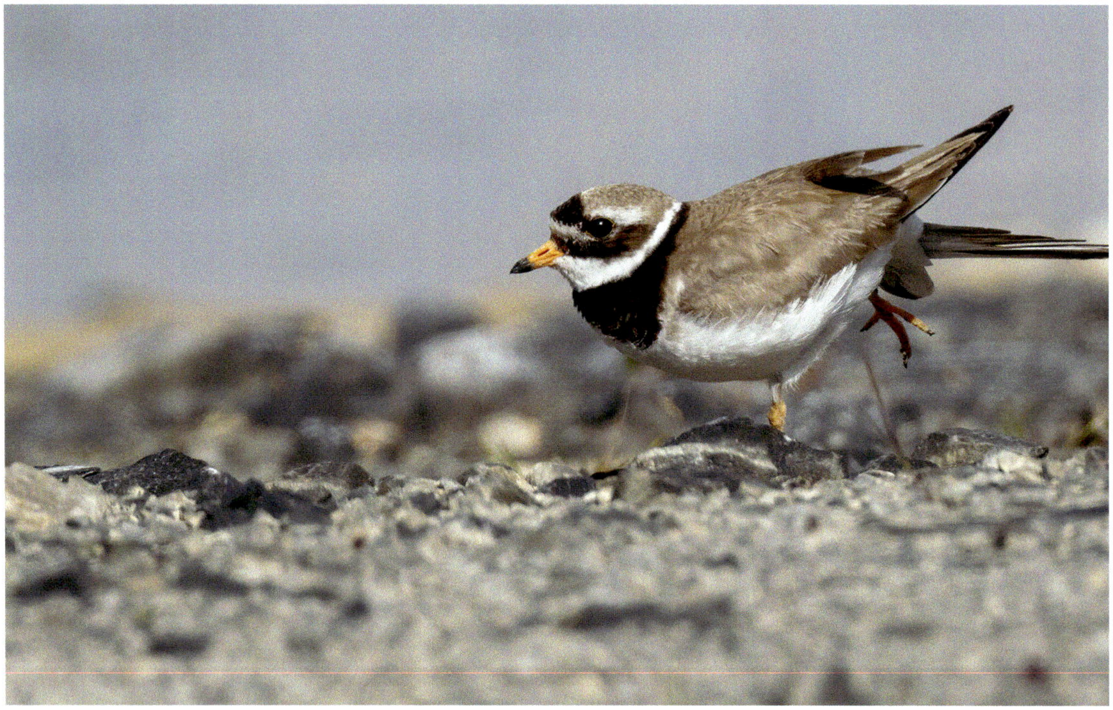

'Ringed plover "tu-li-tu" around, show trailing wings and drunken legs...'

If a potential predator approaches the nest, the adult Tinged Plover (left) will walk away, calling to attract the intruder and feigning a broken wing.

The Green-veined White Butterfly (below left) is especially common in damp and wet grassland and along damp hedges and streams. The female has two spots on the upper side of the white fore-wing (the male has one spot) and both sexes have a dark tip on the fore-wing. The Green-veined White also shows a dusting of dark scales along the veins on the upper sides and undersides of the wings.

Honeysuckle (below) is a woody climber which twines itself over other shrubs and hedgerows, giving out a most heavenly fragrance. From June to October it has distinctive creamy flowers which become pale yellow after pollination, often reddish outside. Its wonderful scent attracts bees by day and moths by night.

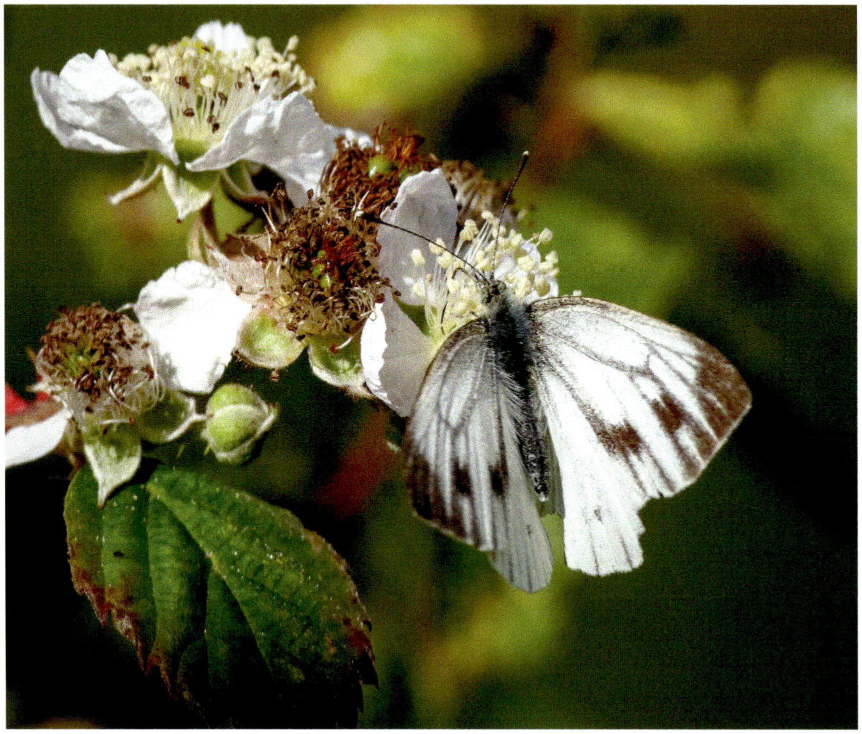

'...to gilly comes the green-veined white...'

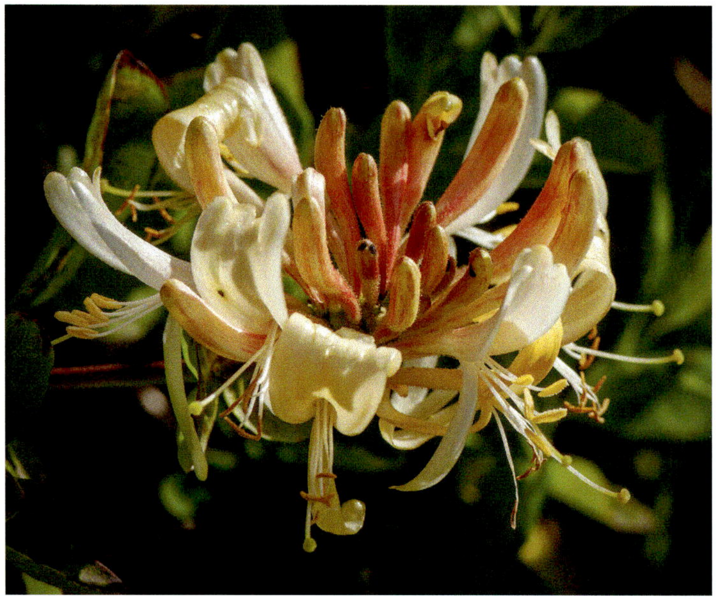

'...sweet honeysuckle bordering near;...'

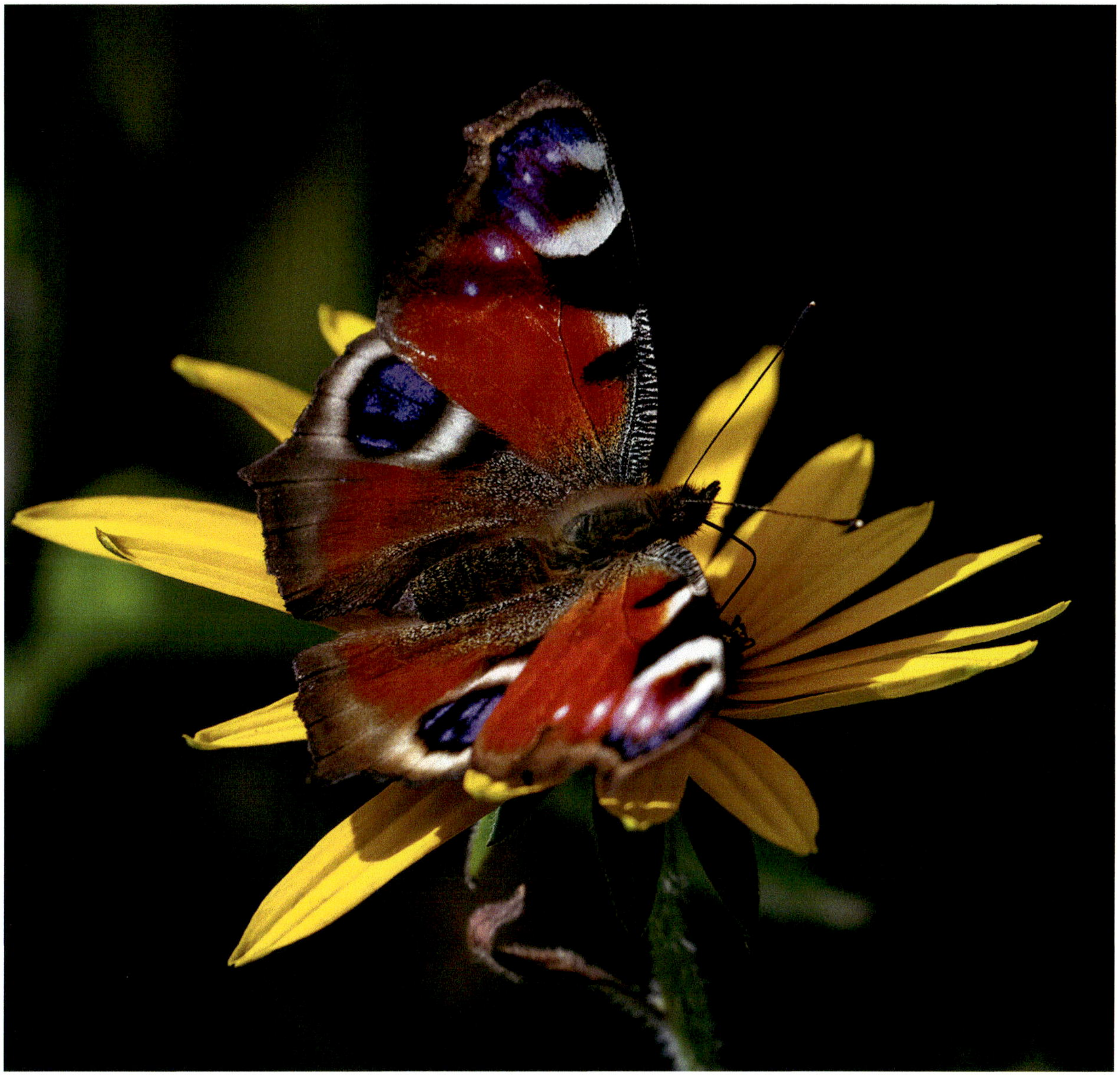

The Peacock Butterfly's spectacular pattern of eyespots evolved to startle or confuse predators, making it one of the most easily recognized and best-known species. The butterfly gained its common name from these peacock-like eyes on each hind wing. They seek out the nectar of flowering plants, especially Buddleia and Thistle to build up body reserves for hibernating. All the eating is done in the caterpillar stage; the actual butterfly never eats anything but flits from flower to flower, sipping nectar.

'A youthful peacock butterfly, dancing in the sunny sky....'

MOSAIC

Upon the waste-lands tangled hem
The nettle glitters like a gem,
Variegated emerald, pink and white,
Each floral curve reflects the light.

A youthful peacock butterfly,
Dancing in the sunny sky,
Alights to take a luscious sup
From the dangling nectar-cup.

As his proboscis sucks the mead
Of the tall leafy stinging weed,
His brown eye-marked wings outspread
O'er its fragrant flowering head.

Brown over green, pink under blue,
Shades and tints of auroral hue;
Butterfly and plant combine
To make an exquisite design.

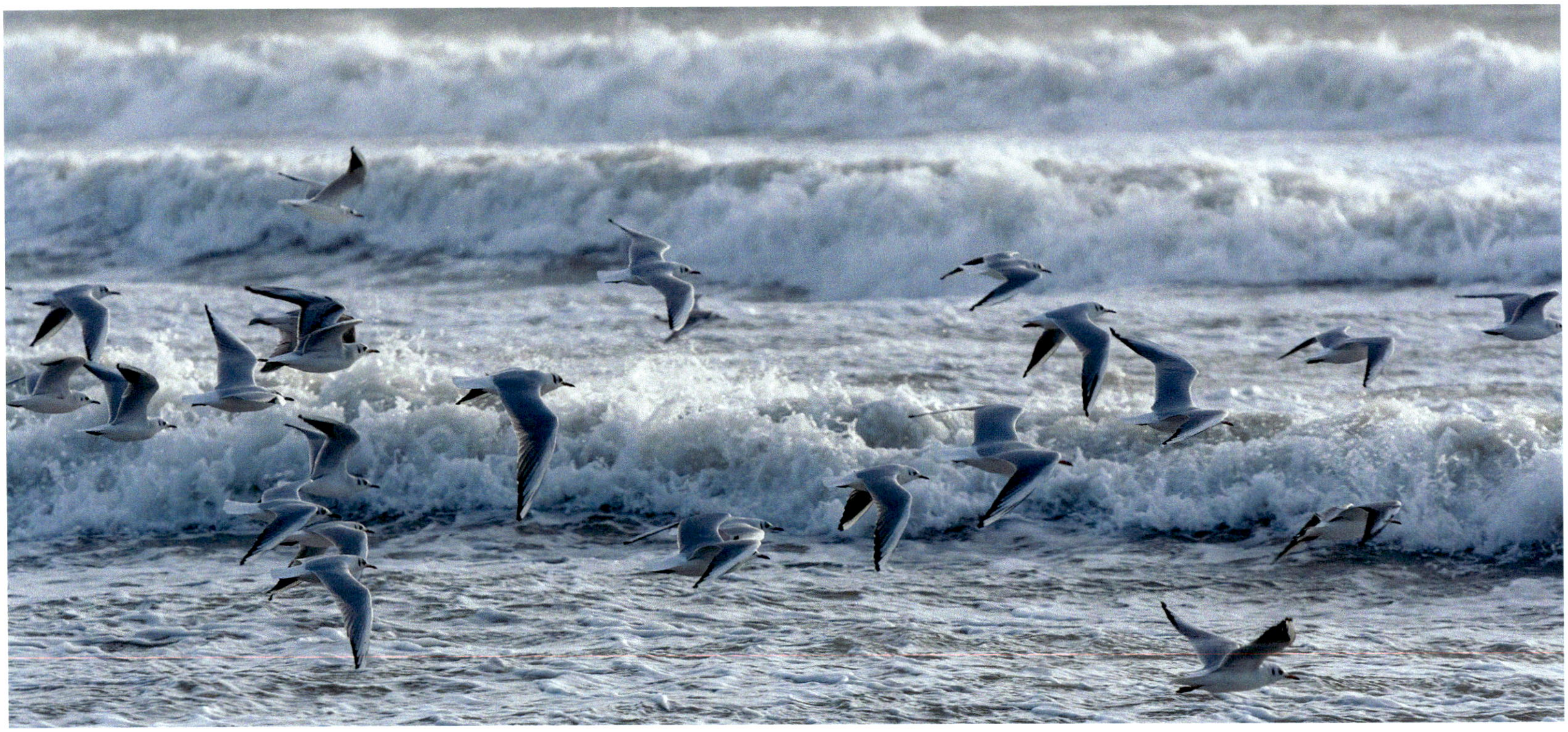

'Each wave that breaks along the shore tears up the beach with thund'rous roar...'

THE GOLDEN SHAFT

This day the world is cold and drear,
The rain pours down, the sky is near,
And all around wild winds do howl
The challenge to man and beast, and fowl.
Close to the hedge the milch cows lie,
And in the grass the beetle and the fly.
With rumps turned to each pelting shower
The sheep upon the hillside cower,
And in the glens way down below
Pied magpies flutter to and fro.
Each wave that breaks along the shore
Tears up the beach with thund'rous roar,
And leaves behind a seaweed layer
Of bubble-wrack, dulse and mermaid's hair.
The idle farmer to his wife
Bemoans the day and farming life;
Whilst on the pier the fishers greet:
"Bad weather for the fishing fleet!"
Then from behind the clouds, Old Sol
Throws down a golden shaft o'er all,
And gives to man, and beast and fowl
New heart—despite the winds that howl.

Sea birds, as in the Black-headed Gulls above in their winter plumage, are adapted to life on the ocean waves, searching for food, often resting and sleeping and for many, travelling large distances across this maritime landscape is part of their annual life cycle. Ireland's rugged and diverse coastline, some 7,500km long, and vast marine waters support hundreds of thousands of sea birds with globally important numbers of breeding Manx Shearwater and European Storm-petrel.

from WEEKEND IN TIRCONAILL

Glazed Dragonflies go flashing by,
Rainbows in a glass-clear sky,
With their front legs held akimbo
As traps for fungus-gnats that go
Sex-dancing where the bindweeds wind
And, mating, perpetuate their kind;
But first each female must drink blood
Before her fecundation's good.
...

Lone jet-slug leaves a well-marked track,
He has no refuge on his back
Like aspersa, his mottled friend,
Who can retire at Autumn's end
By drawing in her horned snout
And sealing her shell-house's mouth,
A seal furnished with breathing hole
Leading to the mantled sole.

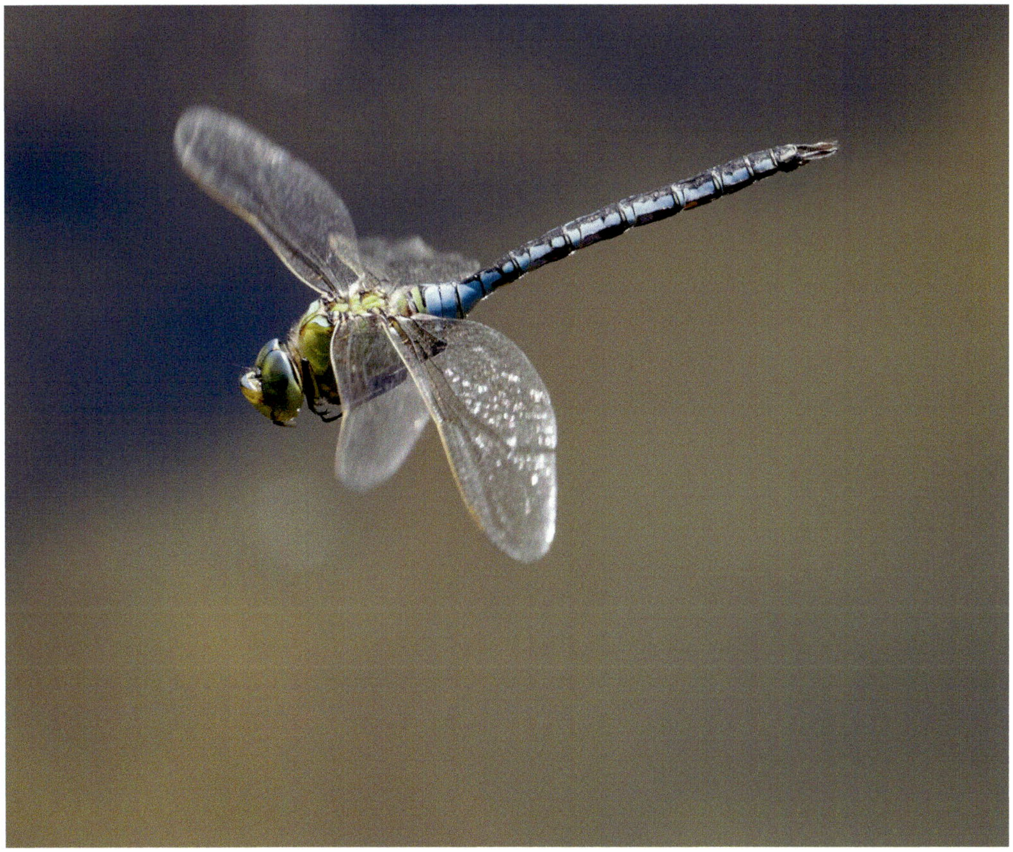

'Glazed dragonflies go flashing by...'

The Emperor Dragonfly is the biggest dragonfly to be found in Ireland. They are bio-indicators of climate change as they expand their range to the north in response to increasing average temperatures. They actively hunt over medium to large bodies of water and rarely settle except to mate and lay their eggs. Dragonflies will consume small prey that can be found in the water, even if they do not typically eat blood.

Cornu aspersum is known by the common name, Garden Snail. During dry or cold weather, it seals the aperture of the shell with an insoluble mucous secretion called the epiphragm, which helps the snail retain moisture and protects it from small predators such as some ants.

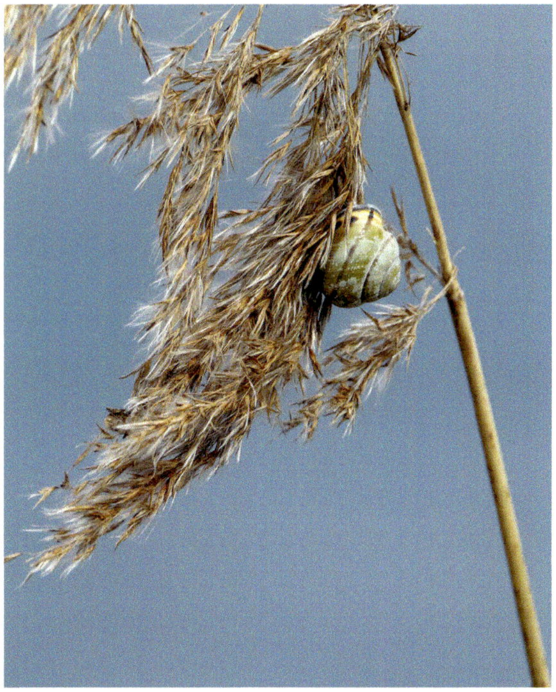

'...aspersa, his mottled friend...'

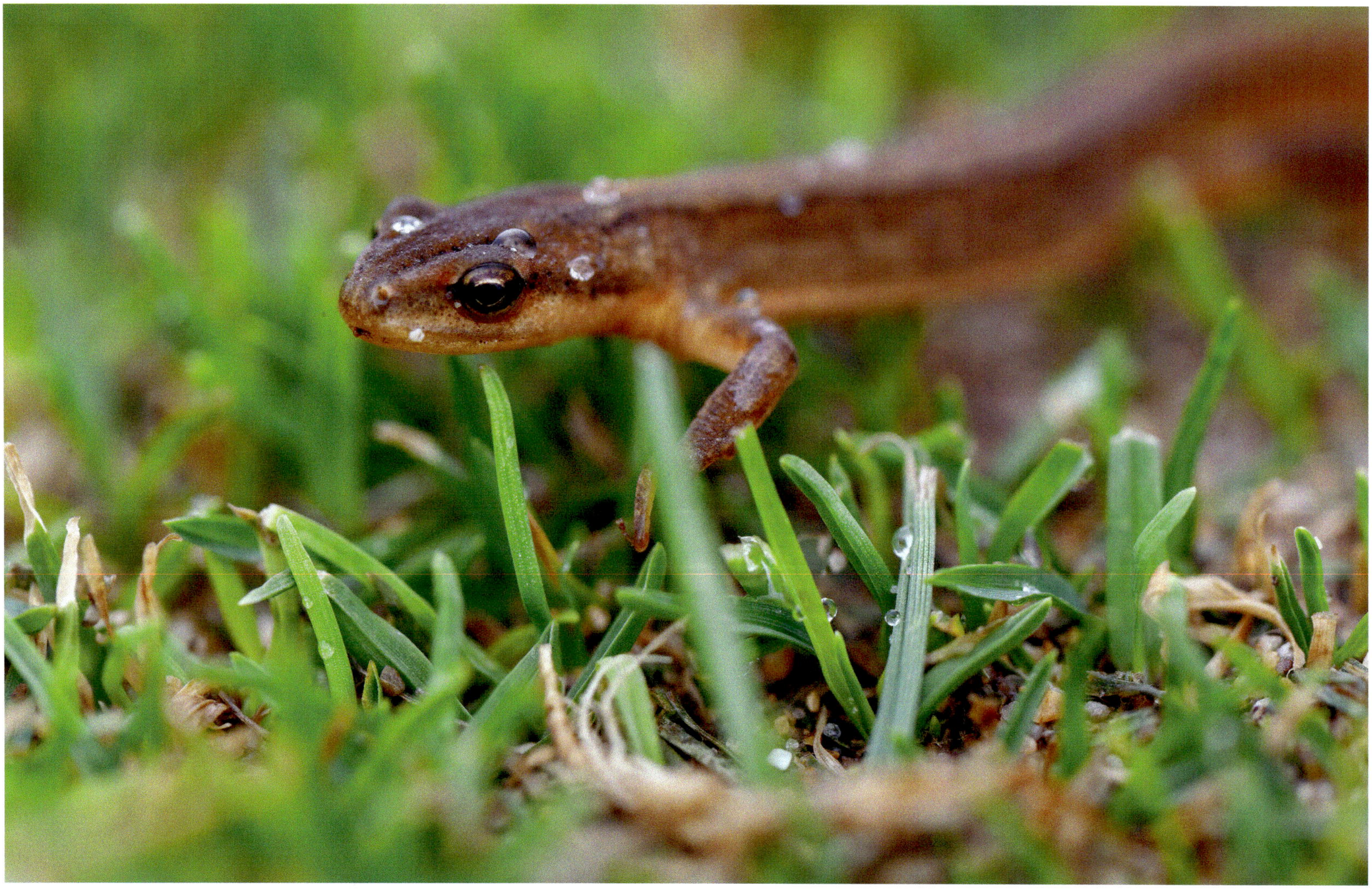

'Brown Lizard lazing in the sun turns colourful, then starts to run…'

Brown lizard lazing in the sun
Turns colourful, then starts to run
In camouflage, across the path,
Twitching long tail, this way and that;
And where the midges gyrate o'er dung
Flicks out his front-hinged tacky-tongue,
Flicks in and out, and in again,
Like lightning-flashes foretelling rain,
Until the insect tribe are gone
And not a sign on any one;
Then waddles to his basking site
To drowse until the fall of night.
…

This is an image of the Smooth Newt. The Common Lizard is Ireland's only native species of reptile. It has no internal temperature regulation system and can often be seen sunning itself on dry stone walls and rocks to regulate its body temperature. At first sight it can be mistaken for a Smooth Newt. However, the Smooth Newt has round black spots on the belly and the tail is oar-shaped and not rounded as in the lizard. It also has four toes on the front feet while the lizard has five.

Return to Earth, where cattle gad,
The warbles driving them so mad
They rush down to the mallard-lake
A panorama of mosaic,
There wallow in the squelching mire
Broad rumps reeking as they perspire
Then, having cooled, return to grass,
Along the spearwort-sprinkled pass,
Pausing before the wagtail's seat
Fresh-budded willow-shoots to eat;
When burdock-burrs stick in their hair
The better to migrate elsewhere.
...
And there, rising from pupal boats,
The mouthless mayflies change their coats,
To dance across the water-pudge—
In places brimming built-up sludge,
Touch its surface with dandling legs,
Grey females dropping pinhead eggs
That hatch tiny transparent shrimps,
In turn becoming yellow nymphs,
Feeding on fragments of green plants,
Or hiding in aquatic haunts
From dysticus and water-lice
Which could devour them in a trice.
...

The Grey Wagtail is slightly smaller than the Pied Wagtail and is more colourful than its name suggests. Its tail is also longer. A very striking bird, with its dark, grey head and back offset by extensive yellow on the breast, belly and vent. It is typically associated with fast-flowing waters such as streams and rivers throughout Ireland.

The Mayfly is known for its extremely short life span and emerging in large numbers in the summer months. Nymphal life is normally one year. When growth is complete, the nymphal skin splits down the back and a winged form, called the dun, emerges and flies from the water. Mating takes place soon after, followed shortly by egg deposition and death all within two days.

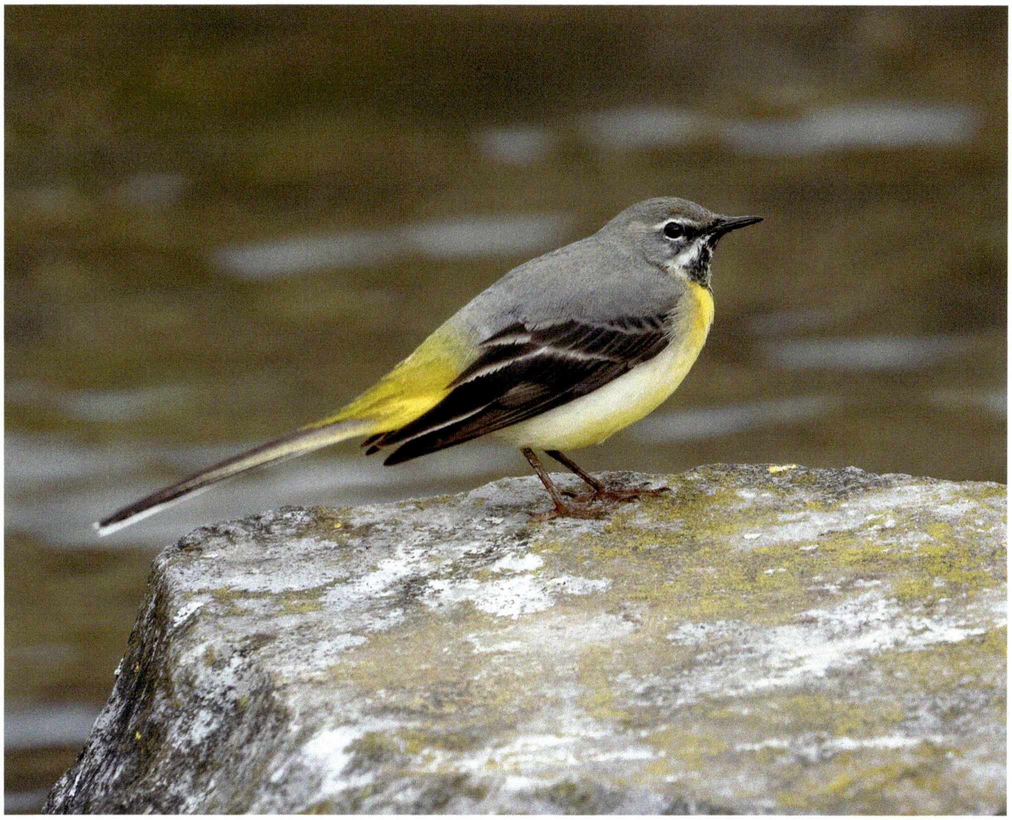

'Pausing before the wagtail's seat...'

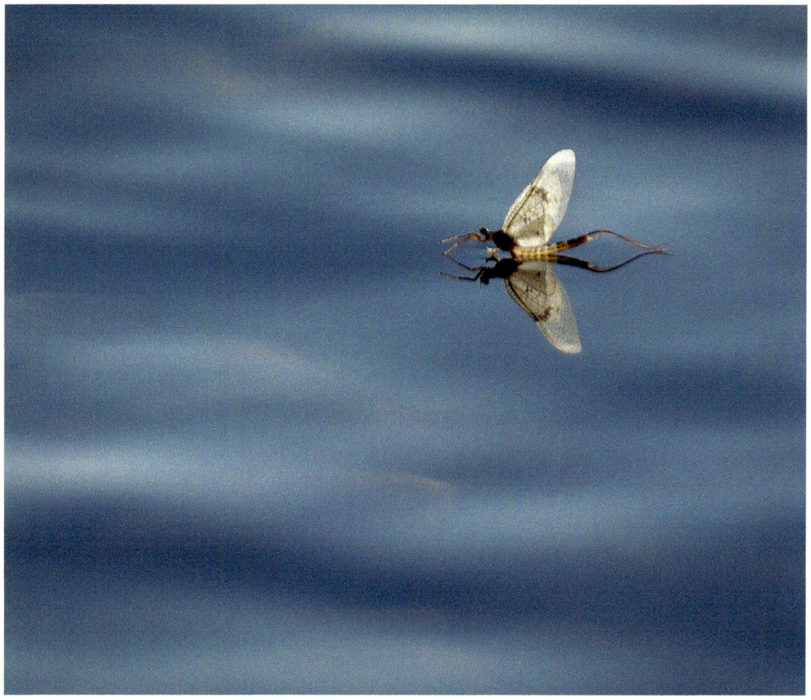

'The mouthless mayflies change their coats...'

So, here we find in everything
God's work: the flower, the midge's wing;
The worms that in clay alleys lie,
Each birr afloat in dappled sky,
Shy badgers' sett by mountain ben,
Dog-fox and cubs outside their den;
Or fern in cryptic crevasse dim,
All giving pleasure, thanks to Him...
...
And so, in bondage of the dark
We slept, until the call of lark
Awakened us to sunlight morn'
The scents of vernal grass and corn;
The stonechat's pebble-bashing song
As he short-hopped the ditch along;
The "moo" of cow, the bleat of goat
With jingling bells hung 'round her throat.

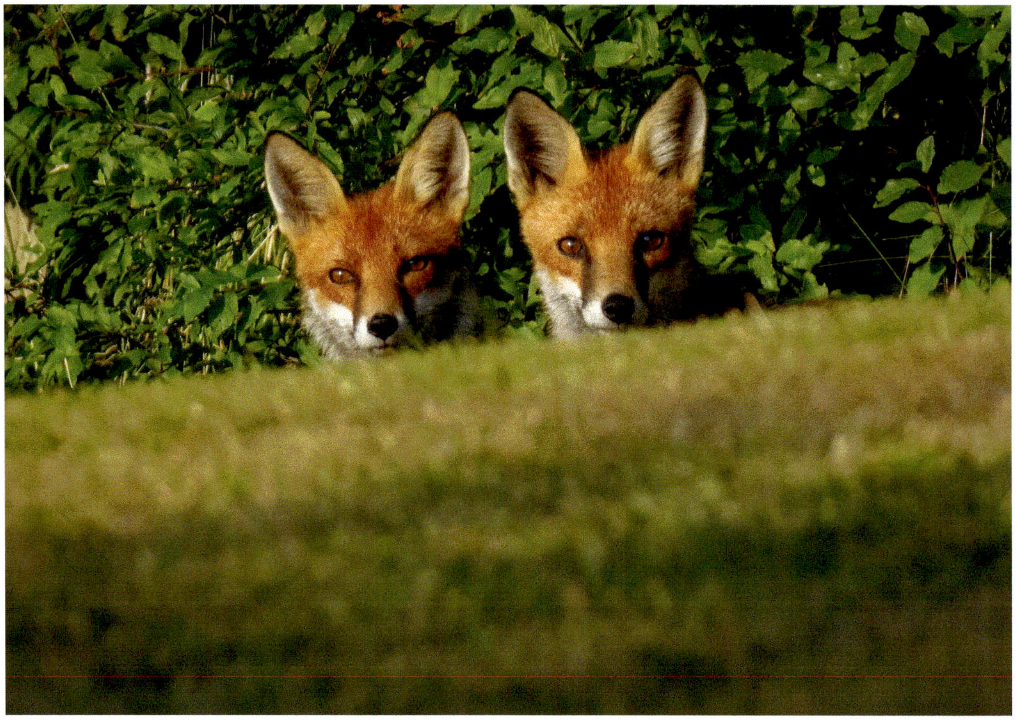

'Dog-fox and cubs outside their den...'

Fox cubs are born blind and deaf in the spring. Their fur changes from dark grey to a dark brown in the first two weeks as their ears and blue eyes open. In the spring, it's normal to see month-old cubs developing their survival skills above ground during the day. They're incredibly smart and have a keen sense of sight, hearing, and smell.

The male Stonechat (far right) has a striking black head with white around the side of his neck. The female Stonechat is similar to the male but does not have the striking black head and back. The female has a brown head and body and its belly is a much paler rust red. As the name suggests, both the male and female birds utter a sharp loud clicking call that sound like two stones being tapped together.

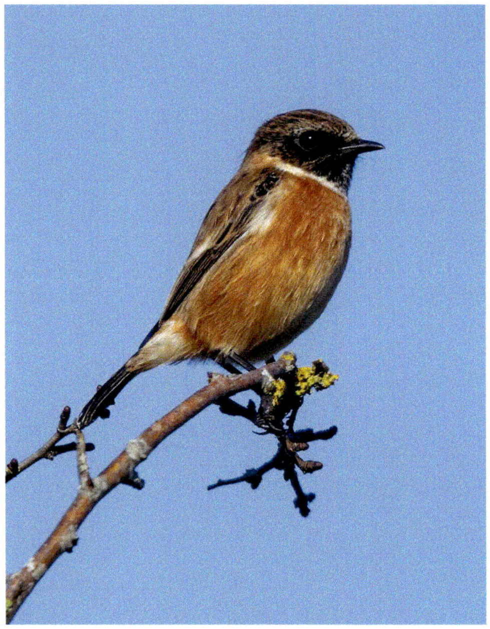

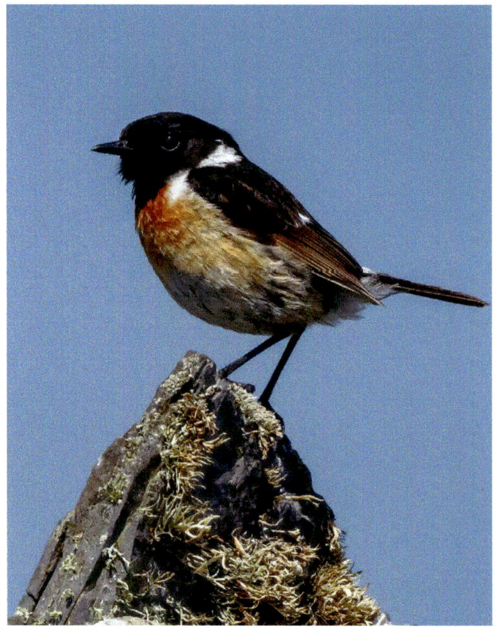

'The stonechat's pebble-bashing song...'

EPILOGUE

THE NEED FOR CONSERVATION

So back to office desk once more—
For wife the routing household chore—
Wild winter comes, we sit and talk
Of pleasures in that summer walk;
Of things delighted in and seen,
Nostalgia keeping evergreen,
And sorting Order out of Chaos,
We place Tirconaill on a dais;
Pray that in this our generation
Wild life be saved through conservation;
Defilement and pollution no more found,
The essence of contentment all around,
Man's home his castle, garden Holy Ground.

(from 'Weekend in Tirconaill')

Humankind has responsibilities for the natural world over which it exerts so much control. Habitat loss has the most damaging effect on all forms of life, even ours. Awareness and action are urgently needed to prevent further environmental damage and preserve the wonder and delight of all life on land and in the water.

Man's relentless capacity to destroy is terrifying. At one time, man had to kill wild animals to survive. Hundreds of years of civilisation have led to the destruction of habitats and their wildlife.

It has taken time for humans to move from birdcatchers and egg collectors to birdwatchers and ornithologists. But progress has brought other threats. Instead of humans plundering nests for food, discarded fishing gear is now harming birds in their nesting colonies.

Gannets collect discarded fishing gear to build nests on Skellig Michael. The unfortunate result of this —a slow, painful death— can be seen on the right. Once a bird becomes entangled in a fishing line, it finds it impossible to free itself.

However, there is hope. Laws have been passed to protect species from extinction. The Badger, Pine Marten, Otter, the Grey and Common Seal are amongst those species now protected by law. There is also hope in the successful reintroduction programmes for species such as the Red kite and the White-tailed Eagle. The designated Marine Protected Areas strive to protect 30% of oceans by 2030. This involves protecting marine life and and its habitats from overfishing, dredging and pollution.

Long stretches of coastline, islands, bogs, and forests have become the last refuges of many animal species. The development and protection of National Parks, and the encouragement of every individual to plant trees, create wild gardens, and build ponds, mean that each of us can make a difference and contribute to nature conservation. People need and want meaningful connections to nature, and those connections nurture a conservation ethic.

Through my photography, I strive to stimulate and excite viewers about wildlife and their environments, and to encourage conservation and prevent further loss of species. Each image captures a precious moment in the life and personality of an animal.

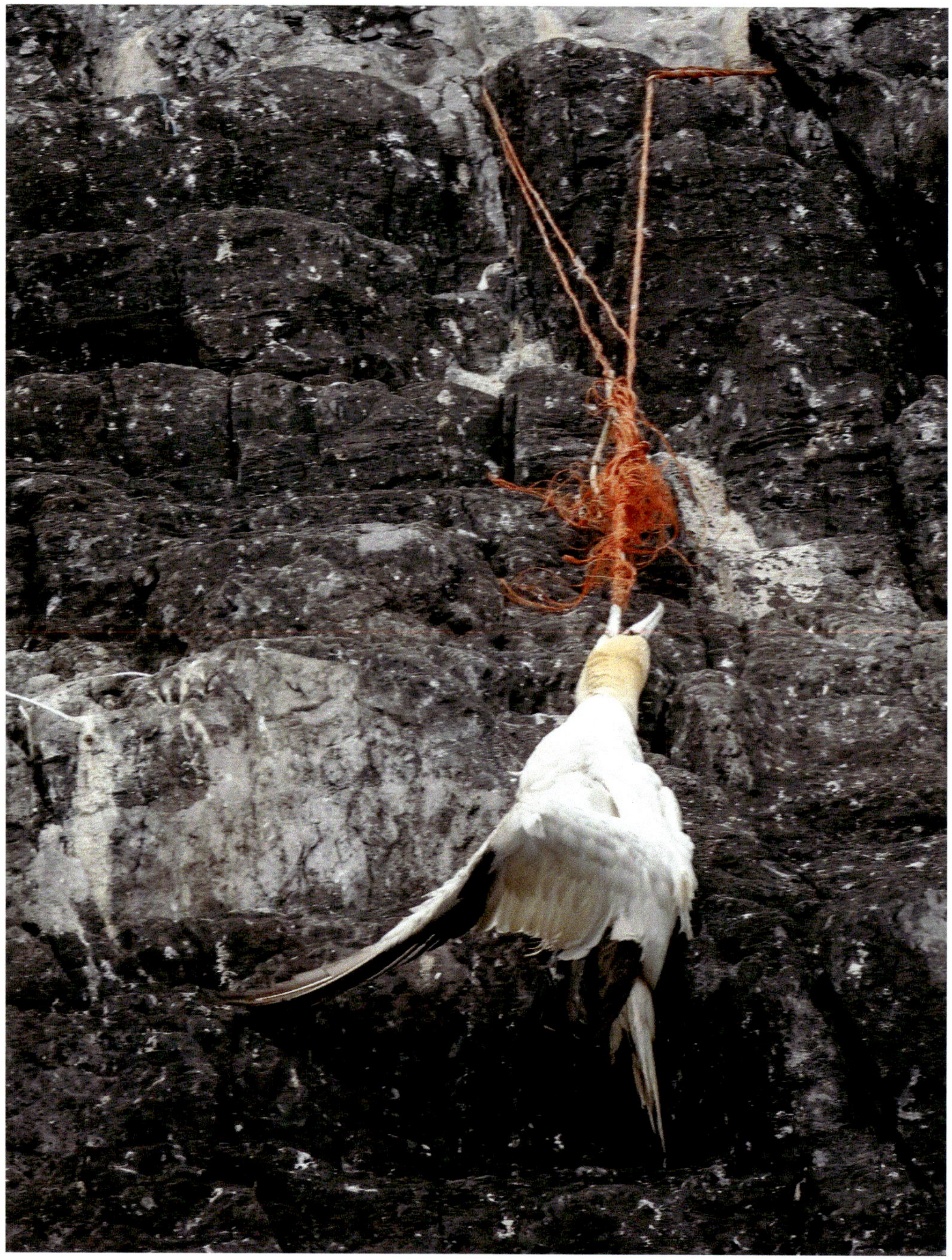

'Pray that in this our generation wild life be saved through conservation; defilement and pollution no more found ...'

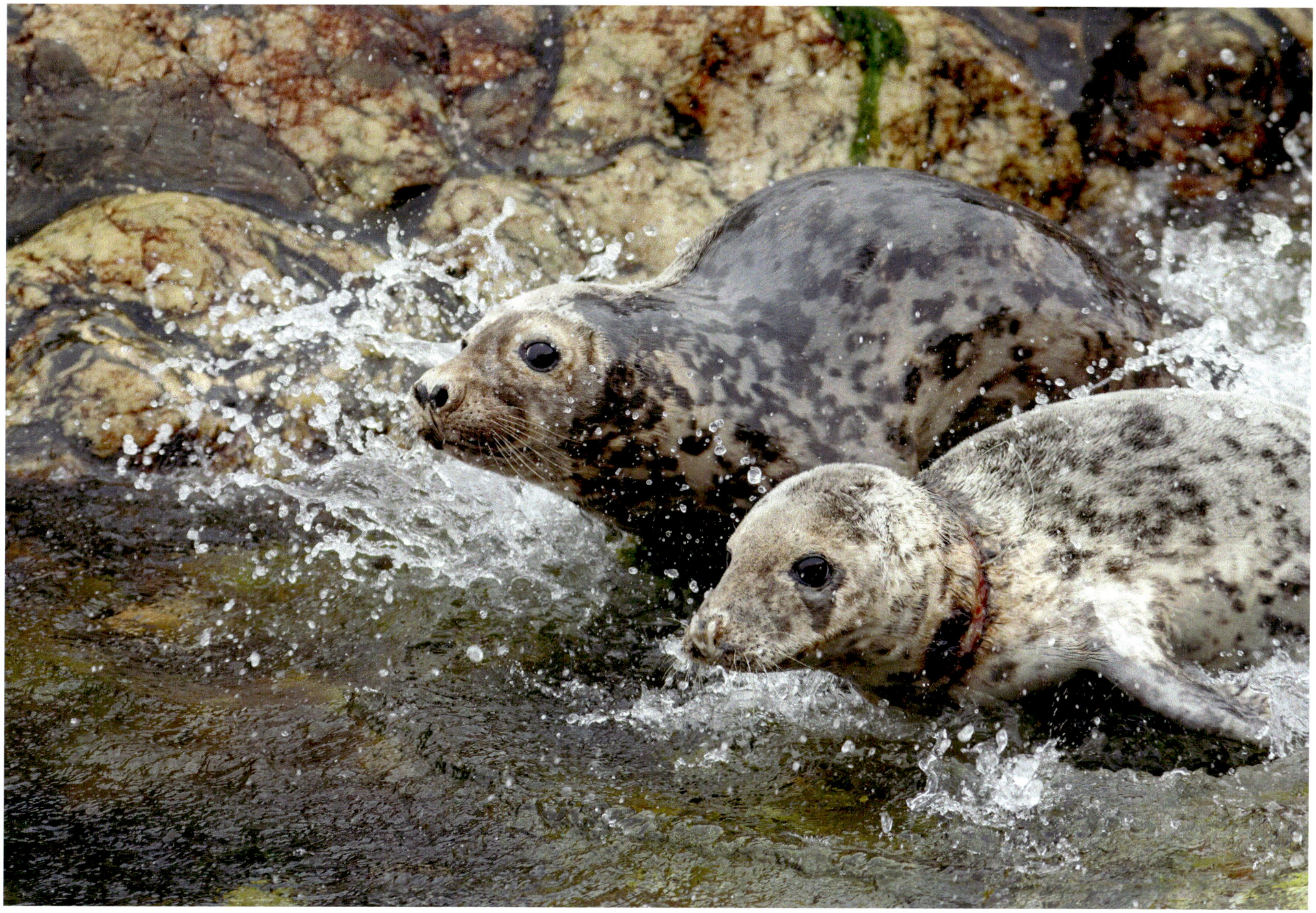

This Atlantic Grey Seal on Inishtrahull is being strangled by a piece of discarded fishing line. It is a protected sea mammal. Every day vast quantities of waste are being dumped into the sea. We need to mend our ways to prevent our wildlife paying the price.

Gannets use discarded fishing gear to line their nests on Little Skellig. Some become tangled in the nets, lines and ropes and come to a tragic end. No doubt bits of line also end up in the chicks' stomachs. Abandoned or lost fishing gear makes up the majority of the ocean's large plastic pollution and wreaks havoc on marine animals.

The photograph below was taken in 2006, and shows how much the problem has grown in 18 years.

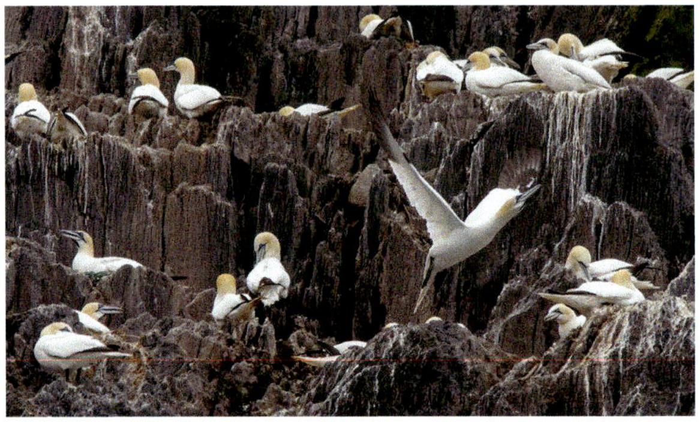

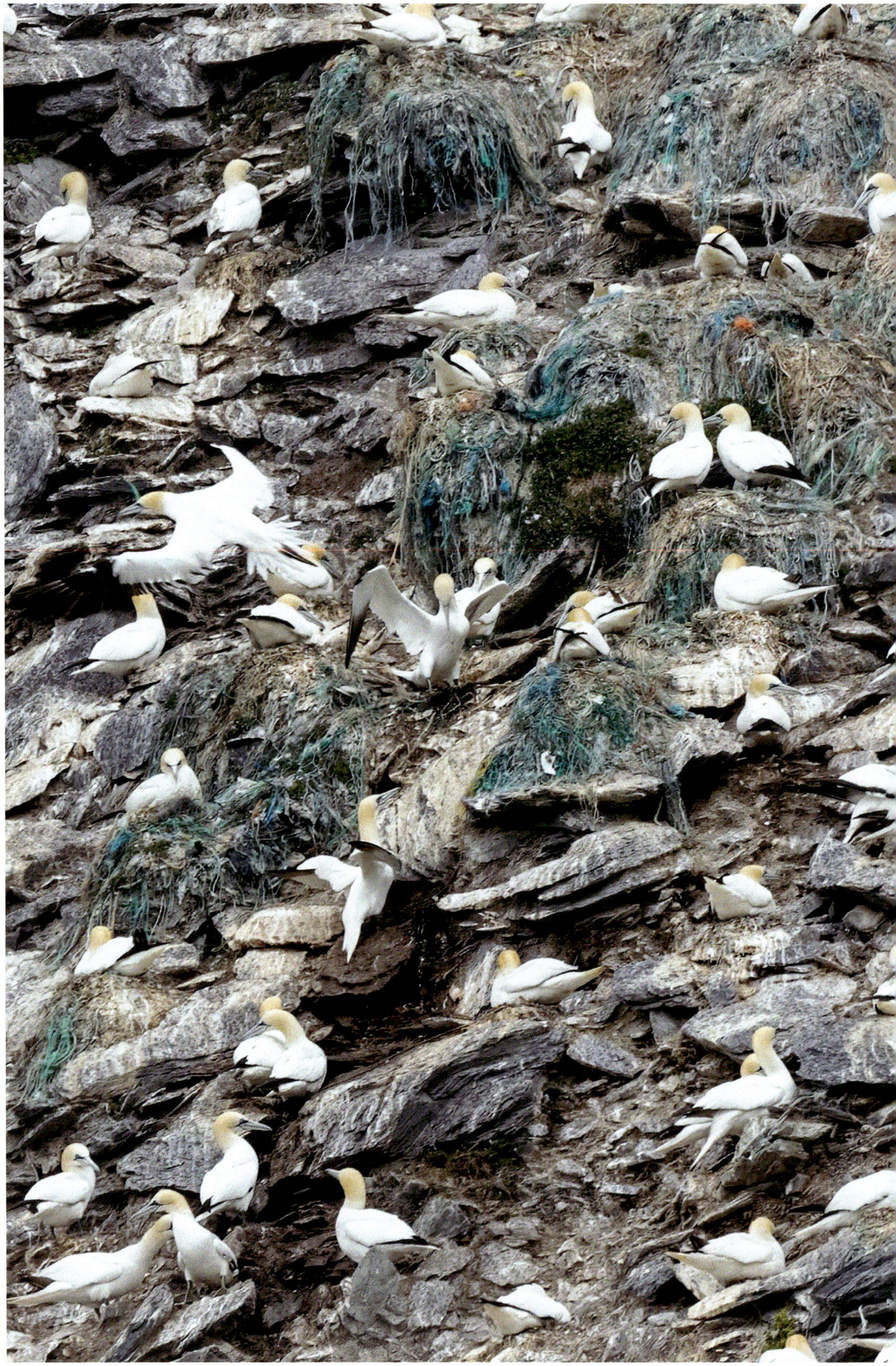

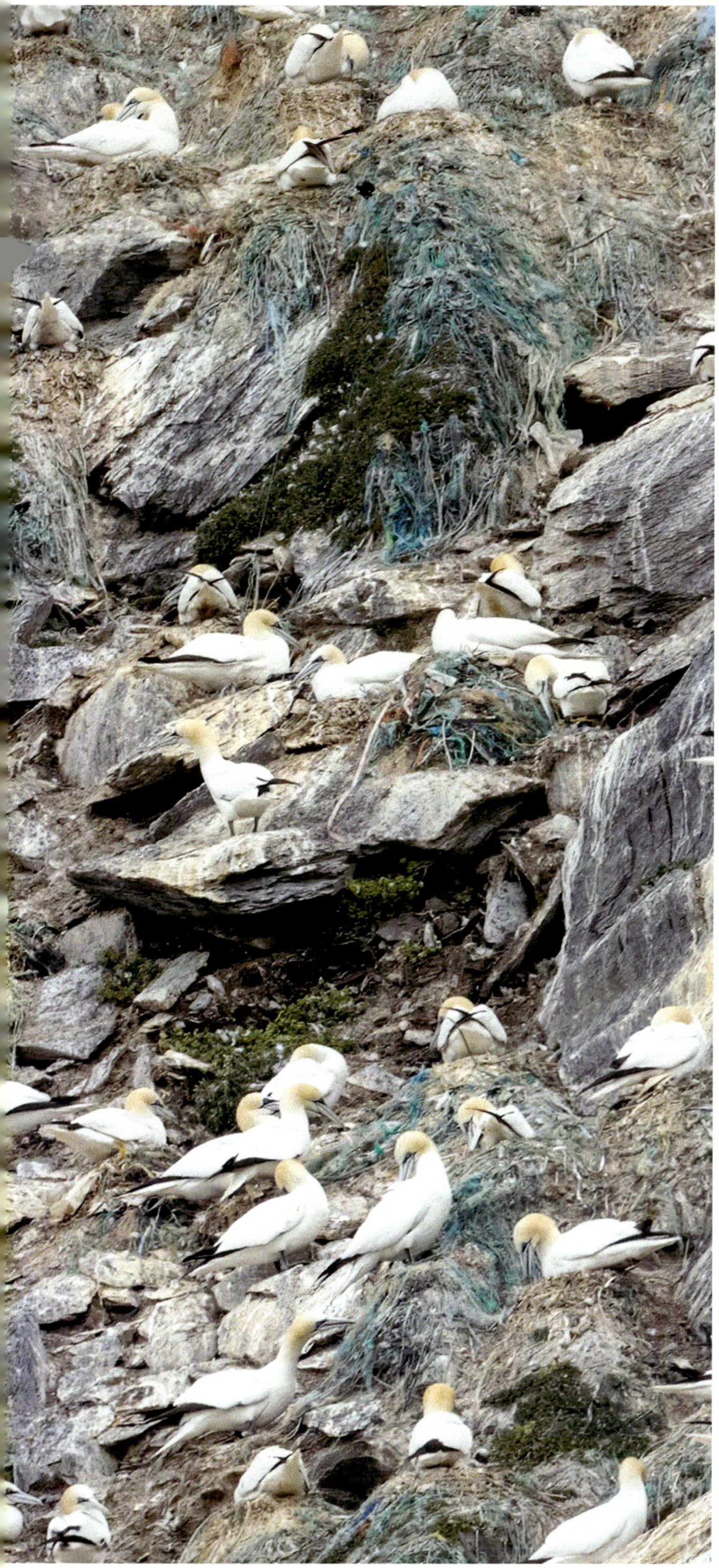

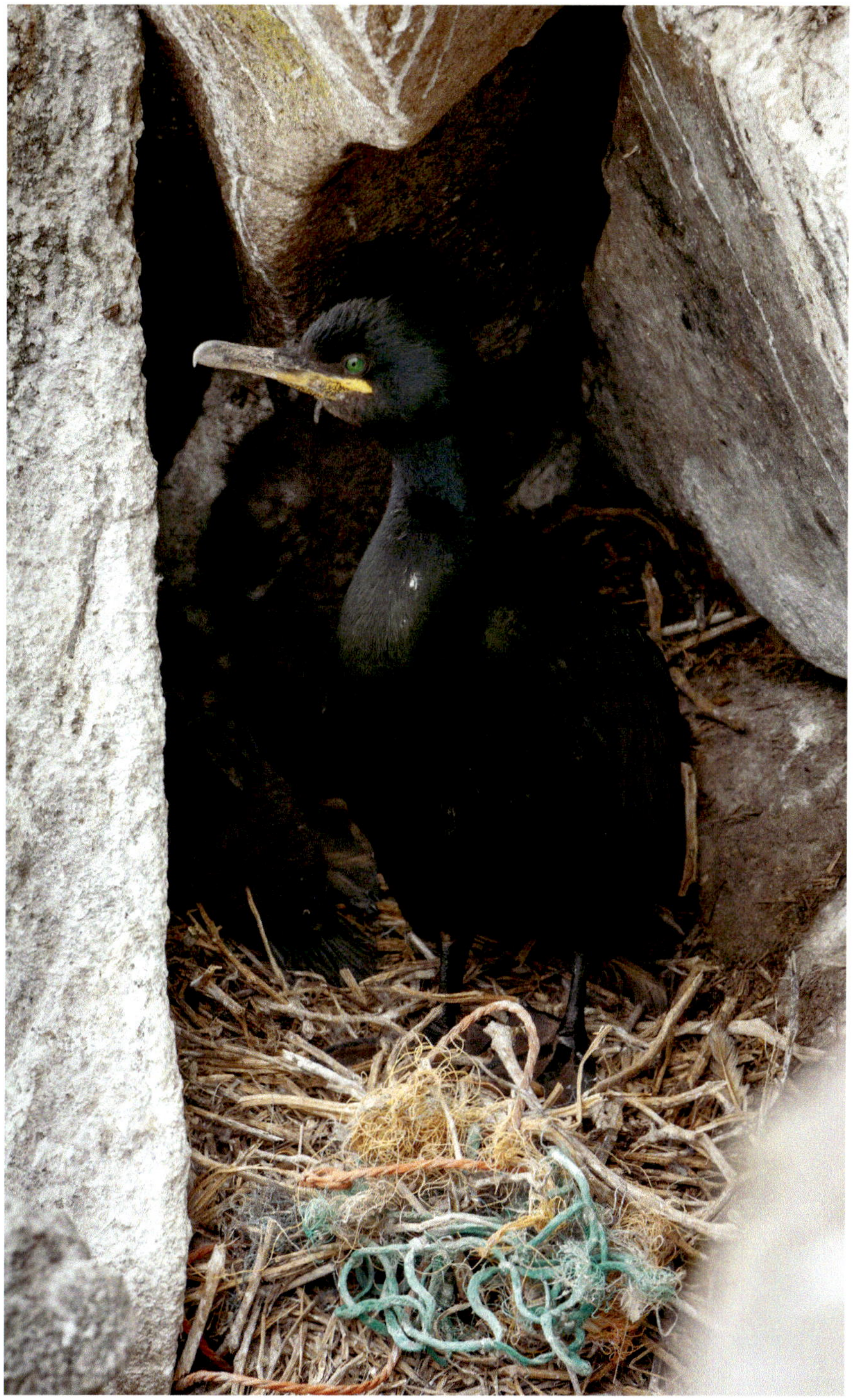

The Shag also makes use discarded fishing material to line its nest.

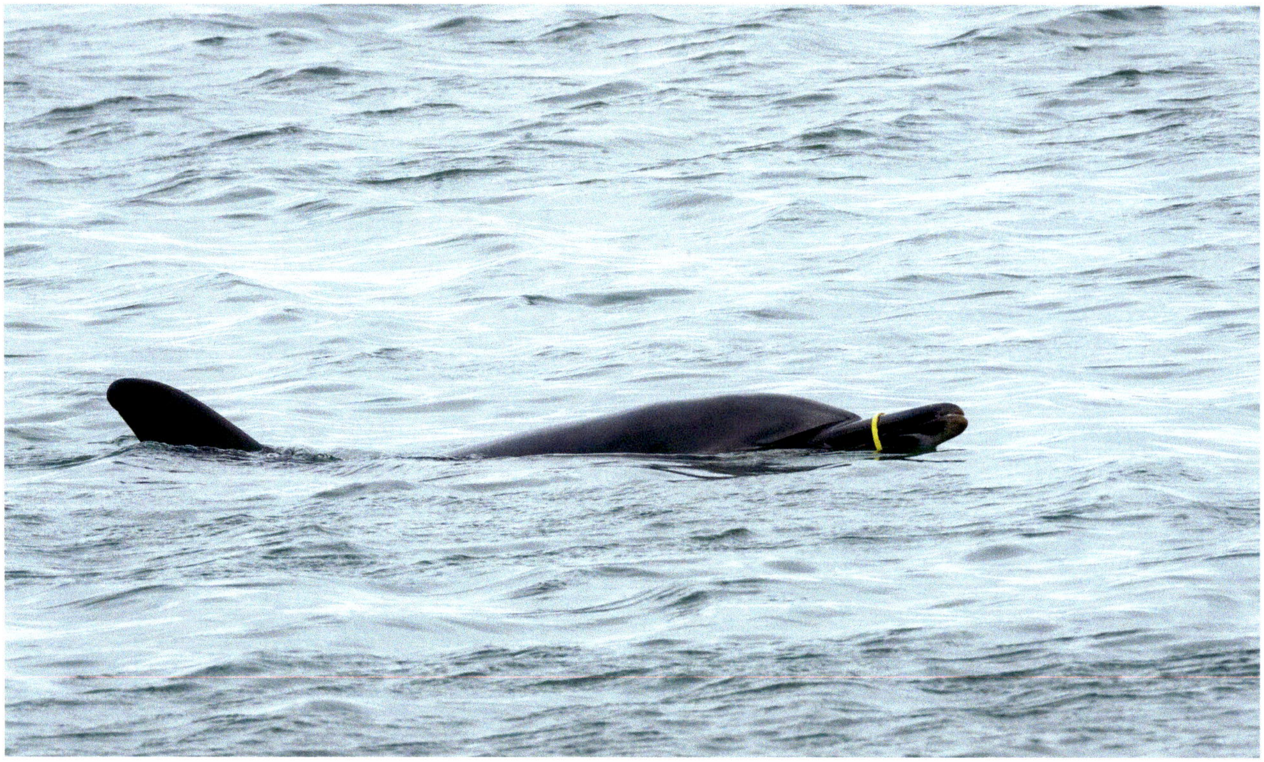

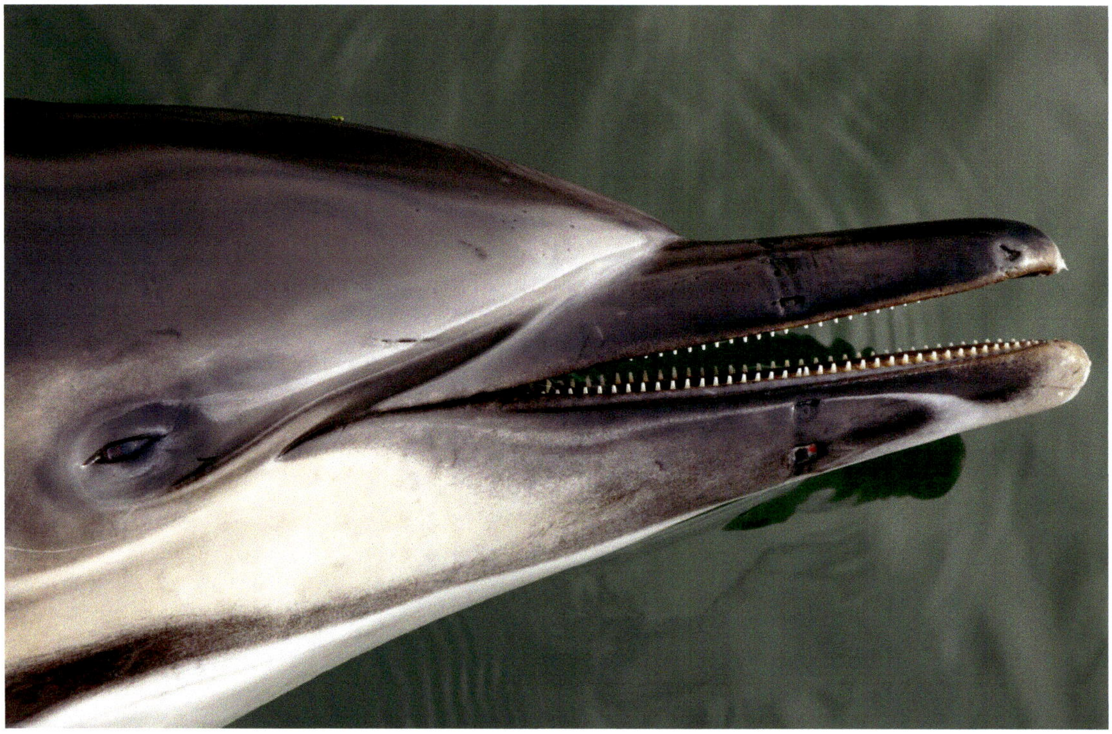

The importance of tackling the scourge of thousands of pieces of marine litter polluting Ireland's coastline is sadly illustrated by the death of this Short-beaked Common Dolphin. This dolphin was alive when I spotted it in the bay in distress because of a yellow plastic ring embedded around its beak. He died soon afterwards in spite of efforts to save him. This loss was clearly the result of careless dumping of domestic rubbish. Sea birds and mammals are particularly vulnerable to being injured by the plastic rings used for packs of beer cans.

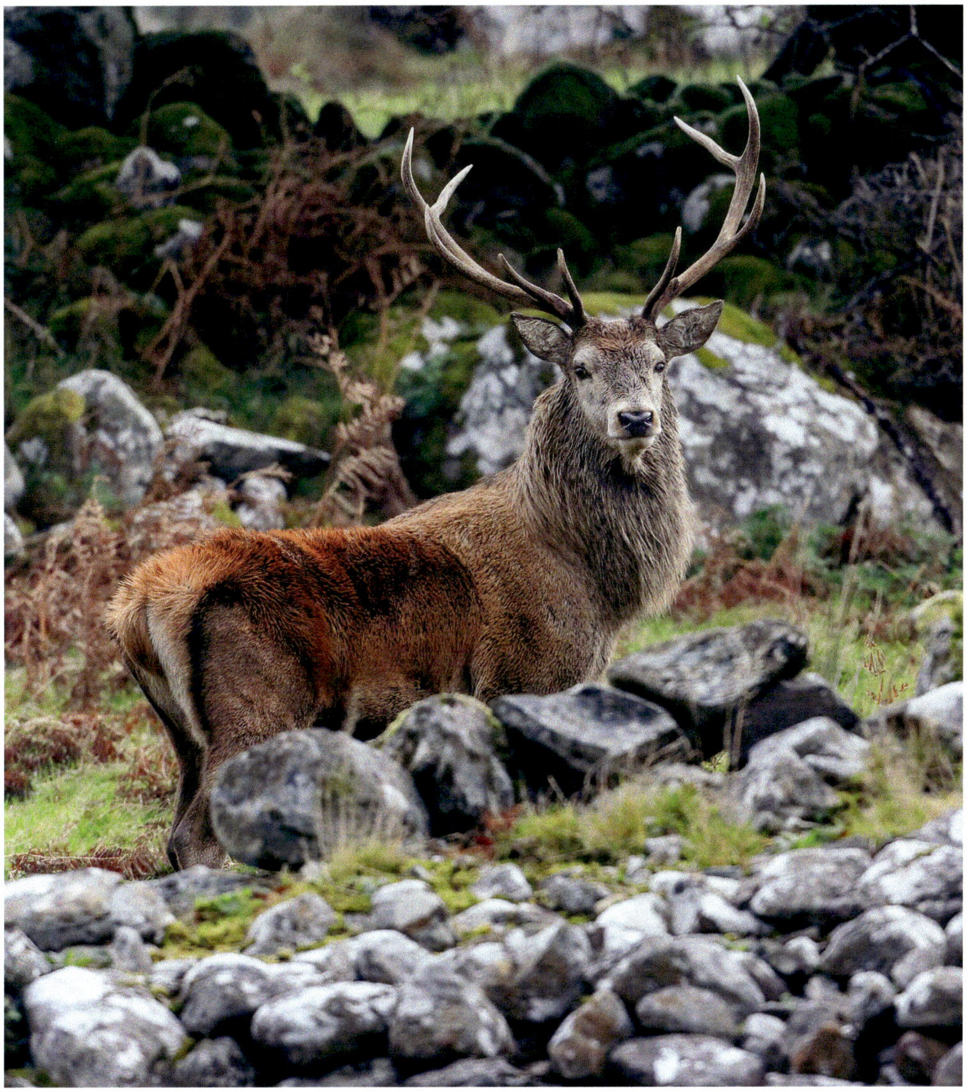

Red Deer have been present in Ireland for thousands of years and are our largest land mammal. The Sika Deer was imported in 1860 to Wicklow. Red Deer and Sika can interbreed and produce fertile hybrid offspring. At present hybrids are found in Co. Wicklow and a significant concern is the potential hybridisation between Sika and Red Deer in the Kerry region, given that the Kerry Red Deer are direct descendants of a Neolithic introduction by humans about 5,000 years ago.

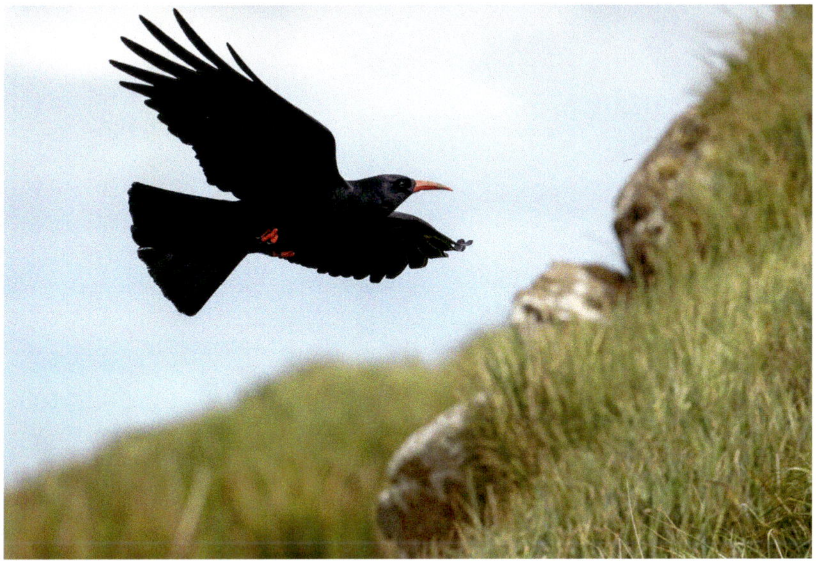

The Chough is a rare member of the crow family and is an amazing character of our coastal skies and a precious attraction of the Wild Atlantic Way. We have a responsibility to conserve this species with nearly 60% of its northwest European population in Ireland. They are associated with coastal fringes from Donegal to Wexford where the frost-free conditions and short-cropped coastal grasslands allow them to find insect food in the soil all year round. There has been a 30% decline of choughs in the whole Beara Peninsula. They live in remote isolation on Dursey Island, and it is hoped that restricting the number of cable-car visitors in August and the creation of defined pathways will help protect this shy and vulnerable bird.

149

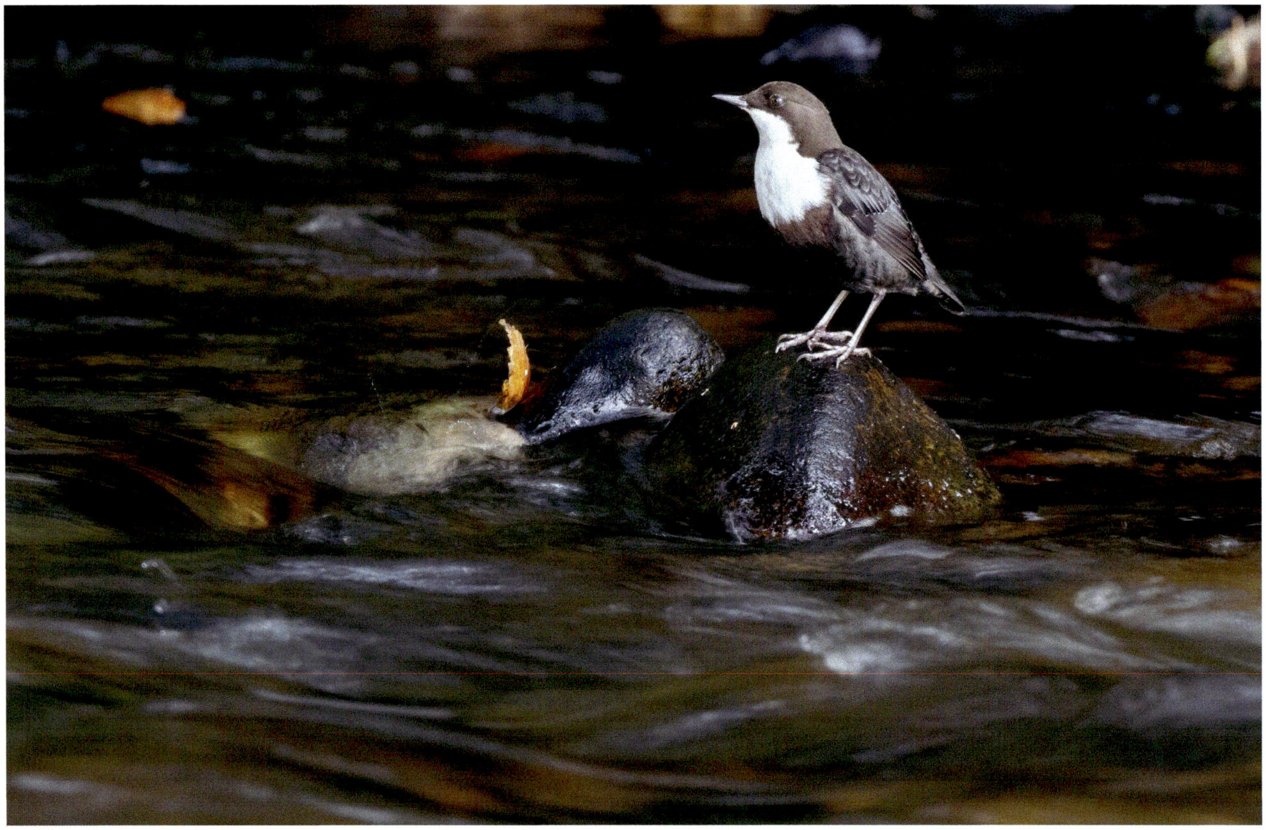

The Dipper (left and below) is the only songbird that swims. To thrive, it needs fresh, clean waterways with safe and quiet nesting areas. It can stay underwater for up to 15 seconds before surfacing, taking a breath, and heading back underwater to find food, such as insect larvae. It dives for aquatic insects swimming underwater using wings for propulsion and can also walk on the bottom of a stream bed. Its third eyelid clears water away from the eye when it resurfaces. If we are to keep our rivers free of pollution, we must address the problem of nitrates, silage effluent and sewage which are contaminating our rivers and streams.

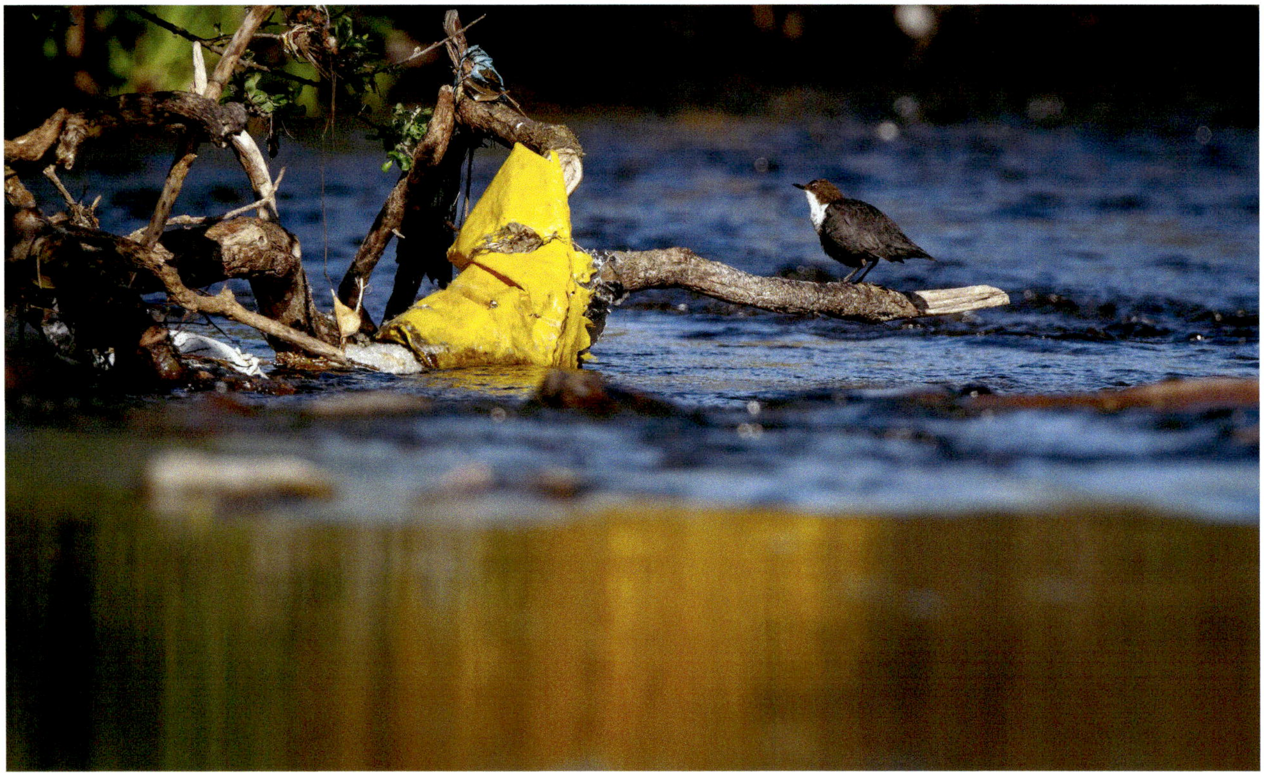

Marine plastic pollution is an issue that has become one of increasing familiarity and growing public concern. It enters the marine environment via a number of pathways including beach visitors, discarded or lost fishing gear from fishing vessels, illegal dumping and via rivers from land-based sources or wastewater plants. Plastic pollution will remain in the marine environment for centuries, harming wildlife through ingestion and entanglement.

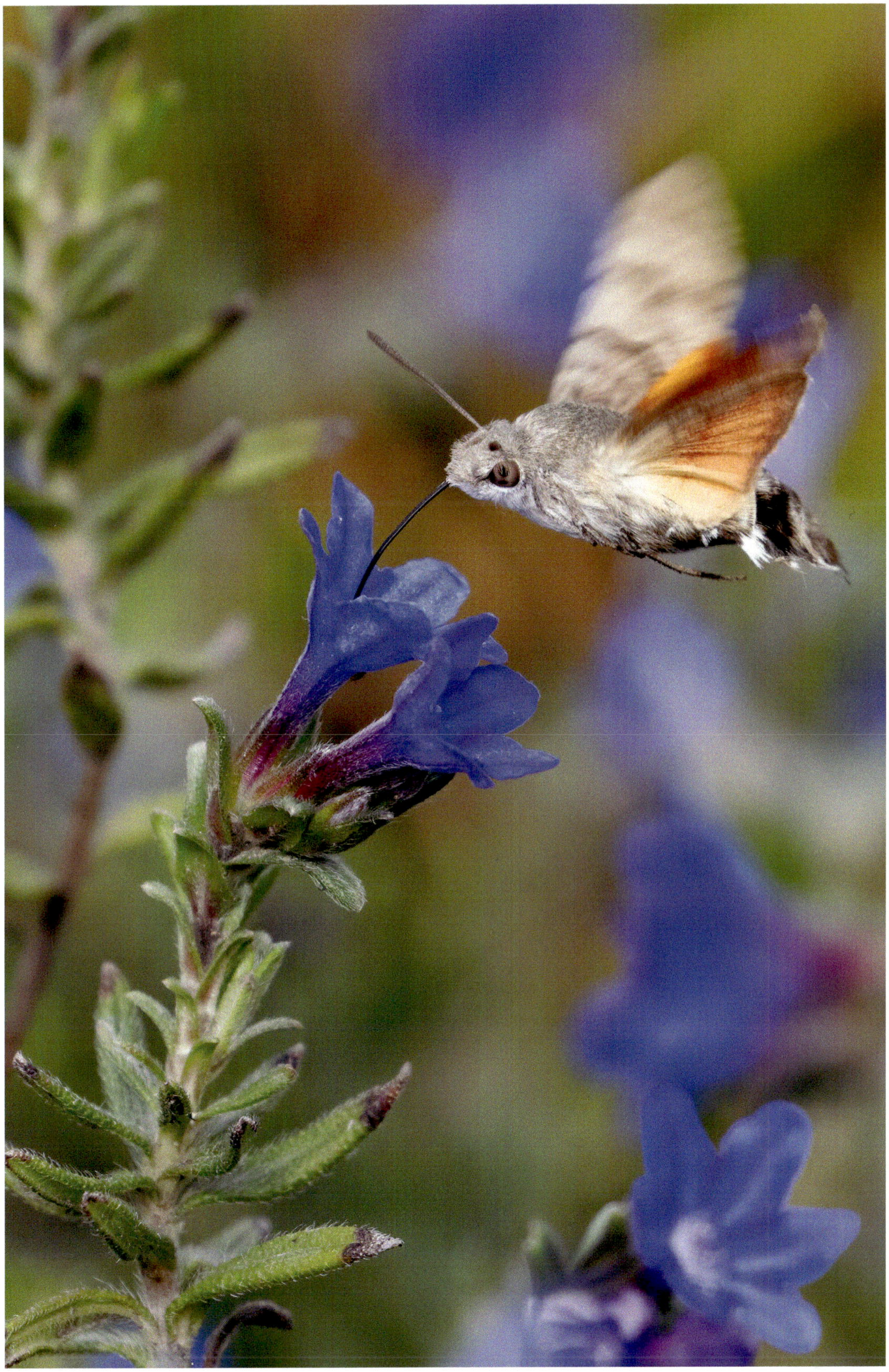

The Hummingbird Hawk-moth is a day-flying species that migrates from Mediterranean countries to Ireland. It hovers like a hummingbird as it uses its proboscis to feed on the nectar of tube-shaped flowers during ours summer months. There is evidence that the population is actively expanding its range, as numbers have been consistently increasing. Warmer temperatures due to climate change allow some individuals to overwinter in Ireland.

ACKNOWLEDGMENTS

I am hugely grateful to Donal O'Sullivan who gave me the copyright of his father's poems. His idea of republishing the poems alongside my images inspired me to create this book.

My thanks to all who helped me in so many different ways. Without their support and encouragement this book would not be possible.

I would especially like to thank the following:

Irish Lights who made it possible for me to visit various islands, to photograph the lighthouses from the air and gave me permission to stay in their lighthouses.

Lighthouse keepers Richard Foran, Donal O'Sullivan, Neilly O'Reilly and Ronnie O'Driscoll, and technicians Stephen Kelly and Phil Lalor who were so encouraging in my efforts to get the shots in often awkward and dangerous locations.

The OPW, in particular retired chief architect Grellan O'Rourke, who gave me permission stay overnight in an OPW hut on Skellig Michael.

The Trustees of the Revelstoke Trust who generously allowed me to spend time on Lambay Island to photograph the rich variety of wildlife there.

Pat Concannon who made numerous trips to Inishshark where the landing and seas could be treacherous.

Others to whom I am indebted are Jim and Una Tracey whose generous hospitality gave me the opportunity to spend more time on Inishbofin as well as visiting other neighbouring islands.

And a big thank you to boat owners Bobby Goodwin and Sinead Foyle for trips in their very special curraghs to various islands where I was allowed to camp.

Spending time on the Great Saltee Island was made possible by the kind offer of hospitality by the late self-styled Prince Michael the First. His is the only house on the island.

My thanks to John F. Atkins for his help in enabling me to observe and photograph otters on the north Beara coast.

Sincere thanks goes to my publisher, Maurice Sweeney of Menma Books, who tirelessly helped me bring it all together.

Finally, none of this would be possible without our natural world which makes life worth living and for which we must all be grateful. I am passionate about the message that my images convey and hope my work contributes to the general appreciation of our precious, beautiful and fascinating wildlife and inspires all of us to protect it. We are blessed to have long stretches of coastline, islands, bogs, rivers, mountains and woods. These are crucial to many animal species and places where, as D. J. O'Sullivan's accurately descriptive poems make us so acutely aware, we may wander, listen and take time to watch.

Sheena Jolley

INDEX OF IMAGES

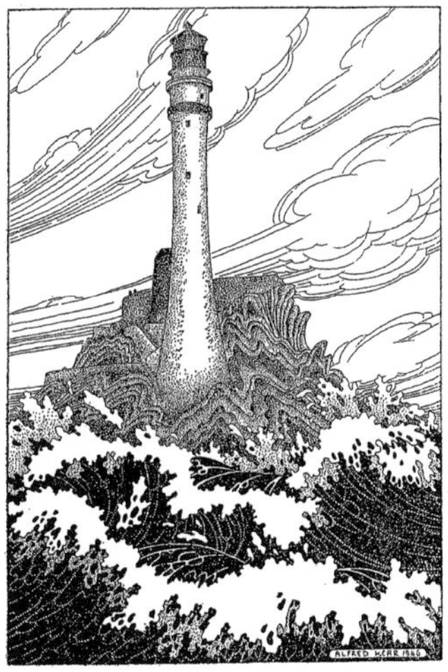

Note on the poems: The poems in this book come from the two collections D. J. O'Sullivan published during his lifetime: *Light-Keeper's Lyrics* (with drawings by Alfred Kerr), published in 1947 by W. Tempest, Dundalgan Press, Dundalk, and *From Fastnet to Inishtrahull* (with an introduction by John Montague), published in 1993 by Lapwing Publications, Belfast.